MITCHELL

Bill in his High River house office, 1965

MITCHELL

THE LIFE OF W.O. MITCHELL

THE YEARS OF FAME

— 1948-1998 —

BARBARA & ORMOND MITCHELL

⟦A DOUGLAS GIBSON BOOK⟧

M&S

Library and Archives Canada Cataloguing in Publication

Mitchell : the life of W.O. Mitchell : the years of
fame, 1948–1998 / Ormond Mitchell and Barbara Mitchell.

Includes index.
"Douglas Gibson Books."
ISBN 0-7710-6108-0

1. Mitchell, W. O. (William Ormond), 1914–1998. 2. Authors, Canadian (English) –
20th century – Biography. I. Mitchell, Barbara II. Title.

PS8526.19765Z728 2005   C813'.54   C2005-903152-2

We acknowledge the financial support of the Government of Canada through the Book Publishing Industry Development Program and that of the Government of Ontario through the Ontario Media Development Corporation's Ontario Book Initiative. We further acknowledge the support of the Canada Council for the Arts and the Ontario Arts Council for our publishing program.

Typeset in Garamond by M&S, Toronto
Printed and bound in Canada

This book is printed on acid-free paper that is 100% recycled,
ancient-forest friendly (100% post-consumer recycled).

McClelland & Stewart Ltd.
The Canadian Publishers
75 Sherbourne Street
Toronto, Ontario
M5A 2P9
www.mcclelland.com

1 2 3 4 5   09 08 07 06 05

CONTENTS

For our children and theirs
Sara, Geoff and Bernadette
Maria and Victoria, Chloe and William

PREFACE

"Who is W.O. Mitchell?" He once gave his own answer to that question: "When I get very tired, I find myself sort of standing apart and the frightening thing is that I don't really care whether this guy rains or freezes. I also wonder, am I the child I was the first twelve years of my life, or am I the guy riding freights back then? So, in answer to that question, 'Who is W.O. Mitchell?', I'm not really certain. . . . No, that's not true. I think in the end you have a pretty vivid sense of your own inner core of consciousness. And as far as anything else goes, of what people think your public facade might be, that's very little of what you are. What you are is parent, lover, dear friend, that's what you are."[1]

In *W.O.*, we revealed some of Mitchell's earlier selves: the "horn-rimmed-spectacled wishbone of a child with the stage presence of an introverted chameleon"; the extrovert "ham"; the "guy" surviving the dirty thirties; the apprentice writer; the lover of Merna Hirtle, daughter of a Baptist minister; the teacher in two small Alberta towns; the freelance writer in High River, Alberta. At the end of *W.O.*, we left the Mitchells just after the stunning success of his first novel, *Who Has Seen the Wind*.

In *Mitchell*, we continue to assemble his various public and private selves, and to show the development and fruition of his writing and performing talents. That fragmentation of himself, that "standing apart," no doubt allowed him to be the spectator-creator he was. He could step out of himself and into the skins of a rich variety of characters and through them he explored various self-truths, including a "frightening" inner darkness that lived alongside his comic self. His themes included death, loneliness, alienation, betrayal, guilt, bigotry, but underlying them all was what mattered most to him – the possibility of bridging with other humans. As self-absorbed as he could be, as he *had* to be as an artist, he also had a magnanimous spirit. Was he certain about who he was? That split-second moment when he said, "I'm not really certain" takes us back to Brian in *Who Has Seen the Wind* and Hugh in *How I Spent My Summer Holidays* and their quests for meaning and identity, for the ever elusive "feeling" and "it," which defy being captured.

I

MACLEAN'S

~ 1948 ~

BILL MITCHELL had a decision to make in the spring of 1948, and it was not an easy one. Freelancing in High River from 1945 to 1948 had been financially precarious for him "with the bankers and creditors breathing down [his] neck,"[1] but he had just been offered the position of fiction editor at *Maclean's* magazine. As he and Merna travelled by train to Ottawa where he would be presented on June 12 with the $500 IODE Award for *Who Has Seen the Wind*, they discussed whether to uproot the family. Financially, it made sense. The proceeds from *Who Has Seen the Wind* averaged out to about $1,100 a year for the seven years he was writing it, not enough to support a family of four. His *Maclean's* salary, on the other hand, would be $5,000 for his first year.[2] Emotionally, however, it was a tough decision to leave the green element of their little foothills town and move to the bright lights of Toronto.

By the time they reached Ottawa they had made their decision. On the front page of the *High River Times*, Mrs. McCorquodale, the editor, noted, "It was just as well he made a clear break when he was in the east. If he had returned to High River and found that the fish were 'biting good' he might not have had the strength to cut loose from the Highwood." The town was sorry to see them go, for they had brought "vigor and enthusiasm to so many phases"[3] of local life. However, it was only to be for two years, just long enough to line the coffers so Mitchell could return to High River and write full-time.

Soon after arriving at *Maclean's*, Mitchell realized that he was part of a significant shift in the magazine's editorial direction. Arthur Irwin had been promoted from managing editor to editor in 1945. For the previous twenty years his vision for a Canadian national magazine had been thwarted by the editor, Napier Moore. For Irwin, the English-born Moore "represented everything that was old, conservative, and colonial about Canada's past."[4] Irwin began reshaping the magazine, and Mitchell was a part of his team of young, energetic editors and writers who came to "be regarded widely as the best editorial staff of any magazine in Canadian history."[5] Ralph Allen was the managing editor and Blair Fraser the Ottawa editor; John Clare, Gerald Anglin, Adam Marshall, Pierre Berton, and Eva-Lis Wuorio were assistant editors. Later in Mitchell's stint at *Maclean's*, Les Hannon and McKenzie Porter were hired. John Clare felt that the *Maclean's* editorial staff became a very effective team partly because many of them were from elsewhere: "*Maclean's* was known in the east, but was run by the west."[6] Their sense of not being part of the Toronto establishment helped this younger generation of journalists to become as close-knit in their social lives as they were at work – and that created a vitality and a collegiality that fed into the magazine.

According to Pierre Berton, Irwin was one of the early Canadian nationalists and he deeply influenced his staff:

You couldn't work on *Maclean's* without becoming a Canadian nationalist. Which is one of the reasons I became one – I wasn't one when I went to *Maclean's*. . . . Irwin felt that *Maclean's* should not try to compete with American magazines on their ground but on our ground. Which is quite right. We should know what our audience was – it was not an American audience – it was a Canadian audience that wanted to read about Canada. And his slogan was interpreting Canada for Canadians. That's what he said the magazine should be.[7]

Unlike Berton, Mitchell already had a Canadian outlook, having learned from Prof. F.M. Salter, his mentor at the University of Alberta,[8] how important it was to write in your own voice about your particular place. It was Mitchell's distinctively western voice and portrayal of prairie life in his writing that first moved Irwin to consider Mitchell for his fiction editor. Under Irwin's policy of aiming for a broad rural and urban audience in all of the regions, *Maclean's* became a truly national magazine. When asked in 1984 what kind of influence the magazine had in the 1940s, Irwin modestly declined to comment; then, after a pause he quietly added, "As a matter of fact, it had a tremendous power in the country at that time. It had a large cross-section readership. When I started in 1925 it had 17,000 circulation and when I left in February 1950 it had just reached 400,000."[9]

When Irwin first met Mitchell, he had asked him why he wanted to become a *Maclean's* editor. Mitchell responded, "'Oh, I have no great ambitions at all to be an editor. I'm a writer. . . . I'm willing to come down here on the fiction desk for two years.'"[10] While Mitchell saw *Maclean's* as a stepping stone *back* to the Canadian west and to writing novels, he was now on the other side of the publishing industry. As fiction editor, he had a major role in deciding what stories Canada's leading magazine would publish – and he was particularly interested in using his position to increase the number of *Maclean's* stories written by Canadian writers about things Canadian. He was proud to be working for a magazine that ranked with the best North American "slicks" such as *Saturday Evening Post, Colliers, Liberty, Ladies' Home Journal,* and *Redbook.* The "slicks" were a cut above the "pulps" in terms of the quality of fiction they published, and above them were the more literary stories published by *Atlantic Monthly* and *Harper's* or the academic periodicals such as *Queen's Quarterly.* Even though Mitchell was given a fair amount of freedom as fiction editor, Irwin had the final say on all stories published, and Mitchell often found himself at odds with a magazine sensibility that, by necessity, pandered to popular taste.

Mitchell's workday began each morning with a bus trip along Danforth Street to the Maclean Hunter building on University and Dundas. He had one of four little offices in the old building facing University. In their second year, the Mitchells bought a car and occasionally Bill would drive to work. Driving with Bill was an adventure – he had no sense of direction and found it difficult to concentrate, for his mind would be on a story or, if he had a passenger, on telling a story. Also, being addicted to tobacco, he was always fiddling with his pipe. One day, on the way to the office, he had to stop for the Orangemen's Parade, a huge event at that time in Toronto. When he struck a match to light his pipe, the whole box of matches ignited. This led to a sequence of events involving a gasoline truck, an elderly lady with an umbrella standing on the street, a King William on a rearing white horse, and Mitchell ending up in the emergency burn unit at the General Hospital.[11] Word of his driving spread quickly and *Maclean's* staff soon learned to turn down his offers for rides home. John Clare claimed that Mitchell was "the world's worst driver outside of Pierre Berton."[12]

Most of Mitchell's working week was spent reading manuscripts that fell into two lots: those submitted by literary agents and those in the "slush pile" (stories personally submitted by writers). *Maclean's* at this time was receiving thirty-five hundred stories a year, about sixty-five to seventy stories a week.[13] As well as the tremendous amount of reading this entailed, Mitchell had to keep up with a large amount of correspondence. While many of the manuscripts required only a short rejection note, Mitchell spent a lot of time corresponding not only with those writers he published, but also with those who showed any promise.[14]

Generally fiction editors read the stories submitted by agents first and then turned to the slush pile. Mitchell, however, gave as much, if not more, attention to the unrepresented writers as he did to writers with agents. He had some readers working for him (among them Matie Molinaro, Joyce Marshall, and Doris Anderson) who would each read about twenty stories a week from the slush pile (for about fifty cents a story). Irwin said "it was a real coup if you found somebody in the slush pile."[15] On Fridays the readers brought in their stories and reports, went over them with Mitchell, and picked up a new batch. Mitchell read all the Canadian fiction himself: "That was the way I found many of my interesting Canadian writers."[16] He took great pride in his eye for writing talent, giving his time generously to a number of writers. He quickly made a name for himself among the *Maclean's* editorial staff as an editor who was "a protagonist, a supporter of quality writing in *Maclean's*."[17] Not all of the writers Mitchell supported were published by *Maclean's*, but he used his contacts and whatever influence he had to set them up with other magazines, publishers, and the CBC.

On Thursday afternoons, Mitchell would meet with Irwin and John Clare to discuss the upcoming issues: "Each week I would have several possibles, the ones that I really wanted. They would go up to Irwin. He would say yes I want that one, or no I don't want that one. And this got us into trouble."[18] Mitchell and Irwin were a study in contrasts – Mitchell, the flamboyant storyteller from the west who looked for open and immediate engagement with people, and Irwin, the reserved Toronto editor. When asked what his impressions of Mitchell were at this time, Irwin said "he was assertive, rather aggressive [long pause], a bit of an egoist, a bit of an actor – he liked the limelight, he liked attention."[19] Mitchell, on the other hand, looked on the older, experienced magazine editor as humourless, as a rather cold fish who did not display his emotions openly, who invited contact only on a professional level. To all of the younger editorial staff he was "Mr. Irwin." He was aloof, on the fifth floor, and he did not join his staff for lunches or social events. Pierre Berton felt that "there was always something of the Methodist in him."[20]

Mitchell had a great deal of respect for Irwin in the area of non-fiction, but in the fiction field they had some fierce arguments. He recalled one occasion when Irwin said to him, "As far as fiction is concerned, strangely, readers want to read stories with a happy ending, with a positive ending – boy-girl stories with a complication and a happy ending." These "formula plus" stories, or what Scott Young referred to as "Roger and Anne stories," were generally what had been published in *Maclean's*. Mitchell soon sensed that Irwin felt "he had made a mistake in me as a fiction editor, once he knew me in the flesh. I wasn't a simple sort of guy. In fact, I was an arty kind of guy, and I would be tending to buy stuff that was beyond *Maclean's* readers and too subtle and not shaped and structured enough."[21]

On one occasion Mitchell discovered a classic slice-of-life story in the slush pile. But there was a problem – it had been written some seventy years earlier by Guy de Maupassant.[22] However, Mitchell was not laughing when another plagiarist's story from the slush pile slipped by his editorial eye: "It turned out it was a guy in Philadelphia or Chicago somewhere, and this guy had simply taken a *Saturday Evening Post* story and changed the title and names of the characters, signed it and sent it in. I bought it. It was a good story. We published it and heard from people right and left – 'Geez, I read this in the *Post* six months ago.'" Irwin called Mitchell and Ralph Allen into his office:

Irwin was really upset. He said, "What are we going to do?" I said, "Well, I'll phone Robert Fuoss, the managing editor of the *Saturday Evening Post*." He said, "Do you know him?" And I said, "Oh sure." And Irwin said, "Well, get him on the line." He had another phone and he wanted to overhear. You see – he didn't believe it. So I got Robert and he said, "Hi ya, Mitch, how are you doing up there in Canada?" I said, "Oh I'm doing just fine. How are you doing down there?" Then I filled him in on how the guy has plagiarized one of their stories and that Irwin was really worried *Saturday Evening Post* was going to hit *Maclean's* for everything, and what do you think of that? He said, "You want to know what I think about it? I've got a good god-damned fiction editor, and *Maclean's* has got a good fiction editor and they can recognize a good story when they see one. When are you going to come down and take over the fiction desk for me, Billy?" Well, Jesus, Irwin could not believe his ears, that this guy actually invited me on a trip to New York to become fiction editor of *Saturday Evening Post*. Barry later told me I was a damned fool not to take the offer, said that's the trouble with you bloody Canadians, you're just not ambitious.[23]

The majority of the writers Mitchell published produced romance, mystery, and adventure stories written to formula for a popular market. *Maclean's* was in a difficult position in the fiction market, for it could not pay as well as the American slicks for first-run stories – only $150 to $300 per story whereas the *Saturday Evening Post* was paying $750 to $1,000 per story. As a result, most if not all of the stories the New York agents sent *Maclean's* had "been kissed and handled all down the line" and been rejected by the higher-paying magazines. So the bulk of Mitchell's work, besides deciding on the stories to be published, "was bandaging and doctoring stories that might otherwise have been taken by *Post* or *Colliers*."[24] On a number of occasions he discovered he had been used as a free editorial consultant – stories he had overhauled were resubmitted to the higher-paying American magazines, which then published them in their improved form.

One of the American writers Mitchell published who had a long shelf life was Ray Bradbury. Mitchell published four of his stories.[25] Up to 1948 Bradbury's stories appeared mainly in the pulps, and *Maclean's* was one of the first quality magazines to begin publishing him.[26] Mitchell admired Bradbury's writing and his effective use of the science-fiction genre, believing that he was one of the first writers to cause science fiction to be taken seriously. *The Martian Chronicles*, Bradbury's second hardcover book, which became a science-fiction classic, used two of the stories that first appeared in *Maclean's*.[27]

A Canadian writer Mitchell dealt with, reluctantly, was W.G. Hardy. A First World War veteran, George Hardy was head of the Classics Department at the University of Alberta and wrote "lusty"[28] historical romances set in biblical, classical, and medieval times. Hardy was an old friend of Irwin going back to the First World War and, before Mitchell's arrival, *Maclean's* had published his work.

When Mitchell rejected Hardy's stories, Irwin called him in for a chat and suggested that Mitchell reconsider and take Hardy, who was in town, out to lunch:

> So, I took George Hardy to Winstons. We talk, and he tells me about how it means more to him to be published in *Maclean's* than it does in an American top magazine. I know Hardy himself was sending me these things after his agent had tried them on *Esquire, Argosy, Cosmopolitan*. So, I may have said something like, "Well, George, we're paying only a $125 or $150, and I imagine with *Saturday Evening Post* you might get $1,500" – and he didn't get the sarcasm. Then he said, "Do you know how many women I've had in my lifetime." I said, "I have no idea, George." He said, "Nine!" I said, "Oh my God, George! Is that *all?*" He looked at me. "You mean you went through the war and all those French ladies – and only *nine?*" Well, he was outraged. So Irwin called me in a day or so later. He said, "You take people to lunch to entertain them, not to upset them." I said, "I think you would have been upset" – you see, Irwin's father was a Methodist minister. Irwin said, "No, there's no excuse for it." I said, "Dr. Hardy asked me, 'Do you know how many women I've *screwed* in my lifetime?'" Irwin's got his horn-rimmed glasses off – and I kept at him and at him and he finally says, "Okay, okay, okay!" That was one that both Irwin and George Hardy lost.[29]

Not quite. Mitchell had to buy Hardy's "Geoffrey and the Lady Gemma," a story of war and romance set in medieval Italy.[30]

Mitchell's recollections of Hardy and Irwin reveal two contradictory impulses in his own personality. On the one hand, he was fascinated by, and at times made fun of, Irwin's Methodist sensibility and his distaste for prurience. On the other, Mitchell was genuinely repulsed by what he perceived to be lewdness in Hardy's writing and, he now realized, in his personal life. Mitchell's sensibility was as stained by his puritan Presbyterian upbringing as Irwin's was by his

Methodist background. He was, as his Aunt Josie had urged him to be, "a good boy." In terms of witty exchanges or jokes and office pranks, Mitchell could hold his own, but when it came to drinking (the daily martini lunches and after-work drinks) and flirting Mitchell was, as Barbara Moon (who was the office receptionist and then secretary to Berton and Clare) described him, an "outsider." The others had "romantic images of themselves as foreign correspondents, as Ernest Hemingways with trench coats. Bill wasn't part of what was rather a jock show – there was a gentleness about him. He never made a pass at me."[31]

Mitchell soon learned that fiction was low on the totem pole within the *Maclean's* hierarchy. The management and the advertising people did not really appreciate the fiction part of *Maclean's* magazine, which they saw as filler. Pierre Berton dismissed most of the fiction being published by *Maclean's* and other slicks, such as the *Saturday Evening Post*, as romance stories: "I hated them, thought they were crap but didn't say much because many of them were written by my colleagues."[32] In fact, a substantial part of the Canadian fiction that *Maclean's* published was written by a stable of former and current *Maclean's* editors such as Scott Young, Arthur Mayse, John Clare (who wrote under the pseudonym James Carver), Eva-Lis Wuorio, and McKenzie Porter.

While Berton was critical of *Maclean's* fiction, he admired Bill's efforts to search out good Canadian stories and to raise the literary quality of the stories *Maclean's* published. But he also felt that Bill "was caught in this kind of vice – between his own sensitivity about what really good fiction was and his need to follow what was considered proper formula."[33] Berton's sense is borne out by Mitchell's comment in a 1984 interview when the titles of the short stories he published were read to him: "Those three years at *Maclean's* as fiction editor, that is when I was most deeply immersed in the commercial stream. I didn't think so at the time. I'm thinking so now, though, when you read me those horrible titles . . . not as a writer, but as an editor, being involved in that system. I was not slumming in writing. . . . I was never slumming commercially when I did those

Jake stories."[34] His editorial work heightened even more the danger Salter had warned him about early on – to make the right choice between writing "*good* stuff"[35] for a serious reading audience and writing popular stories for a mass audience.

The main features of *Maclean's* were its social, historical, and political articles. Mitchell was expected not only to submit some articles himself but to participate in the Thursday-morning staff sessions in Irwin's office on the fifth floor to brainstorm ideas, assign articles, and map out the upcoming "books." Fiction was not discussed at these meetings, which was fine with Mitchell. While he was a vocal participant in these sessions, his contributions were not always constructive. Hannon recalled that "Bill was never really housebroken – as an editor, nor as a human being I suppose. Bill was always the most exotic member of this particular team – in matters of dress and manner." At times his "esoteric humour would completely disrupt the session."[36] On one occasion Mitchell suggested doing a piece on the Bronfmans. This was the only instance he was aware of where management interfered with a project the editorial team wanted to take on. Apparently the Bronfman idea had been tried before "and each time it came up against the lawyers downstairs they said there would be no *Maclean's* if you told the true story of the Bronfmans and their growth."[37] However, a number of his suggestions (often with Merna's input) were used, such as a piece on the Earl of Egmont, and Edna Staebler's article on the Mennonites.

Staebler had impressed Mitchell with her article on swordfishing in Cape Breton. She met Bill when he was speaking at her local branch of the Women's Canadian Club at Waterloo in February 1949, and he had invited her to come to the *Maclean's* offices to talk more with him:

> I was thrilled. He took me down and introduced me to Pierre Berton saying I was the one who wrote the swordfishing piece, "The number one piece in that issue. She lives in Mennonite country – why don't we get her to do a piece about the Mennonites." Pierre asked if I would be interested, and I said I was working on a book. He said, "Why don't you send in an

outline." Then Arthur Irwin came in and took his glasses off and on a few times, and we discussed this thing. I said, "Well, you know I'm working on this book." When we got out of the office Bill said, "Edna, for God's sake here's the top market in Canada offering you an assignment on the strength of your having written only one piece. They just don't do that. Don't say I'm working on a book – you get at it!" I said, "Oh, maybe I should."[38]

Bill drove Edna home – and got lost. Later Berton said to her, "You mean you drove with Mitchell? Did you know you were taking your life into your hands?" This was the first of a number of weekends Edna spent with Bill and Merna: "We talked so much about writing. And the next time I took 'Cape Breton Harbour' with me and he would read some of his and I would read some of mine – it was just such a wonderful thing for someone like me to meet somebody like Bill. Bill, you know, really got me started. So I had these three – Scott Young, Bill, and Pierre. It was wonderful – I couldn't have had better mentors."[39] Staebler did write the article on the Mennonites, after living with a Mennonite family for a time, and it won the Canadian Women's Press Club Award that year.

Given Irwin's serious and quiet demeanour and his desire to keep the Thursday-morning discussions on track, it is not surprising that he was irked at times by Mitchell's antics. Irwin was also offended by McKenzie Porter's penchant for embellishing his articles with sexual innuendo. Mitchell recalls Irwin's justified suspicion of Porter's mischief:

The next time Irwin was willing to go along with Porter was "I Was a Salvation Army Lass." Now how the devil is he going to do something with a dear little Salvation Army lass? Well, Porter could. Irwin would have blue pencilled it before it got through, but the original went, "When she pulls on and feels the harsh kiss of her Salvation Army issue knickers against her thighs, does that tender under skin yearn for the soft caress of silken knickers?" The next thing that came up was Porter's idea – "I Was the Last

Toronto Milk Wagon Horse." Irwin was a great one on nostalgia too. I remember distinctly, "As he pulls his load of clinking milk bottles at the break of dawn" (it was florid!) "down the dreary streets of colonial Toronto, plods his weary way with the clop, clop of his hooves on the unkind pavement, does his mind go to those days, before he had been gelded, to lush pastures with the fat rumps of those lush young mares." Now, I know that this just pissed Irwin off, and I know because we all used to talk about it. We were all amused by it.[40]

While tempers sometimes flared in the Thursday-morning sessions, the editorial team members became very close and developed lasting friendships both in and outside of the *Maclean's* office. There was a lot of hard work and pressure to get the magazine out every two weeks and one way of alleviating that pressure was what Les Hannon called the "element of high jinks and jokes" around the office. Bill, "a light-hearted, unconcerned man," was often at the centre of it or was set up by the others.[41] Over the two years Mitchell worked for him, Irwin took his adventures and office hijinks in stride, and thirty-five years later diplomatically remembered Mitchell as "getting into, ahh, trouble – creating disturbances."[42]

～ "THE ALIEN" ～

House vacancies were limited in Toronto so the Mitchells had been living temporarily on Toronto Island, and it was not until October 1 that Merna located a duplex at 140 Springdale Boulevard, East York. One of the first things she did was purchase an antique writing desk for Bill so he could do his own writing in the evenings and on weekends. His fondness for this desk, which he stripped, sanded, and varnished, is emotionally recounted in *Since Daisy Creek*: "Made of heartwood walnut, eleven feet long and four feet wide, it had hogged a third of the space in the living room area. . . . Except for his first pair of tube skates or his sixteen-inch red CCM bicycle, it was probably the most delighting gift he had ever received" (*SD* 45). Bill could not find a stool of the appropriate height so he stood up to type for the first while. That soon became tiresome, and he sawed down the legs – but he miscalculated and the legs had to be set on blocks. Years later, he propped the desktop on two drawer-size filing cabinets, and it remained his favourite desk throughout his writing life.

When Mitchell came east he brought three finished short stories and two major pieces, his new novel, "The Alien," and a novella, "The Devil's Instrument." Three of the four stories that Mitchell sold in 1948 to *Maclean's* were written prior to his coming to Toronto. "The Day Jake Made Her Rain," published March 1, would go on to have a future on radio and stage. The other stories – "Shoparoon for Maggie" (May 15), "Air-Nest and the Child Herald" (August 1), and "Air-Nest and La Belle Dame" (November 15) – were "potboilers" with little literary value, written out of financial necessity before he landed the *Maclean's* editorship.

"The Alien" grew out of his interest in the Stoney Indians and his experience of living in High River. By January 1947 he had blocked out the narrative in chapters and had completed fifty thousand words of rough material. His central character, Hugh (later named Carlyle), was a half-breed and from the beginning he was conceived of as an idealistic but moody and embittered anti-hero unable to come to terms with his mixed blood. He progressively alienates himself from family and friends in both white and red cultures.

As Mitchell was finding his feet at *Maclean's* in the summer of 1948, he had even less time for serious writing. However, in September 1948 he received an admonishing letter from Salter that caused him to refocus his attention on the new novel, which had been on a back burner for close to a year:

> Mr. Cloud of <u>Atlantic</u>[43] has a number of times complained that he can't get in touch with you, that you don't answer letters, etc. I have tried to soothe him, but I can't go on forever telling him this and that, that you have moved your residence, etc. etc. What's the big idea anyway? . . .

Now you may feel that you didn't get a very good bargain out of them and you would do better to change publishers. Even so, let them know. Let them know where they stand, and don't keep them in the dark. If you have a grievance, out with it in good round manly fashion; the world respects a man, but nobody respects a sulker. Cloud actually used that expression about you some months ago, asking, "Is he sulking in his tent?"

On a more positive note, Salter offered his editing skills: "If you think there is anything left in me that you want, grab it while I'm still around." He also asked Bill to consider one of his student's stories for *Maclean's*, but he closed in his scolding mode: "Well, now, you be a good boy and write to Mr. Cloud. I don't care what you write, so long as it is frank and manly, but write!"[44]

Bill responded a week later, insisting that he had not been sulking: "I think you know by this time . . . , that when I get angry I am constitutionally unable to do so silently. If you will remember my bouts with members of your own faculty some few years ago, the trouble was that I could not keep 'my big mouth shut.' I have not changed very much." Although he admitted he had been disappointed with Little, Brown, not liking their "editing and the wrangling" over *Who Has Seen the Wind* nor feeling satisfied with their publicity efforts, he proceeded to explain the real reasons why he had not responded to Atlantic Monthly Press's letters for more than a year:

The past four years of free lancing have had some pretty precarious moments with the bankers and creditors breathing down my neck; and it has been, particularly of late, irritating to have to turn out pot-boilers in order to keep the family solvent.

About a year ago I asked Little Brown for an advance; they offered me $300, which I disregarded because I felt it would be a good idea, since that was the extent to which they felt they could subsidize me, not to tie myself down when it came to bargaining. . . . I made the mistake last summer in Victoria of telling Salmen[45] the outline of the narrative, and he told me that he was very sorry to hear that the central character died in the end since "negative endings" were poor business as far as novels were concerned. He wondered if it would not be possible for the central character to turn a corner and become regenerated. It is impossible for the central character to turn a corner, as a matter of fact I'm having a hard time to keep him from jumping off Look Out Peak in a most dramatic climax in which he not only dies but kills himself as well. That last sentence looks pretty confused to me, but I'll let it go.

Mitchell was no doubt more resentful about Salmen's criticism of his negative ending than he was about the small advance he had offered, for this brought back memories of how Cloud and Edward Weeks, chief editor of Atlantic Monthly Press, had wanted to change the ending of *Wind* and make it more traditional. He told Salter that he did not want his book to be "tampered with for commercial reasons," and that he would send him a draft of the novel when it was done because, "If I am going to have an objective helping hand, I want yours or that of someone who is disinterested." He never did send a manuscript for Salter to edit. Although he paid his debt to Salter in glowing praise a thousand times over in subsequent years, perhaps he felt that he, now an editor himself, had truly graduated from Salter's mentorship. He enclosed his critiqued story of Salter's student and then closed, "I turn now to being a good boy and to writing Mr. Cloud. I promise that it will be frank and manly."[46]

It took two months, but he finally wrote Cloud: "Forgive me my long silence. It was simply that I did not have a great deal of progress to report on the new book, tentatively titled, THE ALIEN. I have been working on it sporadically, am about two-thirds through the first draft, the pace determined by the necessity of my doing popular pot boilers. . . . I rather think you will like THE ALIEN; it is a little more ambitious than WHO HAS SEEN THE WIND, with a more flowing narrative and a greater appreciation of the importance of conflict and dramatic quality." He hoped to have a final draft done by April 1949. He also mentioned that the past year had been an unhappy one in terms of his own creative writing, but that he completed two short stories and a novella, "The Devil's Instrument," before coming to Toronto and would like to submit them to *Atlantic Monthly*. He closed, saying, "I have not a temperamental bone in my body, and I ceased long ago to consider my work as a personal adornment of the Mitchell ego. Forgive, again, the silence; put it down to poor public relations and not pique."[47] Cloud was very pleased to hear about "The Alien," and told Mitchell to send him the novella and the two stories he had mentioned, promising to keep "a friendly eye on them as they go through the magazine readers."[48]

— "THE DEVIL'S INSTRUMENT" —

The novella, "The Devil's Instrument," grew out of "Peter and the Goose Boss," a short story Mitchell had written in 1945 soon after he encountered two Hutterite boys looking at a mouth organ in the glass counter display in Tom's Café in New Dayton. When Mitchell had remarked how nice it would be to own one, they had responded, "No. It's the Devil's instrument." In High River, he learned a great deal more about Hutterian communal life in the two colonies nearby. Hutterites were a familiar sight in High River, the men dressed in black trousers, shirt, and suspenders with a black felt hat, the women in long black dresses with an apron, lace-up boots, and a polka-dot kerchief covering their heads. When Mitchell went out to fly fish along Willow Creek, he would visit with families at the Macmillan Colony.

Mitchell was attracted to "these people of the gentle persuasion,"[49] by the way their strict religious beliefs were an integral part of their day-to-day life, and by their dogged commitment to a communal life. They had suffered religious persecution for more than five centuries in half a dozen countries before ending up in Canada in 1918. Alberta's Social Credit government was suspicious of the Hutterites' success and their accumulation of land so, in 1942, they banned all land sales to Hutterites. Following the war, they brought in more legislation, culminating in the Communal Properties Act of 1955, which restricted the amount and location of Hutterian land purchases.

But Mitchell was also bothered by some aspects of colony life such as their deep-seated materialism and disapproval of the arts. Their desire for a simple, spiritual life forbade their members from participating in the outside world's lifestyle with its rights of private ownership, politics, educational, and legal institutions. They saw the entertainment industry (radio, movies, and television) as the Devil's tools for tempting sinners away from a life of work devoted to God. However, unlike other religious communal groups such as the Amish and Mennonites who rejected all modern technology, many of the Hutterite colonies embraced new advances in agricultural methods and equipment.[50]

Mitchell was opposed to any authority that repressively moved into another individual's or minority's territory. On the one hand, he was outraged by the bigotry of the Social Credit government's legislation, which infringed on the rights of the Hutterites; on the other hand, he was critical of the power the colonies held over their own individual members. The Bosses controlled every aspect of Hutterian life, including to whom and when a young man or woman married, and that became the subject of "The Devil's Instrument." Using his first-hand observation of Macmillan colony life, Mitchell began expanding "Peter and the Goose Boss" into a fifteen-thousand-word novella in which fifteen-year-old Jacob Schunk rebels against the colony Bosses. "The Devil's Instrument," completed in 1947, explores Hutterian repression of its own members, particularly of a potentially creative adolescent who is denied the opportunity to fully explore and express his emotional, intellectual, and artistic identity.

In the opening scene in the Nu-Way Café a stranger buys Jacob the mouth organ he has been admiring in the display case. Although he has been taught that the practise of any art and the pleasure it gives are sinful, Jacob cannot help himself: "He played it, a youth in a dream, in a trance, exalted and enchanted by the magic of its sound." At the same time, Jacob falls in love with Marta, and Mitchell links his awakening artistic and sexual passions. Though forbidden to meet until they are paired for marriage, Jacob and Marta meet clandestinely behind one of the haystacks. Whenever Jacob thinks of Marta, he feels "a slight quickening of his heart and a breathlessness equalled only when he contemplated playing his mouth organ." For a while he gives up his mouth organ, buries it in the straw stack.

In town, he again meets the stranger who reveals that he is Jacob's brother, Darius, who, years before, had been excommunicated for defying the Bosses. Darius tries to persuade Jacob to leave the colony, arguing that Jacob is not free, that "there are no Hutterite poets, for the colony kills what is beautiful . . . ," and that the Devil is "Boss over all the Bosses!" Jacob does not leave with Darius, but he cannot resist either Marta or his mouth organ. He is discovered, his mouth organ is smashed on the blacksmith's anvil, and Jacob and Marta are sentenced to shunning for three months. The Bosses also decree that Jacob will not marry Marta. When he tries to speak to her, Marta runs from him. Jacob, too, flees, but away from the colony to find his brother, who "would give him another mouth organ." Jacob's self-exile from the colony is an ambivalent victory. Those forces that are inimical to his creative spirit and the fulfilment of his identity in the Hutterite colony are also present, perhaps in more subtle and insidious forms, in the larger colony of the outside society. This is hinted at in Darius's response when Jacob asks him if he is happy: "'I must be honest with you. I am free – "If I forgot thee, O Jerusalem"—' his voice died away. 'Anyway, I am free,' he said again."[51]

One of the Atlantic readers would later dismiss "The Devil's Instrument" as a "period piece" that would not interest a large readership. But Mitchell's intention was hardly parochial. As he wrote in the introduction to the later stage-play version, "Conformity in a puritan society is as much a problem for Jacob Schunk as it has been for other artists since long before the Reformation" (*DWO* 4). Jacob's situation is universal. He is a Hutterian version of James Joyce's Stephen Daedalus, and Mitchell's novella is a portrait of the musician/artist as a young man whose first stirrings of sexual and artistic energies are thwarted by his society. Jacob's final rebellion and self-exile are not as self-conscious as those of Stephen, but he too finally rebels and escapes from his imprisoning island, flies by the nets of religion, materialism, and a powerful hierarchical society that tries to predetermine and control every aspect of his life. Mitchell uses the Hutterian society's repression of creative energy in its young as an exaggerated mirror image of his own puritan and materialistic society's repression of the young, a theme he explored throughout his writing career.

– MITCHELL AS EDITOR –

Mitchell had good intentions to get busy on "The Alien," but he had not yet found his stride at *Maclean's*. As well, the *Maclean's* Fall Fiction Contest and his mentoring of two beginning writers took his attention away from his own writing. Even though Mitchell read every story submitted by a Canadian writer, he was finding very few publishable ones. However, the 1948 *Maclean's* fiction contest netted two impressive stories. "One, Two, Three Little Indians," a story about an Indian couple and the tragic death of their baby in a tourist camp in Northern Ontario, had been submitted by Jarvis Warwick, which proved to be the pseudonym of Hugh Garner. Mitchell was not happy when the judges passed it over. Neither was Garner, and he went to see Bill:

> We had never met before, but when I told him I was the author of the Indian story he sat me down in his office and said, "I don't know what the hell was wrong with the judges, but in my estimation it was one of the best stories we received. Even after the prizes were announced I tried to get it printed in the magazine anyhow, but the editor turned thumbs down." . . . Bill Mitchell showed me a chit attached to the manuscript of the Indian story which he had circulated among the other editors, including Pierre Berton, John Clare and others, and they all had scribbled favourable comments about the story and agreed with Bill that the magazine

should print it. Though Mitchell did his best to get the magazine
to publish it, he finally had to mail it back to me.[52]

Irwin had taken an instant dislike to Garner's grimly realistic story.
When Mitchell could not convince Irwin to publish it, he sent it to
Dudley Cloud at *Atlantic Monthly*. It was rejected but, as Mitchell
wrote Garner, "although they have not taken the story, I think that
you have gone a long way with this one to attracting their attention.
It would be nice if you could send in a dandy to them and thereby
make the Atlantic Magazine."[53] Garner finally sold it to *Liberty*, and
it became one of the most often anthologized of his short stories.[54]

One afternoon, when Merna was helping Bill by reading his
weekly batch of slush-pile stories, she came across one called "A
Penny in the Dust" by Ernest Buckler. She knew she had hit a winner,
and that night when Bill arrived home from work she excitedly
showed it to him. Mitchell wrote Buckler, praising the story's "sure"
characterization and sensitive treatment of a child-father relationship
that is "quite moving without being mawkish or sentimental." He
offered Buckler $200 and asked to see more of his work.[55]

Buckler, who lived quietly in the Annapolis Valley in Nova
Scotia, was thrilled. On November 15, Mitchell telegrammed
Buckler to tell him that another story of his, "The Tablecloth," had
made the finals of the *Maclean's* fiction contest, and to send a photograph and biographical material as soon as possible. Along with
that material, Buckler enclosed a personal letter that ended, "I have
rambled on, haven't I? But I hope you won't mind. I get so pent-up
here sometimes, and somehow I feel that you're a guy I can talk to,
easily."[56] On December 22, Bill sent another telegram, this time
telling Buckler his story had won first place and a $1,000 cheque was
on its way. Buckler responded with another long, exuberant letter
that closed, "This thing has meant a great deal to me, because I don't
think there's anything in God's world like the thrill of placing a story
you really believe in, in a good spot. It makes material pleasures, if you
don't mind me coining a phrase, 'pale into insignificance.' It makes
even your first piece of tail seem like a faded gumdrop. (Julia will

murder me!)."[57] Buckler's winning story, retitled "The Quarrel," appeared in the January 15, 1949, issue of *Maclean's*.

A few weeks later, Buckler submitted another story with a covering letter beginning, "This was to have gone out to you yesterday, but I got tangled up with a fascinating book I couldn't leave. It's a book everyone in Canada should read. Especially those dopesters who keep insisting that there's no such thing as Canadian literature. (I was inclined to agree with them before I read this book.) It's called WHO HAS SEEN THE WIND. Guy name of Mitchell." He continued, "Its beautiful parts are so beautiful they're stilling (for want of a better word to describe them); and its humour and its goddamns are as natural and refreshing as a good, satisfactory, uninhibited, you know what. I don't know when I've come across a book that had so sustained a grip it became almost hurting. . . ."[58] By this time Mitchell and Buckler had dropped the formal Dear Mr —— letter openings and had developed an easy and frank rapport. Bill responded with mutual admiration, "I appreciated your last letter very much; don't worry, boy; when my wife read your contest winning story and when she read 'Penny in the Dark' [Dust], she said, 'I think I could dislike that Ernest Buckler simply because he's more than enough competition for you.' You have a most ardent fan in my wife; I find her a most sensitive and discerning critic. She is not easy to please." Bill, however, dismissed Buckler's new submission, "Love Among the Ogives," as "a clinker; and I mean clinker!" He suggested Ernest take it "and impale it on a nail in the wall of the little house that is at the end of the path going by the woodpile." He asked, though, if he could see any sections of Buckler's novel for a possible story.[59]

Buckler agreed with Bill's assessment: "I put 'Love Among the Ogives' where you advised, but it didn't work. People kept coming in and saying, 'What the hell stinks out there?'" However, he was reluctant to try passages from the novel because it is "very much in the foetal and amorphous stage."[60] Over the spring and summer Buckler sent him a number of stories and light humorous pieces, but with no luck. Yet Mitchell continued to write encouraging letters, and told Buckler that he had mentioned his novel to Dudley Cloud at Atlantic Monthly Press, who might be contacting him.

⊸ "OH GOD WE HAD FUN!" ⊸

When they first arrived in Toronto, Merna was keen to take advantage of the radio and stage acting opportunities, and she auditioned at the CBC for a part. Although she achieved a high score, she did not get the part. To build up her confidence, she decided to go to the radio drama school that Lorne Greene had started. She felt, "It was an in and I could learn from it." Bill, however, was not supportive because he felt she was beyond it, did not need it: "As a matter of fact it's one of the things I hold against him, bless his heart. But you had to become known. And I would not allow Bill to push me. I wouldn't go into anything of Bill's. I could have. Quite easily he could have said to the producer, 'I want my wife to play that part.' I didn't want that because I didn't think it was ethical, so I didn't. So there it was."[61] Merna must have kept these ambitions to herself, for her friends were unaware of her acting talents and background. Claire (Drainie) Taylor, the actress who played Ma on Mitchell's *Jake and the Kid* radio show, later commented,

> I had no idea she was so talented. We had quite a close friend-ship during his [Bill's] short stay at *Maclean's*. . . . But neither of them ever told us that Merna was an actress/singer and accom-plished musician. Talk about hiding that proverbial light under a bushel! Maybe they thought we were professionals and wouldn't be interested. But they were wrong. I can tell you I could never do all the things Merna did, and I think Bill was a much better stage performer than John. With all his talent, John was never really comfortable in front of an audience, so it was fortunate that he lived during the Golden Age of Radio – which I think he helped create.[62]

Merna did act in two stage plays. She played a maid in Goldsmith's Restoration comedy, *She Stoops to Conquer*, a New Play Society production directed by Dora Mavor Moore in October 1949, and both she and Bill played parts in *Pullman Car Hiawatha*, a one-act play by Thornton Wilder.[63]

However, Merna's hopes for an acting career in Toronto did not pan out. While she felt frustrated by this, she had her plate full with other activities. She continued her role as Bill's first editor and often helped him with his reading of other writers' manuscripts. Bill, on occasion, recommended her editing skills to other writers such as Ralph Allen.[64] But most of Merna's time and energy were devoted to running the Mitchell household and organizing a very busy social life.

While Bill and Merna had always planned to leave Toronto after a few years, the circle of friends they soon gathered led them to consider putting down more permanent roots in Toronto. They had become close friends with the Bertons, who lived in an apartment in East York a few blocks away. Jan and Pierre tried to persuade them to join a "co-operative venture – an idealistic community of ten writers and artists and their families living in harmony on forty acres of unserviced land" near Kleinberg.[65] Bill and Merna decided against this, but Pierre and Jan bought three acres in the summer of 1948. There was an apple orchard on the property, and that fall Bill suggested they make apple cider. They picked apples one weekend and took them to a local cider press. Bill got ten-gallon oak barrels and all the paraphernalia. Berton recalled the procedure: "Bill had learned how to make cider, the recipe with sugar and raisins, and he showed me how to work the rubber tubing. Once the bubbling stopped you threw in an aspirin and that fixed the cider so it wouldn't turn to vinegar. And Bill added a couple of pounds of hamburger steak, claiming that this improved the cider. I said, 'Sure, but what does it do to your stomach?' I didn't add any hamburger to mine."[66]

The *Maclean's* people and their families got together regularly for weekends and holiday gatherings. With such a talented group there was plenty of loud talk and party pieces: Berton shouting out

"The Shooting of Dan McGrew;" Bill dramatizing a story in Québécois dialect about a habitant's bull that plunges to its death off a lift bridge with a bugle up its ass; John Clare's mordant one-liners; and McKenzie Porter describing his ride to the Durban Country Club in a Zulu rickshaw. Always there were children running around. The Mitchells hosted Christmas Day parties in their small Springdale Boulevard house. The first year Bill came across some puppeteers on Danforth and persuaded them to come along to the Christmas party and put on a show for the children. It was chaos as Merna cooked the turkey (Pierre insisting that the turkey be basted continually with his homemade cider), while people got tangled in the puppets and strings laid out all over the kitchen floor.

The *Maclean's* people fondly recalled the parties and family get-togethers of these years. At one point when being interviewed about this time, Merna exclaimed, "Oh what a lovely time. Oh God we had fun!" When Les Hannon was told about Merna's comment, he responded that everybody looks back at their youth with similar feelings, and then he added, "Nevertheless, even allowing for the usual colourations, it was really a fabulous decade. There was that sense of camaraderie."[67]

2

RADIO DRAMATIST, EDITOR, WRITER

– 1949 –

I N 1948 when Mitchell arrived in Toronto, radio was well into its golden age, which ran from about 1940 to 1965.[1] In this period the Canadian Broadcasting Corporation (CBC), like *Maclean's* under Irwin's leadership, was developing a national cultural vision for Canada. Under Andrew Allan's direction as national drama supervisor, the CBC put out considerably more Canadian fictional writing than *Maclean's* did.[2] Allan was the director of two national drama series for the CBC, *Stage* and *Wednesday Night*, through which he "nurtured Canadian radio drama into maturity and founded our first national theatre on the air."[3] He focused on quality of writing and acting and, for the *Stage* series, he emphasized Canadian talent, showcasing Canadian writers such as Fletcher Markle, Len Peterson, Joseph Schull, Harry Boyle, and Gerald Noxon. Allan produced four of Mitchell's dramas, but it was Harry Boyle, program director, who brought Mitchell into the CBC fold. Boyle, later a novelist, was a radio dramatist who had forty plays produced on the CBC.[4]

At the same time, John Drainie, perhaps the greatest radio actor in Canada, if not North America, was at the height of his career, playing the lead in many of Allan's productions. Merna and Bill thought very highly of him, and Merna, who had received much praise for her radio acting on CKUA Edmonton (one of the top regional producers of drama), felt that Drainie was ideal for Bill's work.[5] Drainie had an unmatchable versatility, playing roles from Shakespeare, to Ibsen, to Dickens, all the way to Leacock. So, with these opportunities right on his doorstep, and given his love of theatre and his talent for drama, it was quite natural for Mitchell to consider writing for radio.

On January 21, 1949, Mitchell's first piece (which had been written in High River) was heard on radio. It was a fifteen-minute short story called "The Comtesse," and John Drainie was the performer. The story was based on an incident involving one of High River's eccentric personalities, the Countess de Foras. In order to ensure her privacy in the backhouse (safe from the eyes of the training pilots in the little Moth planes), the Comtesse asks the local carpenter (and drunk) to construct a roof for it, but he drinks his wages before doing the job. However, to maintain her dignity, she retrieves her French silk parasol out of her old trunk and, opening the tattered parasol with its panels of "butterflies [that] were the ghosts of their former brilliant selves; . . . [t]he Comtesse Alixe Eduxie Eloise Fernande de la Vergne-Penne, House of Savoy, god-daughter of the king of Bulgaria, old woman – entered."[6]

In this story Mitchell explored, as in much of his work, the confrontation of the civilized with the vulgar, propriety with irreverence – in, short French parasols with backhouses. Writer and poet Earle Birney felt that this little story introduced a new tenor to national broadcasting. On CBC's *Critically Speaking* program, he said,

> I very much suspect that every Canadian "family" magazine . . . would reject this story as vulgar and indiscreet. Yet I also suspect that the majority of those who heard it in the family sitting-room by radio enjoyed it thoroughly and were not shocked. In other words radio can, and will, if permitted, do something to break down the namby-pamby emasculated tradition which continues to exist in our printed fictions, and so provide a stimulus to honest adult writing in Canada.[7]

How correct he was, for Mitchell had given the story to *Atlantic Monthly* for publication soon after it aired. He was proud of its "marriage of elements anything but harmonious: some of Miss Brill [one of Katherine Mansfield's characters] – a touch of Rabelais, or perhaps it's Chic Sale. But that, I think, is Alberta."[8] But three of the four *Atlantic Monthly* readers thought the shift from "sublime to ridiculous" was too much for their readers.[9]

Mitchell's first one-hour radio drama, *The Devil's Instrument*, was adapted from his novella for CBC's *Stage 49*. Broadcast on March 27, 1949, it was directed by Andrew Allan and starred Bill Needles as Jacob Schunk, John Drainie as Peter, the Goose Boss, and Tommy Tweed as the truck driver. In the radio adaptation Mitchell introduces a new character, a narrator whose voice fades into the Devil's. The narrator/Devil's sardonic glosses give the radio play a more comic vision than that of the novella. At the end the listener assumes that it is Jacob's soul that the Devil has come for, but the Devil's final speech makes it clear that he has his eye on the bosses. Mavis Gallant, a young Montreal writer, gave it a very positive review: "William Mitchell, author of last year's *Who Has Seen the Wind*, made an elegant debut with his first radio play, 'The Devil's Instrument.' Where else but on 'Stage 49' do you find stories about Canada which are not cute, coy and self-conscious? . . . [it] was tremendously appealing and the only searching piece about that anachronistic way of life we have ever heard."[10]

The next two radio plays Mitchell wrote were potboilers, "Chaperone for Maggie" for Andrew Allan's *Stage 49*[11] and "Out of the Mouths" for *Summer Theatre*.[12] "Out of the Mouths" had a trivial plot about bets being taken on whether a baby would say MaMa or DaDa first. Mitchell, who played a role in it, described it as a likeable, "cute thing."[13] It seems silly by today's standards, as does the plot of "Chaperone," a romance with a convoluted story-line. Nevertheless, these first four radio plays were the beginning of a long and fruitful relationship with the CBC. As Mitchell put it, "CBC and *Maclean's* – one's the father, one's the mother of writers of my generation."[14]

In the summer Bill and Merna used every opportunity to escape the city on the weekends and holidays. Merna described how the Springdale Boulevard house "would absorb the heat all day and then give it off at night. Sometimes we slept on the floor down in the living room because it was so hot. In the second year when we had a car we would drive with the fishing rods right out of the city."[15] She would pack the boys, Orm, aged six, and Hughie, aged three, in the car, pick up cheeses and egg bread and sliced meats from a delicatessen, and then collect Bill from work. On a couple of occasions they stayed in a bed and breakfast in Peterborough, and Bill discovered a good stretch of stream on Trout Creek. The farmer gave him permission to fish there, but said that he had not seen fish in the stream for years. Bill, however, caught his limit of good-sized brown trout in an hour and had two or three more rewarding outings that season with no one else on the stream. He gave the farmer some of his last catch – which was a mistake. When he came back with Ralph Allen and Greg Clark (a *Toronto Star* writer and avid fly-fisherman) for opening day the next year, word about Bill's success had spread. The banks of Trout Creek were lined with fishermen who were flogging the water with every kind of bait, plug, and metal hardware conceivable. Allen and Clark were not impressed by Bill's secret fly-fishing stream – and did not get one strike. On one of these fishing excursions Mitchell came across a business entrepreneur, Red Edgar, whose Lucky Strike Bait Company had grown from a home hobby of carving fishing plugs out of broomstick handles. He interviewed him and wrote up a light profile article, "He Lured Success."[16]

Another time they came home with a dog. Merna always had a soft spot for dogs and a stray cocker spaniel in the Cavan grocery store won her over. In typical Bill-and-Merna tandem they related how they landed the second of the eight dogs they eventually owned:

MERNA: I walked in and we just fell for each other. She really
    wanted love, you know. And I asked, "Whose dog is this?"
BILL: She comes out to where I was fishing and . . .

MERNA: They said, "We don't know, and if you want her you can have her . . ."

BILL: We didn't realize it, but Maggie was knocked up as well as picked up. She had nine bloody pups – all different. She herself was no pure . . .

MERNA: Bill – Bill, may I interrupt! Bill's mother was staying with us. We advertised we had found her. We were out for dinner when the owner phoned. He said he didn't want her back but said, "Of course you realize that she's pregnant." This is just a few weeks before she was to give birth. Grandmother said, "Well, we know it now!"

BILL: Maggie had the pups in the bedroom underneath the bed. Mother delivered them all. We got home from wherever we'd been . . .

MERNA: Grandma phoned us and said she thought Maggie had gotten under the bed to hide and have her pups. And . . .

BILL: She had nine of them – mother said they just kept coming and coming. And my mother – even having been a maternity nurse in the Bowery in New York – this was something she hadn't anticipated![17]

Bill and Merna managed to find homes for all nine puppies, most of them among their *Maclean's* and CBC friends.

– "A CRITICAL POINT FOR YOUR REPUTATION" –

After the success of *The Devil's Instrument* on radio, John Gray, publisher at Macmillan, asked to see the original novella version right away. Both Gray and Dudley Cloud were concerned that Mitchell had not yet produced a second novel. They felt that it was critical to capitalize on the momentum of the success of *Who Has Seen the Wind* with a new novel within two years – which meant now. On a visit to England, Gray took the novella with him, and Macmillan London indicated interest in it. Gray began preparing to bring out

"The Devil's Instrument" as "a thin little deluxe job to fill the gap between WHO HAS SEEN THE WIND and THE ALIEN."[18]

Mitchell sent the novella to Cloud, hoping that Little, Brown would be willing to "split the gamble in what looks like an unpromising publishing venture." Mitchell was uncertain about the plans to use illustrations and wide margins "so that the thing might look like a novel instead of a novella." He had just signed on with an American agent, Willis Wing, who felt that the place for it was in one of the women's popular magazines.[19] However, throughout June 1949 Mitchell worked on a rewrite, aiming to expand the novella to twenty-five thousand words.

At the end of June, Cloud rejected the unexpanded version, although Gray continued to try to change Cloud's mind. Gray forged on with his own plans to publish five thousand copies about mid-autumn and offered to supply Little, Brown with half the edition at forty-five to fifty cents a copy: "Surely this might be a feasible operation for both of us. I think we shall go ahead whatever you decide, but we should prefer to make it a joint venture."[20] Gray commissioned William Winter, a Toronto artist, to do some preliminary sketches for what was to be a ninety-six-page illustrated book, and he included an entry for "The Devil's Instrument" in the Macmillan fall catalogue, indicating publication in October.[21]

Cloud, however, still had reservations and wrote Bill, "All in all it looks to me as if you are throwing away a good beginning of a novel by publishing this as a little book. We feel that your next book or the one after that should establish you as a serious and substantial author in the eyes of critics and general readers. This is a critical point for your reputation." He asked Bill if he could "build this story into a substantial book?"[22] Bill felt as if he were a Hollywood star being handled by promoters who were moving into his artistic territory. His irritation showed in his reply to Cloud:

> Please know I am not a bloody prima donna, that my only
> reason for doing THE DEVIL'S INSTRUMENT was to write
> a good novella. I did it over a year ago, knowing that it was a

maverick, that it would quite likely find no home in a popular magazine, that I would probably have to wait till I had three of the bastards to make a book. . . .

MacMillans interest is a practical one; I am unable to judge how right or wrong they may be; my interest is simply to have written the story of Marta and Jacob and the Goose-Boss as well as I know how. I agree with you; I don't see how THE DEVIL'S INSTRUMENT could be built into a full dress book. I would like to have it published; surely it will be the material and its treatment, not its length, that will affect my reputation one way or the other.

He encloses an addition of about three thousand words, but says that the total novella will now be twenty thousand, not twenty-five thousand words.[23]

"The Alien" was the book that Mitchell thought would establish him as "a serious and substantial" writer. It had been lying dormant for eight months and now, during his summer holiday in July, he turned his attention to it. Merrill Denison, a writer, playwright, and actor whom the Mitchells had met through Bill's connections at *Maclean's*, invited Bill and his family to spend their three-week holiday at his resort at Bon Echo on Lake Mazinaw in July 1949.[24] Denison's mother, who originally bought and ran the resort, had been an ardent fan of Walt Whitman. When Whitman died in 1919, this "priestess of Walt" and Whitman's biographer Horace Traubel dedicated the Bon Echo Rock to "Old Walt." The dedication, chiselled into the rock face by two stone masons brought over from Aberdeen, Scotland, includes three lines from *Leaves of Grass*: "My foothold is tenon'd and mortis'd in granite,/I laugh at what you call dissolution,/And I know the amplitude of time."[25] Denison's mother envisaged the area as an artists' retreat and, indeed, famous artists did use it, including the Group of Seven.

The Mitchells were delighted to escape the city and the heat. They missed High River and having open country and the Highwood at their back door. Most importantly, Bill looked forward to three weeks of sustained writing on his novel. There was fishing and swimming, and the Mitchell boys managed to create distractions for everyone. Denison was particularly taken by Hughie's "elemental grandeur" that "sets him apart; the primitive male-child, purposeful, indomitable. Last evening, in the course of a beach supper, he almost changed the course of Bon Echo by turning off a water valve. . . . His feats upon a 12 inch tricycle have to be seen to be believed!"[26] Mary Savigny, in her book, *Bon Echo: The Denison Years*, mentions the invasion by the Mitchell savages: "We heard that naked little boys, painted like Indians, had been seen playing near the front gate. Merrill told us later that these were the children of W.O. (Bill) Mitchell. . . . Their mother had used lipstick on their faces and tummies when they played Cowboys and Indians. It wasn't intended they should wander off as far as the gate."[27] The boys swam naked along the lakeshore and, with their "barbaric yawps," yelled and whooped relentlessly at the rock face for three weeks – the echo never disappointed them. Whitman would have approved.

Lake Mazinaw, with its "water so clear you could see right to the bottom,"[28] and the Bon Echo rock face, rising three hundred feet above the lake, transported Bill back to the Alberta foothills and Rockies as he composed the final sequence of "The Alien." Merna always felt that it was some of the most powerful writing he had ever done. Carlyle, the main character, climbs up to the lookout tower perched on top of Mount Lookout's hogback in an atmosphere that is "charged and crackling with the electricity" of an approaching storm. As Carlyle listens to the half-crazed lookout man "droning on and on," he realizes "he looked upon himself – as surely as in a mirror – here he was – this sterile, virgin and demented man – this Aristotle's God thinking its idiot self upon the mountain top."

Carlyle's sense of the futility of connecting with others is strikingly echoed in the lookout keeper's narcissistic monologue, "private words unintended for a listening ear":

"– a sort of epistemological masturbation. The seeds don't come to anything – words can't be any good, of course. Take a word from one mind and plant it in another and it takes on unintended life – a strange fruit – strange blossoms – perhaps it doesn't germinate at all. They never can provoke an exact twin effect. Oh – a loaf of bread is a loaf of bread – a bed is a bed. . . ."

"– sleep in it – procreate in it – would you like – would you have some more similes – metaphors. They are worthless. They are pretty but useless. No use. Why should they have. They are not the thing – the thing is more like itself than anything else, isn't it? Do I bother you?"

The lookout keeper raises an issue that did indeed "bother" Mitchell, an issue that lies at the heart of his own rationale for storytelling. The writer's words should have *both* intended and unintended life – the writer's stories create a shared experience with the reader who is a creative partner. For Mitchell, the writer does not intend his words to aim for "an exact twin effect" but rather precisely for that germination of strange fruit and blossoms that delight and astonish both the storyteller and the reader.

In the final scene Mitchell describes dawn breaking, the sounds of birds, and the movement of a porcupine as it climbs a spruce tree a few hundred feet below Carlyle's body. The scene is caught in the reflection of the lake at the base of Mount Lookout: "Reluctantly, lingeringly the last of the mist breathed from the face of the lake which reflected the sheer mountain side perfectly: the rust and tan and grey of the shale, the dark and sabering trees, the spruce and its porcupine. The reflection gave the illusion of incredible depth; half-way down it held the pine and the broken body at its base – steadily – like a fly in amber."[29] It is ironic that the tragic ending of "The Alien" was partially inspired by a rock face with a Whitman inscription celebrating faith in man's significance in the cosmos.

Soon after writing the final sequence of Part III at Bon Echo, Mitchell hit a major block. He felt that he did not have enough first-hand experience with the Stoneys to convincingly portray Carlyle's life on the reserve at Paradise Valley. When he returned to Toronto from Bon Echo, he wrote to Dudley Cloud, "– there is still one big hole that can be filled only after I have spent my two weeks holiday on an Indian Reservation."[30]

⁓ "ISN'T THAT THE DAMNEDEST THING YOU EVER HEARD OF?" ⁓

"The Alien" had to be put aside. "The Devil's Instrument" was now back on the table. A second reader had liked it and, with the additions, Cloud had changed his mind and began trying to convince his colleagues at Little, Brown to go for joint publication with Macmillan. He liked its warmth and said that the "firmly drawn characterization and description" made Mitchell's work "superlative."[31] One reader reported, "This is one of the most compact things I ever saw. . . . It's a lovely piece of work: sombre, quiet, and amazingly consistent in mood."[32] In an August 18 memo to Little, Brown, Cloud recommended that Little, Brown publish it as a book "because of its high quality."[33]

Then, on September 9, bad news. Cloud wrote Mitchell that the Little, Brown editorial board decided against a joint publication venture with Macmillan. Salmen, all along, had thought the novella was "either a dragged out short story or a dragged out beginning of a novel," and the editorial board felt that it "might well come near to ruining his [Bill's] reputation in our market."[34] But Cloud had worse news:

Yesterday in came a copy of the *Retail Bookseller*, containing this announcement:

The Dream Gate, by Marcus Bach.[35] Bobbs-Merrill. $3.00. A novel based upon the Hutterian colony in South Dakota, a community where no musical instrument was allowed, nor private property. Here little Michael Neumann received a harmonica from a visitor and kept it hidden. His struggles with his conscience, until his father at last persuaded him to throw the harmonica away, provide the plot, but the charm of the story is in its portrayal of a sincere and picturesque religious group. 303 pages.

Isn't that the damnedest thing you ever heard of?[36]

Mitchell was stunned with this news. He strongly suspected plagiarism and immediately wrote Bobbs-Merrill:

Dear Sirs:

In NEWSWEEK for September 12, I have just read the announcement and review of Marcus Bach's novel, THE DREAM GATE. I write to point out a most unfortunate and incredible coincidence in the similarity of this book to my own, THE DEVIL'S INSTRUMENT.

The latter concerns a Hutterite boy, Jacob Schunk, his receiving a mouth organ from a renegade Hutterite outside the colony, his conflict with his conscience, and the resolution of that conflict.

The announcement of THE DREAM GATE comes at a time when my novel is being considered for publication in United States by ATLANTIC PRESS and for serialization by the ATLANTIC MONTHLY MAGAZINE to which I am a contributor. A letter from Mr. Dudley Cloud yesterday, points out that THE DREAM GATE with its similar setting, conflict, and narrative, has automatically ruled out THE DEVIL'S INSTRUMENT for their use.

I am enclosing MACMILLANS OF CANADA'S fall and winter list which shows that a dramatic version of THE DEVIL'S INSTRUMENT was broadcast on the CBC network. This was on the hour length dramatic show, Stage 49, the first week in March [1949].

You can appreciate the horror with which I watch my second novel and over a year's creative effort going down the drain. I would appreciate any information you can give me on the editorial history of THE DREAM GATE, which would show me that its narrative was projected before the broadcast of THE DEVIL'S INSTRUMENT last March.[37]

Mitchell sent a copy of this letter to Cloud and described in more detail how he thought Marcus Bach may have plagiarized from the CBC's broadcast of *The Devil's Instrument*: "This program and another, News Roundup, has a greater listening audience in the States along the border than it has in Canada. The play raised a great deal of press comment in Manitoba and in Alberta where there are Hutterite groups."[38] Furthermore, there was a connection between Mitchell and Marcus Bach through Frank Steele, editor of the *Lethbridge Herald*.[39] It is likely that Mitchell first met Steele when he was living in New Dayton (near Lethbridge) and became interested in Hutterian life. He may also have had contact with Steele when he was in Lethbridge in May 1948 to research an article on George Ross, "The Flying Rancher," for *Maclean's*. At that time, Mitchell was just finishing the fifteen-thousand-word version of "The Devil's Instrument," and he was not the kind of writer who kept secret the details of his work-in-progress. Soon after the radio broadcast of the play, Bach visited Steele in Lethbridge when he was researching the southern Alberta Hutterite colonies, and Steele later told Mitchell that Bach said he had heard the CBC's "The Devil's Instrument" while doing further research on his own book.[40]

Bill concluded his letter to Cloud, "I have just about kissed THE DEVIL'S INSTRUMENT good bye; I doubt very much now that there will be the Canadian and British editions that were arranged for in the first place. Anything that comes out now is labelled a steal from THE DREAM GATE. I am a little bitter."[41] Cloud wrote back a short sympathetic note saying that both he and Weeks thought it was "sheer coincidence" because it would be impossible for Bach to have projected, written, and published *The Dream Gate* between March (when "The Devil's Instrument" aired on the CBC) and September.[42]

However, after checking Bach's book against the radio play, Mitchell and Macmillan were not convinced and considered bringing a $50,000 suit for plagiarism,[43] but Peter Wright, Macmillan's lawyer, asked a question that put the situation in a new light:

> "Now why did you write the book?" And the idea was, did you write it for publicity reasons and to pick up $50,000? I said, "Of course not." "Well," he said, "you understand that if it takes five years and there's been all the publicity, then in the eyes of the public the book that did the plagiarizing will not be the one which came out five years ago but the one which came out five years later, and you will never be able to publish it except under that cloud." And that settled it for me. I said, "Okay we're not doing it."[44]

Mitchell's only reason for writing "The Devil's Instrument," as he had emphasized to Cloud, was "to write a good novella." He was certain of its high literary quality and felt that the best way to proceed was to delay publishing it a few years. By then Bach's novel, which Mitchell felt was mediocre at best, would have been long forgotten.

If Bach did get the idea of the mouth organ and other narrative elements from Steele and the radio broadcast, he probably quite innocently assumed there was no problem with borrowing them for his novel. This, of course, does not diminish the damage, both emotional and economic, that Mitchell suffered as a result of *The Dream Gate* pre-empting publication of "The Devil's Instrument." However, the manner in which Mitchell dealt with this major disappointment was representative of a pattern throughout his life. Although initially angry and frustrated, he invoked a kind of defensive amnesia for major setbacks such as this. He did not dwell on them, but turned his attention to new creative ventures. His buoyancy in the face of what he termed the "capsize quality of life" saved him, over the next twelve years, when his novel-writing ambitions would be repeatedly frustrated.

Although "The Devil's Instrument" had a varied life as a radio, television, and stage play, it never was published as a novella. It was, as Mitchell said, a "maverick," and over the next few years he worked on the idea of a Devil trilogy titled "The Devil's a Travelling Man." The second novella in this collection was to be an expanded version of a short story, "The Black Bonspiel of Wullie MacCrimmon," which he had written in 1947, about the same time he had written the first version of "The Devil's Instrument." By the fall of 1951, probably as a result of becoming reacquainted with his favourite fly-fishing runs on the Highwood, he had mapped out a rough narrative for the third story "in which Satan takes a holiday up the Highwood River."[45]

I recall my father on a number of our fishing trips in the 1950s telling me how this third Devil-temptation story might go. The main character, in his mid-forties, lives in a town on the lower reaches of the Highwood. All his life he has had a passion for fly-fishing, and because he has just been diagnosed with terminal cancer, he knows this will be his last season. Over the years he has had unsuccessful skirmishes with a particularly large brown trout that haunts a series of pools in the Highwood. One afternoon, a stranger appears on the river. To the disgust of the fly fisherman, the stranger seems to be having some success with his spinning hardware and bait. The stranger approaches and watches as the fisherman casts his dry-fly over and over, receiving no strikes. He then offers the fisherman one of his lures, assuring him that it will change his luck. The fisherman declines, saying he only fishes with flies. The stranger persists, offering him a salted minnow and telling him that if he casts it in a particular place in the pool he will hook the largest brown trout that has ever come out of the Highwood, a fish so large it will hold the North American record for years to come. My father played with various endings to this story, one of which was the fisherman refusing to compromise and continuing to cast his fly as the stranger leaves and the evening darkness closes down on the river.

Mitchell never developed this story idea of the Devil as a fisherman of souls any further, though the idea of the Devil trilogy or even duo (coupling "The Devil's Instrument" and "The Black Bonspiel") surfaced from time to time.

~ "YOU ARE A TRUE PROPHET" ~

In spite of the disappointments with his own work, Mitchell continued to be enthusiastic about the writers he discovered through *Maclean's*. Ernest Buckler had submitted "The Harness" in July, but Mitchell had been tied up with "The Devil's Instrument" and then sick with bronchitis. Apologizing for the delay in a letter of October 1949, he offered advice but turned the story down:

> My main objection to the story is that I come away from it with a sense of confusion, that I have to work harder than I am willing, to understand. It may be that my discernment is becoming blunted after over a year of reading popular magazine manuscripts; in any event my feeling is that it is a little too complexly told, certainly for MACLEAN'S readers. I think your inspiration was a real one, because, as with most of your work, I found myself quite believing in the people and reconsidering the ways of like humans known in my own life.
>
> Granting it is a little complex for popular fiction, I still wonder if the story isn't told with a little too much restraint from purely artistic standards? I don't know; the line between obscurity and just restraint will not stay still for me in my own work.[46]

Responding to another story a month later, Bill confided to Buckler that the Mitchells were not happy: "I've got a vitamin compound now that seems to beat this bronchitis thing; if I can get my wife and two children to take it, we could be healthy in Toronto – healthy but unhappy as hell."[47]

Around the same time Mitchell had been very impressed with a story from a young writer named Farley Mowat and had gone to bat for him with Arthur Irwin. In fact, it led to the biggest clash he had with Irwin and was a major part of the reason that Mitchell was disillusioned about his work at *Maclean's*.

Mitchell had been introduced to Mowat's work early in his first year at *Maclean's*, but it was not until 1949 that he tried to publish him. In fact, Mowat's librarian father, Angus, had approached Mitchell in Ottawa at the Canadian Authors Association meeting in June 1948 and, knowing he was the new fiction editor at *Maclean's*, had asked him if he would look at his son's work. At that time, Farley was working for the Dominion Wildlife Service as a field biologist studying wolves and caribou in the barren lands, but his ambition was to make a living as a writer. Mitchell's impression was that Angus was concerned about his son's career plans and wanted Mitchell to assess whether he had the talent and, if he did not, to discourage him so that he would turn his attention to more gainful employment.[48] Mitchell agreed, and soon began receiving portions of a book on "the Eskimos" on which Mowat was working. He was immediately impressed by Mowat's writing and, far from discouraging him, became an enthusiastic and committed supporter. Mitchell must have felt that they were kindred spirits because of their interest in writing about the impact of white culture on Aboriginal people – the Inuit in Mowat's case, the Stoneys in Bill's. Both of them wanted to use their writing to bring to public attention the way in which government policy was exacerbating the plight of Canada's Aboriginal cultures.

Over the course of 1949 Mitchell gave Mowat detailed feedback and advice on his developing manuscript about the Caribou Eskimos. Merna, in fact, claimed that Bill gave Mowat more help than he gave any other writer while he was at *Maclean's*.[49] As he had with Buckler,

Mitchell paved the way for Mowat at Atlantic Monthly Press[50] and Dudley Cloud, on the basis of an outline, bought an option on Mowat's book. Knowing that Mowat was struggling to survive financially, Mitchell took him over to the CBC building on Jarvis Street and introduced him to a number of contacts, including Robert Weaver, which led to Mowat giving six talks called "People of the Barrens" on CBC Radio.[51] After the first two talks, Mowat wrote Bill telling him that the CBC had "upped the ante to six instead of four, and in those that remain to me, I shall have my say about the Indian and Eskimo problem – not too subtly either." Mowat also mentioned in this letter that Robert Weaver "suggested that the three of us get together and talk over the possibility of doing a 'forum-type' discussion over the air, on the Indian. . . . Let me hear, if you think we could do any good."[52] Nothing, however, came of this idea.

In November 1949, Mowat submitted "Eskimo Spring" to Mitchell.[53] This story, the heart of *People of the Deer*, had a lasting impact on Mitchell, who recalled it as "wonderful – it was about the last living human beings of a very small band of Eskimos. It had quite a tragic epic quality."[54] He sent it on to Arthur Irwin and John Clare recommending publication. In the Thursday story session, Mitchell was astonished by Irwin's response to the story:

> I said, "This story is a must," and Irwin said, "Well, it isn't all that hot of a story." I said, "Yes it is, Arthur. It is, take my word for it." He said, "Oh come on now, it is slow moving and there's not much action in it." I said, "Okay, okay," because it's his decision in the end. He said, "You know, Bill, I am right," and I said, "No, you are not right, you are not right at all." And he persisted, saying, "Now come on, admit it. You know that it's not a story for *Maclean's*." And I said, "Arthur, you will never catch me saying to you in the area of non-fiction that a feature article is no good, that I disagree with you, and then try to get you to agree that I am right. Frankly, you really haven't the background, you're not a practising fiction writer and you're not all that good a

judge. You're too simplistic; you're talking about stories with positive endings." At which point I remember John Clare got worried. He said, "Come on, Bill, it's his magazine, not yours."[55]

Mitchell left Irwin's office in a rage. He wondered if there was more behind Irwin's refusal to publish "Eskimo Spring" than his blinkered view of what made a good story. He knew that Irwin did not like Angus Mowat, and suspected that Irwin might be letting a personal dislike for the father influence his judgment of the son's writing. But most of all, Mitchell resented Irwin's pressuring him to admit that his judgment about this story had been wrong. His disenchantment with *Maclean's* had grown to the point that he discussed with Merna whether he should resign.

Mitchell did not resign. He sent "Eskimo Spring" with a covering letter to Peggy Dowst, fiction editor at the *Saturday Evening Post*, and they took it. Mitchell could not resist taking the published story into Irwin: "'Here's the story you felt wasn't good enough for *Maclean's* to publish.' Irwin had a pretty good answer. He said, 'That's all right. We publish a lot of stories that the *Post* turns down.'"[56] Apart from being vindicated in his literary judgment, Mitchell had the satisfaction of knowing that the *Saturday Evening Post* paid Mowat four times more than he would have received from *Maclean's*.

A month after his argument with Irwin, Mitchell received another story, "The Balance," from Buckler. Mitchell felt it needed more work, but he wrote a lengthy and encouraging comment, comparing it in feeling to Katherine Mansfield's "Miss Brill." He felt that the "hearts and flowers ending" spoiled the story and, after suggesting a new direction, closed, "Try that on ATLANTIC and bugger sweet love and positive endings or happy endings or endings on the upbeat or sympathetic characters or any of the other bloody coarse yardsticks of popular fiction."[57] Mitchell was obviously still burning from Irwin's rejection of "Eskimo Spring."

Buckler completed a rewrite of "The Harness" and sent it to Bill in June 1950. He wrote, "I often think that if I could <u>talk</u> to you, we might get points threshed out which could make the difference between acceptance and rejection. The only trouble is, even if I ever were in Toronto I'm so bloody shy I probably couldn't get up the nerve to ask for an interview."[58] Bill responded within a week: "I think it is one of the best stories you have done." But Mitchell's "slight fiction list" (*Maclean's* had now cut its fiction from three stories to only one or two stories per issue) was "overstocked," and he suggested that Buckler try this story "with a quality magazine in the States" such as *Atlantic Monthly.* [59]

Bill continued promoting Buckler at Atlantic Monthly Press, and Buckler was "grateful," as he wrote to a connection at Curtis Brown, "to that wonderful guy and expert writer, W.O. Mitchell, who keeps up a sort of unobtrusive press-agentry for me whenever he gets a chance."[60] "The Harness" was a "near miss"[61] with *Atlantic Monthly,* and after Mitchell told Cloud about Buckler's novel-in-progress, *The Mountain and the Valley,* they made an offer for an option of $250. Bill continued to correspond with Buckler, offering advice on contracts, agents, Canadian rights and publishers, and, in March 1951, Buckler submitted the finished manuscript of *The Mountain and the Valley* to Cloud.[62]

About three months after the *Saturday Evening Post* had bought "Eskimo Spring," Bill and Merna invited Farley and his wife, Frances, for dinner. It was quite a night, with Farley and Bill trading stories about the Caribou people and the Stoneys, and celebrating Farley's recent freelance successes with "Eskimo Spring" and the CBC Radio series. Merna recalled, "Farley had me in tears when he was describing the plight of the Eskimo people in the North."[63] Bill read from his new novel, and, as Mowat wrote in his thank-you note, the evening made a strong impression on him:

> The Mowats are singularly lacking in the social graces. . . . But we both want to thank you very, very much for the evening we spent with you. Fran was particularly taken by your charming wife – and I, the same.
>
> I got hold of a copy of Who Has Seen the Wind and set out to read it, hoping that I could feel pleasantly superior when

I had finished. You know, the way we like to feel about other people's work. It backfired. I read the damn thing through without a pause, and thereby missed the best part of a night's rest. I missed the other part when I did, get to bed, for Brian was still with me. You know, I spent my early years in Saskatoon, and I was as much enamoured by the mystery of the prairies as Brian – and you were. . . .

But, and this is no false praise, your damn book stirred me more deeply than I care to be stirred – at this age of mine. I'm afraid you may do it again with your next. I swear I won't read it![64]

In September, Mowat sent *People of the Deer* to Dudley Cloud, whom Bill had already alerted in order to assure that Farley's manuscript would be given a close reading. Six weeks later Farley wrote Bill, "The book is with Atlantic who haven't made a goddamn sound since they got it. . . . I simply wish to God somebody would open his yap and end the agony. Tell me, how long do they make you sweat it out as a rule? . . . Hope I can sell some stuff fast. Book writing is sure and hell a luxury for struggling authors!" Farley also announced that he had used Bill as a reference for a VLA mortgage: "You were tagged as being in a position to say whether or not we can make a go of writing as a living. I should have asked if you would 'serve' before putting your name down, but I was afraid you would refuse. However, if you are annoyed – and I always am when someone uses my name without permission – you may blitz me."[65] Bill believed in Farley's talent and, remembering his own struggles to survive on the precarious income of a freelance writer, was happy to serve as a reference.

In the end Cloud and Atlantic agreed with Bill's assessment of Farley's work. Bill wrote Cloud in December saying that he was pleased to hear from Farley that he had "joined hands with Atlantic Press."[66] *People of the Deer* was published in 1952 by Little, Brown and three portions of it were serialized in *Atlantic Monthly*. Cloud excitedly wrote Mitchell soon after its publication, "You are a true prophet. Holt is publishing Ernest Buckler's novel, and we have made quite a splash with the Farley Mowat, *People of the Deer*. Have you any other promising writers up your sleeve?"[67]

Throughout his life Bill took very seriously his role as supporter and talent scout for Canadian writing, and he felt genuine delight in the successes of those writers he helped. He saw his editorial work and "press-agentry" as a repaying of his debt to F.M. Salter, who had played such a crucial role in fostering his own writing career.

<u>JAKE AND THE KID SERIES</u>

Episode 1 - The Oldest Old-Timer.

Broadcast: Tuesday, June 27th
8.30 - 9.00 pm T/Can. network

Producer: Peter Francis
Writer: W.O. Mitchell

MUSIC:	*Theme*	THEME FOR JAKE AND KID - EST. & DOWN BG *18*
SOUND:	*grow out of last of music - est briefly & BG*	BARNYARD SOUNDS - WYANDOT CLUCKING - GROW OUT OF MUSIC - EST BRIEFLY & FADE BG

JAKE: *17* You could say the poster started it, Mister, the yellow one
with the oxen and the Red River Cart running along the top, hung
up in MacTaggart's store. He's mayor of Crocus. Kid's Ma trades
there all the time. Me, I'm the hired man. Just me and the Kid
and his Ma. Widda. War. (PAUSE) Real nice poster hung right
over the double-ought gopher traps there - if I'd of known I
wouldn't of read it .. (PAUSE) Trouble. *50*

SOUND: OUT *with speech*

MUSIC: THEME UP & CUT

ANNCR: The place, the bald-headed prairie of southern Saskatchewan ...
the time, the present ... the principal characters, Jake and the
Kid. And here, as the first episode in a new series of radio plays
by the Canadian writer, W.O. Mitchell, is the story of "The Oldest
Old-Timer" ... with John Drainie as Jake. *11?*

MUSIC: *#1* BRIDGE - FADING BG . *10*

JAKE: You see Gatenby - Sam Gatenby - has a half section down
Gover'ment Road from us - yella house - hip-roofed barn - he was
mixed up in it. Mr. MacTaggart was slicing off some meat for
SOUND **MEAT SLICER B.G.**
Mrs. Totcoal - Kid he was looking at a dandy Daisy Air Rifle -
I see this here poster - (FADING OFF) I start reading her off

First page of The Oldest Old-Timer *script*

3

CBC'S *JAKE AND THE KID*

~ 1950 to 1951 ~

O N TUESDAY, June 27, 1950, at 8:30 p.m., people across
Canada tuned in to the first episode of what was to
become one of the most successful radio shows of the
1950s. The program opened with eight bars of jaunty theme music
composed and conducted by Morris Surdin. A rooster crowed,
chickens clucked, and the audience knew they were in rural Canada.
Jake Trumper, played by John Drainie, began:

> You could say that the poster started it, Mister. The yellah one
> with the oxen and the Red River cart running along the top.
> Hung up in MacTaggart's store. He's mayor of Crocus. Kid's Ma
> trades there all the time. Me – I'm the hired man – just me –
> and the Kid and his Ma – widdah – war. Real nice poster, hung
> right over the double ought gopher traps there. If I had known,
> I wouldn't have read it. (Chickens clucking) Trouble.

The theme music picked up again, and the announcer introduced
the show: "The place: the bald-headed prairie of southern
Saskatchewan. The time: the present. The principal characters: Jake
and the Kid. And here as the first episode in the new series of radio

47

plays by the Canadian writer W.O. Mitchell is the story of 'The Oldest Old-Timer' with John Drainie as Jake." A music bridge, western in style (but not hammed up), then some fiddle music, brought the audience into the action of the first of some two hundred and fifty episodes that would entertain radio listeners across Canada for the next six years.

In "The Oldest Old-Timer" Jake and his neighbour, Sam Gatenby, enter the town's contest to determine who is the oldest citizen. Jake claims that he is about seventy-six and that he was eighteen when he wrestled Louis Riel during the 1885 Rebellion. Jake, who is more like sixty-six, certainly does not fool Miss Henchbaw, the judge of the contest. When Gatenby wins, Jake protests that he does not want to attend the fair and see "Old Gate setting up there primpin' and preenin' his self like a banty rooster." However, he is relieved not to have been chosen when he sees Miss Henchbaw treating Gate like an old man, covering him with blankets, and talking of Gate as "the spirit of the old and dying West." As with many of the Jake scripts, this one concludes dramatically and happily. Jake and the Kid, who have been sitting in their democrat watching the events, suddenly find themselves in the middle of the democrat race when the starting gun spooks their horse. They win the race, but, more, Jake wins back his self-respect when he proudly announces, "Not bad for a fellah my age . . . fifty-eight!"[1]

Putting *Jake and the Kid* on radio was Harry Boyle's idea. Boyle, program director at the CBC, called Bill at *Maclean's* one fall day in 1949 and arranged to meet him "at a pungent pub on Jarvis Street."[2] Boyle, a writer himself, had been fascinated by the Jake stories he had read in *Maclean's* since 1942 and recognized that they would make a great entertainment series on radio. At first Bill was hesitant, but Boyle convinced him that he was "a natural for radio."[3] Bill tested the idea on the Drainies, with whom he and Merna had become close friends. Merna recalled they were on their way to a movie with the Drainies when a *Jake and the Kid* radio series was first mentioned: "I was driving and can remember Bill telling John about some of his *Jake and the Kid* stories. John always maintained that he patterned

Jake after Bill, and it was the way Bill presented Jake that night, with that kind of dialect, which persuaded John to do it."[4]

Drainie was perfect for the role and immediately made Jake his own: "Jake's voice is just an intensification of my own when I'm not watching my enunciation. Most of the time I sound like a rather tired Henry Fonda, except that I have something in my voice which is typical of small towns in the Canadian West. I probably caught some of the tones from Mitchell who, at the drop of a hat, will perform the whole show himself in a booming voice."[5] Drainie never sounded as if he was acting, but seemed to totally inhabit the character of Jake Trumper. In some ways John and Bill were very similar, which may explain why John's "Jake" was so perfect. Drainie, like Mitchell, was "childlike and immoderate"[6] and, in fact, Andrew Allan's description of Drainie could as easily portray Mitchell: "Behind the man, behind the artist, behind the communicator, was always the boy in John. This is the secret of creativeness. The boy is the curious seeker, the finder-out, the one who brings home trophies. John, in Shakespeare's sweet phrase, was 'boy eternal.'"[7]

Before the first Jake program was aired, a pilot was produced using the *Maclean's* story, "The Liar Hunter," that was broadcast on May 21, 1950, for Andrew Allan's *Stage 50*. This well-crafted story about tall-tale telling and how oral narratives reflect our cultural and historical identity was, perhaps, better suited for print than for radio.[8] However, William Munro favourably reviewed the play in Nathan Cohen's magazine, *The Critic*: "The play was immensely entertaining, but it was also a not-too-frivolous effort to reveal facets of the character of the Western Canadian. . . . It implied, with superb artistry, a philosophy and a way of life that writers have been trying successfully to get down on paper ever since the first homesteader built his prairie sod hut."[9]

So, it was decided to go ahead with a summer series, with some changes. Although Mitchell said that Andrew Allan was "without peer" as a director, he did not think he was the right director for the *Jake* scripts because "he couldn't hear the rural tunes of speech."[10] Allan directed in a classical style that had worked earlier for "The

Devil's Instrument," but was too restrictive for the *Jake* scripts. Perhaps, too, Mitchell himself had not yet learned to translate short-story narration into dialogue.[11] The music, arranged and composed by Lucio Agostini, was also too classical for Mitchell's work, but the biggest problem was that the Kid, played by a young man, came across as too old and too whiny to become a sympathetic character.

A month before the first series show, "The Oldest Old-Timer," was aired, a new team was in place that would set the mould for the next six years. Only John Drainie from the pilot broadcast was kept on (although Tommy Tweed appeared from time to time, particularly as Daddy Johnston). Peter Francis, the new director, was an ideal creative partner for Mitchell. A year and a half into the series Mitchell had occasion to express his admiration for Francis's direction: "He is intelligent and sensitive and meticulous. . . . Time and again he has shown me and the cast that he is a truly creative producer; his talent for casting, for interpretation of lines, and for the communication to his actors of the meanings he sees, his feeling for pace, his avoidance of cheap farce and Lum and Abner shoddiness, all have realised any illusion or thematic value I have ever tried to write into my dramas."[12] Although he was not from the West, he gave rein to Mitchell's use of the vernacular and encouraged the western regional flavour. He cast Frank Peddie as Old Man Gatenby, an actor, who like Drainie, captured the rhythms and tones of the Western voice. Drainie's wife, Claire,[13] took on the part of Ma, a small but demanding role in that she had to put flesh on a character who sometimes had only a few lines in the shows. Mitchell pointed out that "the Jake and the Kid things were not as simple as they seemed." While he greatly admired Drainie for conveying realistic rural speech without being "vaudeville simplistic," he was constantly on the watch for some of the minor actors slipping into a cliché rural act.[14]

Perhaps the most significant decision was in casting Billie Mae Richards as the Kid. Billie Mae (always credited as Billy Richards), unbeknownst to most of the audience, was a thirty-year-old woman, not a ten-year-old boy, and in that lay her success, for, as

Bill immediately realized, he got the quality of a real boy's voice plus an "intelligent perceptive adult mind" and she was "terrific."[15] Billie Mae had been around radio since 1947 and had frequently been given boys' roles because of her authentic-sounding boyish voice. It is quite probable that, once having heard how well Billie Mae could play the Kid, Mitchell felt confident about expanding the Kid's role. As Richards said, "Once Bill heard my voice in the role, he started literally to work through my head and down into my voice and out."[16] She got into her role by taking her shoes off: "I can't 'feel' boys' parts in heels. When I pick up the script I automatically become The Kid, aged 11. I don't feel like myself at all."[17]

One final ingredient completed the magic that made the *Jake and the Kid* series so hugely successful: Morris Surdin's music. Surdin, a Toronto-born musician and conductor who had experience in both CBC and New York radio, wrote the signature theme, background music, and the music bridges for the series. The music was a vital element of the show. As Surdin explained, it was used to "lift up the words so that it supports them, so that the words . . . become part of a song." The theme music that opened the show was "a simplification, really." Surdin's challenge was to "take all of *Jake* and put it into eight measures. Really, one of the most impossible things to do is to reduce a man's thinking to eight measures." With those eight measures, he created an instantly recognizable insignia for that landscape, so that, even after fifty years, it stirs people's memories of the high-spirited adventures in Crocus, Saskatchewan. The essence of the stories had to be delivered through music that was lively and western without being condescendingly corncob, and, at points, it had to be moving without being mawkish. Fortunately Surdin could not write, as he put it, "schmaltzy" music: "My type of harmonization calls for dissonance, and the older I got, the more dissonant the music for Jake became harmonically."[18] As well as music bridges to provide transitions from one situation or one time to another, Mitchell needed Surdin to translate into sound the interior monologues, particularly of the Kid:

I gave the Kid soliloquies very consciously. You can't get away with this on stage or on film, but you could on radio. It is not unrealistic in radio, and I could ask Morris Surdin for music. We kidded each other about it. And Morris would say, "Jesus, what do you want me to do; do you want me to start writing lines too?" And I would have solid background music behind these thoughts. I was using it in the way a novelist uses atmosphere, emotional staining of a scene. And gee, was Morris good. Could he ever capture sadness or loneliness or delight or bitterness of the child![19]

For Billie Mae Richards, Surdin's music was more than background; it was her Muse:

I was so happy when I had a great big chunk of narration. I would just think – "Oh to hear that orchestra." There is absolutely nothing that inspires you more than starting to speak with an orchestra. All I had to do was look at Morris and I would know that somewhere in there if there was a meadowlark singing I knew as soon as I said that, he would have a flute in there. It builds you up, it takes you down, it makes you cry, it makes you elongate things. Morris was a master at putting music behind.[20]

Morris had an immense enthusiasm for Bill's work: "This man spoke such universality of truths. This was the golden age of W.O. Mitchell's writing. To my mind he never wrote better, with such continuity of thoughts."[21] They also had a great sense of fun and were always verbally sparring. Mitchell wrote specific, and sometimes humorous, stage directions for Morris. In "Brokenshell Flood," for example, he directed Morris to create music to suggest the dam breaking during the flood: "EVERYTHING IN THE BAND WITH FLOOD MUSIC TO GIVE MITCHELL'S CLIMAX THE EXCITEMENT SHE HASN'T GOT IN THE WRITING THEN OMINOUS BG [background]."[22] In "Gettin' Born," he requested the sound of

"THAT BLEEDING DEMOCRAT AND THEM GODDAM HORSES" as Jake and the Kid head home after Church.[23] Although the majority of his suggestions were simple instructions such as "BRIEF BRIDGE WITH MOURNFUL SCOTTISH FLAVOUR,"[24] he would sometimes tease Surdin: "GIVE US THE HEARTBURN AGAIN" or "TAKE IT AWAY YOU CHIPMUNKS."[25]

Along with the mutual respect in the team came the joy of working together. As Harry Boyle remarked, "There was also something special about the production. Bill injected something that was infectious. Actors, producers, technical staff – I know even the sound effects people prized working on the show."[26] In an article for *CBC Times* in 1953 when her true identity was revealed for the first time, Billie Mae Richards talked about how much the actors enjoyed Mitchell's work: "We're always breaking off to howl at some of Bill's remarks or situations."[27]

The shows broadcast through the summer of 1950 firmly established the main characters of the series. Jake Trumper, the hired man, is an imaginative tall-tale teller, an old bachelor who has his foot in both the adult world and the child's world. He is, said Mitchell "a decent and responsible human being" who has "a natural nobility of character."[28] Generally, Jake is called on to solve a problem either for the Kid, for a neighbour, or for his community. His stubbornness and his curiosity usually get him into trouble, and he frequently has to extricate himself from the messes he inadvertently creates. He and his neighbour Sam Gatenby, a farmer of about the same age and cantankerousness as Jake, argue about everything from the weather, rheumatism, and water-witching to love. Jake's nemesis is the stern but fair-minded Rabbit Hill schoolteacher, Miss Henchbaw, who meets Jake head-on over almost all issues in Crocus and who, according to Jake, thinks she "knows everything about everything."[29] MacTaggart, the storekeeper and mayor of Crocus, represents the ordinary citizen of the town. It is usually at his general store or at Repeat Godfrey's barbershop where a Jake story starts, because that is where gossip congregates. Ma, a former schoolteacher and now a widow because her husband was killed in the war, is the voice of reason against Jake's wild schemes and ideas. The Kid is an imaginative nine- or ten-year-old, a more extroverted farm version of Brian in *Who Has Seen the Wind*, whose questions about relationships, history, beliefs, death, and love are at the core of each episode. Sometimes Jake is the narrator, but the majority are narrated by the Kid, especially when Mitchell wants to capture a child's thoughts about birth ("Gettin' Born") or marriage ("Gettin' Married") or life's challenges. Four of the best scripts Mitchell wrote are about a boy's desire to own his own horse, train him, and ride him ("Auction Fever," "Gents Don't Chaw," "Take Her Gentle – Take Her Easy," and "A Deal's a Deal"). The *Jake* stories were great entertainment, but they also had something to say about universal themes – birth, death, and aging; love and loneliness; jealousy and rivalry; the weather and the landscape.

As Mitchell recalled, when the summer replacement series of nine or ten scripts was finished, Boyle called on him again. Mitchell dramatized the conversation:

> HARRY: I've got marvellous news for you. It's going over with a
> bang. We're scheduling it for the rest of the year.
> BILL (hesitatingly): How long is the broadcast run?
> HARRY: Just the thirty-nine weeks.
> BILL: But I only have about fifteen Jake and the Kid stories. And
> we've already used up thirteen of them. Come on, Harry,
> that's one of them every week.
> HARRY: You'll find it easy.
> BILL: I'm going off the end of the gangplank now![30]

The Mitchells needed the money, for they were already talking about heading home to High River and back to freelancing. Boyle persuaded Mitchell to walk that gangplank.

The first series included the summer shows and ran every week for forty-five weeks, from June 27, 1950, to April 29, 1951. Bill would go over to the CBC studios at lunch hour, but he never interfered with the direction. Francis said that "it was not an embarrassment to have Mitchell around, for whatever reason. He didn't bother you. He was frequently enjoying the stuff himself, laughing his head off, and he didn't try to intervene or to throw his weight around in any way."[31] Occasionally Mitchell would be called over to finish up a script, for, as Peter Francis recalled, he would sometimes submit five pages at a time and then have to expand, tailor, add an ending, or just do some fine-tuning to get the required length for the show. Francis noted that Mitchell was "naturally dramatic," a "good actor,"[32] and, on a couple of occasions, he was asked to perform – once as Pipe-fittin' Brown in "Well, Well, Well" and, as Mitchell explained, a couple of times as a gopher:

> In one scene they were in a buckboard or a democrat, and I asked for the creak of harness, grind of the wheels, sound of a meadowlark, and a gopher squeaking. Well, the cocktail bar where the sound effects man worked could handle everything except the squeak of the gopher. The steward with the union who was appointed during that taping said, "You can't have an actor make the sound." The sound man wouldn't squeak like that because it wasn't sound. I said, "For Christ's sake, none of you can do a squeak properly, anyway. I'll squeak and be the gopher." Then both the steward of the soundmen and one of the actors kicked because I wasn't a member of either union. So, they gave me one of those special dispensation slips to squeak like a gopher. And for this I got $17.50 to go, "Eek, eek!"[33]

Just as Mitchell did not interfere with the director or the actors so, too, they respected his role as writer. Peter Francis commented, "It was very much Mitchell's show – that has to be acknowledged. But there was a good deal of empathy between all members of the production."[34]

Mitchell had a very clear concept of territory, which, he claimed, he developed because his mother constantly "invaded" his space when he was a child. Indeed, one of his favourite phrases, used in *How I Spent My Summer Holidays*, was "don't trespass on my territory." As a result, he had, professionally and emotionally, the ability to distance himself from his own work when it was being transposed into another medium such as radio. This turned out to be a laudable quality since much of his work went from prose to the team arts of radio, stage, television, and film. He was quite capable of sitting on the sidelines and watching at rehearsals – even when, as in a number of theatre productions, things were not going well.

Mitchell, as Peter Francis said, was "a kind of disorganized person."[35] He would often work through the night or through whatever confusion there was in the household – and there usually was plenty. Harry Boyle commented that sometimes Mitchell worked on these scripts under "phenomenal circumstances."[36] He recalled one evening when he was at a party at the Mitchell household in Toronto, and Mitchell had a deadline; he was upstairs writing away but would come down, take a drink with his guests, read some lines, and then disappear to write more. This may have seemed "phenomenal" to Boyle but, in fact, Mitchell wrote well under such circumstances. He thrived on an audience and, from his early days of working on *Who Has Seen the Wind*, was able to close out the household confusion of children, visiting relatives, house construction, or whatever distraction there was at the time. In a letter to Surdin, Francis says not to worry about Mitchell "turn[ing] out a script a week" even though he had forced Mitchell, one Friday evening, to come to his house and write more than fifteen pages in order to complete "Scandal, Scandal, Scandal" for the Sunday broadcast. Francis added, it was "an excellent script – one of the best."[37]

As with the *Maclean's* circle, the Mitchells developed some long-lasting friendships with the CBC Radio actors, writers, and directors. They picnicked along the Rouge River with the Drainies and had many informal dinners together. Much of the conversation was domestic, and the children were usually brought along on these occasions. Claire recalled that "Bill was a real nut"; his speaking voice was a yell, he would tell amusing stories, and he would always do the unexpected such as a spontaneous (but graceful) hand spring from one end of their living room to the other. Once when the Drainies arrived at the Mitchells for a dinner party, Bill shoved a jar of shellac under their noses and asked them to find the words to describe its smell: "'I've been trying for a week to describe the smell. And I can't. And, dammit, it's driving me crazy!'"[38] They also became good friends with Ruth and Peter Francis. Ruth commented, "We used to get a good deal of fun out of the Mitchells." Bill would come over to their home and read his scripts. He would sit on the pouf, a large cushiony thing without a back, and would laugh so hard he would fall off it. Ruth recalled John Gray's succinct and apt description of Mitchell: "He lives with all his pores open."[39]

~ SPRINGDALE BOULEVARD NEIGHBOURS
EVICT THE MITCHELLS ~

It was difficult for Bill and Merna to contain the exuberance of their family and social lives in their small house on Springdale Boulevard, and when it spilled out into the neighbourhood it met, from the beginning, with disapproval. In a letter to Bill, his High River banker referred to an incident in which Hughie had outraged the puritan sensibilities of their Toronto neighbours: "Sorry to hear that you still dislike Toronto. . . . I guess possibly you had better come back West where those two boys of yours can grow up in our free and easy environment, and riding a trike, naked or otherwise, [is] regarded as perfectly normal. Anyway it is better than wearing his pants out."[40] Thirty years later, in rough notes for an article on Toronto life, Mitchell detailed some of his impressions of Torontonians during his three years there:

> Sunday mornings – in the narrow little alleyways – all up and down Springdale or Drurie – they were washing and polishing their gleaming cars . . . or phoning the police of East York or West York or Willowdale to tell them that one of the Mitchell boys was out on the street again – naked and urinating into the gutter – or had stepped on the grass wired off with stakes and wire stretched from their tops – or were playing too vigorously and it was the Sabbath. . . .[41]

Hughie was only four years old at the time, but he vividly recalled the police being called because of one such indiscretion: "I remember having my ass kicked outside to play and having a whiz on the curb. This woman across the street opened her front door – 'You nasty little child! I'm going to phone the police!' That was scary, and I hid in a garage for the rest of the afternoon. I never pissed on the curb again."[42]

One particular incident in the late spring of 1950 must have capped off all these small episodes and made the neighbours wonder about the Mitchell family. Merna and Bill had planned a dinner party for the Bertons, the Clares, and a journalist friend from Calgary, Richard Needham. Merna, however, had a late dental appointment and knew that with the Friday-evening traffic on Danforth she and Bill would be getting home late. Bill's mother, who was visiting, was to feed the boys, get them ready for bed, and play the hostess if any of the guests should arrive before Merna got back from her dental appointment. Bill drove Merna to the Medical Arts Centre at St. George and Bloor, dropped her off, and agreed to pick her up at six. After half an hour at a fishing tackle store, he dutifully got in his car to pick her up – but he forgot where she was.

For more than an hour Merna stood on the street corner fuming. A police officer walked by several times, looking at her suspiciously. Meanwhile Needham was in a taxi on his way to the Mitchell dinner party. According to McKenzie Porter, Needham was not sure of the house number and told the taxi driver to drive slowly along the street. "Then he saw a crowd, a fire engine, and a dwelling in flames. Knowing of his hosts' vulnerability to disaster, Needham cried: 'That's it. That must be the Mitchells.'"

The Bertons arrived to find Needham "sitting imperturbably on the front steps. The fire was out, he told us, and so were our hosts." According to Porter's account, Needham had learned from the firemen "that Ormie and Hughie, fighting with wet towels in the bathroom, had shorted a faulty plug and set the place alight." Inside they found a distraught Mrs. Mitchell trying to settle down her grandchildren. The Clares arrived, and still no sign of the Mitchells.

It was 7:30 before Bill found Merna and they arrived home – to the aftermath of the fire. John Clare recalled Merna saying, "'Bill, you've got to do something. Ormie's set fire to the house.' Bill talked to Ormie, but just gave him an absent-minded pat on the ass."

It had not been a fight with Hughie that started the fire. Grandma Mitchell had just put Hughie to bed, and I was having my bath. After I dried off, I climbed up on the vanity and draped the damp towel over the bathroom light, which was just a bare bulb. The steamy bathroom was instantly transformed into an underwater lagoon shot through with shafts of green light that rippled when the towel moved. I thought this was really neat. Grandma called for me to hurry so I brushed my teeth and then crawled into bed with Hughie. The next thing I recall was the bathroom door being slammed shut and Grandma yelling at us to get out of bed and out of the house. Hughie, however, decided he was not going anywhere. In his half-awake confusion and fear, his instinct was to stay right where he was – in bed. He grabbed the brass spindles on the bed head and would not let go. Grandma pulled him by his legs while I pried loose one hand only to have it reattach to a brass rung when I tried to free his other hand. I could smell smoke now. At first Hughie clung to the bed with quiet determination, but when we broke his hold he started screaming and kicking. We dragged him through the smoke-filled hallway, down the stairs (he tried to grab the banister but we had too much momentum for him to stop us), and out of the house. Sirens blaring, the fire truck arrived. Hughie and I stood in our pyjamas with Grandma on the front lawn – along with all of the Springdale Boulevard neighbours – and watched the firemen drag a hose into the house. By this time Hughie had calmed down and was enjoying the excitement of the big fire truck and the firemen in their fire-fighting outfits. It didn't take them long. As they were coiling up the hose, I noticed some of our parents' friends arriving. My parents were not around. I remember going into the bathroom and thinking, How can this mess ever be cleaned up? When I looked in the bathtub and saw the charred remains of my towel – all black, no green – I realized I was in trouble. When my parents arrived, the firemen told them the fire must have been caused by faulty wiring in the bathroom light fixture. That did not explain the charred towel. My parents questioned me, but, if I ever received a punishment, I cannot recall it.

The firemen had shut down the main power switch, but that did not daunt the Mitchells. Merna simply served dinner by candlelight. All went well until dessert, which was preserved peaches. Needham offered to serve them. In the dim light he doled out generous portions of syrupy peaches into delicate white dishes with frilled edges. Only when Merna skidded on the slippery floor did they realize that the peaches had been served in Mrs. Mitchell's beautifully crocheted and starched doilies, which she had earlier set out as table decorations. Perhaps what was most amazing was that, through all this, the Mitchells carried on as if nothing extraordinary had occurred, as if a missed rendezvous, fires, fire engines, blackout dinner parties, syrupy floors, were normal.[43]

It was interesting to interview my parents' circle of Toronto friends some thirty years later. Hugh and I had obviously gained a reputation. Barbara Moon said that we were "holy terrors," and John Clare said many of the wives thought we were "modern versions of Peck's Bad Boy — completely unregenerate." A few defended our parents' way of raising us, "pouring love in one end and hoping that it comes out the other."[44] Others were genuinely surprised to discover that Hugh and I seemed to have turned out all right and were leading normal and productive adult lives. It was a revelation to me because I thought, of course, that we had led a fairly normal family life. But as I looked back through the eyes of these people and remembered in more detail some of the things Hugh and I got up to in our childhood, I realized that we must have been quite a handful. On a couple of occasions we had to get stitches — Hugh in his head when I pushed him out the car window (the car was parked); I in the corner of my eye when Hugh threw a toy metal shovel at me.

Ralph Allen, hearing that best-selling author Bruce Hutchison was going to visit the Mitchells in High River some years later, wrote a note warning him about what to expect in the Mitchell household:

I can hardly wait for the account of your visit with the Mitchells. I shall make a point of assembling the officers and leading members of the Post-Mitchell Convalescent Society to hear your report. I shall try to get you on the agenda just after the ritual opening exercises which begin with John Clare's justly famous recitation of The Night He Nearly Lost His Life To Dear Little Ormie, this being followed by Pierre Berton on The Day The Residents of Three Entire City Blocks Petitioned the Authorities to Have Little Hughie Forcibly and Permanently Removed.[45]

Allen was referring to a dinner party at which "Ormie" crawled under the table and bit John Clare on the ankle, and to Hughie's habit of riding naked on his trike up and down the sidewalks of Springdale Boulevard.

In the summer of 1950, the Mitchells moved to 450 Drurie Street in West York into a large brick house in a well-treed neighbourhood quite near High Park. Cliff Greer, a painter who taught at the Ontario School of Art, lived in the lower half of the house with his wife, five daughters, and dog. Greer was a "tall, irreverent, macho guy," and Bill was amused by, but wary of, his eccentricities. He was "very out-going, and was always screaming about the grocery expenses, with all of these daughters and his wife: 'My life blood is running out into the garbage can in the form of Ritz biscuits!'"[46]

Greer would frequently come up from his basement studio around ten o'clock at night with a bottle of his homemade wine and talk with Bill: "He would look at me doing a *Jake* script and ask, how many pages did you do tonight? How much are you getting for it? He figured out right down to the word how much I got, practically to the letter. He used to say, 'Jesus, Mitchell, you have it so lucky; God, you're rolling in it.'" One day Bill retorted, "Cliff, if you think so, why don't you throw away your brushes and write and make a lot of money!" "What would I do?" he asked. Bill thought a moment and said, "Until I came along do you realize you were the only male in this establishment – including the dog." So, Cliff began writing a piece and getting feedback in his evening chats with Bill. Bill took it along to a *Maclean's* meeting, and it was a hit. "I Live With Six Women" was published in the February 1, 1951, issue: "Well, it was a hell of an article. Cliff was delighted. He had a new career. He thought he could make it with the typewriter!"[47]

Bill developed a rapport with the two youngest Greer children, Patsy and Gail, and began making up stories for them and the boys. Every night Patsy and Gail would join Orm and Hugh on the big bed with Bill:

> I kept, for the full year, the story going of Candy Coyote and the alligator that went down the Dangerous River. Every night I had to figure out how they'd get into a bind – something dreadful like going over a waterfall. The alligator belched a great deal – and when he did [W.O. makes belching sound] out of his mouth would come a bulb, an electric bulb, which he would then screw into his tail – because he didn't have a pointed tail like ordinary alligators, he had a socket. And the bulb would light up and it would stop the falls or would do anything – it was a neat copout when I got them in too much of a bind.[48]

McKenzie Porter described one of Bill's storytelling sessions: "During one party Mitchell persuaded the boys to go to bed by promising to tell them a story. Downstairs for more than an hour guests listened to Mitchell's distant droning. Then there was a silence that was shattered by Ormie yelling for a glass of water. 'I thought you were in bed,' cried Merna. 'We can't get into bed,' bawled Ormie. 'Dad's there, fast asleep.'"[49]

My father often read or told stories to us before we went to sleep at night. I remember in particular Wind in the Willows, Winnie the Pooh, Alice in Wonderland, *and* Black Beauty – *which we liked but he didn't because she was a "self-pitying whiner." He preferred making up stories for us that often grew out of our own adventures. Because he knew how children have a natural fascination with the body and its functions, his stories were at times Rabelaisian. One of these grew out of Hugh's* and my (and, as it turned out, our parents') first experience with pin-worms. Unlike the little foothills town of High River, Toronto was infested with pinworms. Because both Hugh and I sucked our thumbs, it was inevitable that one of us would end up with worms and infect the rest of the family. And the worms came out to play at night. I remember kneeling on the bed, my bare butt in the air, and my father peering while my mother held the flashlight. My father said, "Good God, look at the little buggers." Hugh recalls the story he made up when we complained about the itching: "At night, one worm sticks his head out, looks around, and reports to the others, 'He's asleep. Let's go!' And they all start running around playing tag and Red Rover. Then one says, 'Let's do something else – let's play cards!' So they all take out the tables, put up the legs, bring out the chairs, and get out the cards. They shuffle the decks and then they throw them up in the air like this! That's what's going on in your asshole, he said."

He also told us stories his grandmother had told him when he was a child and ones he remembered from books he had read such as Peck's Bad Boy and His Pa. One of my favourites was about Peck's Bad Boy tricking his father into believing that he had gone blind – when his father falls asleep, he paints his father's glasses with black ink. We were fascinated by these stories about a boy who was always playing tricks on adults. Our father would act them out with dramatic dialogue, yells, and gestures. His stories did not calm us down and seduce us into sleep. Indeed, he often fell asleep and rolled over on the covers pinning down whomever was in the middle. So there you were, wide awake, the adrenalin pumping from his story, and unable to move. You didn't dare wake him up because he was irritable when wakened. So you quietly waited him out and if he didn't wake up on his own, our mother would finally come in and tell him to get up and get cracking on the new novel – or a late Jake script.

~ "THE VOICES OF TORONTO WERE WRONG" ~

From June 1950 to the end of April 1951, Mitchell wrote a *Jake and the Kid* radio script per week, sometimes staying up all night to get it finished. In July he adapted for radio a short story, "The Black

Bonspiel of Wullie MacCrimmon," which he had written around 1947 when he was still in High River. It was broadcast as a half-hour drama for the CBC's *Summer Stage* on July 30 and was so successful that he expanded it into an hour-long radio play for Andrew Allan, slated for the spring. By the fall the *Jake and the Kid* radio series was clearly a success. Mitchell wrote to Ernest Buckler, "I have hopes it's going to get us back to the hills next spring."[50] He was making $150 per script, and at thirty-nine scripts a year this would bring in a comfortable free-lance income and allow him more time for novel writing.[51]

It was a busy fall. In August he had sent two hundred pages of "The Alien" out to his agent, Willis Wing, who was impressed, as was Cloud when he read it in December. But he found it difficult to salvage time for work on the novel. He was barely able to stay a week ahead with his *Jake* scripts and he had another *Maclean's* writing contest to organize. On top of this, he was ill with bronchitis for two weeks. Then the CBC decided they would like a Christmas special *Jake and the Kid* program and he wrote "Frankincents an' Meer," the first of what was to become a regular Christmas one-hour feature.

In mid-November he took the train out to Winnipeg to stay with a Mennonite family and research an article for *Maclean's*. "The Tragic Trek of the Mennonites" describes the mass exodus of seventeen hundred Canadian-born Mennonites from their farms in Manitoba's Red River Valley to "a promised land" in Paraguay in June 1948. The migration had been undertaken because the younger generation were drifting away from their traditional way of life, and because there was growing antagonism in Canada toward Mennonite pacifism. However, for many it was a disastrous venture and within three years more than eight hundred Mennonites abandoned their dream of "a tropical paradise" and returned to Canada. Mitchell was very moved by their experience, and how their "unsuspecting naïveté" led them into a "green hell."[52] This article was more detailed and serious than his earlier articles, and he was proud of the work he did on it.

On February 25, 1951, the hour-long version of *The Black Bonspiel* was broadcast on *Stage 51*, directed by Andrew Allan. Gordon

Sinclair commented in his *Toronto Star* column that the play was "uproariously funny stuff."[53] *The Black Bonspiel* would become Mitchell's most popularly successful drama. Over a forty-five-year period he reworked it in almost every medium, from original short story, to radio drama, to television, to stage, and finally to an expanded novella in 1993.

The Black Bonspiel is a comic version of the Faust legend in which Wullie MacCrimmon, the shoemaker in a small Alberta town called Khartoum, is tempted by the Devil to trade his soul for a victory in the MacDonald Brier, the Canadian national curling championships. Mitchell's depiction of the Devil as a travelling salesman who deals "in Wholesale Souls and Retail Sin" sets the tone for a light-hearted version of the traditional story. Wullie is no great sinner, just "a dawd here, a dawd there," but, in a moment of dreamy self-indulgence he utters aloud his desire to win the MacDonald Brier. In a flash, the Devil appears and a bargain is made in which Wullie and the Devil will curl a match. If the Devil wins, Wullie is bound to curl third for him in Hell; if Wullie wins, the Devil will grant him his wish and Wullie will not lose his soul.

On Wullie's team are the three Jack Browns, differentiated as Cross-Cut (the carpenter), Pipe-fitting, (the plumber), and Malleable (the blacksmith). The Devil's rink in the short-story version was not individualized, but in the radio dramas it consists of: Macbeth (muttering "tomorrow – tomorrow and tomorrow"), Guy Fawkes ("a long thin hungry lookin'" Englishman), and Judas Iscariot ("a cattle buyer from out Gladys Ridge way" who continually jingles loose change in his pockets).[54] Much of the humour is achieved through the incongruity of setting this mythic story in an ordinary foothills town with ordinary working men, as well as playing on the notion of a "black" bonspiel in which everything is reversed.

Mitchell expanded the short story by creating two new roles, the "CBC's wandering reporter" (played by John Drainie) and Reverend Pringle (played by William Needles), who, as minister of the United Church, runs afoul of Wullie MacCrimmon's strict Presbyterian beliefs. This play, unlike the darker and more tragic *The Devil's*

Instrument, is filled with puns and humour: the Devil arrives for a "resole job" on his curling boots; Pipe-fitting's concerns about "C'rrosion" echo the Devil's own business; and many common expressions take on a double meaning – "curl to beat hell," "what in hell's goin' on."[55]

As in *The Devil's Instrument,* Mitchell explores the nature of sin and morality. The Devil tells Wullie that in Khartoum he deals in "petty intolerance – lust for tea-pot power – self-indulgence – sins of omission – snobbery – within-the-family-tyranny." While not flashy in their own right, "it's the accretion that counts," and certainly Mitchell feels that the kind of intolerance shown by the gossip about the schoolteacher going into the Ladies and Escorts is more harmful and sinful than penny ante in the Bluebird Café, curling on Sunday – or Wullie's dream of winning the Brier. Reverend Pringle is a sympathetic character whose more modern religious concept of an inner, psychological Hell and Heaven runs into stiff opposition from Wullie, who believes in a literal Hell, "a three-dimensional, cracklin', actually burnin' hell. . . . Where we may roast in blazin' fire from everlastin' to everlastin'." A continuing Presbyterian with existential undertones, Wullie is a man of democratic sensibilities. After the Devil leaves his boots for repair, Wullie tosses them into the pile on his "shoes-to-be-repaired shelf":

> NARRATOR: . . . laboured felt boots, formless and somehow pathetic child's boots, flat farm boots, ranchers' high-heeled boots, the pebbled brogues of Dr. Hartcroft lying with Mame Harris's (PAUSE) and her disgracefully run-over-heels nudging the bunion bulges of Aunt Lill's sensible English shoes. (PAUSE) There was shocking democracy in Wullie's shoes-to-be-repaired shelf, as though with fine disregard for their owners' social, economic, and moral position he had thrown the footgear there, saying:
> WULLIE: (SIGHS) A boot's a boot for a' that.[56]

The Devil's Instrument and *The Black Bonspiel of Wullie MacCrimmon* approach religion, hell, damnation, and the Devil from different angles. In *The Devil's Instrument*, Mitchell follows the Romantics' vision of the Devil as a positive Promethean figure who, as representative of creative and sexual energy, fosters freedom against the limiting forces of a puritanical and materialistic society. Darius tempts Jacob away from the colony, an imprisoning Garden of Eden, by giving him a musical instrument that unlocks Jacob's innate musical talent. In *The Black Bonspiel of Wullie MacCrimmon*, on the other hand, there is little to admire about the Devil – except his sardonic sense of humour. He is closer to the devil tricksters of medieval legend and to Marlowe's devil in *Dr. Faustus*. He is a bully and a cheat, and the audience cheers when Wullie meets him head-on and beats him at his own game.

Wullie would not have been impressed by Mitchell's blasé curling performances in Castor.[57] However, Mitchell saw that curling had a significant place in the culture of rural and small-town Canada, particularly in the prairie provinces. He was also aware that curling was a political issue across Canada, not least in High River where he heard debates over Sunday curling, women's curling, and fixed matches. Curling became a natural metaphor and plot element for his stories depicting small-town prairie life and, following *The Black Bonspiel of Wullie MacCrimmon*, he would come back to the "noble art of curling" in six of the *Jake and the Kid* radio episodes.

It was clear by this time that Merna was determined to get them back to High River soon. She knew that her boys would be happier in High River than in Toronto, and the excitement of Toronto life had begun to pale for her. She gave Bill an ultimatum, but he argued:

> I said, "Oh, let's stay another year and get a little more fat on our bones." She said, "No, we've got lots of fat" – because we'd cleaned up everything on our house, bought a car, and we had money in the bank. When I said, "No, let's stay another year," her very words were, "Well, you do what you want, but at Easter time

I'm taking the boys and going back to the foothills. You stay on if
you want." So I went into Ralph Allen and said we were going
back at Easter. And Ralph said, "You lucky, ungrateful bastard!"[58]

Besides the financial stability the *Jake and the Kid* series gave them,
there were a number of reasons to head back home. By 1950 it was
clear that the fiction component of *Maclean's* was in trouble, partly
because the magazine had gone from three stories per issue to only
one, and partly because magazine readers' interest in fiction was
being usurped by a new breed of non-fiction feature articles: "The
water was drying up under you. It was not a happy situation to be a
fiction editor in which people are moving more and more into the
new type of feature article which is using many of the skills, styles,
and devices of the short story writer, or the novelist."[59] This meant
that there was even less opportunity for Mitchell to edit and publish
quality short stories, and he had had his fill of working with the
formula-story market.

　　When publicly announcing his decision to return home, he
explained, "Before I left the West . . . I addressed a meeting of the
National Library Association in Vancouver and I told them that I
believed if a writer stayed away from the larger centres, from publishers and radio, he would accomplish more with less dissipation of
energy. Then I promptly settled in Toronto! Now I realize the truth
of my words."[60] But it was not just a case of dissipated energy that
affected his serious novel writing, it was also losing touch with the
geography and people he wrote about. What he felt would be his
major bid as a novelist, "The Alien," had been stalled for more than
two years because he needed to re-experience the Stoney culture that
was at the heart of this novel. Some years later, looking back on his
Toronto years, he said, "The years in Toronto were sterile – I had to
be near my subject – I can't fake it – I have to hear the right voices
and the voices of Toronto were wrong."[61]

　　The cast and crew of the *Jake* series gave the Mitchells a going-
away party. It was held at the Drainies', and the crew had a few
presents for the Mitchells, one of which Merna described:

They all got together and made up a *Jake and the Kid* show — a parody. It was Peter Francis who did most of it. The idea of the show was what's going on between Jake and Ma. Jake still has some sap in him and Ma's a widow . . . so . . . The recording is of the Kid and Jake talking (and you always forget that Billie Mae Richards was a married woman with 3 children). And to hear this kid's voice talking about Jake going in to get some French safes. Ah, it was dirty! And the music — they got a harmonica and a comb that was covered up and it went — [and Merna demonstrates] ooh, ooh, aw ooh ooh![62]

Billie Mae Richards added, "I was never so embarrassed in my life. I hid the whole time they were playing the recording!"[63] The other present was a stop watch for Bill: "The reason they gave me a stop watch was that here I was out west and they would get the script two days before they had to go on and Mitchell is three minutes short or seven minutes long. They claimed I never used the stop watch. But, I would say, 'You can't act! Your timing is wrong. I timed it; it is right on the button.'"[64] Mitchell, however, had a reputation, even when he was in Toronto, for being either too short or too long with his scripts. Francis admitted that he occasionally cut out some of Mitchell's lyrical parts (to save time, and because they were not dramatic enough) and he sometimes added bits once he got to know the characters well enough. Apparently the stop watch did little to correct the situation, for as Francis recalls, "You would see times at the end of script — 40 minutes, or 22 minutes. He was using the stop watch but not the way it was supposed to be used!"[65]

Bill and Merna were well liked by the people they met in Toronto. Some of their friends were shocked at how they yelled at each other and their boys, but many admired their freewheeling relationship and open friendliness. Pierre Berton said, "Merna and Bill never stopped partying and never stopped loving each other. They carried on a cheerful bickering with one another. They both talked a blue streak and were very close. Merna was not really competitive with Bill, was an anchor for Bill, and stood behind him. But she did like to correct him on his stories – and he corrected her – it was both ways. They were a fascinating pair – we were very fond of them."[66]

Although Bill and Merna were excited about going home, they did not regret their time in Toronto, where they had developed close and long-lasting friendships. Quite possibly the *Jake and the Kid* radio series would never have happened had they not been in Toronto. The rich and engaging cultural life of Toronto's media and writing community had its advantages, as Pierre Berton argued when he tried to convince Bill to stay. He felt Bill's creative talents would be stunted in the cultural wasteland of the Alberta foothills. At the *Maclean's* office Berton took bets giving two-to-one odds that Bill and Merna would not last long in High River. Five months after the Mitchells left, Berton was still a confident bookie: "I have a bet on that you will be down here before very long. . . . I am giving you not more than eight months at beautiful High River, garden spot of the Prairies."[67]

High River may have had fewer cultural advantages, but it also offered freedom from the conventional fastidiousness, the puritanical uprightness, that the Mitchells discovered in their Toronto neighbourhoods. Even on their last day in Toronto they ran into trouble. They had bought a second-hand house trailer, a grey twenty-two-foot, two-and-a-half-ton Inglis Schultz, which was to be Bill's office when they arrived back in High River. As they were loading it up for the trip home, the police arrived. An upset neighbour had complained about the trailer being parked on the street in front of the Greer house. If they needed another sign, this second eviction showed them they were not suited to Toronto life. High River was the place to be.

On April 12, 1951, they arrived home. Mrs. McCorquodale reported that the Mitchells and their dog, Maggie, were back, "gladly tossing aside the fleshpots of Toronto for the simple fare of the west."[68] Pierre Berton lost his bets.

4

HIGH RIVER

— 1951 to 1952 —

IT DID NOT take long for Mitchell to settle back into the rhythm of town and foothills life and re-establish his "trap line" for story material. He resumed his morning visits to the post office; he talked with old-timers in the King George Hotel lobby or in the pool hall and barbershop above the New Look Café; he dropped by Jack Brown the blacksmith's as he shoed a horse or repaired a farm implement; he chatted with Harry and Belf at Quon's grocery, with Charles Clark and Mrs. McCorquodale at the *High River Times*, the Kuwatas at the bakery, or Don Blake at the hardware store. Jack Kelly, his neighbour, and some other old-timers, Harry Christianson and George Laycraft, provided anecdotes and rich language for his *Jake* material.

Mitchell had "all his pores open," and over the next seventeen years he soaked up the life of the foothills community. For the most part, he was accepted by the community as one of their own. Much later, during the shooting of the National Film Board biography on Mitchell in 1979, one of Bill's rancher friends, Dave Diebel, commented that Bill "truly loved people" and was just as happy visiting with "some old reprobate or hobo on the street as he was with the Mayor of the town. In fact, he was more interested in them because they didn't cover up – you got to them and found out what made them tick." When the interviewer asked, "What about Bill, did you think he covered up?" Diebel responded, "I don't think he could take the time to cover up. Bill Mitchell bounces off Bill Mitchell before he even thinks."[1]

In the fall of 1951 Bill wrote Ernest Buckler about the contentment of being back in High River: "We are now off the beaten track here and it is much better for work, really. We have come back by choice mostly because a lot of energy gets dissipated in Toronto, arguing about and with talker-writers, talker-painters, talker-musicians, who couldn't describe, paint, or compose their own balls. . . . I count my three years in Toronto almost lost; we breath [sic] again since last April."[2] In the same vein he wrote to Cloud, adding, "Our children no longer look like mushrooms; Orm and I have had pretty good luck with a grey hackle up the Highwood."[3]

I was eight this first summer back home in High River when my father taught me how to fly-fish. I learned how to cast with an old split-bamboo fly rod on our front lawn. My father placed a beer bottle under my arm and told me to squeeze it to my side and not let it drop while I cast. I remember his encouragement and yells – "feel the weight of the line," "get a rhythm going before you let it go," "peel more line out," "keep the goddamn tip up! Don't let the rod go back past one o'clock." Our first outings were on Baker Creek, a meandering stream just west of town. The best fishing holes were difficult to fly-fish because the banks were heavily brushed with saskatoon, willow, and poplar trees. At first my father patiently instructed me and untangled my line when it got caught up in bushes. But when the evening rise began and trout were hitting the surface all over the pool, he excitedly turned to his own fishing. I tried to untangle the mare's nest of transparent leader, the fine loops and knots blurring as mosquitoes whined around my face and rainbows plocked the pool surface. My frustration peaked when my father yelled, "Got one!" He unhooked his fish, held it up for me to see, then saw my frustration. From then on he stayed with me, untangling

my line and telling me where to cast. A rainbow hit. "Set! Set your hook!
Now keep your tip up – play him, don't horse him in!"

He took as much delight in teaching and watching me fish as he
did in his own fishing. Fishing was a passion for my father and played
a significant role in defining our relationship over the years. By the time
I was eleven our outings pushed me into a more than usual adult role
and our relationship became as much one of friends, of equals, as of
father-son. Indeed, increasingly through my adolescence, there were
times when I felt I was the adult and he was the child.

Just before Bill and Merna left for the west, Ralph Allen suggested
that Mitchell do a short piece on Louis Riel. He began researching
the article in Toronto, where he interviewed two very old veterans
of the 1885 rebellion who had stood guard on the tent in which Riel
was kept prisoner: "By word of mouth I got a full description – I dug
and I asked questions, for specifics. I found out that Riel was
suffering from diarrhoea dreadfully at the time."

He continued working on it through May and June, by which
time it had become a major project. He made research trips to
Regina and Winnipeg and while visiting the parliamentary archives
in Winnipeg, he came across some letters of a drummer boy to his
mother. They were filled with fascinating material about General
Middleton and others in that "strange amateur comedy of errors,
that war. In the siege of Batoche, when the men lay on their stom-
achs and fired towards the Métis people, this boy – and I got this
from an old veteran, Alf Burridge, who was still alive in Toronto –
would be crawling up to the men, lying there in the rifle pits, with
hardtack biscuits and food, and additional shells and rounds of
ammunition. A very cheerful little guy he was, too, saying, 'Who's
for biscuits?' "[4]

At the High River Rotary June barbecue, Mitchell gave a talk
to the members and their wives about his sleuthing for the Riel
article. The picnic was held at a farm on the Highwood River Road
southwest of town. He gave his talk after dinner just as it was getting

dark and the fireflies were coming out, flashing against the darkening wood along the Highwood River. "I will never forget how impressive his talk was," Earl Lewis, their neighbour, recalled. "It was the first time I ever heard a really true and authentic version of Louis Riel. Everyone was fascinated. He changed the attitudes of this whole community."[5] The *High River Times* reported that Bill's "dramatic presentation of the frustrations and efforts of this man who so loved freedom, his people and the land of the North West, could never be told in a more appropriate setting and atmosphere. For those who have felt that history had never done justice to the man Riel, it is good to know that belatedly his honoured place in the annals of Western Canada is at last being recognized."[6]

Because Mitchell became so engrossed in the Riel story, it took him much longer to finish the article than he or *Maclean's* had planned. Berton wrote asking where part two of the article was and kidded Bill that if he did not hurry up he would have to turn the project over to McKenzie Porter! Bill was not completely happy with the final shortened two-part version, published February 1 and 15, 1952, in *Maclean's*. In writing to Alberta playwright Elsie Park Gowan, Merna said, "It suffered . . . in being cut from 40,000 to 23,000 to 11,000 and so did we."[7]

In spite of Mitchell's revisionist take on Riel, he felt there was something unstable about him and he became much more interested in Gabriel Dumont, Riel's military leader. Indeed, Mitchell concluded "The Riddle of Louis Riel" with a Dumont encounter that took place some years after Riel's hanging. Chief Justice Fitzpatrick, who had been one of Riel's lawyers, was in London, England, attending a bar convention and one evening went to the Barnum and Bailey Circus. In one of the acts, an Indian attack on a fort is re-enacted. The Indian chief who led the mock attack turned out to be Dumont, still "wanted in Canada, dead or alive, for his part in the Great Saskatchewan Insurrection of 1885."[8] Mitchell's research got him thinking about doing a historical novel on the Riel rebellions but told through two "layers of perception," Gabriel Dumont's and "the innocent eyes" of General Middleton's fifteen-year-old drummer boy.

— THE STONEYS AT THE EDEN VALLEY RESERVE —

Mitchell's research on Riel and the Métis culture fed into his exploration of his half-breed character, Carlyle, in "The Alien," and while working on the Riel piece he began preparing for writing Part III. The Eden Valley subreserve had been established two years earlier when the government finally acted on the Stoneys' many petitions for suitable ranching land and bought the Fraser Hunt ranch. Now, as well as doing haying, fencing, and cattle work for nearby ranchers, the Stoneys were developing their own herd of cattle and, with the other ranchers in the Eden Valley, had grazing rights in the forest reserve. Their traditional nomadic tent life was being replaced by a more static life and most of the families now had houses. Rev. Roy Taylor was the teacher and missionary and his wife was the reserve nurse.

Mitchell drove out in April 1951 and introduced himself to Taylor. During the rest of the school year he occasionally helped Taylor out in the reserve's one-room school and got to know the children. He was delighted to renew his acquaintance with the Stoney families he had met eight years earlier when he supported their petitions for land, particularly the Peter Dixons, Archie Daniels, McFarland Dixons, the various Lefthand families, the Riders, and the Rolling-in-the-Mud family. He struck up a new friendship too, with Raymond Shotclose and his family. Raymond was a Blood who had eloped with his Stoney wife and, once the Stoney community's hostility died down, for they were traditional enemies with the Bloods, Raymond and his family lived at Eden Valley.

In June Mitchell moved his trailer out to the valley, and parked it a few miles upstream from the reserve at Minesinger's Pool, so that he could spend more time with the Stoneys and gather rough material for "The Alien" – and, of course, fish. Access to Minesinger's Pool, one of Bill's favourite fishing holes, was by a rope ladder down a thirty-foot shale cliff. The deep pool, formed by a fifteen-foot falls at its upper end, was named after James Minesinger, who began ranching in the Eden Valley in the 1880s. He was married to a Snake woman and claimed he "was the only man in the North-West who had slept over twenty years with a Snake, and never been bitten," a story Mitchell ascribes to Daddy Sherry in *The Kite*.[9]

Bill and Merna went to the Bar U roundup and branding in late June. Merna, who was "nutty about horses" and loved riding, went out with the crew while Bill looked after the children and chatted with the ranchers and Stoney families who had camped near the branding corrals. It was here that Mitchell met Dave and Rita Diebel, and he discovered that it was on their land, not on reserve property, that he had parked his trailer. This was the beginning of a close family friendship, although Bill soon realized he had different views from Dave on the Stoneys. Dave rarely hired Stoneys for haying and fencing, and he dismissed them as past-masters at conning people who tried to help them. He felt Bill was wasting his time with them.

In the fall Mitchell learned that Roy Taylor would need teaching help in the coming year. Mitchell decided to offer his services as full-time teacher and met with George Gooderham, head of Indian Affairs in Calgary. He told Gooderham he would help out at Eden Valley, but that he could not accept a salary because he did not want his position as an observer and writer to be compromised: "I said, 'I have to level with you. What may come out in the novel may be an embarrassment to Indian Affairs. I'll have to be honest and open about what I find and some of it may be very tragic.'" Mitchell said Gooderham responded, "'I wish you would.' As far as he was concerned, that was going to be a bonus."[10]

For the first few months of the fall term in 1951 Mitchell taught with Roy Taylor, who had become quite disillusioned with the Stoneys during his two years on the reserve. Mitchell felt Taylor was "very hard," and that his derogatory comments about the Stoneys were often racist, perhaps because Taylor sensed that many of the Stoneys had little respect for him. He warned Bill about two individuals in particular who had given him trouble, Allen Dixon and King Bearspaw. Mitchell witnessed one of Taylor's run-ins with Dixon. One evening, when Bill and Roy were washing up dishes, the water tap slowed to a trickle and the sink filled with brown debris. They discovered that Dixon had deliberately staked his horse out by the reservoir for the agency's water supply, and its manure had fouled the line. Taylor was afraid of Dixon and warned Mitchell to watch out for him, that he had been in the army and "was a tough, dangerous cookie who knew how to use his fists."[11]

Mitchell had already heard about King Bearspaw and his Lost Lemon Mine scam some years before when he was on the 1945 roundup at the Macleay ranch: "King Bearspaw was a pretty smart guy. He had given up his Indian status and was the most consummate con man I have ever known in my life. He made a living from the Lost Lemon Mine and also from bootlegging." King was not supposed to be living on the reserve, but much to Taylor's annoyance he slipped on and off all the time. Taylor told Mitchell how King persuaded some High River and Longview businessmen to put up a $10,000 stake for his "find" and how, right away, King's son had a new car and King moved into a room in Calgary's Palliser Hotel from which he operated his gold enterprises. Mitchell found out more about King from Raymond Shotclose, whom King hired to supply pack horses for one of his expeditions. Some of King's investors had become suspicious of the gold mine operation and insisted on seeing the site. King took them on an arduous wild goose chase all through the mountains at the head of the Oldman River. Most of the businessmen were not used to any kind of riding, let alone what King took them through. Raymond said, "He just wore them right down to the ankle bones, frizzed their asses off. When they complained about their aches and blisters, King said 'You see, it isn't easy – this is what I've been doing for you fellas, for our gold mine. And you, all you do is complain and whine.' You never saw any white guys more happy to get back to their warm home and away from that man and that place."[12]

~ "TECHNICAL PERFECTION" ~

Throughout the summer, Peter Francis had written urging Mitchell to get some scripts finished for the second series of *Jake and the Kid*, which was to start on September 30, 1951. Mitchell was now obsessed with Eden Valley, his teaching, and his writing on "The Alien," so it was fortunate that the *Jake and the Kid* series had settled into a well-honed groove. As Francis reported in January 1952, the series had "reached a fair state of technical perfection" – the scripts had become "as perfect as they could be," the actors had become the characters, and Surdin's music had grasped "the spirit of the show."[13] Mitchell had his characters and their town firmly fixed in his imagination. In the first series, Crocus was much like Mitchell's birthplace, Weyburn, but in the second series it frequently took on the character of High River. Over the next five years, a good many incidents were drawn from Mitchell's life in High River, where "the pageant of small town life was vivid for me once more."[14] The range of stories showed an amazing ingenuity although, as would be expected since Mitchell had only a week to prepare each one, the quality varied.

Jake Trumper's character was enriched by foothills people. Bill said he "shamelessly stole" colourful expressions for Jake or Old Man Gatenby from his High River neighbours such as Jack Kelly, a retired rancher: "Every time I talked to Kelly over the fence he would come up with something."[15] Jake's flair for storytelling, his rapport with children, his down-to-earthness are borrowed from Mitchell's own personality. But in other areas Mitchell and Jake part company. Mitchell was not as unsophisticated or colloquial, nor as adversarial or crotchety. More significantly he was not as unbending and traditional in his views. As Mitchell said, Jake was "a man of biases" and was not fond of strong-minded women: "Woman's Lib wouldn't like him at all and he'd be appalled by modern women. That was his blind spot."[16]

By the end of the sixth series Mitchell claimed to have created around eighty characters. One character who came into his own was Repeat Golighty, the gossiping, psychologizing, puritanical barber who says everything twice. He was superbly played by George Robertson and, in time, his barbershop became a more important meeting place than MacTaggart's General Store. Daddy Johnston, the oldest man in Canada, was, perhaps, Mitchell's most popular and successful minor character. He appeared in 1952, played by Tommy Tweed, who could wheeze and sputter to such effect, particularly with his false teeth taken out, that the crew and cast would be in stitches. In fact, Mitchell had created Daddy after hearing Tweed do his old-man routine at a party. One of Mitchell's personal favourites was Noble Winesinger, the con man with a heart, who appeared first on December 2, 1951, but more frequently in 1953–54. He was the ancestor of Heally Richards in *The Vanishing Point*. There were others: the villain, Pete Botten, "a fellah that's a real bad puhtatuh . . . real bad";[17] Mr. Wong, the proprietor of the Sanitary Cafe; Moses Lefthand, the off-reserve Blackfoot Indian, and his family; Mrs. Elsie Abercrombie, the preserver, so she believes, of the town's morals and culture; Mrs. Clinkerby, the dirt widow who tries to snare Jake; and Belva Taskey, the prairie poetess. Jake and the Kid are really the only two characters who are given depth and roundness, but many of the other characters achieve a Dickensian dimension that makes them appear human and not simply caricatures.

The trademarks of this series were Jake's many tall tales, such as the one in which he "wrassled Looie Reel" and made him say Uncle three times (the first in French, the second in Cree, and the third in English), and his cursing, most famously, "It's enough to give a gopher the heartburn" or "It's a shaganappy world we live in." The effect of cursing had to be created without actually swearing because of CBC policy, and the directors had to curb Mitchell's irreverent tendencies: "gopher's ass" had to be dropped; "damn" was usually "dang"; and "hell" was generally "aitch" ("sure as aitch"). "Holy Diddle" was one of Jake's most explosive expletives. Occasionally Mitchell would set verbal traps for Drainie, the most memorable one being Jake's condemnation of the Atheneum Women's Club: "I don't give a damn for the whole clucking flock of them." Just after "damn" in this line, Mitchell added in parentheses, "WATCH IT DRAINIE."[18] He waited with great amusement for the Sunday broadcast to see if Drainie would falter. He did not. Mitchell's scripts were quite different from any other scripts of the time in that he had characters interrupt one another, and used overlapping dialogue. This, said Claire (Drainie) Taylor, "wasn't being done by radio writers that she knew." Just reading it on the page, "the script seemed unnatural to us."[19]

Jake and the Kid *drawings by Duncan MacPherson*
(Duncan MacPherson Estate)

Bill was somehow finding more time to work on "The Alien," but he was still walking the gangplank week after week with the *Jake* scripts. Francis recalled that occasionally the scripts did not arrive until the day of the show, and that sometimes he, himself, would have to cut the stencil on the morning of the Sunday show to make copies for the actors. Merna said, "Bill always got them done, but it was often last minute and I can remember in latter years in the mid-fifties there were times when we would have to drive to Calgary to put a script on the plane so that it would get there in time for the Sunday performance. Then it got increasingly difficult to think of plots, particularly when he wanted to be writing books."[20] On one occasion, Earl Lewis was flying to Toronto on business and he hand-delivered a script to the CBC studio: "The whole bunch of them were set up in the studio for rehearsal and they just took the script and went to work. And Drainie couldn't read his – he started laughing so hard he couldn't read it. The whole crew just thought this was the greatest script they had ever heard."[21] Mitchell always maintained that he never missed a deadline.

One of the major problems with cutting it so fine with the scripts was that Morris Surdin was often pressed for time to compose his music, especially if the script was short and required extra composition. When Bill wrote to say the music for one of the episodes was too loud and made excuses for the lateness of his scripts, explaining he was going through another bout of illness, Morris responded, "Now we have complaints yet!!!! Music too loud. . . . somebody has to cover up the bad literature. . . . And scripts all late and half done and short and badly typed and full of gall bladder trouble. . . . Allegro con fuoco. It's clean. . . . We still love you but where the aitch are the scripts?"[22] Bill replied, "Dear Mozart, I am so sorry I have had to rely on your music in a few of my scripts. Do not worry. I have a plan whereby in the next twenty-six I will need no music at all! Will that not be an interesting and excitingly experimental innovation in radio art circles?" He then goes on to say that the "Rabelaisian nature of the stories has resulted in the Postal department closing the mails to me," but "they don't have to worry about filth because there's a bunch of goddam Methodist sons-of-bitches down there who cut out anything that couldn't be breathed in a Sunday school basement and anyway the lines can't be heard above the brassy din of the musical B.G."[23]

The radio series was broadcast on Sunday afternoons at 5:30. Just after the show, Bill would phone Toronto and congratulate them: "That was great" or "God, Drainie's done it again!" Seldom did he have anything stronger to criticize than that a favourite line of his had been "thrown away" or that a minor character had hammed the role.[24] Many in High River would tune in. As their neighbour Earl Lewis said, "Bill was a guy we were all kind of proud of."[25]

~ TEACHING AND WRITING AT EDEN VALLEY ~

From November 1951 to April 1952, Bill lived alone in the Eden Valley agency cabin, and came home on weekends.[26] When the weather and roads were good, Merna would drive him out on Sunday afternoons and then pick him up Friday after school. On a few occasions Merna drove out with cases of pop for parties for the children. Bill was able to keep in touch with Merna on the Eden Valley party-line phone from the agency or Diebels'. However, the phone line out to Eden Valley was very unreliable, and at times breaks were patched through on the barbed-wire fencelines.

The schoolroom was attached to the agency log cabin: "I just went through a door beyond the stove and was instantly in the school room. I used to keep a big cauldron of cocoa on the stove going and then had camesol biscuits which simply could not be conquered by tooth and saliva." Mitchell recalled, "They were like ship's biscuits I suspect. I imagine that Captain Bligh had some when his crew mutinied and put him into the boat and cast him loose. They were little upholstered things, without the buttons, dimpled. And the whole school would be filled with the sound of children taking them flat in their palms and clapping them at the corner of a desk to try to break them into shards and then hold them in their mouths and swallow the cocoa." These biscuits were the model for Fyffe's minimal subsistence biscuits in *The Vanishing Point*.[27]

At first Mitchell found it difficult to win the Stoney children's trust and get past their shyness, but he had a wonderful ability to engage children on their own terms. He always sent children up to the board in groups of four or five to do math or writing exercises so they would feel less threatened. He also encouraged them to do activities in which they naturally excelled. Every Friday afternoon for the last class, he would turn the children loose with boxes of coloured chalk and, working in teams, they would cover the black-boards with pictures. In "The Alien" he describes their work:

> Even the littlest of the Grade Ones drew excellently; with the girls it was always flowers, exquisitely delicate shooting stars with pointed petal heads hanging, bell-like blossoms of crimson, yellow, indigo; orange tiger lilies with vivid leaves up thin stems. The boys drew pink and scarlet parades of tractors right to the last detail of the exhaust, violet trucks perhaps hauling a horse with red mane flying. With blue chalk they outlined the mountains around their home; in parrot green they harpooned the sides with pines, populated the draws and meadows with incredibly well drawn horses, anatomically perfect; colts caught in true stilting movement, the unmistakably stallion arch of a neck, a sun fishing horse in mid air. (*A* 86)

The teaching went both ways in this small classroom as Mitchell observed and learned about their culture and heard many Stoney stories from the children (as well as from their elders) about Wendigo, Weesackashack the coyote, the backward persons, and the "people with removable hearts that could be hung on tree branches while they slept" (*VP* 13–14). The swing bridge over the Highwood River, which separated the Eden Valley reserve from the outside white communities, took on a special significance for Mitchell and, later in *The Vanishing Point*, became a resonant symbol for two-way bridging between humans and cultures.

We went to Eden Valley in the summer of 1996 and met one of W.O.'s former students, Toots Dixon. When I introduced myself and said my father was Bill Mitchell who had taught here in the early 1950s, his face immediately broke into a big grin and he shook my hand warmly. He said, "Your father taught me – made me think about my inside life."

Toots had not changed much since he was ten years old, a wishbone of a kid with big mouselike ears ("famous" as W.O. described them) and a grin that was so wide it halved his face and made his eyes squint shut. Then he had front teeth – all of which he subsequently lost over his years of saddle-bronc riding in rodeos. He had warm memories about W.O. as a teacher and as a friend of the Stoneys. He said that W.O. wasn't like the "missionary type teachers" because he respected and was genuinely interested in the Stoneys and their culture. Toots had gone to school in Calgary and then to Bible college because his parents thought he should be a minister. Our reminiscing broke free long-forgotten details for me – Stoney kids kneeling on the swing bridge, lowering long thin copper wires with loops in the ends into the river and deftly snaring grayling during their spawning run. When I asked Toots if he remembered this, he slapped his thigh and said, "Now it falls back on me." We asked if W.O. ever told them any stories. He said that he and the other kids often told W.O. Stoney stories. I said, "Like how the birch tree got its stripes?" He nodded, his eyes squinting shut in laughter as he remembered this Rabelaisian tale of Weesackashack the coyote and the chickadees. My father used versions of this story in both "The Alien" and The Vanishing Point *(VP 13).*

One or two evenings a week Mitchell would walk up over the two benches (small plateaus) behind the agency cabin to where the dances were held. He joined in some of the social dances with Susan Shotclose and Mary Rolling-in-the-Mud, and, occasionally, he was allowed to drum: "They let me do things that weren't important, like the Owl Dance or Rabbit Dance. There would be five others there, including the blind head drummer, and we're all holding on to the drum. You couldn't miss your beat with all those sticks going up and down, and getting carried away by it all."[28] But it was the Prairie Chicken Dance that moved Mitchell most, and this dance he only watched.

Most evenings, though, he stayed in the cabin and worked on "The Alien." He described living on the reserve as "one of those heaven-sent situations where what you are living, everything that happens during the day, falls within the circumference of the fiction you are writing. There was an evocation, because I was living there, that was new and fresh and different to me. So that every evening I would be on the typewriter and recording smells, and tastes and touches and sights and sounds, instances, conversations. I was truly a spectator and a listener while I was there for that school year."[29]

Bill's late-evening writing sessions were frequently interrupted by visitors needing first-aid treatment: "'The baby got a burn – sat in the campfire.' And I would dispense ointment for burns. Bismuth hydrate – a great deal of bismuth hydrate – which I was using too. I had a great jug of it which I poured into smaller bottles and put labels on because I also did the dispensary. My bowels were like the bowels of everybody in the Eden Valley community. . . . In all that year there I would be between seized up or running like a goddamn artesian well."[30] However, the medications that Bill dispensed from the agency's supply did little to relieve the symptoms of tuberculosis. He urged those that came to him with coughs to get X-rayed and immunized when the unit came out to the valley and, if they tested positive, to follow up with proper medical treatment. But many refused because they distrusted the "Bony Spectre" machine (*VP* 29–30). Mitchell had a running battle on this issue with Archie Daniels, who had convinced many in the community that it was the X-ray machine that caused them to get sick. TB had decimated some families: "It raced through the Ear family like wild fire. By the time I was there the Ear family had been wiped out except for Wallace, the father, and his son Orville."[31] Despite Mitchell's sense that he connected with the Stoneys in many ways, he despaired over their refusal to address the spread of TB with modern medical treatment.

Archie Daniels both irked and fascinated Mitchell. Archie used a "Socratic dialectic where you push a person further and further back," and he generally had Mitchell on the defensive:

> Archie used to come at you with this sort of wry amusement. His favourite expression was "You whites this," or "You whites that." I remember one time, the summer after I left the reserve, he dropped by the house for a visit. He took a look at the lawn around our home in High River and said, "You whites have got it pretty good, you know. Your grass, your lawn. We don't have that out on the reserve." And his assumption was that grass just grew short in a lovely green lawn for whites, but not for reds. I said, "Archie, if you want short grass like this, that white people have, buy yourself a goddamned lawn-mower and work your ass off cutting it. But before that, scrape it and level it and seed it and put sacks over it and water it." I was pissed off with him. He knew damn well the way you got the grass, but pretended that whites were lucky because they could afford to buy stuff that only grew this long.[32]

Archie Daniels would come back to haunt Mitchell's creative imagination twenty years later when he drew on him for Archie Nicotine in *The Vanishing Point*.

Bill and Merna became particularly close friends with Mary Rolling-in-the-Mud and her family. They looked on Mary as a "real hero." Mary's husband was blind and she supported him, their daughter, Barbara, and her aging father. She was keen to have Barbara, one of Bill's older students, do well at school (Barbara became a partial model for Victoria in "The Alien"). When Bill discovered that Barbara collected discarded biscuits off the floor each day to take home because Mary was short on food, he went out of his way to help her and other families: "Mary told me they needed fat for frying – and for food. Fat was very desirable to supplement

elk, moose or deer."[33] So, Bill brought cartons of fat from the High
River butcher for Mary to distribute among the families. Bill had
discovered an old treadle sewing machine at the back of the High
River dry cleaners, which he bought for ten dollars and gave to Mary
for a Christmas present: "It worked out beautifully for her – it could
drive that needle through corrugated iron!" That Christmas, Mary
gave him and Merna buckskin jackets.[34]

One time, when Bill had finished his teaching at the reserve,
and Archie dropped by the house for a visit, Bill discovered that
there had been rumours on the reserve about him and Mary:

> Archie was in really fine fettle and he said, "Well, I guess we're
> going back now. Got a full load." And I said, "A full load of
> what?" "Been to the butchers – all that fat." I said, "Oh." And
> he said, "For your girlfriend." And that really got to me. He
> meant it – he figured I was climbing into the goddamn kinick-
> inick with Mary Rolling-in-the-Mud. I said, "Archie, are you
> sitting in my living room and telling me you think I'm screwing
> Mary Rolling-in-the-Mud? She's not my girlfriend, she's my
> friend." "Well," he said, "that lovely fur coat [Bill and Merna
> had given Barbara an old fur coat of Merna's], that sewing
> machine, all this fat."[35]

Bill kept in touch with Mary over the years, although she rarely
came into town. Bill and Merna's concern and affection for the
Rolling-in-the-Mud family left a mark on Barbara as well. She
named her first daughter after Merna and her first son after Bill. But
Mitchell recalled that he learned this from Mary, not from Barbara:
"There was that distance, always that distance. You couldn't get
beyond the eyes with many of them. But I know damn well nobody
else has been there, except for this guy John [Laurie] that ever got
any closer to them than I did, or they to me."[36]

Over the next fifteen years while the Mitchells lived in High
River, members of the Eden Valley reserve would drop by the house
to pay a visit or to drop off some beaded leatherwork. Bill and

Merna became salesmen for Stoney dry goods, keeping their relatives and friends in a good supply of moccasins, fringed gloves, white doe-skin shirts, elk, moose, and buckskin jackets throughout the 1950s. Innocent visitors, particularly from Toronto, following a drink or dinner suddenly found themselves captive audiences for Bill and Merna's sales pitch, the living room filling with the pungent smell of wood-smoked buckskin. Sometimes the Eden Valley people would come by because they needed money. They often pawned their saddles with High River merchants for money for groceries or gas, and once or twice, Bill held saddles as surety for a loan. But more often he would buy some of their dry goods or cover their debts at the grocery store or gas station: "Merna and I felt that it was simply a condition of our association with them – if they're going to be in a bind, I can afford ten or twenty bucks."[37]

Merna, however, had a serious concern about one of the visits from some Eden Valley people. During a High River rodeo, Bill and Merna had a party at the house for some of the Stoney kids and their families who were in town camped out at the rodeo grounds:

> There were about a dozen people in the living room. We had cases of pop and those marshmallow cookies with the chocolate puff cover – they'd kill for those. Wallace Ear and his son Orville were there, and Orville was coughing and coughing and coughing. After they left, Merna said, "That boy was really coughing." I said, "Yeah, he's got pretty active TB." Well, Merna was furious with me. She said, "Don't ever let that happen again." She was thinking, How could you do that, this kid in here coughing around sputum and everything and little kids here and what if Ormie and Hughie pick up TB. She was right.[38]

On our first research visit to Eden Valley, in the summer of 1986, we met Webster Lefthand. He was a band councillor then, sixty-six years old, and had a very distinguished air about him. He recalled W.O. in some detail: "Your father was a fine man – he could talk to us Natives. It's not so easy to do that. I remember him well — he knew how to get along with the Natives — a lot of people did not." I said that from what I understood he was very good with the children, and he immediately nodded, saying that W.O. had taught one of his children. He also remembered that W.O. had supported the establishment of the Eden Valley reserve in the 1940s. When we said goodbye, Webster shook our hands and said, "Your father, he was a fine man — and you can say that to anybody."[39]

— "A POWER IN THE LAND" —

The first crisis with *Jake and the Kid* came in December 1951 when Harry Boyle wrote to tell Mitchell that Peter Francis was leaving the CBC for a position at *Mayfair* magazine. Francis was getting fed up with CBC management politics and was deeply concerned, as many were, about the effect on the CBC of the Royal Commission on National Development in the Arts, Letters and Sciences (the 1951 Massey Report). He worried what might happen to a series such as *Jake and the Kid.* Harry Boyle, too, seemed to think that the Massey Report, what he called "Masseyitis," would promote high culture ("candlelight and old poetry") at the expense of "that culture [that] comes from plain ordinary reflection of everyday living."[40] Mitchell was "terribly upset" that Francis was leaving and wrote Boyle insisting that he find some "unorthodox way"[41] for Francis to continue to produce the shows after he left for *Mayfair.* Boyle prevailed on CBC management, and arrangements were made for Francis to continue on a freelance basis.

In fact, *Jake and the Kid* had become so popular that, as Francis noted in a letter to Bill, an "outcry" would have gone up if the show had been stopped. Arthur Phelps, a professor of English at McGill University who gave radio broadcasts on literary subjects, had commented that the series was "culture in the making," and Francis wrote "Jake, although by no means the program with the largest listening audience . . . is certainly the CBC's prize prestige-making show." He added, "You, sitting there in High River, have invisible lines of power and influence radiating out from you, whether you realize it or not. I like your stuff simply because it's good, but there is an influential group of people in this country who regard you as our chief cultural prop."[42]

Mitchell was having his own minor crisis in simply getting the scripts written. How was he going to produce sixteen scripts between January 6 and April 20 when the season was to end? Francis wrote to say that Harry Boyle would allow only one repeat show so that meant fresh material had to be dredged up. The myth in the East was that Mitchell was "a fast man with a buck," had to be "prodded," and had a penchant for reusing material.[43] All three accusations were true – at times – but in this situation Mitchell came through. He created eighteen new episodes, repeated only two shows, and the series ran longer than planned, until May 25.

Partly as a result of Merna's input, a few of these episodes took on a more political tone. Mitchell considered himself politically naive, like Jake who, in "Prairie Flower," seems oblivious to all the town activity surrounding the visit of Princess Elizabeth. Repeat Godfrey calls him "a idiot" in the ancient Greek sense of the word, "one who is without political awareness."[44] Merna, however, was very interested in political issues at all levels of government. She regularly read the newspapers, including the *High River Times*, and would cut out interesting stories and file them "under Politics, meaning town politics."[45] On one occasion she was so annoyed at what she perceived to be anti-francophone editorials and an anti-female one in the *Calgary Herald* that she wrote a letter to the editor. Merna's lively interest in political issues led Bill to think about the possibility of Merna taking over the writing of some *Jake and the Kid* stories starting in the fall of 1952. Although nothing came of this, it is clear that Merna was instrumental in suggesting story ideas to Bill during this period.

Some of the issues that Merna steered Bill toward were small-town politics. But, on a more universal level, Mitchell dealt with issues of racial prejudice in episodes such as "One Hundred Percent Canadian" (April 29, 1951), which concerns Moses Lefthand, a Stoney

Indian, moving into town from the Indian reserve, and "Curling Fever" (April 15, 1951), about Wong, the Chinese café owner, being ostracized from the curling team. A couple of episodes had an even more satirical bite to them such as "Going to a Fire" and "Crocus Under the Microscope."

"Going to a Fire," broadcast on January 13, 1952, was, as Mitchell said, "my slap on the wrist of intolerance."[46] It concerned racial prejudice against the Kiziws, a Ukrainian family. When the Kiziws begin to prosper, their neighbours feel threatened and exclude them from social gatherings. The climax comes when the Kiziw house catches fire, but, proud and determined, Mr. Kiziw will not allow the townspeople to help him: "First falla step forward wit' bocket – I brain him wit' axe! . . . You ain't gonna halp before with kind word – well, you ain't gonna halp now" (*AJ* 194). The show was applauded by many, including the Canadian Citizenship Council, and the Honorable James Gardiner, minister of agriculture, who telegrammed Mitchell requesting a copy of the script. Arthur Irwin, who had left *Maclean's* to become commissioner of the National Film Board, also wanted a copy of the script for a film project.

"Crocus Under the Microscope" (February 24, 1952), which caused an uproar, was instigated by Merna and Mrs. McCorquodale. They were upset about a study by a University of Toronto sociologist, Dr. Jean Burnet, who had visited Hanna, a small town northeast of High River, to study how the Social Credit government took root in small depressed western towns. The results of her study had just been published in a book, *Next-Year Country*.[47] She was critical of the quality of the town's professional people and their lack of leadership, and of what she perceived as the town's racial intolerance, its stratified social life, its stultifying cultural environment, and its incestuous sexual mores. Basil Dean, a *Calgary Herald* reporter, was indignant about the "merciless clinical dissection" of this community and quoted a number of passages in his column to illustrate why the townspeople would be "outraged."[48]

Mrs. McCorquodale picked up on his points and wrote an angry editorial in the *High River Times* entitled "Under the Microscope," in which she questioned Burnet's methods.[49] Because Hanna was such a small community it was inevitable that the anonymity of its residents, particularly the professionals who were discussed, would not be protected. Bill recalled, "I was so outraged, having gone up goose hunting and having taught for a year at Castor which is in the same area as Hanna, that I did the most deliberate, political, propaganda, pulpit thing I have ever done."[50]

"Crocus Under the Microscope" satirically attacked not just the premise that a community could be scientifically measured, but the casual, unscientific methods adopted to seek and present information, and the callous disregard for the individuals involved in the study. It certainly was a different kind of *Jake* script: social-conscience drama. As Francis wrote to Bill, "It's not particularly entertaining, it certainly isn't funny, and it is not very heart-warming either, except the final recitations at the end."[51] The script Bill sent off, with an unusual ten days to spare for rehearsal, caused Francis great anxiety. Mitchell had changed Hanna to Crocus, but Burnet was only thinly disguised as Dr. Campbell, a lecturer on sabbatical who had written "Next Year Town." Francis made Campbell a male, removed the name of the book and of the university, and deleted a few passages he thought were risky such as Ma saying that Campbell must "be terribly twisted."[52] Francis was still nervous and wired Bill asking if any of the quotes from the fictional Dr. Campbell's "Next Year Town" were direct quotes from the real book. Bill assured him that they were not quotations from *Next-Year Country*, and Francis thought they would be safe from any potential "libel."[53]

"The next thing I knew," said Mitchell, "is that the Anthropological and Sociological departments of the University of Toronto are threatening me and the CBC with libel."[54] A University of Toronto sociologist, probably a colleague of Burnet, wrote an angry letter to which Francis had to respond.[55] It turned out that Mitchell had quoted from the book – at least indirectly, for he quoted from Basil Dean's newspaper report, which contained direct quotations from the book. CBC management was up in arms, and Francis had to do some fancy footwork to calm things down.

Within a week the tables were turned. Oswald Hall, chairman of McGill's Sociology and Anthropology department, weighed in on the debate. He wrote Mitchell a two-page complimentary letter, saying that he felt Burnet's book had broken a policy of anonymity that he and other sociologists in the field had been attempting to codify in the last few years. In his view, the *Jake* program was justified: "As a spokesman for people whom I feel have been victimized in this case, you certainly let us have it – both barrels, plenty of powder!"[56] Hall also wrote Francis saying that Mitchell had helped to "clarify a problem" and was "owe[d] a debt of gratitude."[57]

Francis, who believed that a couple of the top brass at the CBC were always trying to sabotage the show, was delighted with the turn of events, and enthusiastically wrote to Bill:

> . . . all this steam over the sociological piece is resulting in the program attaining not merely greater notoriety but greater eminence. I am telling you the simple truth when I say that Jake really has become something of a power in the land, and that almost anything said on the show seems to bring repercussions in high quarters – fortunately most of them favorable. I feel slightly awed at having anything to do with it. One of your beer-parlor characters makes a crack about the Liberal government, and Agriculture Minister Gardiner asks for a copy of the script – and ten thousand farmers cheer and feel they have a voice. Stevie Kiziw's house burns down, and the film board and the Ottawa citizenship people think the cause of tolerance has advanced several notches. And so on. As I said, an invisible web of power radiates out from you in your reservation out there, and it will be a pity if you ever stop spinning it.[58]

On another occasion, Mitchell's satire ran afoul of the Canadian Pacific Railway. In the episode "Prairie Flower," about Princess Elizabeth's eleven-minute train stop in Crocus, Mitchell parodied the purple prose of the CPR's travel brochures in Weighfreight Brown's description of the princess's train route across Canada: "Down the broad St. Lawrence, past quaint habitant Quebec to the hist'ried city of Montreal —. . . . Through the garden the Dominion — Niagara peninsula — North shore mighty Superior where green-clad pines stand their sentinel watch. . . . Take the Saskatchewan prairies faster'n a greased gopher through a thirty-six-inch thrashin' machine. Eager to catch their first glimpse of the soft swellin' beauty the Alberta foothills."[59] In one of his *Toronto Star* columns, Pierre Berton recalled how "some nameless idiot [in the CPR] corporation took it upon himself to write Mitchell a pompous letter." Mitchell replied saying he "was sorry . . . that he had hurt the CPR's feelings," that "Crocus . . . would immediately be moved off the CPR line and on to the CNR line. Never again would he mention the CPR in any of his writing. Even prunes, which are colloquially known in the West as 'CPR strawberries,' would henceforth be called 'CNR strawberries' in all scripts." Berton claims, "The CPR hierarchy pleaded, cajoled, apologized. . . . Platoons of vice-presidents were called in to make amends; it was no use. To this day, I believe, Crocus is a CNR town."[60]

The week before the "Crocus Under the Microscope" episode, Mitchell stirred up more trouble with "The Grim Gash of Death," a story about a travel-writing celebrity. St. Clair Jordan returns a hero to his hometown of Crocus, claiming to have "scaled the Matterhorn – faced cold steel in that grim gasha death which is known as the Khyber Pass –" However, when this worldly adventurer gets lost going in a straight line along Government Road and cannot face a barking dog, he is revealed as a "two-handed deliberate phoney."[61]

St. Clair Jordan was a lampoon of Gordon Sinclair, the feisty broadcaster and writer. Long before Sinclair made a name for himself as one of the panelists on *Front Page Challenge*, he had become immensely popular for his colourful and suspenseful travel stories of man-eating tigers, crocodiles, and cannibalism (he claimed to have encountered them all).[62] Through his four daily radio broadcasts on CFRB in Toronto and his *Toronto Star* "Radio" column, Sinclair had created a reputation for being entertaining but abrasively opinionated.

While still in Toronto, Mitchell "was wont to dart from office to office in *Maclean's*, waving a Sinclair clipping and shrieking."[63] When Sinclair attacked Sylvia and Ben Lennick in two of his "Radio" columns,[64] Mitchell decided to create St. Clair Jordan, who first appeared in "Woman Trouble."[65] At first Sinclair just laughed off the St. Clair Gordon caricature. Mitchell recalls, "I got a letter and on the back of the envelope it said 'St. Clair Jordan, Station Pain.' It was just a card and it said, 'Dear Mitchell, for Christ's sake get my by-line right.'"[66]

But when Mitchell resurrected St. Clair Jordan in "The Grim Gash of Death," Sinclair was not happy and he hit back in one of his columns saying that Mitchell was "drying up"[67] – which prompted another St. Clair episode. After the fourth episode, Sinclair got riled up enough to go and speak to Arthur Hiller, who was then directing the series. Mitchell describes the conversation:

> Gordon Sinclair said, "This has got to stop. Mitchell has made me out an inaccurate reporter, he has made me out a liar, he has made me out a chicken, he's made me out a guy that ground sluices ducks." And Arthur said, "Well, Gordon, that isn't you. His name is St. Clair Jordan. He works for the Crocus Breeze. He was born in Saskatchewan. You didn't write 'How I Saved the Maharajah of Minoor' in a gouting bath of tiger blood when you jumped from a tree. It's a fictional character. You know, Gordon, you must be a very vain man to think that Mitchell is slashing at you specifically with that fictional character."[68]

Mitchell did only one more St. Clair Jordan show after this,[69] but he recalled that Sinclair used to periodically attack him or the program in subsequent years. The remark that Mitchell remembered most, because of his mother's response, occurred in 1959 when the NFB decided against making a television series of *Jake and the Kid*. Sinclair wrote, "Like CBC television producers, I could see no merit in this saga of the unwashed. To me, Jake was repulsive – not because he gave me the feeling of dirty socks and soiled overalls; but because he was essentially a cruel and malicious failure, contemptuous of people who had made the grade. Get lost, Jake!"[70] Much to Mitchell's amusement, his mother sent a note to Sinclair that simply said, "Get lost, Gordon!"[71]

— "THIS THING IS AS GOOD AS MOBY DICK" —

While Mitchell worked with the Stoneys at Eden Valley from the spring of 1951 to the summer of 1952, he filled in most of the "big hole" in Part III of "The Alien," which had stalled him in 1949. Carlyle seems to have found his vocation and relaxes into a more fulfilled life with his family and his teaching, pinning his idealistic hopes on a young girl, Victoria Rider, who becomes the first Stoney to complete high school. But he soon falls back into his despairing moodiness, broods about the impossibility of communicating with others, and withdraws from his wife and children. He loses faith in his mission on the reserve and sells out the Stoney community when he persuades them to sign a power deal with a hydro company. This is the last straw for Grace, and she leaves Carlyle, saying, "You've just never grown up to contain the world, that's all! Or the other people in it. Me – your own children – you stop at the outer edges of yourself!" (*A* 306).

A few nights later Carlyle walks up to the dance tent. He sees Victoria and, "stirred and dazed by the fierce assault of drum and liquor,"[72] he joins in the Rabbit and Owl dances with her, then takes her outside the dance tent and makes love to her. They leave the reserve and ride to the valley just below Mount Lookout where they camp. Growing more and more disgusted with her silence, her cultural habits, her features, and her smell, Carlyle sends Victoria back to the reserve. He then rides up to Mount Lookout, where he meets the lookout keeper and then plunges to his death down the mountainside in the storm.

Carlyle is a figure cut in part from the cloth of such Romantic tragic heroes as the Poet in Shelley's *Alastor* and Manfred in Byron's *Manfred*. Like Shelley's Poet, Carlyle is unsatisfied with the mundane and petty world. He closes door after door on humanity in a selfish and alienating quest for the ideal, which is symbolized by Mount Lookout, whose resonances draw in part on Shelley's "Mont Blanc." In the early rough notes describing Carlyle's motivation, Mitchell refers to Shelley's "Adonais":

> A hunger for the eternal – a dissatisfaction with the transient nature of the tactual the audible the visual.

> Shelley: The One remains, the many change and pass;
> Heaven's light forever shines, Earth's shadows fly;
> Life, like a dome of many-coloured glass,
> Stains the white radiance of Eternity.[73]

Carlyle in the end takes the advice Shelley offers in the remaining lines of this verse: "Death" will "trample" the "many-coloured glass" of life to fragments, so, "Die,/If thou wouldst be with that which thou dost seek!"[74]

Mitchell had a problem. A year earlier he had written Cloud (who had just finished reading Part I) that his "main concern has been whether the reader would find sympathy in himself for Carlyle, and I'm awfully pleased you like him, for the book is a tragedy and you can't purge worth a damn if the central human is a heel."[75] Although Mitchell indicated that he was going to add "fire and colour" to his character, Carlyle had grown more and more negative.

During this period, both Cloud and Willis Wing were frustrated by lack of news from Mitchell on "The Alien." Wing wrote to Cloud, "If there ever was a cat who walks alone Bill is it. I have not yet discovered what magic must be had to prod him successfully."[76] Mitchell finally wrote Wing, after ten months and three unanswered letters, explaining that the move from Toronto and pressure of *Jake* scripts had held up progress on the novel.[77]

Bill, however, did keep in touch with Ernest Buckler, giving him whatever help and advice he could on finding a publisher for *The Mountain and the Valley*. When Holt & Co. accepted the novel, Bill wrote back, "Hurrah – hurrah! for Holt and up Atlantic's dirty kilt! As soon as I read your letter Merna and I toasted the book's success — she in Calgary lager and I in my three o'clock eggnog, having just discovered that my ulcer had broken open again before Christmas. I suppose I could have toasted it in pregnant mare's piss which is what the doctor wants to have me take. The trade name is Kutrol and it will give me a new stomach lining for only two hundred dollars."[78]

Mitchell had been diagnosed with a stomach ulcer about seven years earlier. As a result of this last attack, they cancelled a trip to Mexico in February and, as Merna wrote to John Gray, work on the book had been slowed by "ulcers, flu, sinusitis and two relapses." However, she reported, "I am very excited about the work Bill has done. It has material that as far as I know has never been touched; and it has everything — humor, pathos and wonderful atmosphere. There is an excitement in Bill too, which I think will give the work a good pace and he won't stop till the book is finished. There is less interruption and he keeps better hours. He's feeling much better."[79] Mitchell pushed himself hard, spending about five weeks out on the reserve trying to get "The Alien" ready for the fall lists.

In July 1952, he wrote Cloud that he hoped to finish Part III of "The Alien" in three weeks, after which he would do a rewrite of Part II. He was excited and confident about the novel:

> I think it is excellent and may be my major bid as a novelist. Nothing like it has ever been done. . . .
>
> The last section in which Carlyle is an agency teacher and supervisor is not the Maugham in the English colony or Bates in Burma or Green among the British African exiles sort of thing. My natives are real; I have known them for ten years now, have been living on the reserve and teaching them for the past winter. . . . The INDIAN QUESTION or WHAT SHALL I DO ABOUT MY MISCEGENATION does not form the core of the book at all any more than Melville concerned himself with the current evils of the whaling industry primarily.

This thing is as good as Moby Dick and I appreciate your patience throughout my rude silences.

Mitchell enclosed a copy of his Louis Riel article and described plans for his next novel, a long historical one growing out of his research on Riel, "done with the Lord Jim now-you-see-me-now-you-don't-technique and using a fictional central character for focus. I think I can do a dandy for my next book, since I was born and raised in Riel country, and now know exactly how Riel spent his Montana interludes as a teacher at an Indian school." His only problem, he wrote, would be his "ignorance of the religious side of his life," and he jokingly added that spending six months in a Franciscan's retreat northwest of Calgary taking a "short course in Catholicism studied in the cell they have waiting for me, should clear that up."[80] John Gray was intrigued by this idea, and urged Mitchell to do a short juvenile novel titled "General Middleton's Drummer Boy."[81] Nothing, however, came of this project for, as Mitchell explained, "generally a novel does not begin for me like this but with a 'ding,' an idea, some insight that grabs me about the ways of humans and the universe. But very quickly it also is a person and, of course, a context. It grows and comes out of that rather than all of this historical harness and event. So it peed away into the sand."[82]

~ FORT QU'APPELLE CREATIVE WRITING WORKSHOP ~

The seed of what was to become a significant part of Mitchell's philosophy about teaching creative writing germinated this summer at Fort Qu'Appelle, Saskatchewan, where he was invited to give his first writing workshop from August 18–31, 1952. Each morning was allotted to two-hour informal talks about the techniques of writing, followed by individual consultations in the afternoons and evenings. What was important, he told the students, was to get it down, to "write fast and even in a slip-shod fashion." Students were encouraged to "grow antennae," to observe the world around them and record the sensual experiences in a notebook. As they started fine-tuning their work, it was important to develop "the art that conceals art," which became one of his most significant messages. Finally, he said, "Don't give up." Although "none of us made it big time," wrote one of his students, "I don't think many came out of Bill's class without a positive obsession to keep on writing." Because Bill was encouraging, charming, and funny, he could "let us know clearly what he thought of our writing, but he was never harsh."[83] Another student, who later sold some of her stories to magazines and published a novel, said that "he had a wonderful knack of taking someone's poor little story, and with a few suggestions making it into something publishable."[84]

By coincidence, Florence James was the drama instructor at Fort Qu'Appelle. Mitchell had known of her and her husband, Burton, in Seattle around 1935, where they had founded the Seattle Repertory Theatre and the first Negro Repertory Theatre Group. Florence and Burton had also taught summer workshops at the Banff School of Fine Arts, where Merna, then an aspiring actress, had met them in 1938. They were victims of the McCarthyite Washington State Committee on UnAmerican Activities, whose investigations closed down the James' theatre. In 1953 the Arts Board of Saskatchewan's CCF government ignored the blacklist, and she became their first drama consultant.

That summer Florence rekindled Mitchell's love of performance and the stage: "she made me a playwright again." She put on Stephen Vincent Benet's *The Devil and Daniel Webster* and asked Bill to play Mr. Scratch, the Devil, and Merna to play one of the townswomen. Years later, Bill recalled some of her advice to him: "For God's sake, PROJECT: And don't ham it up – it's like an orange – don't you squeeze out all the emotional juice – leave some in there for the audience."[85]

My father played Mr. Scratch too convincingly from my nine-year old point of view. At first I was confused that that was my father with the sinister eyebrows, villain's moustache and goatee, my father who triumphantly swung his black cape around and terrorized Jabez Stone and his bride, Mary. My shame and guilt became total terror when the stage and theatre went completely black, except for the Devil's disembodied and ghostly green face that floated centre stage as his doomsday voice summoned his jury of notable sinners from Hell. In the last scene, as the townspeople (including my mother) ganged up on Mr. Scratch, kicking and hitting him as they drove him out of town, I remember crying out, "Don't, don't!" Then the curtain call – and there was my father smiling with pleasure as the audience clapped and cheered the cast. When I went up on stage and he saw how upset I was, he hugged me, saying it was all pretend. Then he showed me the flashlight with a piece of green clear Cellophane taped over the lens that was attached to his chest inside his black vest. He told me to turn it on and his face was again grotesquely transfigured. And it was his delight in showing me how the trick had been done that calmed me down.

Mitchell returned to Fort Qu'Appelle the next year and continued teaching there until 1956. Florence James persuaded him to adapt his radio drama, "The Day Jake Made Her Rain," for the 1953 summer's stage production. This story had its genesis in Mitchell's "fascination with rascals," with con men, evangelists, and demagogues.[86] Jake boasts that he had been an accomplished rainmaker, and Gatenby dares him to prove it. Jake, himself, is not a demagogue, but Mitchell plays with the idea of a man working magic on a crowd and restoring their faith. The trick was that Jake "made her rain" with the help of Jimmy Shoelack seeding the clouds with dry ice.

The play "worked out beautifully" Mitchell said, "and we had a lovely rain-making machine – a bloody gas engine that went 'puckety-puckety-puckety.'"[87] It hadn't rained for weeks in Fort Qu'Appelle, and, right on cue, following Jake's rain-making exhortation, a tremendous thunderstorm hit the area. The theatre's sound effects for thunder and lightning were redundant. As reported in the *Regina Leader-Post*, the rain came down in torrents as the audience left the theatre.[88]

5

"THE ALIEN"

— 1952 to 1954 —

MITCHELL MOVED back out to his trailer at Eden Valley after his Fort Qu'Appelle course and worked Monday to Friday on "The Alien." When the weather turned colder, he moved into the shack in the bull pasture at Dave and Rita Diebels' ranch. After having dinner and conversation with the Diebel family, he did not look forward to his walk back to the shack – not only because "The Alien" was waiting for him, but so too, he feared, were Dave's Hereford bulls.

This was the fall that Dave Diebel, a hunter of some note, introduced Bill to duck hunting on Frank Lake a few miles east of High River. Frank Lake was really a very large slough, but it was on the edge of the central flyway. Surrounded by grain and summer fallow fields, it was a favourite stopover for migratory game birds. The thousands of ducks that fed in the local barley and wheat fields caused huge losses to the farmers, who often got pre-season permits and gave hunters free shotgun shells to hunt in their fields to keep the ducks and geese away.

I was nine when I went out with my father on his first attempt at duck hunting. He had borrowed a single-shot 12-gauge Cooey, and Dave had given him pointers on how to hold the gun and "lead" so the duck would fly into the shot pattern. We hid in some bulrushes at the south end of Frank Lake and, as evening came on, flight after flight of ducks and geese flew out for their evening feeding in the surrounding grain fields. The noise of their feeding chuckles and wings was stirring. My father fired a lot of lead shot up in the air, but no ducks came down. As we walked to the car in the gathering dusk, I remember consoling him and saying next time he would get one. He didn't need any consoling — our first outing had us both as hooked on hunting as we were on fishing. My father hated the "stun" of the foothills prairie winter and had always found fall a melancholy and foreboding season. But now he looked forward to fall hunting as much as he did to summer fishing. His description in "Roses Are Difficult Here" of Matt Stanley's excitement about the approaching fall hunt was his own:

> . . . on sibilant wings they launched their punctual assault against the dawn and sunset skies. Daily they welcomed the splashing arrival of each new contingent of pintail, mallard, and canvas-back from the North. Thread after thread of snow geese unravelled from the far horizon, grew loud and shrill as they circled over Cooper's Lake, broke formation, then, still calling, fell like snowflakes through the sun. There came a late September night when the two-note plaint of Canada honkers drifted down to ordinary mortals far below. Their high, wild call lifted Matt from sleep; in his pyjamas, and barefooted, he rushed outside the kitchen door to stand in the chill fall night, and to stare upward with pounding heart. The next morning they would be riding the far centre of Cooper's Lake, magnificent as Nelson's fleet before Trafalgar. (RD 224–25)

That Christmas my father bought my mother a 16-gauge Ithaca pump shotgun and she returned the favour with a 12-gauge Ithaca pump for him. Hunting had become not only a preoccupation for my father as a sport, but also a significant element in his stories. His first Jake and the Kid hunting story, "Duel at Dawn," was broadcast February 1, 1953.

The November 20, 1952, *High River Times* reported that Merna and Bill Mitchell and the Diebels went goose hunting at Bassano (seventy miles east of High River) over the weekend, "with luck." The *Times* had obviously been given an edited version of this hunt. The Mitchells had taken their trailer, parking it by a large reservoir where they spotted some geese sitting in a swampy bay. Young Petey Diebel was the only one to score – his first Canada grey goose – but it dropped a hundred yards out in the water and they did not have a retriever. Bill, seeing Petey's excitement turn to utter disappointment, stripped down to his underwear and swam out in the frigid November water to retrieve it. He came back shivering and covered in mud from the slough, but triumphantly holding Petey's goose. Bill could not remember where he had put his clothes, and as he looked for them he walked into a pile of cactus. Merna was up all night with him, pulling cactus thorns out one by one. The next morning when they stopped at the local service station for gas, they discovered they had been hunting on a migratory game bird sanctuary.

Mitchell continued to be upbeat about work on "The Alien" through September 1952. He wrote from 7 a.m. to midnight, but frequently dropped by the reserve to visit with the Stoney community. In October, however, he was not as confident when he sent Part III to John Gray:

> Honestly, John, I cannot tell whether the thing is competent, bad, or good; I've been too long with it. I know it's authentic, for I spent most of the winter and fall living with the Stonys; like Carlyle I taught them; his disillusionment in the hopelessness of work with them is very nearly autobiographical. I am now a regular drummer for the Owl and Rabbit dances. I am seriously thinking of getting out a tape recorder then arranging to have little plastic discs cut to be inserted in the book jacket. One side would be the chicken dance to be read before the chapter in which Carlyle leaves with Victoria for the bush; the other side would have the Owl dance and the Rabbit dance.

He also told Gray that he was in financial difficulty and had to arrange an overdraft: "I have almost ruptured myself financially to get seven months work in on this; I have just finished bleeding all over the floor of the Royal Bank." He asked if Macmillan could increase his $500 advance to $1,500, but adds that he realizes this is steep and "your decision would not change my regard for MACMILLAN."[1] Within three weeks Macmillan sent Bill $1,000.

The reason for all this "blood" was that Mitchell had gone six months without a cheque from the CBC. The 1951–52 *Jake and the Kid* season wrapped up on May 25, and Francis wrote to say he would no longer be allowed to produce the show on a freelance basis. Mitchell, fed up with all the CBC bureaucracy, refused to continue with a third series. Also, he wanted to concentrate wholly on "The Alien," and he had moved into his trailer out at the Eden Valley. When *Jake and the Kid* did not reappear in the fall of 1952, the radio audience was not happy. As journalist Vicki Fremlin wrote, "A roar of protest went up from coast to coast in Canada, with reverberations from below the border. From Prince George, B.C., to Bridgetown, N.S., listeners wrote in to beg or command their return. Letters came from large cities, small towns, minuscule villages and rural routes."[2]

A new director, Arthur Hiller, was asked to get Mitchell back into the fold. In the fall of 1952 Hiller flew from Toronto to visit Mitchell, but when he arrived in High River he discovered he would have to drive another thirty-five miles out to Eden Valley to Mitchell's trailer. The trip was worth it. Mitchell approved of Hiller, and the series started up again beginning with a one-hour Christmas day episode, "All is Calm, All is Bright." With two hundred dollars coming in every week, Mitchell was solvent again.

In early February Mitchell interrupted his work on "The Alien" to read Ernest Buckler's *The Mountain and the Valley*, which had been published the previous fall. He wrote Buckler that when he saw the dedication, which included him, "it made me cry." In a long and intimate letter he praised the book, describing reading it as "at first wonderful then a saddening and then a wonderful experience." He marvelled at Buckler's accomplishment, and then he felt "selfishly sad:" "I contemplated my own coarse net, knowing that I was just a hack angler after words, that all my own fish were just lethargic pike and yours were thrilling and beautifully fierce rainbow and cut-throat." Finally, he described how the satisfaction of having written a fine novel can break the loneliness that is the writer's lot, but he wondered if that was enough for Buckler:

> You're my dish and it worries me; I've had Merna and the children the past ten years; now that we're back from Toronto and its unique and stultifying depression, I have our home and the mountains and the Highwood River. In your book and in your letters I sense a loneliness that pretty nearly matches mine in the old days; my remembrance of it has been sharpened by my three months in the mountains with only Maclean Powderface dropping by the trailer to gather cattle. . . . I'm leaving Mern and Hughie and Orme to go up there again this week and take what I hope to be a month's last run at the novel; the walls of the cabin will be listening tirelessly and I will be reminded again of riding freights and sleeping in pogies and hotel rooms and boarding houses, wondering what the hell is the dull point of it all. The answer now is with Merna and Hughie and Ormie and almost as paramount – in my writing. With THE MOUNTAIN AND THE VALLEY between covers you have that satisfaction and the realization that you've reached a lot of <u>right</u> ones. If you're as like me as I think you are, you can touch the book now and again like a child with his hand in the pocket that holds his first jack knife; I think it's loneliness that withdraws ever so little then.
>
> We love you dearly, Ernie, and we feel we know you the best we know anyone – which is almost magic since we've never met you or talked with you – hell, that's all wrong, for the true understanding has little to do with such unimportant things as the height, weight, appearance of a friend. As long as I have known her, I've promised Merna we'll get to Nova Scotia and Mahone Bay where she was born. I think we will within the next year; perhaps we shall see you then.

Good luck to the book and God Bless the true people in it. . . .[3]

Mitchell's praise for Buckler's book, his comments on the writer's loneliness, and his self-doubts about his own writing are revealing and poignant in the context of his struggle with "The Alien." At this time Mitchell was imaginatively "living" in Carlyle's existential and cultural loneliness, but to a certain extent, in his lonely life out at Eden Valley, he was also actually living it. Unlike his character, though, Mitchell was a "yea sayer" who believed deeply in human "bridging," in family connections, and in the potency of words. While Carlyle finally feels that there can be no real communication between humans, not even between father and son or husband and wife (let alone between alien cultures), Mitchell believed strongly that there could be. He argued here, as he would throughout his life and work, that writing assuages loneliness, that it is a positive gesture against the defeatist attitude behind the question, "What the hell is the dull point of it all." The power of connecting through writing is made clear in Bill's remark that even though he and Merna have not met Buckler, they feel they know him, through the magic of the written word, "the best we know anyone."

Perhaps Mitchell's intense and lonely retreats into himself and his fictional worlds partly explain his love of talking with people and, later, of performing for an audience. He was like a trapper who, after a long lonely winter, would come back to human community and not stop talking for three days straight. Merna understood this process and supported Bill in his inner retreats, acted as a buffer to the interference and distraction of the outside world. But, she must have felt at times that Bill stopped at the outer edges of himself — and perhaps he sensed this in himself, in his obsessive desire to write (and fish and hunt) and in his, at times, explosive outbursts against others invading his inner territory. At the same time, unlike his character Carlyle, he had an omnivorous appetite for experience and human contact, and an ability to focus on things outside himself.

— "REJOICE — REJOICE! . . . IT IS DONE AND
I LIKE IT STILL AFTER SEVEN YEARS." —

Mitchell stayed out at Eden Valley for February 1953 and completed Part II of "The Alien." By this time he had also grown a beard, which he refused even to trim until the novel was finished. He and Merna had planned a holiday trip to California in March, and just before leaving, Mitchell wrote Cloud that he would shortly be sending him the completed nine-hundred-page manuscript (about two hundred thousand words). The following day, he wrote Gray, "Rejoice — rejoice!" Even though he still wanted to do some revising, "the main thing is that it is done and I like it still after seven years."[4]

Macmillan liked it very much (although they had some questions) and wished to publish part or all of it. There was some talk of publishing Parts I and II in the fall and Part III as a separate book the following year. Pierre Berton wrote a perceptive and detailed reader's report on it for John Gray. He noted some flaws (the motivation for some of Grace's and Carlyle's actions and the melodramatic ending), but praised the novel's characters, particularly its minor characters, prose, and imagery: "It is easy, lively reading, full of surprises, and it captures the reality of the foothills country as no other book has done."[5] Gray wrote, "It is fine work, Bill, and taken as a whole much the best you have done I am sure." He was still concerned that the reader does not "warm" to Carlyle enough and felt it would take "just a few lines here and there" to correct this.[6]

It was a different story in the United States. Dudley Cloud and his wife, Jeanette, wrote mixed reports for Atlantic Monthly Press, although they recommended further consideration, but the trade editorial reports from Little, Brown were all negative: "It would seem well to reject and let the author go."[7] In April, Cloud wrote Mitchell, "This is a sad letter for me to write — and a disappointing one for you to read, I'm afraid." He explained that their major concern was Carlyle, who "by his outrageous actions . . . sacrifices our sympathy." While Cloud said that he hoped another publisher might "make a success of it," his letter was a rather perfunctory one that offered no suggestions or hope for the novel; he did not invite Mitchell to resubmit it after another rewrite.[8]

Mitchell was devastated by Cloud's rejection letter. Seven years – and such hopes. He had dreamed of this book, his "Moby Dick," being serialized or making the Book of the Month Club so that he could drop writing *Jake and the Kid* radio scripts and get on with his Riel book. He had never thought that Atlantic would flatly turn it down. He stopped working on "The Alien," and seemed to have stopped working on his *Jake* scripts, for the final two of the season were repeats. It was three weeks before he could write John Gray:

> The wounds have been well licked now for some three weeks. I lost myself in laying three thousand brick on the new patio and outdoor barbecue, so I can write this letter and, I trust, a gentlemanly one to Dudley Cloud.
>
> Their decision set me back on my heels, particularly a unanimity I suspect, with which Carlyle struck them all as <u>outrageous</u>. I felt I had the most tragic character flaw of all in this man, alienated by his own attitude to his miscegenation.[9]

Mitchell did not write Cloud.

For the next two months Mitchell continued to lose himself in work on the new house addition, which included two bedrooms, a large study, garage, and full basement. Not even winning the University of Western Ontario's President's Medal for best short story for 1952 raised his spirits. When Mrs. McCorquodale reported in the *High River Times* that "The Princess and the Wild Ones" had won, she added, "At the moment Bill is working on a new addition to his High River home, and feels that he is much more expert in running cement than in the literary world."[10]

Mitchell did get some satisfaction when the house addition was completed. For two years he had worked in makeshift spaces in the small house, mainly in the kitchen nook or on the kitchen table. When the new study was finished, he set up his Underwood typewriter on his Victorian bookkeeper's desk, which had been in storage for two years. On the flat part of the desk along the wall and behind the typewriter were lined up his eleven pipes (his favourite a "goose-necked pipe with its sterling-silver ferrule and amber mouthpiece"), tobacco pouch, pipe cleaners, and box of kitchen matches (*Eve* 201). He was surrounded by books, now tidily collected on shelves. The family shotguns hung on the wall on mounts made by Dave Diebel from mountain-sheep feet, cured in L shapes. His fly-tying vice was set up on the right side of his desk, the materials in the drawer below. His fishing rods leaned in the corner by the door, handy for pick up when he slipped out to catch the evening rise on the Highwood three blocks from the house – if he could get by Merna.

About two weeks after Cloud's rejection letter, Bill and Merna read the following article in *Saturday Night*:

> One of the major misconceptions held in this country is that, to earn a living [as a writer], you must spend a good part of your time turning out pot-boilers to formula.
>
> When I was just beginning the job of writing, I had an interview with the editor of a Canadian magazine, and I told him of my ambitions. He looked at me sadly for a moment and then said, "Well, you can try. But let me give you a tip. If you hope to eat regularly, don't bother with anything that doesn't fit into the boy-meets-girl-5,000-words-happy-ending pattern." Now, that man was also a writer, and a good one. But he believed what he told me.
>
> I was sufficiently depressed, but I had a story on hand – only one – and my wife and I were getting hungry. I sent the story to the CBC and received it back in the next mail. Then in some desperation I sent it to my editor friend. I hoped he might have forgotten his dictum – but he hadn't. He wanted no part of a story that dealt with starvation amongst a group of Canadians, and which ended on a tragic note.
>
> . . . But then a lucky accident happened. Acting on a random suggestion, I sent my story out of the country. . . . The agent to whom I sent the story promptly sold it to the *Saturday*

Evening Post for a sum about five times that which I would have received from the Canadian magazine.[11]

The writer was Farley Mowat, the magazine was *Maclean's*, the story was "Eskimo Spring," and the editor was Mitchell. Although Mitchell was not mentioned by name, it was clear to many in the writing community that Mitchell and *Maclean's* were being used as examples of how parochial and second-rate Canadian editors and magazines were. Mitchell was stunned by Mowat's attack, which completely misrepresented his role in Mowat's development and success as a freelance writer. The attack must have been particularly hard for him, given the recent rejection of "The Alien." Merna was furious and wanted to write *Saturday Night* and Mowat, but Bill insisted on following his Grandmother McMurray's advice – ignore the person who does you injury.

Mitchell had been mulling over changes to "The Alien." On May 23 he wrote to John Gray describing his plans for restructuring the novel and changing the ending. The climax now would be the Prairie Chicken Dance, not the "tragic descent ending in his [Carlyle's] death where no man can reach him." Most importantly he wrote, "Altogether I shall warm Carlyle; he shall not do things I would not do myself."[12] Shortly after this letter, "The Alien" won the first *Maclean's* new novel award, and over the next three months Mitchell turned his attention to condensing Part III into nine instalments for *Maclean's*.

Winning the *Maclean's* novel award for *The Alien* bucked up Mitchell's spirits. He wrote Gray, "The honor of the *Maclean's* award is inspiring and the check [$5,000] impresses hell out of the wolves. . . . Slightly unsteady with it all, I went into the bathroom and shaved off the beard, an act I have been contemplating ever since you told me that Farley Mowat had one. All approved except Hughie, who dissents always."[13] He added that he thought he could send him and Wing a complete rewrite of the novel by early September, and wanted Wing to begin submitting it to American publishers beginning with Viking.

In August he told Buckler about his rejection from Cloud: "I hope I never have another shock with other books I do to approach what Dudley's letter did to me. . . . By God, it shakes a person! And it shouldn't." He still had his sense of humour, though, as he went on to describe their life in High River, including his adventures in horse breeding: "Two months ago I handled Cochrane Girl while she was bred. . . . It was my first assist as they say in hockey and midwifery; I was not sure which of us was getting bred, having just received Dudley's letter." In an earlier letter Buckler had told Bill of the slump he experienced when finishing *The Mountain and the Valley* and Bill replied sympathetically, obviously describing his own experience as well:

I know how you feel after THE MOUNTAIN AND THE VALLEY; there comes an awful lassitude, almost unwilling but too great to get the muscles moving again. Looking back over the years and the endlessness of a long work, you even find yourself telling yourself that you simply can't strike out again. But you will. If you're like me, it starts with formless note making, shapes itself into a theme, gathers people around itself; you leave it and come back to it and two years have passed and you have quite a body of work done and you're in the goddam bog and you can't call it off and there's nothing to do but go back to it for a month, then leave it tired and disgusted again to come back again. By this time people are asking you when you're [sic] next is coming out and you tell them in a year or so and your conscience is bothering you and you begin to welcome the time to get at it and it's a little easier because you've been coming back to it again and again in your mind while you're shingling or fly fishing the Highwood or dropping off to sleep at night.[14]

My father did a lot of building and fishing that summer as a means of getting out of the "goddam bog." This was the summer he took me to the canyon on the upper reaches of the *Highwood River*, one of the last refuges of cut-throat trout. Earlier, in the spring, at the kitchen table after supper, he showed me how to tie flies using clumps of buck tail that would stay afloat in the fastest runs. The canyon was a special place for my father, and he later attributed its appeal to Carlyle in The Vanishing Point (VP *108–9*). Through my father's stories, the canyon became a special place for me before I ever saw it.

The canyon lived up to my father's descriptions. I was in a ten-year-old's fishing heaven. But there was one particular moment that became a touchstone between us for the rest of our lives. We had compared our catches over lunch and begun working our way down the lower half of the canyon. I saw a big rainbow hit the surface and I started dry-casting and walking through the rubble of boulders toward the pool's edge. The rainbow struck on my first cast and I yelled, "Got one, Dad! Need the net!" As I ran along the river edge, I tripped and smashed my knee on a boulder. Instantly my excitement turned to excruciating pain — and then to utter disappointment as I realized I had let my line go slack and the fish was gone. As I wept, I was aware of my father sharing my pain and loss, consoling me, splashing cold water on my bleeding kneecap. Later that evening I insisted my rainbow would have been the largest catch of the day. He asked, "What hurt more, Ormie — your knee or losing the fish?"

There is an intense absorption in the outer world of fishing that distracts you from others and your everyday self. As you read the water, you paradoxically turn inwards. You may go fishing with someone, but there is very little overt communication until the end of the day when you compare catches and trade stories about big ones that spat your fly out or broke your line. Looking back, I realize that on this trip to the canyon my father's intentness on his fishing was directly related to his struggle with "The Alien." He was recharging his creative batteries, vacuuming his mind clean in preparation for doing battle with a manuscript that had grown to Moby Dick proportions, and which was threatening to pull him under.

⁓ "LIFE ON THE BRICK DOORSTEP" ⁓

In spite of Bill's disappointment with "The Alien," he and Merna were happy in High River. As Bill told a Rotary gathering, "Life on the brick doorstep teaches you to learn to appreciate that material things are not so important. . . . I wanted and continue to want the kind of childhood for my children which is not available in the cities."[15] The Mitchells' brick doorstep, patio, and barbecue created a place of great social activity. Bill had scavenged a large cast-iron griddle from the alley behind the New Look Café that was ideal for pancakes as well as steaks. On Sunday mornings he would mix up his special pancake batter, a recipe used by roundup and thrashing crew cooks (the secret ingredient was a large dollop of Roger's Golden Syrup). He would yell out to anyone who happened to be passing by to join the family for a breakfast of pancakes, topped with Merna's homemade saskatoon or chokecherry syrup. Bill was very proud of his pancake cooking, but Merna found it more trouble than it was worth, for Bill was constantly shouting from the kitchen for things he could not find, and it was her chore to clean up the kitchen, which looked like a scene from a Three Stooges movie.

In the fall of 1953 Merna became pregnant with their third child. They had postponed this decision until they were well settled back in High River so there was a considerable gap between this child and Orm, now ten, and Hughie, seven. Bill so much wanted a girl that the unborn child was pre-christened Little Annie, and every few nights he would tell his boys another instalment of the adventures of the adorable, mischievous Little Annie. The stories always reflected what was going on in the Mitchell household, and many of them dealt with Little Annie's desire to have her own horse. Bill had bought Merna an American Saddler, Cochrane Girl, in June 1952 and over the next three years Cochrane foaled three colts (Robin, Ginger, and Poppy). Cochrane's second colt, Ginger, was born a few months before Little Annie.

Hugh and I would lie with our parents on their bed and put our ears to our mother's belly to hear Little Annie's heartbeat, and later we put our hands on her stomach to feel the kicks ("Gosh! She kicks like a horse!"). It was an exciting time for us and we could hardly wait for the birth of our sister. In our father's stories, Little Annie was a female version of Peck's Bad Boy. He acted out dialogue exchanges such as:

"Little Annie, would you like a jelly bean?"

"I would like the whole goddamn bag!"

I remember particularly the stories about Little Annie's pleadings for her own horse. When she is finally given a horse, she wants it to live in the house and sleep in her bedroom.

"But, Annie, horses live in stables or out on the prairie. We can't have a big horse running around in the house."

"Why not?"

"Well, think of all the mess from the hay. And the horse turds."

"I don't care!"

"But we do."

"I promise to clean it up."

Of course, Little Annie got her way, which led to dozens of plots for our bedtime stories. Hugh and I delighted in Little Annie's antics. These stories must have filtered through to our gestating sister for they were strangely prophetic regarding her identity as a wilful, spoiled, and undisciplined child.

For the 1953–54 school year, at Merna's and Bill's suggestion, Larry Diebel roomed with Mrs. McCorquodale and had his meals with the Mitchells so he could do his last year of high school in High River. He recalled "a quality of total chaos" that made mealtimes with the Mitchells "interesting." Bill and Merna would "just pitch into one another and unload: 'It is damn well time you started pulling your share around here and I am not going to carry the responsibility for this whole family' and 'What are you talking about?' and words to that effect. If you were an outsider you would be thinking that this was a marriage breakup situation." However, "three minutes later it was all gone. In retrospect I see it was an exceptionally strong relationship." Larry thought that Merna was the aggressor as she tried to straighten Bill out. Her pregnancy at this time would not have made it easier living with Bill, who was struggling with revisions on the "The Alien" and just barely meeting weekly deadlines for the *Jake and the Kid* radio scripts. Larry also recalled Bill's insensitive treatment of his mother on one of her extended visits: "She was a distinguished, almost aristocratic lady, very proper. But she wasn't in good health and he was really hard on her at times." She had false teeth and when she ate they "really clacked." At one dinner Bill said, "'Jesus Christ, Mother! You sound like a goddamn gravel crusher.' It was funny but he didn't mean it to be funny. That poor old lady was really devastated by that – even to the point that she got up and left the table."[16]

Much of this was indicative of the pressure Bill was under. He was optimistic, however, that he could revise "The Alien" in a few months, and had convinced himself that the book would be published in both the United States and Canada. Indeed, in his August 4 letter to Buckler he said, "I have a feeling that it is going to make a major book club."[17] But he was unable to substantially revise the manuscript and sensed that the new ending he had written for the *Maclean's* version was a spliced-on *deus ex machina* that was out of synch with the novel's essentially tragic vision and protagonist. In the fall of 1953 he made a few cuts to the manuscript, and it was submitted to Viking and Random House in New York, but was rejected by both. Gray had hoped that Bill would do "some drastic cutting, especially in the earlier material" and was "a little appalled to find revisions so meagre." He said that Macmillan was still willing to publish the novel as it stood, without an American publisher, but it would be "without complete confidence and enthusiasm" and only "to get it out of your system and your way since it has been there too long."[18]

Willa Lynne was born July 31, 1954, and was doted on by all the family. Bill telegrammed John Gray, "FILLY, DAM MERNA, SIRE W O." and signed off, "LOVE FROM WILLA LYNNE."[19] Gray visited the Mitchells the following week and wrote to Dudley Cloud at Little, Brown, "Merna had a baby girl in August and the affectionate

Mitchell household is just filled with joy at the event. The little boys contend for the privilege of holding the baby and all the neighbouring children and their puppies come in two or three times a day to see the baby. It is really a wonderful place."[20] Willa always held a special place in her father's heart. In 1967 when Mitchell was answering a young student's questions about *Who Has Seen the Wind* and family life, he replied that yes, indeed, he had wonderful children and that his two sons were away at university: "But at home still I have the most important one, Willa Lynne, thirteen. Perhaps I shouldn't say most important, because I love all three – but after all Willa is a girl and the fact that I came from a family of four boys, makes a girl pretty important alongside a boy."[21]

Mitchell abandoned "The Alien" in the fall of 1954. He realized that there was something deeply wrong with it that cosmetic changes, including splicing on a positive ending, could not rectify. He had become too intensely involved with the Stoneys and had begun to see them from Carlyle's point of view, had himself "become despairing philosophically." He later recalled that this was his first close-up and sustained "exposure to human anguish:" "Being with the Eden Valley people had one hell of an impact for me. When I came away from that I said thank God I'm not a social worker, thank God I'm not in the business of supporting losers, thank God I'm not in the Indian Affairs, thank God – and the reason I said this then was because I despaired of anything happening to these people except to go down, down, down."[22] It would be another thirteen years before Mitchell gained enough distance to undertake a major rewrite of "The Alien."

~ KING OF ALL THE COUNTRY ~

During the six years of the *Jake and the Kid* series, there were three directors: Peter Francis (June 27, 1950, to May 25, 1952), Arthur Hiller (December 25, 1952, to February 14, 1954), and Esse Ljungh (February 21, 1954, to April 26, 1956). Because Francis had set the mould for the show in its first two years, and since all the actors stayed on, the transitions to Hiller and then Ljungh were not greatly noticed. However, Hiller's and Ljungh's direction tended to be broader than that of Francis, and lacked Francis's subtlety in mixing dialogue with Surdin's music. At times they also failed to rein in some of the actors taking minor roles. Nevertheless, Mitchell admired all the directors of *Jake and the Kid*, and while he felt that Francis was the most inspired, he was fond of Hiller and Ljungh and seldom criticized any of them.

Ljungh enjoyed Mitchell's sense of humour immensely and he played up the farcical elements in the scripts, in particular Tommy Tweed's Daddy Johnston. Ljungh urged Mitchell to create more episodes around Daddy, and Mitchell, who tended to exaggeration and to the creation of eccentric characters on his own accord, may have been led further in that direction, not only by Ljungh's style of direction, but by widespread audience approval and the pressure to produce scripts on a weekly basis over such a long period of time.[23]

"King of All the Country," directed by Ljungh and broadcast on November 7, 1954, was one of Merna's and Bill's favourite *Jake and the Kid* radio plays. It began with an ongoing argument between them over hunting. When they first took up hunting, Merna had been as passionate about it as Bill:

> You know, I will never forget the excitement, the electricity in the air from that sound! In those years the ducks were so numerous — and their wings — whssss whssss whsss. It was almost tactile; it was as though you were plugged into an electrical current and it stimulated your whole body, and they were just marvellous to look at and to see. It was beautiful and it was good physical exercise, too, because we had to walk quite a way, and I can remember that I would put ducks in the oven and stuff them with an apple dressing so that when we came back from hunting we would have a drink before dinner and then we would eat the ducks that I had put in the oven before I left and they were so delicious. Yes, those were good times.[24]

They were good times. Hugh and I were blessed with parents who played with us well into our teens. Many fall afternoons and Saturday mornings were spent on family hunts. Dad had constructed his own goose-caller, and I remember the family "concerts" we played at 4:30 a.m. in the kitchen as we got ready to leave for a hunt — my father working his goose caller, Hughie blowing on the duck caller, I working the action of my Ithaca shotgun, Beau, the dog, barking and jumping at the back door, and Mom laughing and hushing us, trying to rein in her orchestra and not wake the neighbours.

A major part of the atavistic pull of the hunt for my father lay in working with dogs. Our first hunting dog, a blond Chesapeake Bay retriever, was named Beau (a silly name for a hunting dog because it rhymed with basic commands such as "no," "go," and "whoa"). My father, as with all of his projects, immersed himself in the literature and lore of training retrievers and did a creditable job with Beau (and later with Plato, a golden retriever). He trained Beau to have a soft mouth by getting him to retrieve a balled-up sock with pins in it and then raw eggs without breaking them.

The Ithaca pump my father originally bought for my mother turned out to be too big for her to handle, so he bought her an over-and-under St. Etienne 16-gauge with which she became an excellent shot. In the fall of 1955, my parents went out for an evening hunt, and using his cigar-box goose caller, my father pulled in a small flight of a dozen Canada grey geese to the decoys. He called the hunt perfectly, waiting for them to circle over the pits three times. Then, their wings set, their feet stretched out for touch down, he yelled, "Take them!" He fired three shots. Not a goose dropped. He looked round at my mother and saw her standing in her pit, her gun aimed at the receding geese. He yelled, "Jesus, Merna! Shoot! Shoot!" She held a few more seconds and then fired one shot. Two geese dropped. My father was gobsmacked.

There was celebration over a goose meal the next day and over the years my father and mother, interrupting each other, my mother insisting this was her story, would recount what happened that afternoon — my father exclaiming about missing, and yelling at Mother to shoot before the geese were out of range, and Mother saying, "And I didn't, you know.

I knew they were too close — that's why Bill missed. And I just waited."
And she was right. When he fired, his shot pattern was too tight and he
missed them completely. My mother became a legend in High River
hunting history.

Goose hunting for Bill was a passion and he wrote at least seven *Jake*
and the Kid scripts that centred on the goose hunt.[25] In an unpublished article, "How to Shoot a Goose and/or a Movie," he wrote,
"To hunt the Canada Grey Honker is an atavistic compulsion;
mountain climbing must have the same passionate imperative. The
Canada goose is almost unattainable; his pursuit is a fair and even
contest; when he falls it is as though the hunter has defeated gravity.
To kill is not the thing; strangely the goose hunter learns empathy
for his quarry."[26] But, very soon, Merna began questioning the
object of the hunt: "Merna hunted with me and then she quit. We
got into a conversation and I said, 'Why won't you go shot gunning
with me?' And she said, 'Because it bothers me. It is killing.' 'Not
really,' I said. 'That is not the important thing of it.' And that argument with Jake and Ma is exactly the kind of exchange I had with
Merna that was the genesis [of "King of All the Country"]."[27]

In "King of All the Country," Jake decides it is time to get the
Kid his own gun, even though Ma objects to both the hunt and
the gun. Seeing the Kid's excitement about the hunt, Jake cannot
help himself, and he takes the Kid on a hunt. Just as the geese are
about to come in, the Kid's Ma comes running across the field and
Jake hauls her into the pit. She becomes so caught up in the excitement of the hunt that she takes the Kid's gun and shoots her first
goose. Jake says, "She looked down at it sorta dazed. Then she
looked up at me an' I seen the wind had tooken out a lock her hair
an' I seen the tears too."[28]

When asked to account for this abrupt change in Ma's character, Mitchell replied, "It is a very inadvertent and tragic thing that
Ma, too, is caught up in that passionate episode."[29] Ma had failed
to realize, Mitchell said, that all the intellectual and honest disgust
is not enough to overcome the excitement of being there in that pit

when the geese come over. Mitchell was not trying to win any arguments with this script. He says that he had no denouement in mind when he began – just the argument. However, when interviewed twenty years later, Mitchell commented, "I would have to say that Jake was probably coming down on the wrong side of the matter – and me too."[30]

At the time, though, Mitchell looked on the hunt as "ritualistic as any art – each portion of the ritual from sighting to spotting to the catharsis of the hunt itself – equally fascinating and exciting. For the gray goose hunt has pattern – it has suspense and it has climax – it has a beginning and an ending – and in a sense possesses an art form as surely as does a short story – a play – or a novel. It has its center – for me – meaning. . . ."[31] Never a trophy hunter, he believed in a hunter-hunted contract of mutual respect, and the hunt intensified his deep sense of the mortality of all things.

～ DROPPING THE "RADIO TIGER'S TAIL" ～

Mitchell still had a year and a half to go before he "dropped the radio tiger's tail"[32] that gave him a wild, but profitable, ride for six years. Most of his best stories had been written by this time, and over half the remaining episodes were repeats. For the final show on April 26, 1956, Ljungh chose one of Mitchell's best scripts from the first series, "Take Her Gentle – Take Her Easy." Mitchell had written four horse scripts for the first series that centred on the Kid and Jake buying an unbroken colt, Auction Fever, training the colt, almost losing the colt, then racing him and winning. Through the Kid's narration in "Take Her Gentle" the audience felt what it was like to conquer a fear and to be one with a horse, the wind, and the prairie: "He was runnin'! With his mane flyin' an' his shoulders poundin'. An he was smoother'n anythin' I ever sat on! Smoother'n a rockin' chair – smoother'n cream pourin' – I sat back an' it was just like waves washin' an' liftin' me to the tune of his gallop!"[33]

Mitchell wrote 155 to 165 different episodes in the *Jake and the Kid* series. This number does not reflect repeated programs, nor does it include his other radio drama. Mitchell always claimed that he wrote anywhere between 300 and 400 radio dramas, a figure that, though inflated, represented all performances, including repeats. It is impossible to obtain an exact number because scripts and recordings are missing and because some episodes are either reworkings of a previous plot with minor changes or are repeated episodes under a new name.[34] But, whatever the exact number, Mitchell produced an impressive number of radio dramas, many of excellent quality. He was the first to joke about being the "Rerun King" (though he did not like anyone else reminding him of this). His repeats often required a fresh opening or ending or changes of topical and timely references, and, in his mind, this constituted a new show. Figuring the way Jake Trumper would (twenty-five pages per script for six years would equal forty-five hundred pages), he argued that this writing would have amounted to ten novels. In fact, over the years the *Jake and the Kid* material would yield an excellent crop. There is no question that Mitchell created some of, if not *the* best radio drama of the 1950s. Harry Boyle said that the *Jake and the Kid* series became a "part of broadcast mythology," and that the close rapport of the Jake team – the actors, the directors, the writer, and the musician – led to its "unparalleled success in CBC drama."[35] In fact, Jake, the Kid, Ma, and Crocus became more than a part of broadcast history, they became a part of Canadian cultural mythology.[36]

In its first season, the hard-nosed critic Nathan Cohen, on his radio show *Critically Speaking*, enthusiastically compared Mitchell to William Faulkner, the American writer of the 1920s and 1930s who had immortalized his southern United States landscape in the mythical county of Yoknapatawpha:

> Now granted that Faulkner is most concerned with the horrors of existence and Mitchell with its humors, there is a surprising similarity in method, technique, and plotting. . . . Faulkner is a regional writer, the stories he writes form an extended chronicle of Mississippi life; Mitchell takes onto himself the topography of the Canadian west. . . . Faulkner's tales, no matter how thin they

may seem to be, always have something significant to say. Mitchell too has this ambitious aspiration. Localized as his stories are, they try to draw always on sources of universal truth. A theme that runs through all of Faulkner's writing is the idea, the importance of honor. Nothing is quite as important in the Mitchell plays as the notion of self-respect, dignity. Both men have a rabelaisian streak . . . in the sense that they are willing to exaggerate, because they see life in distorted, comic perspective, the better to reveal it in an intense, uncorrupted reality. Sentiment is cardinal to Faulkner; Mitchell would be lost without it. Both men are race-conscious. Faulkner is haunted by the presence of the American Negro. The best play in the Mitchell series was one wherein Jake Trumper has to deal with prejudice against the Canadian Indian.[37]

Peter Francis, too, felt that this body of work was significant and that, "if the scripts were produced in some more permanent form," Mitchell would be put "on permanent record as one of the few authentic humorists, better than Leacock and in a class with Mark Twain."[38] In fact, first in 1961 and then in 1989, Mitchell published in book form twenty-nine of his best *Jake* stories and won, for each book, the Stephen Leacock prize for humour.

Although Mitchell himself never thought of his *Jake* radio drama as profound literature, he was, as Merna said, "never ashamed" of it: "Even though *Jake and the Kid* is not what you would call high quality writing in the sense of a poem or a novel or a stage play, they were still damn good."[39] Mitchell rejected the suggestion some critics later made that *Jake and the Kid* was glib:

Because of the seemingly simple nature of the radio dramas the perception was that I was doing a more popularized thing. Well, there was nothing simple about those things. People were rather homespun but not simple. The thematic concerns and observations I was trying to put in the things were serious and complicated. . . . But it is this graceful kind of thing that hides its complexity. . . . People keep coming back — with a sense of astonishment — to these stories.[40]

Although Mitchell admitted that he was "forced into [radio writing] by the exigencies of going freelancing and making a living," he was adamant that "not in any way did I adulterate and corrupt what I did."[41]

The *Jake and the Kid* radio series was so successful across Canada that later on, particularly in the 1970s, Mitchell had some misgivings about its popularity. He would refer to it as his albatross and resented the fact that he was known more for it than for his novels. The series also gave him some international exposure. It was heard by Americans along the border and was broadcast in Australia by the CBC international service. Bernie Braden, a Canadian living and performing in England, did two series of eight shows for the BBC in 1957–58 (he played Jake, his son the Kid, and Barbara Kelly, his wife, Ma).

The six years of writing *Jake and the Kid* sharpened Mitchell's dramatic skills and gave him a name as a playwright. This was a critical period in his life when he was experiencing success with *Jake and the Kid* and disappointment with his novel "The Alien." For the rest of his writing career he continued to feel the pull between drama and novel writing. If cultural conditions had been different in the 1950s Mitchell might well have written his next two novels as stage plays. Indeed, *The Kite* became a radio play in 1964 and then a stage play in 1981. Merna commented in an interview in the 1980s, "If there had been a number of professional [theatre] companies in Canada during the 1950s when Bill was writing for radio, he would have been writing plays, because he enjoys it enormously. He finds it much easier and less demanding than the novel, of course, and he loves it because he was an actor first."[42]

6

TELEVISION

~ 1955 to 1959 ~

Τ HE MID-1950S to the early 1960s were tremendously active
years for Mitchell in film and television. The television arm
of the CBC, the NFB, the BBC, and American film and television companies were all clamouring for a Mitchell script. As early
as April 1953, when *Jake and the Kid* was in its prime on radio and
still had three years to go, Mitchell was approached by the Jaffe
Agency in California, which wanted to market it for television in the
United States. For the next few years Mitchell attempted to break
into the American and the international markets.

Film and television work in Canada was already taking off, and
in the spring of 1955 Mitchell received a number of interesting offers.
Budge Crawley signed him on to write the script for "The Face of
Saskatchewan," a thirty-seven-minute documentary narrated by
John Drainie, which was released in 1955. The NFB asked him to
write several scripts for the television show *On the Spot*, including
one on curling and one on the Hutterites. Crawley had also taken
out a six-month option on the *Jake* material for a possible television
series. Mitchell was riding a wave, at least in Canada.

Quite unexpectedly, on April 19, 1955, Merna's father died of a
heart attack at the age of fifty-seven. Merna's mother, Evelyn Hirtle,

was visiting in High River when they received the news. Merna was devastated and her mother, who became hysterical, had to be sedated. The next morning Merna and Bill accompanied her back to Vancouver by train.

When he collapsed Mr. Hirtle had been on a visit to a newly purchased farm in Surrey on which he planned to retire and where he hoped his son, Spud, would be happier. Mr. Hirtle had been distressed for some time about Spud, whose schizophrenia had become increasingly difficult to handle.[1] A year earlier Spud had lost control and thrown a chair through the front plate-glass window of their house and, four days before Mr. Hirtle's death, Spud had another episode in which he smashed a mirror. As a result he was to be sent for long-term psychiatric treatment to Shaughnessy, the Veterans' Hospital in Vancouver.

Her father's death was a dreadful blow for Merna, who had been very close to him. On top of that, she was now left to cope with her mother and her brother, both psychologically fragile and dependent people. After the funeral Mrs. Hirtle came to stay with Merna and Bill for a while. She was distraught about her future, and Bill wrote a letter on her behalf to the Veterans' Pension Fund asking for more money: "Her need and her grief in the double tragedy which has struck her in the past two weeks with the commitment of her son and the death of her husband – are great."[2] Although only intending to stay a few weeks, Mrs. Hirtle stayed on until June.

Three to four years later, when Mitchell was asked to expand the character of June Campbell for his next novel, "Roses Are Difficult Here," he provided June with parents who were similar to Merna's parents. June's father, like Merna's, had "a straight clear gaze" and "the hair-splitting honesty of [a] clean and logical mind." The description of June's mother cuts close to home as a portrait of Mrs. Hirtle: "Her father's strength – her mother's weakness. Such undignified and debasing weakness – and with it a frightening and contradictory wilfulness that won cheap trophies every day, won them with tantrums and coquetry" (RD 236). Indeed, Bill knew that "Merna's big guilt was in not loving her mother," and he had reassured her time and time again that Mrs. Hirtle "was not lovable."[3] Merna must have felt, as June did, how "intolerable [it was] to be leaned upon, till life became like a dream of pursuit in which she could move her arms and legs so slowly – oh, so slowly" (*RD* 237).

After teaching at Fort Qu'Appelle in August, Bill, Merna, and the children drove, with their trailer, to the Kootenay Lakes area in British Columbia and stayed at Grey Creek. Mrs. Hirtle joined them. This was becoming a favourite summer spot for them, and, again, in 1956 they went for the month of July to the Kootenays, followed by Bill's workshop at Fort Qu'Appelle. It was during this summer, when Mrs. Hirtle joined them again, that they discussed ways of dealing with Spud. In September, Bill and Merna loaned $1,000 to a neighbour of Mrs. Hirtle, who had agreed to set up a chicken business with Spud. The hope was that some steady occupation would help rehabilitate him, but by the spring it was evident that he was not well enough to handle the duties involved in running a chicken farm, and the project was abandoned.

Mrs. Hirtle and Spud generally came to the Mitchells for Christmas, and the Mitchells made an annual Easter visit to the coast in return. Spud and his mother had a precarious symbiotic relationship. He would miss his pills, become violent, and Mrs. Hirtle would put him in the hospital, but she would not allow him to stay in long enough to stabilize. Bill made a number of trips out to Surrey to help straighten out messes. Just before Mrs. Hirtle and Spud came to High River for one of their visits, the neighbour who was working with Spud on the chicken-farming venture phoned Bill to warn him to keep his eye on Spud. Spud resented being "bossed around" by Bill and had told the neighbour that one of these days when Bill took him hunting again out to Frank Lake there would be a hunting accident. From that point on, when Spud visited during summers and at Christmas, Bill used a skeleton key on his bedroom door to keep it locked at night.[4] Given Spud's condition and Mrs. Hirtle's dependent and, at times, hysterical behaviour, this was a constant and serious burden for Merna and Bill.

In June 1955, Merna and Bill were visited by the Hutchisons. Bruce Hutchison had come to High River in search of the "flavour of early Alberta" for a *Maclean's* article he was writing.[5] Bill introduced him to a number of the High River and Eden Valley old-timers as well as to the Diebels. The Mitchells and the Hutchisons became immediate friends. Hutchison inscribed a copy of his book, *The Incredible Canadian*, "To Merna and Bill Mitchell, most Incredible of Canadians because they live as they please between the mountains and the plains."

The Hutchisons were so taken with the ranch country that, for the next two summers, they holidayed at the Stampede Guest Ranch. It was during a visit with them in the fall of 1956 that one of those Mitchell happenings occurred that delighted their friends and prompted, as Ralph Allen joked, the formation of the "Post-Mitchell Convalescent Society." At this time the Mitchells' four horses were pastured on a farm just a few blocks from their home. On this evening, just as they sat down to one of Merna's well-prepared meals, someone exclaimed that a horse had just galloped by the window. Merna and Bill both leapt up and ran out of the house in pursuit of their four horses that had been incited to escape, the Mitchells felt sure, by a strange pinto that had joined in the fun. What else could the Hutchisons and the other guests do but abandon their meals and join in the roundup.

On October 9, 1955, the first Mitchell television drama, *The Black Bonspiel of Wullie MacCrimmon*, was broadcast. It was directed by Robert Allen for CBC's *Folio*, with Frank Peddie (who played Gatenby to Drainie's Jake on the radio) as Wullie. Mitchell probably recognized that the transition from radio to television had not yet been perfected with this script. Nevertheless it sparked interest from the CBC, who wanted five scripts to be adapted for *Folio*. Television was just becoming an exciting new creative medium, and Mitchell's plays were considered major literary pieces. All this activity had John Gray a bit worried that he was losing a novelist: "I hear that you are on the point of great prosperity in the T.V. field and I am delighted. But what of Daddy Johnson [Johnston] and Dr.

Weinberger? And what of General Middleton's Drummer? . . . I'm sure you are wondering, as I am, when you are going to get your books written and, of course, only you can decide, but I would hate to think that you have abandoned the book field or even half considered doing so."[6] Mitchell had already discarded the idea of a novel about General Middleton's drummer boy, but still planned to do one with Daddy Johnston at the centre. Through all this he was keeping the *Jake and the Kid* series going, although, noticeably, there were more repeat programs.

Mitchell was indeed being seduced by exciting and lucrative offers, such as the "invitation from the producers of the LASSIE series to write their scripts"[7] and interest from Twentieth Century Fox in employing him as a writer for its projected *Flicka* series of horse stories. Spurred on by all the American interest, he decided to try them out with "The Devil's Instrument" and sent a copy in February 1956 to the Jaffe Agency. He was gunning for the larger American audience with the *Jake and the Kid* material as well. None of this materialized, unfortunately, and Mitchell turned his attention back to the Canadian market to begin negotiating with the NFB and the CBC, where there was great excitement about doing *Jake and the Kid* on television, the first joint project between the NFB and the CBC.

In June the Mitchells said goodbye to their friend, Mrs. McCorquodale, who was retiring from the *High River Times*. June 24, 1956, was designated Mrs. McCorquodale Day, and Bill and Merna helped organize the celebration in her honour. The main event, a montage of "the voices of people for whom Mrs. McCorquodale has spoken over the past fifty years" through her newspaper work, was put together by Bill and Merna and narrated by Bill.[8] Only the work and excitement of preparing for the day concealed Merna's sadness at seeing her dearest friend prepare to leave for her retirement in Trail, British Columbia.

In October, Mitchell signed a six-month option with the NFB for a *Jake and the Kid* television series. For the first time Mitchell engaged lawyers (a firm in Montreal) to haggle over contracts, and he was advised to form his own company, W.O. Mitchell Ltd.

Feeling jubilant after six months of negotiation, he wrote to his lawyer, "I only wish my ten year old son [Hugh] had the maturity to appreciate the formidable forces against which his Dad has pitted himself; I am sure that Davy Crockett, Gene Autry, Roy Rogers and Wild Bill Hicock could not have come off so well against the might of the National Film Board Commissioner, the CBC, Department of Citizenship, Department of Justice, Treasury Department and their minions."9 At $1,000 per script, it was the financial break he had dreamed of as he wrote John Gray:

> . . . the series is not simply our living, but . . . is much more than that: CBC use alone guarantees me $39,000.00 for a season of 39 and National Film Board could not undertake it on a Canadian basis only – they expect to distribute in the U.K. and the U.S. to triple that amount. I mention these astronomical amounts of money because this thing is the equivalent of what we had hoped for in the novel field: either a major book club selection or a movie right sale which would give me security to give full time to novels. . . . Our delight in all this is not the money but the time – as much as perhaps nine months of the year in which I can work on novels.10

At the moment, with *Folio* ready to televise five of his works (though only two were done) and the promise of the *Jake and the Kid* series, he truly felt that "CBC Canadian writers are the luckiest artists in the world."11

"The Devil's Instrument," the first of the projected package of five dramas, appeared November 21, 1956. He wrote his mother about the production:

> They did a pretty good job on THE DEVIL'S INSTRUMENT. . . . That young man, Douglas Rains was terrific as Jacob and David Green[e] is a most imaginative director. My only difference with them would have been that they did not allow a

little more of the laughter and gayety of the colony to show through. Marta was directed a little too solemn an interpretation so that the mood was somewhat unrelieved and somber. Otherwise it was terrific.[12]

CBC Folio won a first at the Columbus, Ohio, awards chiefly on account of *The Devil's Instrument*'s "inspired television writing."[13] On March 11, 1957, it received from the Canadian Council of Authors and Artists an award for the most distinguished artistic and creative achievement in English radio, TV, and cinema for 1956. It tied with Arthur Hailey's TV drama *Flight into Danger*. Bill joked that "Ollie Snodgrass Machinists and Welders have [the statuette] now mounted on the radiator of my car. It is a twelve inch sort of Winged Victory with very hard tits."[14]

In the fall of 1956 another Mitchell script, "Going to a Fire," was filmed and then shown on CBC's *Perspective* February 17, 1957. It tested the waters for the NFB's and CBC's joint *Jake and the Kid* series. At first Mitchell was very involved, recommending ideas for his scripts and for locations. But, through the first months of 1957, with the CBC and NFB haggling over whether to use "Political Dynamite" as the pilot show, Mitchell saw the first signs of the flip-flopping that was going to plague the project. He and Merna realized they were dealing with a different breed of people from the radio group: "At the moment they're [NFB] wrangling with the Actor's Union over wages. Before that it was the directors and before that it was the C.B.C. who were protesting the high cost of the pilot. I guess we'll eventually get used to film people. We've had three lots of them here for conferences and found them all completely mad. We Mitchells are, I'm convinced, quite sane."[15] With all this delay, it became too late in the season to shoot "Political Dynamite," a curling script, and as no replacement film had been decided on, and the six-month option was about to expire April 22, 1957, everything was in limbo.

— "MY WHOLE DAMN FUTURE" —

Following the failure of "The Alien," Mitchell had tried to get started on two new novels using material from the *Jake and the Kid* stories and, with the conclusion of the radio series in April 1956, he had begun to focus on them. Though the Daddy Johnston book ("Egypt in My Bones") germinated first, Mitchell set to work on a different novel, "Roses Are Difficult Here,"[16] around the end of 1956. Once started, it moved along quickly and was half-done by April 1, 1957 when Merna wrote to Frank Upjohn at Macmillan explaining how it had begun: "In reading through the middle unpublished portion of THE ALIEN we noticed that the lonely people, such as deaf Aunt Fan, Mr. Oliver, and the Napoleons, could all be salvaged and worked into a new narrative involving the general theme of communication between people."[17]

High River is the life-model for "Roses." Mitchell raided the lives of his family and community for plot and characters, and he kept his High River friends well amused with readings from the developing manuscript. Frances Fraser, a writer friend who farmed east of High River, was one of his most faithful listeners.[18] Bill would telephone her every couple of days and read a section from the new novel. He did not realize, at first, that he was reading not to one listener but to about ten, for Fraser was on a party line and, as she said, "Bill had the most appreciative and interested audience ever."[19] It was like overhearing some of the district's most interesting gossip — and, indeed, some of it was actual gossip and scandal that Bill had picked up in his conversations with High River people. Fraser, though, was slightly embarrassed because, although the scandals Bill was using "may have happened thirty years ago, some of these people were still alive!"[20]

Gossip and its potential harm was a theme Mitchell explored in both his *Jake and the Kid* series and "The Alien," and it was a fact of life in small-town High River. There was always gossip circulating about Bill not holding down a real job and about what "poor Merna" had to deal with living with such an irresponsible person. In "Roses,"

Matt thinks that being under the constant surveillance of the towns-people is like "taking up residence in the underwear section of the Hudson's Bay catalogue."[21] As Mitchell pointed out in a speech to the Rotary Club, "When you are in underwear before the populace, there is no pretension, no pompousness, no dignity – the neighbors know all."[22]

Bill was less certain about the success of "Roses" than he had been about his previous two novels. Perhaps he was defensively pro-tecting an ego already battered by the failure of "The Alien." He wrote to Bernie Braden in London, "I know how the female ele-phant feels after her three year gestation period is over, except that she has some dim sort of confidence in the growth of her foetus, while I don't know that mine will emerge with the right number of legs, heads, trunks, tails, liver, gizzard, and lights!"[23] He had prom-ised John Gray the new novel by the end of October, but he was distracted by other work – the scripts for the television series and now a potential stage play for a London West End stage production. Braden's BBC *Jake and the Kid* radio shows had been well received in England, and he had asked Mitchell to send him a three-act drama based on two of the *Jake and the Kid* stories.

Another of the *Jake and the Kid* episodes, "Honey and Hoppers," which grew out of the Saint Sammy story from *Who Has Seen the Wind,* was shot live in the studio and broadcast November 7, 1957, on *Folio* with John Drainie as Jake, Johnny Washbrook as the Kid, Douglas Rain as Matthew (Saint Sammy), the prairie eccentric, and Jack Creley as Albert Douglas, the villain. Mitchell and the director, Frank Lalor, had had different ideas about adapting the scripts. Mitchell felt characterization could carry the narrative, whereas Lalor wanted, as Bill noted on one script, an "over-disciplined <u>plot</u> con-structed according to all the copy books' rules and regulations."[24] Not surprisingly, Bill was angry about the studio feel of "Honey and Hoppers," its presentation, and the artificiality of the setting (painted rocks and backdrops), though he had praise for most of the acting.

Merna was helping Bill with the television adaptations, and they had submitted twenty-four of the twenty-six. They had spent seven months negotiating with the CBC, and Mitchell was not happy that the contract he signed November 25, 1957, allowed the CBC to produce the series live (in a studio) rather than on film. Furthermore, he and his lawyer overlooked the clause giving the CBC "exclusive, irrevocable and perpetual television rights."[25] However, as the CBC continued to assure him that they still wanted to do the series on film, he was optimistic. In fact, he was banking heavily on the success of the television project: ". . . a great deal depends on this first series, my whole damn future, and I don't mean television writing. If successful, I'm home free in the matter of security, will be able to finish the novel I'm on, and, I trust, be able to do others I've projected."[26]

In December, Mitchell contacted Edward Weeks and then Dudley Cloud at Atlantic. He confessed to Cloud, that after four years of silence, he must seem "a truculent bastard." But he had good news; he would soon be sending the manuscript of his new book (still untitled). He was guarded and excited at the same time: "If it should fail, the disappointment could not be nearly so devastating as it was with THE ALIEN, for now I can see clearly to the next book and the next and the next." He predicted that he could write five novels in five years, all drawing from the "semi-polished reserve" of characters and plots that were a part of the *Jake and the Kid* radio series.[27]

— MERNA: "A GIVING AND A WARMTH" —

Merna was the anchor in Bill's life. Though she could be as buoyant and adventuresome as he, she had a stability, a practicality that buffered her and her children from the vicissitudes of Bill's extremes. That, and her sense of humour and lack of ego, made her a perfect partner for Bill.

Around 1956 Merna had begun to explore ways to assume a more active role both in the community and in Bill's work. Willa was two, and Orm (thirteen) and Hugh (ten) could be depended on to help with babysitting. Probably her role as one of the chief organizers of the Mrs. McCorquodale Day and the departure of her friend, which left a gap in Merna's life, were catalysts for her becoming more involved in other activities. In the fall of 1956 she began to help with the scriptwriting for the *Jake and the Kid* television series. When W.O. Mitchell Ltd. was formed, she became secretary-treasurer, which not only gave her a professional status but a small salary. She jested about her new position when she wrote a friend in the spring of 1957: "I am now the official sec.-treas. of W.O. Mitchell Ltd. I don't like the name. It implies that Mitchell became limited when I became the other half of the partnership. It isn't so." In fact, this job pleased her: "I now help with the adaptation of scripts to the point where Bill feels I can handle them alone, do the correspondence, and take care of his files. I'm enjoying it enormously and it's good for my morale."[28]

However, working with Bill was not always easy. She sometimes had to bear the brunt of his injured ego when she criticized a draft and made suggestions. She often had a good sense of what was wrong with a passage or a character, and because she was close to him he could unleash a few more expletives on her than he could on John Gray or Dudley Cloud. Especially in later years he would explosively denounce her suggestions, but then, a few days later, when he tried out another draft on her, her suggestions had been blended in. Merna, of course, was not a writer, and Bill resented it when she crossed the line into his territory and attempted composing lines, imagining endings, expanding characters. That was when the tension level increased and the yelling started. Restraint may have been a credo for his writing, but not for his life. Bill always expressed his emotions spontaneously and openly with Merna, and people were often shocked at the way he yelled at her. The walls of the house did not do much to contain Bill's voice, or Merna's for that matter, and neighbours maintained they heard them a block away yelling at kids, dogs, horses, or each other. Merna discovered that sometimes the best way to handle Bill's outbursts was to retreat into what he called her silent Baptist sulks.

Merna, though, understood the pressure Bill was under with his writing (heightened by deadlines for pieces on which their livelihood depended), and she realized that his yelling was a way of releasing that pressure and not an indication that he did not respect and love her. She described how she learned this early on in their relationship:

> I can remember when he was having problems writing, and I wondered if I and the kids were not in a sense his hostages that kept him from fulfilling himself. And when I finally got the courage to say this to him, he said that that was completely wrong. He felt it was essential if he was to be a good writer, and a writer who always said yes to man, to have a normal life with wife and children and family, because to him it was the most important unit in the world.[29]

Merna was much like Ruth of "Roses Are Difficult Here," and Ruth's thoughts on marriage were close to Merna's: "That was what a marriage was for, to allow a man an opportunity to be a hero; to permit him to be one to himself at least, the illusion deliberately assisted by his wife and his children" (RD 108–9). Merna, like Ruth, had "a giving and a warmth" that made for a successful marriage. In Bill she recognized something unique, and her strength came from allowing her "hero" to fulfill his potential. When asked if she felt Bill's creative energy and the demands it made on her had prevented her from fulfilling her own career aspirations, she replied, "No, no. I felt lucky because we have been lucky. Bill is a very interesting man to live with, and I don't think that he overpowered me because I can be pretty tough too. When he talked he had something to say — mind you, at times he would go on and on and beat it to death, but that was all right. He was just in a sense doing another draft of what he had been thinking or talking about."[30] Merna had a fierce loyalty to and protectiveness of Bill. It was, indeed, this latter emotion that bound them together so strongly and that took precedence over her own self-interests. While it could never be said that Merna existed only in Bill's shadow, she was content to live within his sphere rather than establish her own. But within it she preserved for herself a strong and individual character.

Because of the combination of Merna's protective instincts about Bill and her feisty nature, she occasionally stepped into the fray to protect her hero. Generally she worked quietly behind the scenes, protecting and manoeuvring, but an attack on Bill in September 1957 drew direct fire from her. She and Bill received a short note from Peter Francis attached to a clipping of a Scott Young *Globe and Mail* column: "Don't know whether you saw this. I don't know much about it, but I do recall your trying to help that quaint little bearded character – even bringing him round to the CBC and rooting for him, so I felt this column was unfair."[31] Young's column was about Farley Mowat's first meeting with Mitchell. Young described Mitchell as "an excellent writer who, however, as an editor [at *Maclean's*], was given to frequent periods of deep disillusionment and mopery." He then proceeded to tell the fictionalized story that Mowat, himself, had put in print four years earlier about Mitchell's rejection of Mowat's story and his advice:

> What Mitchell told him would be a severe shock to some – that he'd have to write boy-girl stories if he wanted to sell. He further lectured Mowat on the formlessness and general ineptitude of the story he was rejecting.
>
> The effect on Mowat was wonderfully good. He came away knowing Mitchell had to be wrong on the boy-girl count, at least. Such advice was just too ridiculous to be right. This first loss of blind faith in the omniscience of editors is the most single leap forward in many a writer's career.
>
> So he submitted the story to CBC, who also turned it down.
>
> Whereupon Mowat sold the story to Saturday Evening Post. . . .
>
> In a world where aspiring writers' noses often are tweaked, and few bite the tweaking hand, this was a satisfying crunch.[32]

Bill, as before, refused to respond to the misrepresentation of his role in fostering Mowat's success as a freelance writer. He could not restrain Merna, however, from writing to Scott Young:

> This is a letter from one of those 'female of the species', an angry
> wife. I'm angry at my husband's hurt because a man he admires
> is labouring under a misconception of his character and he's too
> damn proud to do anything about it himself. I'm angry because
> Farley Mowat told you a lie and although as far as I'm concerned
> he can lie as much as he wants to, when it involves my husband's
> integrity as a writer and teacher in the eyes of his friends I feel I
> have to do something about it. . . . perhaps Bill's attitude has
> more dignity. But to hell with dignity – I'm mad.

She went on to explain what had occurred and what Bill's advice
was, suggesting to Young that he contact Ralph Allen and look at a
sheaf of correspondence from Bill to Farley if he wanted verification
of Bill's advice.[33] Merna claimed that Ralph Allen said that when he
went through the files "it was tremendous the number of letters
written and comments that Bill had done – and the thickest file of
all was Farley Mowat's."[34] Merna never got over this public bad-
mouthing from Mowat and Young.

Two months later Pierre Berton wrote saying he wanted to do
a profile on Bill for *Maclean's*. Bill facetiously replied, "As you know
my first choice for [doing] this profile would have been Gordon
Sinclair; Farley Mowat's name springs to mind as well, since he has
again lately been showering me with fulsome bouquets, and I know
that if he is tender towards Eskimos, deer, and malamutes, he would
be especially understanding with Mitchell."[35]

— FAMILY LIFE —

As Mrs. McCorquodale noted, Bill was a family man: "It is impossible to think of Bill as an individual. He is always identified as one
of a family. The Mitchells, as they are invariably known, not only
love one another but they enjoy one another's company. Whether
they are hunting, fishing, gardening, picnicking, riding or even kite
flying they are as one."[36] He spent a lot of time with his children,
perhaps partly because of his own childlike love of life, but certainly

because he was keenly preoccupied (both in life and in his fiction) with nurturing the growth of a child's creative sensibility.

Given the solidity of the Mitchell marriage (in spite of the shouting), it is interesting that in only three of Mitchell's novels do a married couple appear together as main characters: Maggie and Gerald O'Connal in *Wind*, Grace and Carlyle in "The Alien," and Matt and Ruth Francis in *Roses Are Difficult Here*. In his other novels, short stories, and plays, his main characters are frequently widowed, and although they may have had fulfilling relationships, that is not his focus. The family situation in "Roses" is most closely based on the Mitchell family. Ruth and Matt are so in tune that "they conversed with each other by telepathy. . . . a voice shade, the touch of a hand, a reticence, the quick lift of similar feeling, a perfect anticipation."[37] Merna had exactly this intuitive sensitiveness about Bill, although Bill would often say about Merna that, while he loved her dearly, he did not always understand her.

Bill usually did what he wanted, fishing, hunting, building, gardening, as the whim moved him, and it was left to Merna to regulate family life around these whims. At times she was annoyed by his impetuousness, but by and large Merna understood Bill's temperament and adopted her own subterfuges to deal with him. She, herself, had an element of spontaneity. On one occasion neighbours Earl and Helen Lewis were over for a drink, sitting in the kitchen listening to Bill explain how he was going to paint knots on the cupboards so they would look like knotty pine without having to pay for the real thing. Then Merna started talking about how they could enlarge the kitchen by taking out the small bedroom next to it. When Helen came over the next morning for coffee, the bedroom wall had been ripped down: "They probably stayed up all night and got it done."[38] Bill lived, as Merna said, "intensively at everything. He didn't do anything that bored him, so that no matter what he did, he got a great deal out of it – it enriched him and it enriched his work."[39] While Merna recognized how fortunate a situation this was for both him and the children, she was at times frustrated. She never took up fly-fishing and in the late 1950s her interest in hunting waned.

Part of this, she says, was "because Bill was so over-enthusiastic that it sort of killed my interest, because I felt that he spent too much time at it for one thing, and I wasn't going to compound it by being interested as well. Not only that – I couldn't. When you've got little kids to look after you have to watch them every second."[40]

In the summer of 1957, the Mitchells, who had become good friends with a neighbouring family, the Northeys, decided to join them in Kenora for a summer vacation. Unfortunately, the weather was so rainy and cold they were kept indoors with the wood fires going. Shirley Northey recalled a scene with Hugh and his father that illustrates something about the Mitchell family dynamics and attitude to discipline, and about Bill's ability to quickly step from a father's to a child's consciousness. One evening as they were sitting around the fireplace, Bill asked Hughie, who was eleven, to get a wagonload of firewood. Reluctantly Hughie went out into the rain, returning shortly with only a few sticks in his arms. Bill yelled at him to get back out there and bring a whole wagonload. Hughie shot back, "Get it yourself, you stupid goddamn bastard!" Shirley was aghast: "Who is used to their little kid saying things like that?" Bill leapt to his feet, and Shirley thought that Hughie was going to get it. But Bill grinned and said, "I am not stupid!" For that moment Bill had stepped into Hugh's shoes, remembering how much he, too, had hated to be ordered around by his mother.

As if that rainy vacation at Kenora had not been enough, the trip home provided another Mitchell adventure. Merna, as usual, was driving, Bill giving advice. Ever since it had been purchased, their 1956 Pontiac station wagon's wiring had given them grief.

Hugh and I were in the back seat playing with Willa when Mom said she thought she smelled smoke and that none of the gauges were working. I looked out the back window and yelled, "We're on fire!" Trailing a cloud of billowing black smoke, we looked like a hit fighter plane from a Second World War movie. Dad yelled, "Jesus Christ, Merna! Pull over! Pull over!" Mom braked and pulled off to the side of the highway, but we had to coast the last bit because the brake line had burned through.

Hughie jumped out his door, I grabbed Willa, and carried her to the other side of the highway. From the ditch I could see flames billowing underneath the car. I screamed for everybody to get further away from the car, that it was going to blow up. But Dad stubbornly rummaged around in the back of the station wagon looking for his only copy of "Roses Are Difficult Here." Two large transport trucks had stopped, and one of the drivers came running up with his fire extinguisher and put the fire out. As Uncle Dick drove us home, Dad lamented that the "Goddamned fire extinguisher had worked, and the Goddamned car hadn't blown up."

As the children grew older, Bill and Merna spent time talking to them about ideas — literature, philosophy, politics. It was clear in the family that teaching and art (whether writing, music, dance, or painting) were the most favoured careers, but Bill and Merna did not impose their own literary predilections on the children. Indeed, Orm was almost failing English in grade ten before his father took him in hand.

Up until I was eleven, my father had read children's classics to us at night or made up his own stories for us — the last ones were the "Little Annie Mitchell" stories as our sister was gestating. Hugh and I received the new crop of Macmillan books for children and adolescents each Christmas from John Gray, but I rarely read them. Instead, much to my father's dismay, I was more interested in comic books — which were not allowed in our household. So I would go over to my friends' houses, squirrel myself away in a corner of their rooms, and gorge myself for hours on Tarzan, Archie, Batman, Superman.

By grades eight and nine, my main interest was trying to be part of the in crowd at school, and reading books was not going to help me out there. I was relegated, often quite cruelly, to circling the outer fringes of the in-set. I had some close friends, one on one, but when we were a group those friends were doing exactly what I was trying to do — only more successfully. In grade ten, my first report card showed that I was in trouble in English. I remember my father taking me into his office and asking

*me what books I had been reading lately. I said I couldn't remember —
maybe something by Zane Gray. He said, "Well, son, I think it's time you
started to read some real books." He handed me three from his bookshelf —
Salinger's* Catcher in the Rye, *Saroyan's* The Human Comedy, *and
Steinbeck's* Tortilla Flat. *He suggested starting with* Catcher in the Rye.
*I did, and it had quite an impact on me. In retrospect I realize that my
father probably knew more than I realized about what I was going
through with my peers. The book's humour, Holden's refusal to buy into
the teenage or adult worlds, his campaign against phoniness — all this
really hit me.*

*I had a new world now, and conversation with my parents often
involved books as well as fishing and hunting or sports. I recall the
excitement about Howard Fast's* The Winston Affair *(1959) when it first
came out and our discussions about its portrayal of paranoia. I began
exploring my father's bookshelves and reading Steinbeck's* Of Mice and
Men, *Ernest Dimnet's* The Art of Thinking, *Thoreau's* Walden Pond,
and Hemingway's The Old Man and the Sea. *That conversation with
my father was a defining moment in my life. I ended up doing my
master's thesis on John Steinbeck and going on to an academic career. In
a symbiotic twist, my Steinbeck thesis would reintroduce Steinbeck to
my father at a crucial point in his writing career.*

The Mitchells entertained a tremendous amount, often people of
importance in the literary world, but also their own relatives and
friends. During the 1950s when they were hunting, Merna would
often cook a couple of the ducks or geese or some of the trout Bill
had caught. They did not have a formal dining room. In fact, early
on they did not have a proper bathroom, which was a great source
of amusement to their visitors. Dinner had the joyful informality of
a picnic; indeed, the table looked like a picnic table with two
mahogany door slabs for a top. Except for Bill's chair at one end and
Merna's at the other, everyone sat bunched together on the benches
on either side of the table. It was classy informality though, for the
dishes were Royal Doulton Wedgewood and the talk was rich. This
was Merna's show. It was not simply the good food; she had the

knack of making people feel warm and important. If Bill's way of bridging was through his art, hers was through the dinner party. This was her stage, and the spotlight was on her.

— "ROSES ARE DIFFICULT HERE" —

In February 1958, Merna and Bill (and Willa, just three and a half) went to Montreal for nine weeks to work on the *Jake* scripts. Merna recalls this as a hellish time:

> Bill was working on scripts, and I was helping. I was in on script conferences, as it were, and trying to be an ally to Bill. The scripts became so convoluted. Part of the charm of *Jake and the Kid* was it had very simple episodes. Sometimes it didn't need an episode; it just needed a situation between two characters of personality conflict. The television people thought it needed a lot of action which I think was one of the reasons why it just didn't succeed in those days. [Bill was trying to do something] like Mary Tyler Moore, Barney Miller — the good ones. They were very simple. And it's conversation between people and the sparks fly from what happens there. That's the important score.[41]

"Political Dynamite" was released this spring, but Mitchell was unhappy with it, to say the least: ". . . it stank. It stank because of the inexperience of the National Film Board people with feature films, but mainly because . . . they went ahead and got one of their documentary writers to re-write a script which should never have been chosen for the pilot at all."[42] To top it off, their apartment was robbed, and Merna's fur coat and her emerald engagement ring were stolen. That summed up, too, how they felt about the handling of the *Jake and the Kid* property – they had been robbed.

In March, while still in Montreal, Mitchell sent a completed manuscript of "Roses" to Gray, who immediately telegrammed to say that it was "wonderful authentic Mitchell of best vintage."[43] Atlantic Monthly Press received it two weeks later. "Roses Are

Difficult Here" concerns the virtues and vexations of living in a small town and the collision of personal ambitions with family commitment. Matt Francis, the editor of the *Shelby Chinook*, is jolted out of his complacency by Dr. June Campbell, who has come to prepare a sociological report on small-town life. This plotline grew out of the *Jake and the Kid* radio episode "Crocus Under the Microscope," in which Campbell's slanderous report shocks the town. Around this central story are woven a number of other narratives, largely borrowed from Part II of "The Alien" and from *Jake and the Kid*. Through Rory Napoleon, the town's nuisance man, and his wife, Mame, Mitchell addresses the issues of social and racial discrimination, and sets up his usual antithesis of spontaneous, natural forces opposed to puritan, civilized order. In the end Matt helps reunify the town through his newspaper response to Campbell's report. Mitchell, however, does not conclude sentimentally. The Napoleons leave town, and Matt takes a jab at the puritan forces that cause them to leave with his remark that it was Mame who won the championship cup at the annual flower show for her perfect rose: "It was a supreme achievement, for roses are difficult here."[44]

The novel is resonant with small-town life, although the various plots, drawn from seven *Jake and the Kid* episodes, are not entirely successfully shaped into a cohesive structure.[45] Matt and Ruth are not strong-enough central characters to hold together this diversity. In fact, much of the creative energy of the novel resides in the deftly handled vignettes of the ten or so minor characters who represent the townspeople, such as Joe Manley, the young bachelor schoolteacher, and old Aunt Fan, the lonely, impoverished spinster. Mitchell's glimpses into their interiors are movingly and surely done, giving them an individuality that is very rich overall. Dealing with the same themes he approached in "The Alien," the limitations of communication and bridging with people, he works, however, from the opposite angle in this novel where the community becomes the central character, rather than the tragic individual, and, here, the outcome is positive.

The vitality of the novel was what most impressed the Macmillan reader, who thought it was certainly publishable:

> On the whole I think this book comes off pretty well. . . . In fact I read it with such enjoyment almost to the last that I find it hard to say exactly why I'm a little disappointed now I've finished it. . . . When Bill just lets go and lets characters come alive by themselves and express themselves in their marvelously articulate way, everything's fine. But when he uses people to carry his themes a forced and hollow note creeps in.[46]

Macmillan did not think any major changes were needed and offered to draw up a contract. Readers' reports from Atlantic Monthly Press, however, were harsher than those from Macmillan. The consensus was that the main Ruth-Matt-June plot was not successful, and Atlantic readers found the theme about small-town virtues to be "hackneyed."[47] It was interesting that the American and Canadian readers differed so dramatically on the total impact of the novel, for the Atlantic readers found the book "subdued and lacking in vitality."[48] They declined the book, although they said they would look at it again if Mitchell undertook some revisions.

In April, Gray wrote regarding a difficult money matter. Mitchell had been advanced (in 1952) $1,500 against "The Alien," which was never published, and Gray, admitting that Macmillan could forfeit this advance, asked Mitchell if he would consider it as an advance on the new book.[49] Mitchell readily agreed to the latter and was warmly thanked by Gray: "It is what I expected of you, and I think it is of a piece with our relationship, but I am still grateful for it – a good deed in a naughty world."[50]

Television was exactly that, a "naughty world," and it, and later the film world, brought out the worst in Mitchell. The delays and the misinformation that came from "dealing with a large and anonymous group of civil servants"[51] often pushed him to the explosion point. Although Mitchell had the CBC and NFB people on his doorstep from May through to July 1958, and although he went down to Montreal himself in July, and declined teaching at Fort Qu'Appelle and pushed aside his revisions on the novel, all in hopes that the series would begin in the fall, he was let down. In September 1958, nearly a year after the contract was signed and two years after negotiations began, the CBC and NFB could still not make up their minds about a shooting schedule, about which scripts to use, and about whether they were going to produce it on film or do it live. The CBC and NFB were using Mitchell as their battleground to carve out their territories. In the middle of all this uncertainty and tension, on September 7, Bill and Merna were called to Vancouver, where Merna's mother was having a uterine cancer operation. They stayed with her for ten days, and looked after Spud, arranging for him to go back to Shaughnessy again. A month later Mrs. Hirtle came to High River to recuperate.

By October 1958, Mitchell had completed the twenty-six adaptations of *Jake and the Kid*, but because it would be another four months before the CBC paid him, he was $10,000 short on his personal finances. He had to cast around for other ways to draw in money. Budge Crawley had an idea for an RCMP television series, and Bernie Braden paid $1,200 for an option on some non-*Jake* short stories. Ralph Allen offered $600 for a *Jake* short story for *Maclean's*. So it was back to piecemeal work to tide him over. The most promising venture was the three-act stage play he was working on which dealt with the visit of Princess Elizabeth to Canada in 1951.[52] Braden was excited about putting this on in both Canada and the West End of London, but in the meantime, Emrys (Casey) Jones, head of the Drama Department at the University of Saskatchewan, approached Bill to see if he could mount a production of this play for the university's Golden Jubilee birthday celebration. Frank Holroyd, who had directed Bill in Calgary Theatre Guild during the 1930s and who was now in the university's drama department, was to be the set designer. By fall the Saskatchewan production was a sure thing.

With the CBC and NFB still dithering over the *Jake and the Kid* television series, Mitchell decided to show the material to an agency in the States. For over a year David Freedman (International Literary Agency in Berkeley, California) had been phoning and writing him, eager to get his hands on the *Jake* property and market it in the States. Mitchell felt this was his chance with the international market, and in November 1958 he requested from the CBC and NFB copies of his twenty-six adaptations to send to Freedman. The CBC warned Mitchell against this, and Mitchell in frustration asked Willis Wing to take over the matter:

> It sounds like a hell of a hassle and it has been – could only have happened with CBC and NFB – and perhaps a lot of it has been my fault for dealing with them in the first place, but I am a Canadian, and I felt that I would enjoy an artistic control I would not have in Hollywood. I am so fucking angry at the mismanagement of this thing – there is a reservoir of over three hundred radio scripts – the projected series' budget for writing is over three-quarters of a million dollars and I am the only writer young enough and healthy enough to write them all myself.[53]

This was a crucial point. However, the CBC refused to renegotiate the contract, so Mitchell's hands were tied by the "in perpetuity" clause and he could not deal with the Americans. All the promise of a quality and marketable series had been dashed, and the only bright light was the CBC's assurance to Mitchell that they intended to work on the series in the summer of 1959.

~ ROYALTY IS ROYALTY ~

Royalty is Royalty opened before the fellows of the Royal Society of Canada, the University Board of Governors, and many civic dignitaries on June 1, 1959, at the University of Saskatchewan. The play was about Crocus's plans to honour Princess Elizabeth and Prince Philip on their ten-minute train stop in the town. Community pride, jealousy, and racial discrimination are exposed as the townspeople argue over which child would hand flowers to Princess Elizabeth. In the end it is Moses Lefthand, whose grandfather had signed the treaty with Queen Victoria, and his son Lazarus, who conduct themselves with grace and decency and make the biggest impression on the Queen. Jake Trumper has the final word: "Whether they feed on elk an' bannock or breast of them royal swan – thousands crown 'em or millions – wherever you find it – royalty has a way of being royalty."[54]

This was Mitchell's first major stage production, and it was a very exciting event. Their neighbours Helen and Earl Lewis drove the Mitchells to Saskatoon in their new Cadillac, and they were chauffeured to the theatre in style. Merna wore her new, second-hand mink stole (which wheeler-dealer Bill had bought through a newspaper ad, but, eight sizes too large for Merna, it had to be resized). Bill's brothers, their wives, and his eighty-four-year-old mother drove up from Weyburn. This was a moment of great pride for Mrs. Mitchell, who collected every item about the play in her scrapbook. Mitchell thought the play was "terrific" and was impressed with the "enthusiastic reception of the audience."[55] Some reviewers found the play "first class entertainment," but there were also criticisms: "Mr. Mitchell probably because of his radio experience thinks in terms of dialogue not of action."[56] Mitchell could see that there were problems that needed work before it could become a London production, and he wrote Braden,

> I saw . . . the terribly invitational trap that lies in the characters and the situation core of the play; it woos and seduces towards corn and slapstick. The director and actors in Saskatoon, particularly the women and MacTaggart, ran for that trap. In a sense they did not fall into it, but they did achieve high folk comedy, a rather thin illusion, and no realization whatever of the thematic reason for the play: dilineation [sic] of what constitutes nobility of character: compassion and generosity and unselfishness.[57]

Mitchell turned back to "Roses Are Difficult Here" and finished the revisions that he had intended to get to fifteen months earlier. They were mailed off to Macmillan and Wing in the first week of

September 1959. He called it "a major overhaul job – almost a hundred pages longer than the first version – : the book is now almost completely in the envelope of Matt Francis' person and has a much stronger and unbroken narrative current."[58] Macmillan felt it should be published as it was, although there was still some concern about the characterizations of Matt and June. Atlantic Monthly Press, however, rejected it again. As Wing reported, the American readers felt that "the background is developed in such depth that it becomes the foreground."[59]

Gray sent the manuscript to Lovat Dickson at Macmillan in England and, while he acknowledged that Mitchell was a good writer in Canada, he said that English readers would not be interested in the book. Gray responded to Dickson's comments about Bill: Bill's "real trouble is not that he has been unproductive for years, but that he has been doing largely radio scripts and doing them well, but perhaps damaging his talents."[60] "Roses" did not have the overall perfection of a book like *Wind*, nor the potential of "The Alien," but its individual minor characters were as good as any he had created. Where it is possible to see the damage done by radio writing is in the various plots, some of which are contrived and trivial. He had shifted away from the meditative and almost plotless characteristics of *Who Has Seen the Wind* and the intense interiorizing of "The Alien" to more plot-oriented material. However, it was probably the devastating rejection of "The Alien," rather than the radio work, that forced him, financially, and even psychologically, to turn to what had provided him with success – his *Jake and the Kid* material.

"Roses" is, in fact, about background rather than foreground, about ordinariness, the unheard voices in a community. Sections in the unrevised (1957) manuscript are poignantly presented in the envelopes of consciousness of the lonely people (Aunt Fan, Joe Manley, Millie Clocker, Rory Napoleon) and these are sensitive and beautifully done. In fact, Mitchell, who has frequently been criticized for his flat handling of women, does some of his best work with a Katherine Mansfield–like touch to Millie Clocker and Aunt Fan. These sections, lifted from "The Alien," were finished at least by 1952 and have about them the same tone and impulse that Brian Moore very successfully employed in *Judith Hearne* (1955), similarly about the lonely spinster figure. While the various American publishing house readers argued against the manuscript because of its mundane, daily events, Mitchell's point was that these were the very things that defined community life – dog poisonings, gossip, imagined love affairs, church suppers, drunken binges – the type of events that he had characterized so well in *Jake and the Kid*. Nevertheless, the fact that he could not interest the American editors and readers in the book suggested that he had not yet found the format to talk about the ordinary. "Life ain't art" became one of his most used phrases when addressing his creative-writing students, and in "Roses" he had not quite been able to make art out of ordinary life.

With all the concern about his failed novels over the past six or seven years, perhaps it was a slight consolation that *Who Has Seen the Wind* was being used in high-school and university classrooms all over Canada. This renewed interest started John Gray thinking about reissuing the book. At first he was interested in producing a deluxe version of the book with illustrations by James Smith, but that proved to be too expensive. He asked Northrop Frye for his opinion about preparing a school edition. While Frye thought highly of *Wind*, he felt that it should be on a supplementary reading list because some parts (Saint Sammy, Uncle Sean, and the Ben) might not be considered appropriate for high-school classes.[61] Gray suggested to Mitchell that he tone down some of the language for a school edition. Mitchell replied, "After thinking about changes in the re-issue projected for WHO HAS SEEN THE WIND, I have come back to my first response: it really shouldn't be changed. . . . The whole family seems to share this feeling with me; Orme was particularly strong: 'Just look at CATCHER IN THE RYE.'"[62] A standard edition was published in August 1960 and a school edition, with notes by Ruth Godwin, was published in 1961, and, although Macmillan did not remove any "goddamns," they did use the American version with Mitchell's (rather distracted) permission. This was cheaper because it shortened the book by about seven thousand words, and Macmillan did not have to reset all the type.

– THE GREENHOUSE –

Mitchell claimed he had the tropics in his veins, an allusion to his having spent four years in Florida: "My original forty-below-proof Saskatchewan blood was replaced by a dilute tropical variety with very tender corpuscles." To find some respite from what he called the stun of foothills winters, he had built a greenhouse on the south side of the house. He would spend considerable time (too much time, Merna thought) puttering around in the warm, humid environment with his "eighty-five orchid plants blow-torch[ing] pink and lavender and yellow" and with "the utterly pure blossoms of gardenias breath[ing] a heady and immoral fragrance" and the "flamingo flowers lift[ing] scarlet as arterial blood."[63] He would proudly show visitors his orchid blossoms, saying if "you hold one of these big babies up to the light, there is an internal incandescence to them, as though the petals were all crystal. It's a cold kind of light, like one of those screens they use for home movies." He was also fascinated by orchids' immortality: "There's just something about the mystique of them, the fact that there is new growth each year as the old growth dies off. I can imagine orchids living as long as the olive tree."[64]

He became very adept at growing orchids, even contemplating propagating them until he read about the procedure that both fascinated and amused him: "I read it in a book on orchid culture – and couldn't believe it – I fell out of bed laughing – it broke my wife up too." After gathering up all the instruments and materials that first had to be sterilized, and getting the bathroom steamed up like a Swedish bath, the propagator was then to undress and sterilize himself: "They didn't say you had to shave your armpits and pubic hair and paint yourself purple . . . but it might be a good idea . . .

now this is where your wife comes in — she takes the spray and she sprays you from head to foot to sterilize <u>you</u>. . . . you dash into the steaming bathroom — and as quickly as possible do it — fertilize — no — they've already been fertilized and it's time to put the seed into the flasks and cork them for the beginning of the gestation period. . . ." It took ten years from germination to first bloom and he, fortunately for Merna and the family, concluded that he was too old: "It is much simpler to buy a mature orchid plant."[65] For a while he toyed with the idea of doing a fantasy short story in which a propagator using this method cross-breeds himself with an orchid, resulting in blossoms that bear his features.

I first met W.O., my future father-in-law, in December 1959 when he presented me with an orchid corsage. I had been invited by Orm to the high-school Christmas banquet and dance. Merna, whom I had met before, and my piano teacher had played match-makers for this date, but I had never formally met W.O. and did not know, in fact, that he was a "famous" person. Orm had been asked to bring me home to meet him before we went to the banquet. Merna and W.O. were watching a hockey game in the basement rec room, and as I tottered down the narrow basement steps in my unfamiliar pumps I was unnerved to hear great hurrahs and Judas Priests shouted out. I stood uncomfortably in front of them, but was soon glowing from all their warm compliments about my dress and the sparkles in my hair, which fascinated W.O. They had the gift to hug you with words. Then W.O. presented me with an orchid. I had never seen an orchid before, and it was simply stunning. But I was not sure what to do with it, for it was not done up in a corsage with delicate greenery and a bit of ribbon and a hidden pin. No. It was stuck in a slightly discoloured test tube of water with a rubber stopper, and I was told not to remove it from that tube. It was in that vial so it could survive, not only the dance, but the next two weeks, possibly even the next month. I, on the other hand, was not sure I could survive the next four hours with a test tube hanging on my beautiful strapless gown. Somehow we got it fastened on — with makeshift tinfoil, tape, and a safety pin. I did survive. It was a conversation piece, and for the next few weeks I held it up to light and admired its crystal incandescence just as he had shown me.

By the end of the year, Mitchell had no news on whether *Royalty is Royalty* would be staged in London, no solid news about "Roses" from Macmillan, and still no movement on the television series — two seasons had come and gone without the series even starting. Even this year's New Year's party seemed to conspire against success when his plumbing system in the greenhouse started leaking in the middle of the party. When he put in the heating system, he had used salvaged two-inch galvanized piping he picked up on a deal. He had borrowed Chuck Wong's plumbing tools and put the system in himself (almost giving himself a concussion at one point when a three-foot length of pipe snapped out of the pipe rethreader and hit him on the head). So the corroded pipes in the system periodically sprang leaks. Just before midnight, in his best suit and white shirt, with wrenches and ball-peen hammer in hand, he crawled under the plant shelves and beds to fix the leak. He emerged, grimy faced with earth and manure-coloured water stains all over his white shirt, to rejoin the New Year's celebration only to find that two of the guests were standing nose to nose in a drunken argument, and were about to resolve it physically. Certainly roses, carnations, orchids — not to mention novels and scripts — had been difficult for him to grow during the last few years.

7

JAKE AND THE KID AND *THE KITE*

~ 1960 to 1962 ~

"I HAVE gone through all our savings," Mitchell wrote to Gray in February 1960. "Roses" had been turned down by Viking as well as by Atlantic Monthly Press, and the only bright light was a new novel he had begun in October 1959:

> . . . perhaps it has been the uncertainty about ROSES which has slowed me down on the Daddy Johnston novel, tentatively titled: EGYPT IN MY BONES [*The Kite*]. Over the years I have told myself that the important thing is to write the work as well as I can – that if it is publishable that's very nice but not nearly so important. It is not nearly so easy to manage this detachment honestly when it involves a third novel.

At the end of his letter, he asked Gray for advice on applying for a Canada Council Grant, an idea that to him after so many years of freelancing was "quite repugnant."[1]

Although Mitchell never gave up on "Roses," it slipped into the background and was all but forgotten for nearly thirty years. Looking back on why Bill did not publish it when Macmillan had accepted it, Merna explained, "They felt it needed more work and when Bill looked at it he felt it shouldn't be published because it did need more work. But he also felt that it wasn't an important enough book to spend a lot of creative energy on because in a sense it was the result of spleen. He was furious with what the sociologist did to the community."[2]

Wing was still negotiating on Mitchell's behalf with the CBC, which seemed prepared to accept a deal if they could recover part of the $26,000 Mitchell had been paid for the twenty-six scripts. However, Mitchell was too immersed in his new novel to get involved, so he asked Wing to carry on. Mitchell felt so positive about the new novel that he did not pursue the Canada Council grant. In July, *The Kite* was sent out to Gray and Wing, who both responded quickly. Wing thought it was "quietly touching," and Gray wrote that it is "that rare thing – a good book which is also popular."[3] Mitchell set to work on the minor editing that Gray had requested.

Picaresque in form, the novel is layered with anecdotes about Daddy Sherry's adventures, all of which originated in the *Jake and the Kid* radio series. Through Daddy, Mitchell celebrates the art of living: "There is life art and there is art art . . . life art . . . is in conversation, being a good husband, a good father, a good lover, a good friend, fly fishing, growing orchids, sailing. These are life arts. Art art is only part of life art."[4] Mitchell admired a character like Daddy whose life was an acrobatic art and whose secret for longevity was "never settle for anything less" (*K* 209–10). He continued to be preoccupied with the theme of mortality and with the very young and the very old. Given that at the age of seven Mitchell's father had died, it is probably not coincidental that he created a character, called Daddy, who is the oldest man in the world, who has lived a very long and active life, and whose closest relationship is with a young boy whose father is dead.

All the incidents of Daddy's colourful life are set in the frame of David Lang's journalistic mission to write a magazine article on Daddy's secret of longevity. Lang is based to some degree on Bill's friend, Pierre Berton, who, in Bill's opinion (and this is ten years before Berton wrote *The National Dream*), was wasting his talents writing journalistic pieces. Lang's dissatisfaction with "the fleeting nature of most of his work" (*K* 2) is also relevant to Mitchell's own situation: three years working for *Maclean's*, two failed novels, the ephemeral *Jake and the Kid* radio shows, and the wasted time with the television series. But the parallel stops there, for Mitchell was not as hesitant about life, nor as afraid to alter his life-course as Lang is. Life for Mitchell, as for Daddy, was not "a spectator sport at all" (*K* 201).

Daddy's birthday celebration is the highlight of the novel. It is a very entertaining, but also a well-conceived, scene. Mitchell wrote in his rough notes "THIS IS THE SECRET**DADDY CANNOT BE A SYMBOL — ALL DADDY CAN BE IS A REBEL AND AN INDIVIDUAL — SO HE SMASHED THE CLOCK."[5] The townspeople see Daddy as a "tribal shaman" (*K* 70) and a "Methuselah" (*K* 71), so when Daddy smashes the "sheeted monolith," as though it were "a deadly snake coiled and reluctantly dying on the community stage" (*K* 203, 206), he is not simply being petulant, he is objecting to being idolized. Countering that scene is Keith's present to Daddy of the kite, which allows Daddy to be simply human. With Daddy's instruction about how to fly a kite, so "she'll be strong an' she'll be steady an' she'll be acerobatic too" (*K* 209), Lang recognizes that that is the way to live one's life. He decides to leave Toronto, strike roots in Shelby, and commit himself to serious novel writing, which parallels Mitchell's decision to leave Toronto for High River and then to leave radio in 1956 and turn again to novel writing.

Lang is Daddy's opposite, attempting to produce art without having lived artfully himself, without having put up the life-kite. Some twenty years later, when Mitchell was compared to Daddy Sherry, he responded, "It's true that I'm probably difficult to live with, I'm certainly getting older and I definitely subscribe to Daddy Sherry's never-settle-for-less credo. But it just ain't that simple."[6] As Mitchell pointed out, through Lang, "the pity of it was that longevity had ordained Daddy with apostolic succession, but it had bequeathed him such a wistful fragment of historic truth to hand on" (*K* 105). Mitchell balances two kinds of truth, and both have their validity: Daddy's tales, that rich fund of those lived-truths about foothills western people, history, and culture that are handed down through oral narrative; and Lang's reporting, that equally rich repository of history that has been reflected upon, examined and written about.

~ DEATH OF HIS MOTHER ~

Mitchell's mother had a heart attack in early September 1960. Bill and Orm took the bus to Regina and then hitchhiked to Weyburn. Mrs. Mitchell was in hospital for a couple of weeks before she died at the age of eighty-five on September 20. She had been Bill's biggest fan, wanting to hear about all his successes, writing letters without hesitation to people in his literary circle, whether in anger to Gordon Sinclair or in admiration to Hugh MacLennan. She would ask Bill, "Are there any new developments?" and he would happily fill her in. In boyish delight, he would address letters to "Dearest Mother" and excitedly brag about all of his victories, particularly mentioning the monetary advances he was making.

Mitchell recalled sitting by his mother's bed in the Weyburn hospital and telling her all about *The Kite*, which he had just finished. Even though she had suffered a stroke and could not speak, he was convinced that she understood everything he said. His Aunt Josie, who came into the hospital to see her sister a couple of times a day, told Bill there was no use talking to his mother because she was paralyzed and could not understand a thing:

> I said, "Yes she can, Aunt Josie. She understands every word I'm telling her. I know her well enough that I know when she's getting what I'm saying to her – she just has difficulty getting back out to me." [As we argued I heard] Mother grunt, "Yeah, Bill, give her shit." And then Josie says, "But she's paralyzed." It was hot, mother just had the sheet over her, and as she lay in the

bed her bare foot was out like this. She moved her foot. I said to Josie, "I told you." At which point Mother kicked Josie right under the chin, caught her a dandy right under the chops. And then I looked and Mother sounds as if she was just laughing her ass off. God, those two hated each other's guts.[7]

As a part of the grieving process for a mother he both loved and criticized, Bill was tolled back to his childhood years, and over the next year he began writing reminiscential pieces in which she figured prominently. One of the first of these, "Lincoln, My Mother and Mendelian Law," concerns his mother's efforts to have him follow in his father's footsteps as an elocutionist. Bill and Merna sent a copy of this to Mrs. McCorquodale. In the covering letter he says, "it is almost the truth as these things generally are" and explains that he is doing a number of this sort of thing with a view to gathering them together for hard cover.[8] "Of Tar Paper, Shiplap, and Shingles Made"[9] is an elegy to his mother and the house he grew up in, and "The Day I Caught Syphilis" (*Eve* 123–5) concerns his mother's Victorian prudishness.

There were other pieces in which his Grandmother McMurray was the key figure. "The Shocking Truth About the Undefended Border" humorously related a number of encounters Bill had with border officials.[10] The most poignant of these stories, and the one written immediately after his mother's death, was "Those Detestable Middy Suits."[11] Reflecting his nostalgic mood, it evocatively describes the Christmas his grandmother did not make the usual Christmas present for him, the detested middy suit out of hand-me-down clothes, but gave him his first pair of long trousers made of new grey flannel.[12]

In "Of Tar Paper, Shiplap, and Shingles Made" Mitchell describes the three-storeyed house on Sixth Street, the home that held "solid" for him throughout his childhood years. The metaphor he employs throughout the piece is of the house as a living body, "another and outer self." His visit to the house on the afternoon of his mother's funeral evoked this memory:

> On a September morning two years ago [1960] when the fall
> wind went ticking through the leaves of the poplar for which I
> had once carried pail after pail of water – the lone survivor of eight
> – I walked up the porch steps with my youngest brother. . . . I
> glanced at my brother and from the stilled look upon his face
> I knew that the same realization had happened to both of us at
> the same instant. Her death had become a fact for us, and we
> knew truly that this afternoon she would take her place in the
> prairie cemetery beside her own mother and our father.
>
> As each child grows up and leaves it, a house dies by bits.
> The house of a child must have vivid permanency. When a
> mother dies it's time enough for it to take its final and mortal
> blow. (*Eve* 91)

His mother's death affected him deeply. Her extraordinary pride in his
achievements and her constant interest in his life left a gap. In later
years her prudishness, her authoritativeness, and her invasion of his
psychological territory had all lost their sting, and she became more
benignly revered than alternately loved and hated, as she had been in
earlier times. Her death, coming at a time when he was emotionally
vulnerable because of the failure of his novels and the convolutions of
the *Jake and the Kid* television rights situation, left him in particularly
low spirits. With little success to buoy his spirits, little money coming
in, a son nearly ready for university, and his future hanging in the
balance, the retreat to his childhood was his therapy. Merna described
his writing them as "a personal exploration . . . and in doing that he
got over the bad time. But it took a long time."[13]

The last of these pieces, "Melvin Arbuckle's First Course in Shock
Therapy," was written in 1963.[14] Here he recalls how five bored boys
on a hot August afternoon attempt to build an underground fort. The
inspiration for the climax of this tale came from a story Larry Diebel
had told him ten years earlier. Larry's father had told him to dig a new
outhouse hole and, when he hit big tree roots, he used a stick of
dynamite with dramatic results – a large nine-foot hole laced with bare

cottonwood roots.[15] Some of these pieces, such as "Melvin Arbuckle's First Course in Shock Therapy," are reminiscential tall tales. Others, such as "Take One Giant Step" and "Of Tar Paper, Shiplap and Shingles Made," are closer to the kind of nostalgic childhood memories perfected by Dylan Thomas in "A Child's Christmas in Wales" and "A Visit to Grandpa's." Because of their poignancy and humour, they were easily transformed into reading pieces that became the backbone of Mitchell's career as a performer. Later, four of them furnished Mitchell with scenes for three of his novels.

With his increasing exposure as a result of the *Jake and the Kid* projects, his performances of the reminiscential pieces, and his facility to give entertaining and interesting interviews, Bill was becoming sought after as a speaker and an interviewee. He and the family had been the subjects of a twelve-minute television profile on *Graphic*,[16] and McKenzie Porter had written "The man behind *Jake and the Kid*," a *Maclean's* profile, in September 1958. In 1959 *Maclean's* asked Bill to write an article on a family weekend holiday in Calgary, illustrated with pictures of the Mitchell family dining out, going to a concert, visiting the park and zoo.[17] Pierre Berton came out to High River with a film crew to do a program on Bill for CBC's *Close-Up* in June 1961, and the following year he appeared on Berton's television show three times. Mitchell was fast becoming a celebrity, which, in turn, encouraged his career as a public performer.

— "PAPIER MÂCHÉ BLOODY ROCKS AND KMART BULL RUSHES" —

The fall of 1960 brought disappointments for Mitchell. *The Kite* was turned down by three American publishers in November, and the television and stage projects had come to a standstill. There were, however, firm plans to do a *Jake and the Kid* collection of stories for a fall 1961 publication, and in November Macmillan sent a very welcome cheque for $1,000 as an advance against this book. To buoy up Mitchell, Gray wrote, "one way or another there should be a Mitchell book out next Fall in Canada at least,"[18] and Kildare Dobbs, the editor for the collection, wrote to Bill that it would be "a delightful and popular book."[19]

In early June, Pierre Berton came to High River to interview Bill for CBC-TV's *Close-Up*:

> Pierre said, "I won't let you know the questions beforehand." I said, "That's all right because you don't know my answers beforehand, either." We sat down and I got relaxed and I had underestimated Pierre because he said, "How does it feel to realize that *Jake and the Kid* is hitting the airwaves on television in two weeks time." And I just exploded. It was the most rude thing that has ever been done to me in my life. They [the CBC] hadn't told me.[20]

The CBC immediately apologized for their negligence. However, as they had been working on the budgets since February and had rehearsed the first show in April, this was a suspicious oversight, suggesting they had not wanted to involve Mitchell in the film process.

Murray Westgate was cast as Jake, Rex Hagon as the Kid, and three directors, Ron Weyman, Ray Whitehouse, and David Gardner, divided up the shows. The twelve-episode series ran weekly beginning with "The Day Jake Made Her Rain" and ending with "King of All the Country."[21] Gardner wrote Mitchell that he hoped "the flavour and personality" of the scripts would come through in the productions, but that it had been "a great personal frustration . . . to try to put the Saskatchewan prairie and Crocus into a television studio."[22] As Mitchell had predicted all along in his earlier arguments with the CBC, many of the episodes, more than one-third, could not be done on videotape and in a live television studio.[23] Gardner said that "King of All the Country" was his "favourite" (*ML* 285), but staging a goose hunt in the studio was challenging. The camera had to move quickly from stock shots of geese reproduced on telecine to the faces of Jake and the Kid looking upward (they were actually reacting to shots of geese shown on a television monitor) and then to Ma running across the field. Ma's shooting of the goose was accomplished by showing a prop goose dropped from the lighting grid in the studio. All this, of course, had to be meticulously cued. In spite of the many problems, Gardner felt "the heart of many of the shows was there."[24]

The majority of reviews of the first show, "The Day Jake Made Her Rain," were unenthusiastic. It was described as slow, unpoetic (unlike the radio series), and "self-consciously rural,"[25] although one commentator felt that this series had "the makings of a tremendous hit for Canadian television."[26] Unfortunately, as Gardner noted, "only the first episode was noticed and it was not the strongest entry."[27]

Corresponding with Mitchell soon after the series ended, Gardner agreed with him about the quality of the CBC scripts:

> I couldn't agree with you more about the severe damage done in reducing the scripts to basic plotlines and evaporating off the character touches, mood nuances, and "colour" bits. Wherever possible (if the script was short at all) we reinstated from the originals whatever speeches, odd tiny moments, even adjectives that we could. . . . I know I speak for Ron Weyman and Ray Whitehouse when I say we thoroughly enjoyed producing the series, and only wish a) we could have worked directly with you, and b) that we could have got outdoors with film and tape to capture some authentic rather than studio prairie atmosphere.[28]

When Bill talked about this fiasco much later in the 1980s he would explode with rage at the "missed opportunity," and the waste of five years fighting with the CBC and NFB, but he was also able to place it within the context of not only his own career but the growing pains of the CBC:

Those bastards took those scripts and rewrote them and the casting was most unfortunate. The agreement was that they were to be done on film and they did them studio. Christ, they did the goose hunt with papier mâché bloody rocks and Kmart bull rushes. But it would be Hugh [Kemp, national script supervisor for the CBC] and Frank [Lalor] who were really responsible. . . . Merna says I am unforgiving, but it was a matter of some money which would have been nice then. Creatively it didn't mean anything. I never ached very long after that. It was a missed opportunity, but not an important one. I didn't sting very long from it. And I can't monolithically blame the CBC.[29]

The sting and the anger at the time were more intense than he remembered. Bill and Merna's biggest complaint when all the dust had settled was that they had not been kept informed of CBC decisions, and that it had adopted a dog-in-the-manger attitude about his making a deal with American television. With all the false starts, the haggling between the NFB and CBC, the infiltration of other writers, a union strike, and the costs issue, it was a hard five years for Mitchell, all of which, in the end, was wasted energy.

As we watched some of the Jake *television shows together in the summer of 1961, W.O. paced and fumed, making it rather difficult to follow the programs. He would hook his fingers in pretend overalls and strut in front of the television set, imitating Murray Westgate doing Jake Trumper. He ranted about the sets, and the lack of innocence in the Kid. The sorest points for him were the rewriting of the scripts and the acting that, he felt, made his prairie characters' attitudes quaint and their language corncob. Of course, his expectations were very high, for his dream had been for the series to be filmed on location, and ultimately to go to the United States and England. We shared those disappointments. But, reviewing "The Day Jake Made Her Rain" in a CBC office, fifty years after it was made, we felt less resistant, more protective toward it, for it seemed to carry, if somewhat shakily, the mood of the prairies of the 1940s*

*and 1950s. Perhaps it looked better now that the memory of the superior
radio version and John Drainie's portrayal had dimmed, and it certainly
felt more authentic than the glossy, beautified Global-Nelvana television
series of 1995–97.*

‑ GRIZZLY HUNT ‑

In the late 1950s Mitchell had begun playing with an idea for a novel
involving a grizzly bear hunt. The idea for this story began with an
incident he heard over the dinner table at the home of Dr. Harry
Jennings. Jennings was an avid big-game hunter who, in the fall of
1948, had shot "the grizzly of the grizzlies,"[30] a giant bear of nearly
eight feet in height. He sent it away to be dressed by the taxidermist,
and invited his friends to a party to toast the unwrapping of the
hide. Instead of the magnificent hide he had sent away, out fell a six-
foot hide. His son recalled the scene: "I can still remember vividly
the look of amazement when my father unrolled the hide and then
probed the hair where he knew his bullets had gone."[31] Jennings
sued the taxidermist for $5,000 in a court case that was "one of the
most interesting trials in Alberta big game history,"[32] but in the end
the judge awarded him only $300. Jennings was convinced that the
taxidermist's son had made the switch, the judge felt there was negligence, but nothing could be proved. Bill was excited about this
story and told Jennings he would like to use it as the basis for a
novel. Graham Greene, the British novelist, visited the Jennings in
1955 and he, too, was interested in using it. He thought it would
"make a fine movie."[33] Mitchell, however, thought he had first dibs,
and recalled that Frances Jennings told Greene, "No, you can't use
that because Billy Mitchell's using it."[34]

    With *The Kite* now being shopped around, Bill turned his
attention to the grizzly novel. He had learned a lot about bear
hunting from Dave Diebel, who had shot quite a few brown and
black bears to protect his stock and in the 1950s had tangled with
a grizzly. Hearing stories like this gave Mitchell a healthy respect for
grizzlies, but he felt he would have to go on a grizzly hunt, that he

couldn't fake it. Diebel set one up in late March of 1961. He shot an old horse up Cataract Creek to use for bait and called Bill when he saw that bears had been at it. Bill drove out to Diebel's for his first grizzly hunt. Instead of a gun, he took a pencil and pad of paper.

I remember my father's mixed excitement and fear about this venture. When he came back from the hunt, he was brimming over with what he had experienced. He told us how unnerving it was walking the three miles in to the blind in the late afternoon, waiting in the hide for the bears to show, and when they didn't, walking back to the truck in the pitch dark and wondering if they would run into one of the grizzlies that would be working its way into the horse's carcass. He described how Dave and Petey sighted their rifles before the first outing and that when they got in the hide, about a hundred yards downwind from the carcass, they could only whisper. Dave was to take the first shot. If he only wounded or missed the bear, Petey was backup. My father asked, "What if you both miss and the bear charges us?" Petey said, "You can shove your pencil up her ass." We all laughed at this, but my father said it was neither funny nor reassuring at the time.

On their way in to the blind on the third evening, they saw tracks, "great flapjack depressions in the spring snow – the front of each combed with claw marks," and a grizzly appeared. The notes my father scribbled down describing the bear are ascribed to Dr. Bruce Lang, the narrator of "Green Thumb – Red Finger," a radio show that aired about ten months later.[35] "He sauntered out – arrogantly and yet comically too – ravens swooping over his head – diving at him – lifting and wheeling to dive again. He reared up on his hind feet under a tree standing by itself in the clearing – swatted at the ravens as one would at bothering flies." When the bear reached the dead horse, "he leaned forward, plunging his fore paws into the carcass – he leaned back and heaved – shuffled his hind feet to gain better purchase – working and pulling and lifting – his great rear sashaying from side to side – for all the world like some gargantuan plumber straining to uproot a stubborn toilet bowl!" Dave whispered that it was just a three-year-old. My father was amazed at its strength, for it picked the whole horse carcass up and flipped it over. As it turned out, both Dave and Petey missed their shots. My father found the walk back to the truck particularly harrowing (as Doc Lang says, "The current had been turned on along my nerves" and "every pine had taken on a new look for me — become part of a gestalt — me-tree-escape").[36] *Dave later discovered that the scope on his gun had been jarred awry when it knocked against the truck door.*

⁓ TWO BOOKS IN TWO YEARS ⁓

There was a concerted effort to get Mitchell into print after his long hiatus. *The Kite* was still making its rounds with the American publishers, but it had been decided to publish the collection of *Jake* stories in Canada only. *Jake and the Kid* had been Gray's idea, and from conception to galleys was a short five months.

Jake and the Kid, published in September 1961, contained thirteen stories, all of which had appeared in *Maclean's* or *Liberty* in the 1940s with the exception of the final two stories, which had been published in 1952 and 1955. Although the book was subtitled a novel, the order of the stories was simply dictated by the date of their original publication. Mitchell had wanted to edit the pieces but, as everything needed to be completed quickly in order to get it out for the fall, the Macmillan editors simply standardized some of the colloquial spellings and removed some repetitious material. It does not have the typical rising action, the character exploration, or unity of structure of a traditional novel, but, like Alice Munro's *Lives of Girls and Women* or Margaret Laurence's *A Bird in the House*, it is a suite of stories in which the Kid, like Del and Vanessa, undergoes an education of the imagination. As it happened, "The Liar Hunter," with its discussion of the significance of creative storytelling, is beautifully positioned in the middle of the group of thirteen stories. Although the Kid does not mature in terms of chronological age (remaining ten to eleven years old), he matures imaginatively as he learns to differentiate between kinds of communication, specifically between Jake's tall tales and Miss Henchbaw's factual history and, in the end, recognizes the value of both approaches to telling stories about ourselves.

Mitchell received the 1962 Stephen Leacock medal for *Jake and the Kid*. The reading public and newspaper critics liked the book. Joan Walker of the *Globe and Mail* wrote, "There is a deceptive simplicity about W.O. Mitchell's writing that is actually extreme sophistication and touches the hem of genius."[37] Margaret Laurence, in her review of the book for *Canadian Literature*, described the impact of these stories when she first read them in *Maclean's*: "These stories were among the first that many of us who lived on the prairies had ever read concerning our own people, and our own place and our own time. When grain elevators, gophers, or the sloughs and bluffs of the 'bald-headed prairie' were mentioned, there was a certain thrill of recognition. The same applied to the characters who inhabited Crocus. A prevalent feeling on the subject was, as I recall – *that's us; he's writing about us.*" However, she criticized the stories for being too sentimental, for containing no real villains, and she felt that the collection would become a Canadian classic only "as a book for children."[38] Mitchell, of course, never intended the book for juveniles: "I know it speaks and means a great deal to young people; it was not written as such. I don't like these divisions and I labour, maybe it's under a misunderstanding; I think older people are interested in things that involve people who are younger than they are . . . I'd have been up the creek if only kids listened to *Jake and the Kid*."[39] After *Who Has Seen the Wind*, *Jake and the Kid* was Mitchell's most popular title for many years, and to date has sold about a quarter of a million copies.

By September there was still no action on *The Kite* from American publishers. Mitchell reported to Gray that he had decided on a Canada-only publication after a talk with Pierre Berton: "I am even firmer about this than I was a year ago, after talking with Pierre Berton this Spring; [Berton] said that he has assumed that a Canadian audience is the most important one and that . . . he has gone ahead with simply Canadian editions. So should we."[40] Gray disagreed with Mitchell about the advantages of American publication: "I believe that ideally your books should cross the border fairly easily – that is they should appeal to an American audience."[41] However, *The Kite* did not appeal to American editors, and by the end of the year it had been turned down by ten publishing houses, although it was a near-miss with some, like Viking. Generally, the readers found fault with the David Lang frame device, though they were impressed with the Daddy Sherry character. Gray asked Mitchell to consider reworking the opening chapter. Mitchell responded, more quickly than usual, that he and Merna had reread the beginning carefully, adding, "perhaps we are losing our critical grip," but he really felt that all is "quite natural."[42] So, without alteration, Macmillan decided to publish it in the fall of 1962.

– FOOTHILL FABLES –

The *Foothill Fables* series began because of a mutual need: the CBC needed drama scripts and the Mitchells needed money. Esse Ljungh asked Mitchell if he had any ideas for an original radio series and Mitchell, early in 1961, sent Ljungh thirteen scripts for considera-tion. Ljungh felt they were too close to the *Jake and the Kid* stories, and he was justifiably concerned. Mitchell had changed the names of the town and the people, but many of the plots came directly from the *Jake and the Kid* series. However, of the twenty-six episodes, broadcast between December 25, 1961, and January 19, 1964, about half were completely original, and the others were altered to some degree. The frame device of *Foothill Fables* gives it a distinctive tone. Dr. Bruce Lang, a newly conceived character, introduces the story in a contemplative and sophisticated manner without any of the *Jake* colloquial earthiness. He is a blend of David Lang, the journalist-narrator of *The Kite*, and Doctor Harry Fitzgerald of "Roses."

The series opened on Christmas Day 1961 with "After Mary's Boy," a poignant story about parenthood. In September there had been a shift in the Mitchell family when Orm left for university. Merna wrote him a note three weeks later: "We all miss you very, very much. Hugh and I manage to be a bit restrained about it but Willa and your dad are <u>terrible</u> – especially your dad. However, the emotional experience has inspired your dad into writing a beautiful Christmas script."[43]

"After Mary's Boy" opens as Doctor Lang and his wife, Sarah, return home from dropping off their son, Hugh, for his first year at university. They are suffering from "sonsick[ness]."[44] The scene jumps ahead to Christmas time, where preparations are in place for their son's return, including Lang's trip to Paradise Valley reserve to cut down the Christmas tree. However, because of a blizzard, he has to stay on the reserve. Fortuitously, this means he can help to deliver an Indian baby, which prompts him to contemplate the vast difference between his own son's advantages and those of the Indian child: "The accident of parenthood – one baby feeds on formula – pablum – orange juice and cod liver oil – the other sleeps in a yo-kay-bo – suckles the amber breast of a tribal mother – is weaned on an elk bone – runs the obstacle course of rickets – tuberculosis – the deep dusk of trachoma blindness."[45]

The story was poignant and sombre and reflected Bill and Merna's mood that fall and Christmas. In October, Merna wrote her "dearest Davie" McCorquodale, who had been hospitalized in Trail, giving her news of *Foothill Fables, The Kite,* and the family:

> The biggest change in our lives is having our first fledgling leave the nest. It leaves quite a gap; but at least it's under pleasant circumstances – no war yet – no depression – yet.
>
> People around here seem terribly disturbed by the climate of war and fall-out. My own feeling remains the same. My faith in humans won't let me believe they're stupid enough to commit suicide. If they use the monster I hope to be under the first one they drop. . . .
>
> This turns out to be a most dull and factual letter. Bill's words will provide the sparkle I don't have. I love you very much – sparkle or not.[46]

Bill added a bit of "sparkle" about a goose hunt and his tropical plants, and enclosed one of his reminiscential pieces. This was their last communication with Mrs. McCorquodale. She died a few months later in Trail. The funeral was held in High River with the reception at Merna and Bill's two days after Christmas. Bill wrote to his friend John Clare, "It was pretty rough for Merna, who loved her more than she would a mother."[47]

Mitchell drew on his grizzly bear hunt material for three *Foothill Fables* episodes, which explore a male character's obsessive drive for a trophy grizzly. In "The Trophy,"[48] the most serious of the three, Mitchell began to explore some of the character and thematic issues that would later appear in *Since Daisy Creek*. Donald Armstrong, an obsessive bear hunter, is mauled by the trophy grizzly he shoots. When he recovers, he holds "a grizzly party" to celebrate his victory over "Master Bear." As he asks his guests to toast his trophy and the parcel is opened, there is consternation that fades into Doc Lang's narrative voice: "There in the middle of Donald's living room rug I saw [a small brown bear hide] . . . not much more than a cub. (LONG PAUSE) Oh my, oh my!"[49]

The cast for *Foothill Fables* was, on average, four characters rather than the six to eight in a *Jake* episode. This cost-saving measure led to lengthy monologues from Doc Lang, which made the episodes more static. Unlike the *Jake* series, there was not always a continuity either of events or character from one episode to another. Some of the *Foothill Fables* episodes became individual character studies, as with "Stylite," a study of the loner, or "Sons and Fathers," a study of a disgruntled son. Mitchell referred to 1961 as a dry year, suggesting that he, himself, knew that he was plodding, not creating with fresh energy. The series, however, was popular on the International Radio Service, with seventy-five orders (seventeen from abroad) placed for the first run, but it never gelled the way the *Jake* series had.

When one of W.O.'s programs was on the air, it was sacrilege for anyone in the family not to hear it, and when I began going with Orm I was expected to participate. On one occasion we were on our way to my grandmother's for Sunday lunch just after church, and we knew we could not miss a Foothill Fables *episode without a guilty conscience, especially as we were expected to report back on what we had heard. So Orm and I parked outside grandmother's house and listened to the whole episode (not what most teenagers in High River did when they "parked"). Other Sunday afternoons we would all be seated around the antique burl-walnut radio cabinet in the Mitchell living room listening to the latest episode. I can recall Merna and W.O. laughing uproariously, making loud comments throughout, all the while saying "Shh! shh!" to each other. In my opinion* they *were the show! When it was over, however, and after a general appraisal, that was that. W.O. did not egotistically carry on about the shows. He wanted the magic of a participatory audience – not fawning praise.*

— "THE MAGIC OF THE GREEN ELEMENT" —

The "atavistic hunger of the city sparrow for the vista of leaf and blade and water"[50] led Merna and Bill to think about a summer cottage. In the summer of 1961 they heard through High River friends Howard and Mary Garrett that there were lakefront lots for sale on Mabel Lake, near Vernon, in the Shuswap area of British Columbia. It was a good bargain: for only $1,000 they had a seventy-five-foot lot, and for $5,000 more they had their cottage. When Bill saw the property for the first time, he exclaimed, "Jesus, Howard, you said the place was nice." Howard was taken aback. Bill grinned, "It's gorgeous!"[51] Writing about it ten years later, he said, "I fell instantly in love with Mabel – thirty miles long and two wide – fed at her south end by the Shuswap River, which flows out again where my sons and I built our cabin."[52] Twenty-five miles from the nearest town and a short boat trip across the river mouth, it became a seductive family retreat.

During the winter of 1961–62, Merna and Bill pored over plans in cottage magazines, and Bill began ordering and collecting the materials. He had discovered the Unclaimed and Damaged Freight Sales in Calgary and the auctions became not just his favourite shopping centre but his regular form of entertainment. He purchased many unnecessary objects – gaudy lamps with orange moulded plaster bases; Inuit soapstone sculptures, all with broken parts, which he ineptly attempted to mend; green or orange glass vases with long spearing prongs (one or more snapped off). More usefully, however, he outfitted his cottage with a hot-water tank, sinks, toilet, light fixtures, window glass, mattresses, sofa, and chairs for next-to-nothing prices. Indeed, Bill was so in love with the thrill of a bargain at the Unclaimed and Damaged Auction that, for the next twenty years, his household – and his married children's households – were furnished with appliances, plumbing fixtures, and furniture from the auction – all with dents, cracks, unfortunate colourations, and rips in upholstery (but easily fixed, he argued). As a result of one sale, Bill outfitted almost every room in his house, including the bathroom, with crystal chandeliers, most of which had broken arms that he fixed with fibreglass (which discoloured) or just left to tilt crazily. Once, as a joke, he bought fifty pounds of dental moulding plaster for fifty cents and left it on the front steps of his High River dentist (who later told him that it was worth about $500). Other used items for the cottage came from High River stores. He got old cupboards from Quon's grocery, and a pane of glass for one of the front windows of the cottage (which is still there) from the top of the New Look Café's display cabinet. Clouded by scratches from thousands of coins passed across it, it somehow seemed fitting that Mabel Lake was filtered through some of High River's heritage.

In the spring and summer of 1962 both Orm and Hugh worked at different times with their father in building the cottage. For the first few years there was no electricity, just propane appliances, a wood stove, and kerosene lamps. There was no telephone, and even when it was available, the Mitchells resisted for a while because this place was their retreat from the busy world. For the next twenty-five years, they spent two months of every summer there. It was, as Bill noted, a lure for his children and his grandchildren. It was also the source of many humorous incidents, especially when innocent reporters or film people attempted to interview him there. Bill soon became obsessed with salmon fishing: "A half hour with a 20-pound spring salmon in the pool below our cottage is my notion of an orgy." But most importantly, as Bill wrote, "it is a place where a man can knit together again his own sacred and individual self. This is the magic of the green element in which Canada is so rich, and which seems to be valued so little."[53]

When Bill was not fishing he was sailing, a passion that resulted in his building an eighteen-foot Y-flyer sailboat with Hugh. In the winter of 1962 Bill found an ad in the Calgary newspaper for the hull of a Y flyer, and over that winter and spring, he and Hugh built a sailboat. There was some tension because, as Hugh discovered, "Dad was sloppy" and would resist Hugh's suggestions,[54] but they got her built for the summer's sailing. She was christened *The Kite*.

The first boat they had was a utilitarian skiff. It had a small British Seagull motor, which Mrs. Hirtle gave the Mitchells when she and Spud came out in the summer of 1962. Although Bill described it as the Rolls-Royce of outboard motors, it was complicated to operate. Spud loved to drive the boat, and Bill did not object because it kept him out of trouble. Hugh described one of Spud's outings with Mrs. Hirtle:

> She had a little sunhat on and sat in the front of the boat, as Dad described it, "priming and praming." Spud did not follow good marine common sense and get the motor started and then untie the boat. I am standing on the dock watching because I know there is going to be trouble. Spud does everything – except he forgot to open the gas valve. As the current takes them down towards the river mouth, he gets it started, and then it quits because it is not getting any gas. I am now offering useful advice from the river bank, and Spud says, "Shut up. I know what I am doing." He sits there and he is pulling, and pulling, and pulling, and Grandma's getting worried, and Spud is getting madder and madder. And Grandma says, "Spuddy, you fool, get the boat started. We are going to go down the Chucks" [unnavigable rapids]. Spud gets fire in his eyes. He climbs out of the boat, up to his chest in water, swearing and cursing at me, calling me a

little shit as if I am to blame for the boat not starting. Grandma says, "Spurgeon, stop that swearing," and she picks up the oar and whack whack, "Leave Hughie alone. You fool," whack, whack. Spuddy figures out that if he lets go of the rope she can't hit him with the oar anymore, so he lets go of the rope and she continues drifting downstream. I don't know who saved her, because as soon as Spud got up close to the bank, I was out of there.[55]

Incidents like this were humorous in retrospect, but at the time they produced a great deal of distress, especially for Merna, who constantly had to deal with Mrs. Hirtle's self-centredness and with Spud's anxiousness, compulsions, and violent outbursts at his mother's "bossiness."

— THE KITE —

The Kite was published in September 1962. Newspaper reviewers liked the "everyday philosophy"[56] and enthused about the humour, the character of Daddy Sherry, and the story, one even proclaiming that *The Kite* showed "more than great promise and will be more popular than his first novel, *Who Has Seen the Wind*."[57] A couple of negative reviews, however, stung Mitchell: "W.O. Mitchell Fails to Hoist 'Kite' Aloft"[58] and "Go Fly a Kite, Daddy," which dismissed the novel as a "sentimental, romantic picture of a kind of prairie foothill Never-Never Land."[59]

The academic reviews were mixed. *Queen's Quarterly* acknowledged Mitchell's "technical competence and control" but felt that Daddy Sherry "cannot really bear the philosophical burden of the novel," and the *University of Toronto Quarterly* dismissed it as "a collection of local colour sketches."[60] Margaret Laurence, in her *Canadian Literature* review, also had reservations, but concluded that the novel "somehow comes off . . . because of the character of Daddy Sherry. Mitchell has not, thank goodness, idealized him or made him quaint. Daddy Sherry seems to me to be quite the best and most complete character Mitchell has yet created. I am grateful for the existence of this one old man, who strikes me as a genuine holy terror."[61]

Mitchell, himself, knew that *The Kite* was not the complex book that "The Alien" was, but he always felt that *The Kite* had been too easily dismissed. He had not intended to be didactically moralistic, but he had set out to provide "an answer" in this novel as he explained in a 1962 interview with Patricia Barclay: "It's quite a serious novel with a picaresque surface. Any novel will probably involve a search, and a questioning – and, in most cases, an answer. When I wrote *Who Has Seen the Wind*, I didn't have an answer. It was just a question, which is a perfectly fine reason for writing a novel. In *The Kite*, there is an answer, in *The Alien* there is an answer, and in 'Roses Are Difficult Here' I try to make an answer – three answers to things I believe in."[62]

In fact, the "answer" in *The Kite* is more complex than it would seem. Daddy is not the moral centre of the novel, as some readers too easily think. While Daddy offers good advice about spontaneity and living life to the fullest, his attitude of not "giv[ing] a damn whether . . . you live or die" (*K* 191) does not completely reflect Mitchell's own beliefs about the art of living. But, of course, Mitchell did not want to violate the character of Daddy and make him into a philosophizing intellectual. Rather, it is David Lang who represents the more rounded adult, and who, at the end of the novel, integrates Daddy's existentialist message (to never settle for less) with his own more reflective philosophy of life. In theory, Lang vies for centre stage with Daddy, but, in fact, he is too shadowy a character, in comparison, to carry the weight of the theme of self-exploration that Mitchell intended.

Mitchell always found it difficult to win favour with those critics who were suspicious of humour and sentiment, but Michael Hornyansky argued that "complexity and scope" should not be confused with "depth" and that Mitchell with his "parable" has been able to "map and shape our human world." Comparing *The Kite* to two other books of the same season, Hugh Garner's *The Silence of the Shore* and Brian Moore's *An Answer from Limbo*, Hornyansky concludes that Mitchell has "written a better novel" because it is not pretentious and has a "freshness of vision" and "ability to haunt the mind."[63] Ten years later, noting that *The Kite* had received little attention, then or now, Catherine McLay in "A Study in Immortality" argues that it is "an enduring contribution to literature."[64]

— "ONE OR THE OTHER OF US IS GROWING UP." —

Earlier that year Mitchell had successfully pitched an idea to the CBC for a docudrama film on a goose hunt, and it was shot in October 1962.[65] The $900 he received for the script and narration was icing on the cake, for he and his son Hugh, now sixteen, got three weeks' goose hunting at CBC expense. It was, however, hard work, digging pits large enough to accommodate a "behemoth" camera, and doing take after take: "Time after time Hughie leaped from the pit and ran over the stubble after his first Canada goose. Beau retrieved the same dead goose twenty-seven times. . . ."[66]

Against the background of a goose hunt (spotting the geese, digging and camouflaging the pits, setting out the decoys, calling the geese, and the shoot itself), Mitchell weaves the drama of a father-son bonding experience through the ritual shooting of the son's first goose and the "moment of revelation when a boy's innocence gives way to an understanding of the mortality of all living things."[67] As Bill narrated in the film, "You couldn't hunt any better than with a father and a son." Bill and Hugh had their arguments, but Bill was proud of Hugh. He had a more tempestuous relationship with his second son, who took a different approach to his father's whims, demands, arguments, and yelling than did his first son. Whereas Orm had learned to humour his father, Hugh resisted him, and there was a constant contest of wills. However, a letter to Orm in December indicates that their work on the film together had been a bonding experience:

Peter Kelly and Ken Black [producers] have twice written to say that Hughie is wonderful in it. I can't see how they could have any usable footage that didn't show him – a. Scratching his ass. B. Picking his nose. C. Sucking his thumb. D. Chewing gum with his yop wide open. Actually I think he is probably the new Marlon Brando of the foothills. He would certainly do a wonderful Macbeth – which he is by the way reading for Literature now . . . that is if Macbeth dunked his doughnuts and sloshed his soup and dipped his bread in his soft boiled egg. He and I have had hardly an argument for six months now. One or the other of us is growing up.[68]

It had been a busy but less anxious year of freelancing than the previous few. Mitchell had finally broken the spell and published a novel. He also continued to drum up work in magazines, radio, and television. He always had a "quiver" full of stories for *Maclean's* or for his friend, John Clare, at the *Star Weekly*.[69] *Foothill Fables* brought in a regular income, and he narrated seven of his reminiscential pieces for Robert Weaver's CBC *Wednesday Night*.[70] He also had two television plays this year, *The Black Bonspiel*[71] and *The Devil's Instrument*,[72] which was a powerful production directed by Eric Till.

The CBC were very pleased with *The Devil's Instrument* and tried to hook Till and Mitchell up to adapt *Who Has Seen the Wind* as a television movie. Mitchell invited Till out to Mabel Lake in August 1962 to discuss this project. Till, who had not met the "great gentleman," thought it proper to arrive in suit and tie. Just as he arrived, a strong wind came up and Mitchell had his mind on only one thing – sailing. Assuming that all Englishmen by their very nature could sail, he promptly ordered Till into the sailboat to crew the jib. Till recalled, laughingly, that he did not know a thing about sailing and that he had a perfectly "horrid" time.[73] When Mitchell yelled "Coming around!," Till was nearly knocked unconscious by the boom, and when they arrived back at the cabin Till was soaked through. He was amazed that Mitchell was much more concerned about salmon and sailing than he was about the movie project, and it was a few days before he could even bring the subject up. But he refused to go sailing again in what he called Mitchell's "sailing submarine." Although he could not get Mitchell to deliver a script for *Who Has Seen the Wind*, he became Mitchell's long-time friend and associate in various other film ventures.

Judging from Mitchell's tone in his December 5, 1962, letter to Orm, the year was winding down to a quiet close – he had just met his deadline for his annual Christmas radio drama,[74] his orchids "nod in their moist atmosphere" (the Vanda has a spray of eight blossoms but the Jeanne d'Arc blossom had been half-chewed through by a "great son-of-a-bitching slug" that he carefully salted), and he was looking forward to doing a profile article on a Hutterite girl. He signed off, "Mother has been skinning bushels of almonds – dicing them – stirring till her arm is ready to drop off – making countless Christmas cakes and puddings – all this goddam house is geared to your pimply home coming. We love you very much and miss you now and again."[75]

8

THE DROUGHT YEARS

~ 1962 to 1967 ~

MERNA HAD begun to take a more active role in High River community affairs in the 1960s and was enjoying it. Bill kept himself free for writing – and fishing and hunting. He was not a Club man. He had once joined Rotary but, after missing three meetings in a row, had been banished. He ran for school board trustee in September 1958, but placed last in the running. Merna, on the other hand, directed the United Church choir, belonged to a book club, played bridge, occasionally gave talks at book club or other organizations, helped her friend Shirley Northey with Young People's Drama for two years, served as an elocutionist judge at the community "Amateur Night" talent shows, and, informally, gave some coaching in speech-making.

When I was seventeen I entered a public-speaking contest (the grand prize was a three-week bus tour culminating in a visit to the United Nations in New York). I was required to write a speech about an international subject and present it, first at the local Home and School Association level, and then at the District level. Merna offered to coach me, though I was so nervous about speaking in front of this articulate, accomplished woman that I almost did not accept. But she had already coached one speaker into the winner's circle. Four years earlier Joe Clark had won the Rotary contest and a trip to Ottawa (which may well have inspired him to become prime minister!). In later years, much to Merna's annoyance, Clark always credited Bill with the coaching. It was lucky for me that W.O. did not do the coaching. My speech was on emerging African nations, and the only thing I remember about it was the last line, which I intended as the dramatic, emotional clincher: "As Cecil Rhodes said on his deathbed, 'So much to do, so little done.'" In those days, Cecil Rhodes was a hero, not an imperialistic marauder. Merna's advice was to be natural, not to memorize lines but to know *what I was saying at all times. During practice sessions with her, W.O. was working in his office, but apparently he overheard my speech. One day (fortunately after I had won the competition) he mortified me with his parody of my last line, "Cecil Rhodes 'rared up'" – and W.O. 'rared' up himself – "on his death bed and said" – and with mock seriousness W.O. finished the pompous lines – "So much to do, so little done!" Over the years he never let me forget my last line, and he eventually immortalized it in a scene on famous last words in* How I Spent My Summer Holidays.

In 1960 Merna became one of the key organizers on the High River Recreation Committee. The town had been granted $22,000 from the Alberta government to create recreational areas for the town and district, and Merna immersed herself enthusiastically in this volunteer work. She polled the citizens, researched costs, and arranged for architectural plans for artificial ice, a swimming pool, and a site for baseball, lawn bowling, and sports. She was largely responsible for the report that went before council in October 1960. A board was formed to co-ordinate these recommendations and to fundraise, and she was named secretary. But she was frustrated by the struggle it took to raise money. Nevertheless, in October the vote was won to finance the pool, and the installation of artificial ice was finally completed in December 1961. Bill proudly wrote to Orm, who was away at university, that Merna had been very busy preparing for the vote and that the success was "a staggering achievement in any community let alone High River."[1] Years later, though, looking back on those few years, she sadly commented that she had felt terribly let down by the lack of commitment on the part of the townspeople.

Occasionally Bill and Merna would be invited into Calgary to hobnob. In the letter bragging about Merna, Bill also described a party that began at the Calgary Petroleum Club. He and Merna were guests of Ron Brown (president of Home Oil) and his wife, Dorothy. The Browns and Mitchells had been socializing for some years; Bill and Dorothy, a poet, had been reading each other's man-uscripts since the early 1950s. Bill described the party: "Ronnie's brother, Bob, was there with a party, and sent two bottles of Pommery champagne over to us. Mother got very drunk; at least she does not recall doing the twist with Ronnie, while Dorothy and I back at the table, discussed whether or not free will is an illusion." After dinner, they were invited over to Bob Brown's home, where they continued partying in the ornate "Chinese Room":

> There your Mother in her best Baptist pulpit style told [Bob] that he could have been a great Canadian if he'd let his con-science be his guide, that it was not too late for him to pull up his pants. Later – too many drinks for him later, he told me that he was a bigger man than I was and I said he wasn't and he said, "How much are you worth?" And I said, "How much are you worth?" And he said he wasn't sure – "Fifty million anyway." "Well, then," I said, "I guess in monetary terms you're worth fifty million and my Royal bank three thousand dollar note more than I am and I'm a much bigger man than you are." He said, "I'm a bigger man than you are or ever will be." I said, "You've got fifty million three thousand dollars more than I have but it is just money, which I generally piss on, and there are at least a thousand men of your material stature in North America but there is only one of me which is namely W.O. Mitchell." . . . He said, "You are just a goddam intellectual and I hire them by the dozen." I said, "I'm a mostly sober intellectual and I never noticed you hiring me." He said, "I could." I said, "You

couldn't." . . . The pity and irony of it was that your mother was not there for me to have her applaud.[2]

Bill recounted in his letter how he ribbed Merna at three in morning as they drove back to High River:

"Now that you've had your La Dolce Vita evening on the town, I think I must tell you that I'm going to devote the next five years to making a lot of money." She said, "That's nice." I said, "I mean a lot – two or three million." She said, "Go ahead, Dear." I said, "Don't you think I can – if I tried real hard and concentrated on it?" She said, "I'm sure you could, Dear – only I'd leave you." "All right," I said, "I guess I won't make five million in the next five years." She said, "You just write three fine novels." I didn't immediately say I would, for it is harder to do that.

Please do not misunderstand – your mother conducted herself in a most ladylike fashion the entire evening – there was no head holding or anything like that to be done for her. Her conscience still bothers her now and again today. Some day I may understand your mother as well as love her.[3]

Bill's humorous account of this egotistical jousting match over the relative worth of the artist and the millionaire suggests that at this time he had an unshakeable belief in his worth as a writer and as a human. This was not so.

— "I SUDDENLY DESPISED MYSELF" —

The last ten years had tried Bill's confidence more than he realized. The two projects on which he had pinned his hopes for success, "The Alien" as a literary achievement and the televised *Jake and the Kid* as a financial cache, had collapsed. He had failed with "Roses Are Difficult Here." *Jake and the Kid* and *The Kite*, while commercially successful, were not the profound novels he had hoped to write by now. In spring

1963 he became depressed, and he did not regain his equilibrium for about two years. In a 1966 letter to Hugh MacLennan, Bill wrote, "My last two years [of writing] have been singularly sterile, and I sometimes wonder if I shall ever be potent again."[4]

His mood had been up and down throughout the 1950s and early 1960s, but he differentiated this feeling from the psychological crash that now shook his "inner climate." In retrospect, he compared these few years of depression to what his character Colin Dobbs (*Since Daisy Creek*) suffered after a divorce, a writing block, and being mauled by a grizzly bear: "Colin Dobbs's turmoil, spiritually, psychically is such a ringer for what I went through in those two years. Now, at that time, I'd gone through the ice. I should have had professional assistance. I know it. I suddenly despised myself." Bill said that it was his "mother's death and quitting smoking that precipitated those two bloody years." The quitting smoking may seem "unimportant," but it was "a completely new dimension in my life because I was missing the stimulation and the boost of the constant and heavy use of nicotine."[5]

For nearly thirty years he had been a "poly-addict, smoking almost a pound of pipe tobacco a month and a package of cigarettes a day."[6] He customarily smoked nine pipes in the morning, went down to the post office, returned home, filled the pipes, and chainsmoked them again until four o'clock. Bill claimed he stopped smoking on April 4, 1963.[7] In "Stopping Smoking" he describes how he kicked his habit by substituting one addiction for another – from pipes, to Mackintosh's English toffee, to chewing gum, to chewing Merna's cigarettes, to the real thing, plugs of Black Strap snoose and Old Stag chewing tobacco. The old "morning-glory" spittoons had gone out of fashion, so Bill had to carry makeshift spittoons with him everywhere he went – crumpled paper towelling, Dixie cups, and Campbell's soup tins. His dinner invitations fell off sharply.

The chewing stage of my father's battle with nicotine lasted about three years – much to family members' and friends' dismay. My father could never get the hang of spitting his discard cleanly, let alone accurately. He did not have palsy like the old confederate civil war veteran he describes in "The Day I Spoke for Lincoln," but his aim was as bad if not worse. Amber spittle ended up on his moustache, chin, shirt front, and random places within a three-foot radius of his mouth. At my mother's insistence, he kept empty soup tins in every room of the house and in the car so he could spit directly into them. But he dribbled on friends' car doors, on neighbour's white carpets, in friends' coffee mugs – soon his High River friends also kept tins handy to protect their rugs, furniture, pets, and children. Once, I knocked over a tin sitting on the car floor; it is impossible to completely remove tobacco spit from suede Hush Puppies.

One summer out at Mable Lake, Aunt Betty avenged us all. She decided she would clean out my father's brass spittoon, which he had received as a gift after one of his dinner speeches. But when Aunt Betty checked inside and saw it was three-quarters full of disgusting brown mess, she had a better idea. She sprinkled some left over rice on the surface and exclaimed, "Good God in heaven, Bill! Look at this!"

My father yelled from the bedroom, "What's wrong?"

"Come here and look – there's maggots growing in your spittoon!"

"Bullshit!"

But when he looked in the spittoon, he gagged, and it wasn't until he emptied it out at the dock that he realized Aunt Betty had set him up.

His final and lasting addiction was to snuff, a habit introduced to him by Burl Ives, who used Mother Rumney's Eucalyptus snuff. After experimenting with various brands, he settled on Joseph and Henry Wilson's Finest Menthol snuff. He was well hooked on it by 1968. This indulgence, he rationalized, provided him with the nicotine high but not the cancer risk. He said it would have to do until someone invented a nicotine suppository. He began collecting antique snuff boxes (eventually accumulating about fifty), and snuffed away for the next thirty years. It, too, was a filthy habit, for it covered his fingers, his moustache, his shirt, and even his white hair as he ran his fingers through it. Various methods were employed to keep him clean – paper towelling, baby bibs, a Black & Decker dust buster, a small silver spoon with which to deliver the snuff –

but, to Merna's dismay, nothing worked. Whenever Merna was with him on his reading tours, the last thing she did before he went on stage was, with a "For God's sake, Bill!," brush or vacuum the snuff off his shirt and jacket. Somehow it seemed a fitting bad habit – with its mix of earthiness, unusualness, and antiquity. He delighted in offering a pinch of snuff to curious novices, including his three-year-old grandson, whose first small sniff led to such a violent sneezing fit his nose began to bleed. When he was being interviewed by Hana Gartner on CTV, she asked him about his snuff habit. He offered her a pinch, which she unwisely took. Her immediate sneezing fit prevented her from being able to ask any questions for five minutes – which was not a problem, because Bill just kept talking.

The nicotine withdrawal and his mother's death were the precipitates, but Merna felt that other things combined to make this period a "psychologically bad time" for him.[8] She felt that Bill, at forty-nine, was going through a midlife questioning of his accomplishments. Bill, however, argued that that was a normal experience, "the vanishing point, the time when a person realizes his own mortality and thinks, Jesus Christ, I've had 40-45 years and what have I done, really, and I have fewer years left."[9] He insisted that his depression was something much more severe.

Along with his feeling of worthlessness came an insecurity about his marriage. He recalled, "I was absolutely certain that Merna was betraying me" and that "I was a totally unlovable phony person and that nobody could possibly care for me."[10] Merna explained what contributed to Bill's concerns:

> One of the things that I think aggravated Bill's loss of confidence in himself and his writing was the fact that I got involved with choir work. They needed a choir leader desperately so I did it. Then I got involved in the formation of the Recreation Board in High River, and it involved a lot of work and it was something that for the first time I was not engaged in with Bill. I didn't know it at the time, but this upset him terribly. He told me afterwards that he thought I didn't love him any

more which just astonished me, and it was because I was so busy
with the house and doing these other things that I didn't have
the time, or as much time, to spend with him.[11]

Although Merna was not "betraying" him as he feared, she was
receiving considerable attention from members of her committees
and her choir. The recognition, in particular from the young energetic businessmen she worked with on the recreation committee,
pleased her and, as an attractive, intelligent, and competent woman,
she made a larger impression on some of them than she was aware
of at the time. Living in the shadow of such a star performer as Bill,
Merna welcomed being in the limelight herself, and she felt that her
involvement "in something that was outside him for the first time"
partially caused his depression. Bill disagreed: "Merna chooses to
believe this, but it wasn't a part of it."[12]

This period of Merna withdrawal was as intense as the nicotine
withdrawal. Bill's bereft feeling may have started some years earlier
when he was writing "Roses" and Matt's feeling that Ruth is pulling
away from him may, in part, reflect a loneliness and confusion that
Bill himself was beginning to feel: "Never before had he heard this
persistent off-key note in their marital harmony. It was an indefinable
drawing apart from each other. . . . For all its vagueness it was
real. . . . It was the saddest thing he could think of for himself, to be
excluded from her fondness. And there was nothing he could do
about it, for it seemed to him that mention could only magnify it"
(*RD* 285). Certainly something crucial in the dynamics of Bill and
Merna's relationship occurred around this time. The loss of attention,
and, Bill thought, love from the two most important women in his
life precipitated a desperate feeling of worthlessness and abandon-
ment in him.

Bill said he did not talk to anyone, not even Merna, about his
depression. In an interview twenty years later, Merna said, "It
makes me sad to think of that [time] because I hate to think that
he was going through such a turmoil and I didn't recognize it."[13]
Instead, Bill made a conscious decision to "go in on that typewriter

every god damned day at that slant topped long desk and keep going." But he did not produce new material: "That is when I began to do adaptations. That's when I did the Peter Kelly documentaries, *The Goose Hunt*, *A Saddle for a Stoney*, and *Ron Southern – Master Builder*. And in that time I never did anything from a standing start creative. It was taking something in one mode and translating it into another."[14]

Peter Kelly, who had directed *The Goose Hunt*, also directed *A Saddle for a Stoney*, which was shot in May 1963 and shown on CBC's *20/20* on July 14, 1963. It was to be a simple docudrama about an Indian boy of twelve or thirteen who desperately wants to win the grand prize at the High River Little Britches Rodeo, a hand-tooled black saddle decorated with silver. There was, however, nothing simple or predictable about the filming. With great difficulty and no professional actors, they shot two days of film at the Eden Valley Reserve. One of the young Lefthand boys, a champion rider, had been specially chosen for the role. Against Mitchell's advice, Kelly paid the boy for his first two days of shooting and, as predicted, the boy, with money in his pocket, took off the next day to attend a rodeo at Fort McLeod. They found another boy, Wattie Dixon, but Mitchell was hard-pressed to keep him around between takes.

They struggled through the shooting at the reserve, but, at the rodeo, when Wattie caught sight of the roan horse he had drawn for his wild bronco ride, he took off like a shot and disappeared into the midway crowd. Bill was sympathetic: "It was a huge roan with pretty bloody wild eyes, a ring-a-ding because it kept rearing up. I wouldn't have wanted to get on that horse." The crew finally found Wattie and got him back to the chute:

Harry Makin was outside the gate with his camera all set up on the tripod, trained and ready to go. Well, Wattie kept complaining and wouldn't get down on the horse. And I remember saying to Wattie's father, "I'm awfully sorry, McFarland, it is embarrassing. And I know how a father would feel if – I know how I would feel, if either my son Orm or Hughie were lacking in guts the way Wattie evidently is." Well that annoyed McFarland, and he just brought both arms down on top of Wattie's shoulders and knocked Wattie down on top of the horse and Lou yelled open the gate and the horse went out of the gate. Wattie had no intention of staying on that horse. He went down before the actual first buck. That's what Harry Makin caught on his camera.

Bill tried to assure Peter Kelly that all was not lost – they could shoot Wattie in the calf-roping event, or the wild goat milking event, but "what we got shot could not in any way show that this Indian boy had won the grand champion prize against all the other white boys and Indian boys." In the end, Bill had to rewrite the story so that the boy wins "twenty dollars and fourteen bruises" and goes to the saddlery and buys a second-hand saddle.

An important element in the film was to show "another great hunger" of this boy, the desire to be a fine Prairie Chicken Dancer. A big party was held at Eden Valley, and the CBC bought "all the pop and fine cut and Copenhagen snoose and cookies, and potato chips." Bill sadly recalled how much things had changed at Eden Valley:

> Many things had happened to the Stoneys in that ten years. From a band of people who had very little alcoholism or drinking when I was there ten years before, they had discovered alcohol. Word of the party had gone out, and from the Morley reserve north forty miles away had come relatives and friends, and they also brought bottles with them. So there were quite a few people who were drunk. Not only that, but by the time we were wanting the Prairie Chicken Dance, the beaded costumes and everything else – there weren't any. In the ten years since I had been there, they were no longer interested in doing the Prairie Chicken Dance and there was nobody left who had any costumes. There certainly wasn't one to fit young Wattie Dickson.

Mary Rolling-in-the-Mud told Bill that she never went to the dances any more "because everything had gone downhill – beatings, fights." Ironically, for the dance scenes in the film, the CBC had to hire, with some difficulty, dancers from the Sarcee Reserve, the traditional enemies of the Stoneys. When the filming wrapped up, Peter Kelly scolded Bill, "Don't you ever again get me into something with a variable – with an unpredictable – with a ring-a-ding element which can wreck the entire film and cost tens of thousands of dollars."[15]

～ THE END OF THE CBC WARS ～

Except for "dream[ing] all winter of Mable [Lake],"[16] Bill's morale was very low. On November 22, 1963, American president John F. Kennedy had been assassinated, and Bill and Merna were thrown "all out of stride" and feeling "emotionally drained."[17] Esse Ljungh, his *Foothill Fables* producer, detected that Bill was not himself: "It distressed me to find you a bit at loggerheads with your good Muse."[18] Mitchell's scripts were coming in short, some even by five minutes.

The situation with the *Jake and the Kid* television series was still eating away at him. A year earlier Arthur Hiller, who, after his *Jake and the Kid* radio days, had gone to Hollywood and was working for ABC television, wrote, "Alright – enough of this nonsense – let's get Jake on T.V. here! . . . I'm positive Jake can make a contribution to American T.V. & more so to the American audience. God only knows they need some of Jake's & friends' lessons."[19] Mitchell sent scripts in December and, in June 1963, Hiller had contacted Willis Wing requesting a one-year option on the property. However, in November 1963 Wing wrote Mitchell that the CBC was stonewalling and demanding full recovery of the $26,000 in script fees it had paid Mitchell. Exasperated by this prolonged, deceptively civil, negotiating game, Mitchell wrote Wing that he was going to file suit against the CBC.[20] In the meantime, though, Wing had become increasingly unhappy with Mitchell's understanding of their agent relationship, and in January 1964 he cancelled his contract with Mitchell.[21]

Money was tight again, and Mitchell had no big projects underway, which made it all the more frustrating that the *Jake and the Kid* deal with Arthur Hiller had fallen through. When he was in Toronto in March he blasted the CBC in an interview with the *Toronto Star*, claiming that someone there was deliberately "bucking" him.[22] Mitchell claimed that the publicity of the article, his threatening legal suit, and the firing of his agent finally cleared the air, and he regained the rights to his *Jake and the Kid* scripts. The CBC release, signed on April 30, 1964, was conditional on the repayment of $14,950 to the CBC – which Mitchell considered blackmail. He paid the sum and continued to hope for a break with the American networks, but he sensed that "the crest of opportunity with the A.B.C. network" had passed by him.[23] He was right. There would not be any serious interest in a *Jake and the Kid* television series for another thirty years.

It had been eight years since Mitchell first optioned *Jake and the Kid* for TV rights to the NFB and CBC. What had seemed like such a golden prospect for Bill resulted in nothing more than twelve live shows during a CBC summer series. The CBC had severely tainted the property with their long delays over production and with their refusal to release the rights for an American series. Mitchell's hope that this saleable property of more than 150 *Jake and the Kid* scripts would bring him financial stability brought instead six years of frustration and rage as he watched a number of television opportunities "piss away in the sand." In the end, Mitchell made $11,050 for adapting twenty-six scripts (fifteen of which were produced). This was a far cry from the $840,000 that he had imagined collecting back in 1957, not to mention the international recognition and financial stability he had dreamt of.

— THE STONEYS AND THE HUTTERITES —

Mitchell's sense of how the Eden Valley community had changed for the worse fed into a trilogy of *Foothill Fables* episodes that aired later that fall. The three plays, "Hurrah for Civilization," "The Soft Trap," and "The Wrong Trail," deal with Peter Powderface's decision to give up his treaty rights and move his family off Paradise reserve into Shelby's white "civilized" world.[24] The narrator, who sees the reserve system as a "soft trap" that offers the security of government support but also an inadequate and dependent livelihood, supports Peter Powderface's decision. However, although quite successful in the white world, Peter becomes disillusioned with it, and moves back to Paradise Valley. Peter, a Stoney version of Henry David Thoreau, tells Doc Lang that "Master Clock" tyrannizes whites, turning them into materialistic conformists and blinding them to the natural rhythms of the seasons and their fellow humans' suffering: "That's going to get you people in bad trouble some time." Peter concludes that white civilization took a wrong fork in the trail. As he leaves for Paradise Valley, he tells Doc Lang about a cave in one of the Spray's cutbanks, and that "people could be snug in there, Doctor – for a long time":

> NARRATOR (LONG PAUSE): Just what do you mean, Peter?
> PETER: Oh – some day – you and your wife – you might visit us out there. (PAUSE) Not for fishing. (PAUSE) Not for hunting. (PAUSE) In that cutbank hole with running water – us Powder faces we'll move over for you.
> MUSIC: #9 ATOMIC FINALE.[25]

The October 1962 Cuban Missile Crisis was still very much on people's minds, and the "atomic finale" direction was a direct answer to a comment made by one of the film crew members on the shoot for *A Saddle for a Stoney*. He had become so frustrated with the confusion and delays that he commented, "if they had an atomic bomb and they didn't know whether it would work or not, this would be a good place to try it out, right over this reserve. If it went off, all it could do was good."[26] Mitchell's view of red and white cultures was much more complex. He was too much of a realist to buy the "noble savage" and back-to-nature cults, yet he despised the arrogant attitude that assumed that white culture was more "civilized." Again, Conrad's *Heart of Darkness* was looking over his shoulder.

A few months after this episode aired, Mitchell gave permission to the United Church of Christ (North Dakota) to use it for a Conference on Youth that was studying Indian-White relationships. Associate Minister Lester Soberg wrote Mitchell that the reaction of the 210 young people, including thirty Indians, was "marvellous" and completely fulfilled his expectations regarding the "problem of two divergent cultures coming to terms with each other."[27]

Mitchell was fascinated by the Hutterites for the same reasons he was fascinated by the Stoneys. In both cases he used these ethnic minorities to explore the paradoxical and complex tensions of a love-hate triangle: an ethnic minority, the larger majority demanding assimilation, and the individual caught between the two. In the 1950s and 1960s, the Mitchell house had become "a regular port of call" when Hutterites came into town to sell fresh vegetables, ducks and geese, and goose down. Mitchell recalled one time, just before Christmas, when a Hutterite visited the house:

> I can remember when I was working on "The Alien" and had promised myself I would not shave until it was done – so I had a beard. And I had my usual winter siege of pneumonia or bronchitis or flu. Hearing somebody at the front door and thinking it was one of the neighbors visiting, I just yelled out, "Come on in." I heard these hesitant footsteps and no answer. I got up and as I looked around the corner of the partition, this guy looked around the partition and it was a Hutterite with a goose in each hand – and a beard. I looked around at him and I don't know who was more shocked. And as my bearded face came opposite his bearded face I said, "Do you want to buy a goose?" Just as he said, "Do you want to buy a goose?"[28]

When Mitchell was teaching at Eden Valley and living in the unheated shack, Merna decided that he needed a goose-down sleeping bag, so Bill ordered the best down: "'How much would you like,' Elias asked. 'Oh, ten to fifteen pounds,' I replied. He looked startled, so I said, 'Okay, twenty-five to thirty pounds.' And he looked even more startled. I assumed that wasn't very much. So I ended up getting fifty pounds. The pickup truck was piled with burlap sacks full of down, and I just stacked them in the front entrance right up to the ceiling. I knew then that we had more down than we needed." Merna began to make king-sized sleeping bags, sewing tubes in the ticking for the down to be inserted. Realizing the work involved in that, Merna "got the brainwave" that she could use the vacuum cleaner to blow them in: "We instantly had a blizzard. No feathers went into the tubes. It was like an early-spring snowstorm. The whole inside of the living room was filled with feathers." Merna diligently made sofa cushions with down-filled upholstery, two double-sized sleeping bags, pillows, and down-filled jackets, but it still took Bill several years to hock the leftover feathers to various people.[29]

Bill and Merna became staunch defenders of the Hutterites in the 1960s. At that time the Hutterites were legally contesting the validity of Alberta's Communal Properties Act, which prevented them from buying more land. Bill saw this act as racist: "It is more than a single arbitrary piece of legislation: it is the crystallization of antipathy and opposition that has been building in Alberta ever since the Hutterites moved into Canada in 1919."[30] He felt that Diefenbaker's bill of rights passed in 1960 was toothless, and he realized that the Alberta government would not reinforce it, because it would lose them votes.

Anti-Hutterian feeling and distrust grew to open hostility in the High River area when the Hutterites applied to buy land for a third colony. Five hundred people came out to the community centre to show their opposition. When the Hutterite application went forward to the provincial government, it was rejected under the Communal Properties Act. In response, Bill wrote "No Man Is," a radio drama for the CBC's *Summer Fallow*, broadcast on May 29, 1961,[31] which showed the positive value of the Hutterian people and their colonies. In December 1961 the Hutterites made another application, which was similarly rejected.[32]

Two years later the same situation arose in Brant, a nearby town, and many people in High River pledged to stop Hutterite expansion. Mitchell responded again with a radio drama, "Ladybug, Ladybug."[33] Later that year Bill worked with CBC director Peter Kappele on a television documentary on the Hutterites. *The Strait Gate*[34] showed the audience the inside working of a colony. After it was broadcast, Kappele wrote Bill that although, on the whole, he was not pleased with it, the show received a positive response. In the postscript, Peter wrote, "Maybe the next time we find ourselves up to our asses in bigots, we can provide some more calculating humor and rout the Philistine bastards."[35] A few months later, Mitchell wrote a satiric letter to Mr. Ernest Manning, premier of Alberta, attacking his government's treatment of the Hutterites, in particular Mr. Hooke's (one of his cabinet minister's) comment that relaxing the Communal Properties Act to allow Hutterites to buy land "would be like letting a pack of starving dogs off their leashes."[36]

In December 1962, Merna had noticed an item in the *High River Times* on Judy Walters, a young Hutterite girl attending junior college in Lethbridge, and suggested to Bill that he do a profile on her for *Maclean's*. In the article he describes colony life and dispels the various misconceptions about the Hutterites held by small-town and rural Alberta. He then tells Judy Walters's story, pointing out that inflammatory meetings held in rural districts where a colony wishes to start up cause even the more liberal colony Bosses to close ranks and make it difficult for individuals such as Judy to bridge the two worlds of colony and outside life, with its opportunities for education. He describes Judy, the first Hutterite child to attend a school outside the colony, as a "one-girl breakthrough," and hopes that such "little elastic compromises" will continue. Judy went on to complete her bachelor of education and teach off the colony. In his concluding paragraph, Mitchell shows his sympathy for the Hutterite's struggle to maintain their way of life within a dominant culture that may be headed for disaster: "One thing is certain: so long as they can resist the worldly influence, they will continue as gentle, stubborn Christians sharing love and possessions. They could just possibly be the Lord's ace in the hole for a new game of civilization, if this one comes to an atomic end."[37]

Throughout 1964 and 1965 Mitchell remained in a slump. He was busy, but mostly doing documentary-type projects. In one burst of energy on March 11, 1964, just after arriving home from Toronto, he wrote six letters, drumming up short-term projects. To Peter Gzowski, articles editor at *Maclean's*, he complained about the "paltry $200" that he was being paid for "All Westerners Are Snobs," an amusing tongue-in-cheek one-page article that differentiated each western province by its particular brand of snobbery, from the first-family snobbery of Manitobans to the climate snobbery of British Columbians.[38] When in Toronto for the CBC negotiations he had met with Gzowski, but confessed that after "four martinis at the Benvenuto, I am understandably a little vague about the other pieces. . . . I will stay off martinis so that I will not get the little Hutterite maiden and the Grizzly Bear mixed up. . . . I hope that my conflict with the grizzly gets decided this spring – one way or the other."[39] However, no grizzlies showed up at this spring's hunt and Mitchell filed away the material he gathered from it and his previous hunt for future use.

With this spurt of energy he wrote John Gray in March 1964 suggesting two possible books – though they were not new novels. He dredged up one of his old ideas to combine "The Devil's Instrument" and "The Black Bonspiel" under the title of "The Devil is a Travelling Man." More interesting to Gray was Mitchell's idea for a collection of his reminiscential pieces. Mitchell described this book as a fictive memoir, "not fiction, but . . . not exactly fact, perhaps something like a cross between Stegner's *Wolf Willow* and Steinbeck's *Travels with Charlie*."[40] This was a strange combination. The nostalgic pieces he had written were close in impulse and, at times, tone to *Wolf Willow* (1963) and may very well have formed the core of a similar fictive memoir. But Steinbeck's account of his travels with a poodle across the United States to feel the pulse of America bears little similarity to the sort of book Mitchell was contemplating. He probably linked *Travels with Charley in Search of*

America (1962) with his new project because of his theory that Steinbeck had written this kind of free-fall diary in an attempt to restoke creative fires that had been dead for some time. Some months later Mitchell sent Macmillan a number of his pieces along with some tapes of his reading performances. One reader liked the collection very much and urged that it be published in the spring of 1966, but a second reader's report was negative and Mitchell lost interest in the project.

Two months later, in May, three pieces came out together in *Maclean's* under the title "Three Random Scenes – Complete with Cast and Plot – from the Unfolding Drama of W.O. Mitchell."[41] The first random scene is a hilarious, largely autobiographical story that was later titled "How I Sold Lingerie in a Prairie Whorehouse." This piece became one of his most popular performance pieces. The second was similarly a slightly heightened autobiographical event about the day he set the car upholstery and himself on fire while he was driving to work in Toronto. The third scene described his recent attempts to conquer the nicotine habit. In June, CBC Television's *Take 30* taped "The Day I Spoke for Lincoln" and liked it so much they taped five more of his reminiscential pieces. Mitchell collected $300 for each script and performance.[42]

The Kite had been adapted for radio in June 1964, and in 1965 Mitchell adapted it for television, working with the story editor, David Peddie. David Gardner directed the one-hour show broadcast on CBC's *Show of the Week*.[43] Mitchell went to Toronto to attend some of the rehearsals and was pleased. Although John Drainie was originally cast as Daddy, he became too ill to continue, and Jack Creley, a forty-year-old actor, was made up to play the role of the 111-year-old Daddy Sherry. The newspaper reviews were mixed. The *Toronto Daily Star's* Bob Blackburn complained that "everything [Mitchell] writes for television comes out Jake and the Kid."[44] Blackburn was correct in noting the echoes from *Jake and the Kid* in this production, but he must have missed *The Devil's Instrument* and *The Black Bonspiel* in 1962 and *The Goose Hunt* and *Saddle for a Stoney* in 1963. Nevertheless, Mitchell himself acknowledged that these were not creative years. Although he was writing, he was not moving ahead, not staking out new territory.

In a more documentary vein, he wrote "Holiday Trails of Canada: The Kananaskis," published in *Maclean's* in June 1965 and, once again, worked with the director Peter Kelly on *Ron Southern: Master Builder* for *Telescope* with Fletcher Markle as the host.[45] Ron Southern was the president of ATCO, a Calgary-based company, that built prefabricated house trailers and shipped them all over the world. Mitchell, Southern, and the film crew travelled by chartered jet to various sites of preconstructed ATCO buildings "on an island opposite Anchorage, at a pulp mill town on Vancouver Island, at an American air force base at San Francisco and in the rugged California interior."[46] Mitchell even had a series of vaccinations, in preparation for a possible trip to Venezuela and the Virgin Islands.

Bill was fascinated by Southern's business, but there was also a bonus to this project – an opportunity to construct a fibreglass motorboat. Bill located a Sangstercraft mould, and ATCO allowed him and a friend the use of the ATCO fibreglassing facilities to make two hulls. Bill and Hugh then moved the boats to a neighbour's garage and finished them off. The following year, 1965, they built three fibreglass canoes (two to sell). Over the next five or six years, the Mitchells launched the largest flotilla on Mabel Lake: "The name of Mabel has never held much magic for me – like Helen, for instance – yet Mabel caused us to build an eighteen-foot planing sloop, a run-about, to acquire a canoe, a floating patio boat, a skiff, surf board. Helen launched a thousand; six isn't bad for a girl named Mabel."[47]

In the fall of 1965 Mrs. Hirtle was diagnosed with a brain tumour and Merna and Bill went out to Vancouver. She was not expected to live, but after four operations and two months of recuperation with Bill and Merna by her side, she made a miraculous recovery. Mrs. Hirtle's illness was compounded by Spud's schizophrenia. Mrs. Hirtle and Spud had, as the psychiatrists noted, a precarious interdependence. He liked to live at home, but his mother's bossiness upset him. Spud was not happy to see Mrs. Hirtle return home, and now that she was so unwell it became an increasingly difficult problem for Merna and Bill to handle. They brought her to High River to recuperate, but when she went home she had a relapse and was back in the hospital in spring 1966. Spud could not cope on his own and was again sent back to the Shaughnessy psychiatric ward. Merna did not talk much about this difficult time; she simply bore it quietly and stoically, as was her custom. She dealt with the medical arrangements as best she could, but she was torn by the guilt that she did not feel more emotional ties with either her mother or her brother.

Fortunately Mitchell was back in his stride by this time, and it was with great personal pleasure that he took on his next freelance assignment. He had been commissioned to write the script for a half-hour interview with Wallace Stegner for CBC's *Telescope*,[48] and in February 1966 Bill met with him in San Francisco. Stegner, an American writer who had spent six of his childhood years in Eastend, Saskatchewan, had published *Wolf Willow*, a fictive memoir about those years that was as evocative of the prairies as was Mitchell's work. Although they never became close friends or regular correspondents, Mitchell, early on, had admired Stegner's *On a Darkling Plain* (1940) and *The Big Rock Candy Mountain* (1943). They first made personal contact in November 1957 when Mitchell wrote to recommend a student from his Fort Qu'Appelle summer course for Stegner's creative-writing program at Stanford University. Aside from the referral, Bill wrote, "I welcome an excuse to write to you," and invited Stegner to visit him in the foothills, "for you are our favourite North American novelist."[49] Stegner was equally flattering when he replied, complimenting Bill on *Who Has Seen the Wind*: "There was more Saskatchewan in that than anything I have read."[50]

As part of the interview Stegner took Bill on a tour of the Stanford campus and introduced him to his creative-writing class. Once again Mitchell was working with Peter Kelly, their fourth television production together. If Kelly had not been too comfortable out on Eden Valley, Bill was even less comfortable at the nightclub performance by the infamous Carol Doda (a.k.a. "Candy Cupcakes") that Kelly dragged him to one evening. Her strip dance at the Condor had gained some notoriety two years earlier when she and other strippers were charged with obscenity. Her lawyer, Melvin Belli, won her case by arguing that her performance was artistic and therefore her nudity and movements could not be construed as obscene. Her act, which began by her being lowered from the ceiling on a white grand piano, made her queen of the topless dancers who, following their court victory, became the rage in San Francisco nightclubs. On this particular evening, as her piano descended, she stripdanced to "Michael Row Your Boat Ashore." This folksong, made famous in the early 1960s by Peter, Paul, and Mary, was a favourite in the Mitchell household, often sung by Willa accompanied by Merna. The incongruity of Candy Cupcakes' gyrating strip dance and his eleven-year-old daughter's lovely rendition of this folksong, plus a few too many martinis, was too much for Mitchell and he impulsively stood up and yelled, "Sacrilege!" The Condor bouncers immediately descended and escorted him and the CBC film crew out of the club.

~ *WILD ROSE* AND OTHER PLAYS ~

Novel writing was still on the back burner through 1966, but Mitchell had three plays on the go. In November he was especially pleased to attend the first stage production of *The Black Bonspiel of Wullie MacCrimmon*. Earlier in the fall Macmillan had published a textbook for schools, *Three Worlds of Drama*, which contained *The Black Bonspiel* along with *The Caine Mutiny* and *The Glass Menagerie*.[51] Although this was the television version of *The Black Bonspiel*, Andy Harris of the Lakefield Boys' School felt it could easily be adapted for stage and asked permission to do it with his drama group. Mitchell was enthusiastic about the performances and, indeed, the play went on to win the Ontario Drama League Award for the year.

He was also invited by Robertson Davies to collaborate on a Centennial Play in which five playwrights would create pieces representing their particular region of Canada. As Mitchell informed Hugh MacLennan on January 21, 1966, "I have just finished my portion of a projected Centennial Play that Nicholas Goldschmidt felt you might be contributing to. I am beginning to understand

W.O. with Morris Surdin, the composer of Wild Rose, *May 1967*

why you passed the opportunity up."[52] MacLennan and Joseph Schull had signed on in January 1965, but dropped out within nine months. Mitchell completed his piece by December 1965 but was never comfortable with the concept of the project. Although Davies had created a frame to unify the individual pieces, the styles, tones, and intentions of the five writers were too disparate to coalesce effectively into a single play.

The trial performance took place at the Lindsay Academy Theatre on October 6, 1966. Mitchell's section was a three-part skit about con men: the medicine man (Professor Winesinger from the *Jake and the Kid* stories); the rainmaker (from "The Day Jake Made Her Rain"); and the modern-day "politician cum professor cum evangelist,"[53] a new sort of Winesinger who, in revival-meeting style, attempts to "stir a little sunshine" into the lives of his audience by suggesting that the gopher be adopted as a talisman of happiness. The evangelist skit was his only totally new piece of writing, and it was a hodgepodge of ideas. Mitchell was not particularly proud of his contribution, and felt that the entire production was an embarrassing flop. Only Davies's schoolroom scene, Mitchell's rainmaker section, and the dancing in the Quebec skit received any positive commentary in the reviews. Reviewers were dismayed that five of Canada's best writers could not do better than this. Using his Yogi Jorgensen accent in a high falsetto, Mitchell would mercilessly re-enact a particularly melodramatic scene from the pageant in which a pregnant, early Viking settler tears open her bodice and whets a sword across her breasts to scare away marauders. He was delighted to see this scene and other serious scenes hammed up by the actors in the Lindsay production so that the pageant became total farce. That was its only salvation; it never, he said, rose above being a "church basement pageant."[54] When it went on to play at the Ottawa Little Theatre – as straight drama – it was panned.[55]

Mitchell, by this time, was immersed in plans for a musical comedy based on his stage play *Royalty is Royalty*. He and Morris Surdin had been batting this idea around since the early 1960s. By February 1966 he had composed five "lyric gems" that Merna made him read aloud to the poet Eli Mandel, who was visiting at the time. Bill exclaimed, "I could have wrung her neck. Truly. I have suffered from nice Saskatchewan ladies, who insisted on reading me their poetry; I am not at home in this medium – yet."[56] By May plans were well underway for the musical, now called *Wild Rose*. Eddie Wong, the young boy whom Mitchell had taught in Castor, Alberta, in 1942, had become involved in theatre production in Calgary and Edmonton, and Mitchell pitched the venture to him and a group of MAC Theatre production people. In his customary repartee with Morris Surdin, Mitchell (who could not sing a line) bragged, "They are all very excited about 'Wild Rose,' after I read it and personally sang all the songs to them."[57] It demanded considerable work on Mitchell's part to get this play into production. In May he tried to get Esse Ljungh to direct it; in June he wrote to Bernie Braden in London, England, pitching the musical as a possibility for the West End. With remarkable unawareness of his usual unbounded optimism he wrote, "I am almost never enthusiastic about work, whether it be play, script or novel, but Morris and I know we have a once-in-a-life-time winner in this."[58]

By the end of 1966 Mitchell had surfaced from his depression, revitalized by *Wild Rose*, but especially by work on his reminiscential pieces. In October he wrote to a former cottager on Carlyle Lake, where he and his family had gone every summer in his childhood, describing how revisiting his childhood haunts revived him: "Everything seems to have shrunk alarmingly; I went to where our cottage once was, stood for some time behind the Grosses while forgotten, long forgotten, feelings and sense fragments drifted to the top of my consciousness. I have never had a session on a psychoanalyst's couch, but these nostalgic minutes peeled off the years and tolled me back to childhood as no analysis possibly could."[59]

There was a national groundswell of emotion in 1967 when Canada celebrated its centennial, and Mitchell was swept up in it. Aside from the disastrous centennial play collaboration, about which Mitchell was more amused than upset, he was asked to contribute to a number of cultural events planned by the centennial commission, as well as to some events that were simply a part of the festive spirit of that year. Weyburn, Mitchell's birthplace, was renamed Crocus for a week, and July 6 was called W.O. Mitchell Day. Mitchell felt especially touched by this event and by the oil painting of Crocuses with which they presented him and which, unlike some mementoes, he proudly displayed over his fireplace mantel. He was asked to give a number of readings and addresses that year, and he prepared the text for the Western Canada section of the Centennial Train and Caravan exhibit. He also wrote an article, "Prairies: The Poetry of Earth and Sky," that appeared in *Century*, a centennial magazine insert that came out with most newspapers in February 1967 and that included representative writers such as Hugh MacLennan, Farley Mowat, Max Braithwaite, Anne Hébert, Thomas Raddall, and Robertson Davies. In this article he personalizes the history of the prairies over the last one hundred years with references to his grandmother and Sheepskin, an Assiniboine Indian he knew from his summer cottage days at Carlyle Lake, and with references to his own half-century of life on the prairies: "So much has happened in such a short time to this country that people of my generation have a living thread of apostolic succession back to the beginning of Canada." Yet, he wrote, some things remained the same: "The ululating hysteria of the coyote lifts in the foothills night amongst the Eiffel towers of oil rigs; in spring the prairie crocus opens blue and the gopher squeaks his impudence to the ageless Saskatchewan wind."[60]

He must have been working on this article when he received a letter from a Vancouver schoolgirl who told him that her life had been changed by reading *Who Has Seen the Wind* and that she wanted to spend her life on the prairies. He replied, "It is important to be able to hear 'the poetry of earth' and it does not have to be <u>one</u> kind of poetry; it will sing to you and make you want to cry on the sea shore – in the mountains – the foothills – lake country. The important thing is to be able to hear that poetry. . . . Don't ever forget how."[61] "Prairies: The Poetry of Earth and Sky" is a signature piece expressing Mitchell's credo about the powerful impact of place on the senses, and about how and why he became a writer.

Wild Rose excited him as he had not been for years and made him "very serious about returning to [his] first love, which was playwriting."[62] Perhaps it was coming out of a period of depression that made him so manic, so disproportionately exuberant about this play that, in the end, did not measure up. He again wrote to Braden, saying, "I have never been so sure or so excited with anything I have done since my first novel."[63] Of course, salesman or con as he was, he always knew the selling power of such exuberance – and Braden did fly in from London for the opening night. In spite of a severe bout of hepatitis and a pancreas problem early in the year (probably related to subsequent gall bladder problems), Mitchell thrived on the activity. *Wild Rose* was commissioned by the Centennial Commission and produced by Edward Wong with MAC Theatre. On May 24, 1967, it was given its world premiere, a royal command performance before Princess Alexandra and her husband, the Honourable Angus J.B. Ogilvy, at the Jubilee Auditorium in Calgary. It played for four days and then moved on to Edmonton for two days.

Wild Rose is about the visit of royalty to the small town of Wild Rose and the delicate problem of which child shall hand up the flowers to the visiting princess – Mariel, the mayor's daughter; Cora, the socialite's daughter; Bud Morgan, the top school student; or Lazarus Lefthand, the Indian child. Dave Morgan, the hard-swearing rancher and single father, and his tomboy daughter, Bud, who refuses to wear a dress for her royal performance, were the new additions to the basic story line of *Royalty is Royalty*. Miss Henchbaw is transformed into the lovely young schoolteacher, Margaret, who eventually falls in love with the rancher.

Mitchell was proud of the twenty lyrics he wrote for the musical, some of which are poignantly memorable such as the schoolteacher's solos, "Other Mother's Little Ones" and "Arithmetic of Love." "Rope Me a Lie" sung by Dave and his cowboy friends parodies the traditional cowboy songs. The most poignant song, "The Wrong Trail," is the final number and is sung alone by Mrs. Lefthand: "Man walked this trail/Long time ago/Come to the fork/Long time ago. . . . Who chose the right one?/Long time ago/Who chose the wrong one?/Long time ago." *Wild Rose* has the ingredients of a charming, light-hearted musical with the love element and the drama of a royal visit alongside gentle satire of small-town snobbery and racism.

Georgie Collins, a relatively inexperienced Calgarian actress and director, took on the directing duties. John Hirsch was to be advising director, but, unfortunately, he was there in name only. The cast included Wally Koster as Dave Morgan, Joan Karasevich as Margaret, the schoolteacher, and Len Birman as Moses Lefthand. Aside from the daughter-father relationship that Mitchell took great delight in writing, Moses and the race motif are the strongest elements. Jamie Portman, reviewing for the *Calgary Herald,* was particularly impressed by Birman, who gave "the finest performance of the evening," playing the role with "quiet humor and dignity."[64]

The politics of small-town egotism and jealousy played themselves out both on and off stage. Just as one of the main conflicts in the play revolved around a father-daughter situation with Dave insisting that Bud, his young, bright daughter, should be the one to hand up the flowers, so, too, did Mitchell insist that Willa, his twelve-year-old daughter, would be the best choice to perform the role of Bud. Willa was musical and had taken piano, dance, and voice lessons. She auditioned and performed well but was less professionally trained in dance and voice than Julia Lewis, who also auditioned for the part. As Willa recalled, the whole situation "was painful": "Dad was too subjectively involved. He probably shouldn't have suggested that I be involved in it and left it to the director, Georgie Collins. It was a dynamite situation that was bound to blow up."[65] And "blow up" it did. Willa was unaware until the advertising was released that she was being treated as an understudy and would have only two shows to perform, and certainly not the opening night performance. Bill was as hurt as she was and always felt that Willa was superior in the role. It was uncharacteristic of Mitchell to interfere so strongly in a production, but, as Collins noted, Willa was "very special to him" and he could not be objective when it came to her. Also, as Collins admitted, the problem was that she and her team were "green," and they found it difficult to argue with Mitchell, who had had much more theatre experience: "To say anything against the play was a bit like hitting W.O.'s baby in the face with a wet rag."[66]

Jamie Portman reported that on opening night the audience of 1,700 rose to a standing ovation when Mitchell and Surdin came on stage following the production. While he felt that the relationship between the characters lacked depth, he liked the dialogue, plot, lyrics, and the satire on snobbishness and racism that, "although never malicious, nevertheless cuts deep."[67] Nathan Cohen, on the other hand, savaged it in the *Toronto Daily Star*: "The libretto is a mess. . . . there is no construction, no characterization or conflict or momentum of development," and the "clumsy and threadbare lyrics are rendered to ordinary and hackneyed music composed by Morris Surdin."[68] Mitchell, nevertheless, believed that the play had been a huge success and that, with some rewriting, it would be a hit on London's West End. Braden went back to London and lined up a producer and a theatre, but the producer suddenly died and he was unable to generate enough interest to mount another package.

— "YOU STAND OR FALL ON YOUR OWN TALENT" —

Mitchell said his first love had been playwriting, even though he prized novel writing above playwriting. Akin to writing for the stage was being on stage himself and reading his own work before live audiences or on television. With the success of the *W.O. Mitchell Reading Series* on CBC Radio in the summer of 1962 and subsequent requests for appearances on television, he began to recognize not only how much he enjoyed doing these performances, but how they could generate a substantial part of his income.

His performance at MAC Theatre in Calgary on February 20, 1965, was the first of his one-man shows. For two and a half hours he "enthralled" the audience with "hilarious descriptions of human situations."[69] He read six pieces, ranging from the satiric "All Westerners Are Snobs" to the poignant "Going to a Fire." "How I Sold Lingerie in a Prairie Whorehouse" was a hit – according to Mitchell, a woman laughed so hard she vomited in the aisle and two ushers had to help her to the ladies washroom. What Mitchell liked about speaking performances was what he liked about novel writing: "You stand or fall on your own talent, no script writers, no directors, just yourself."[70] And he had talent. Mitchell did not simply give a reading, he gave a performance that was more in the tradition of the stand-up comedian or the turn-of-the-century elocutionist. In a convocation address he gave at the University of Alberta in 1975, he said, "As a child I wanted to be an acrobat. I also wanted to be a magician and a ventriloquist; the ham genes must have been strong on both sides of the family. Today I am an acrobat *manqué*, a performer with a sense of audience responsibility both as a writer and as a teacher."[71]

As he walked out onto the stage, frequently in a suit and bow tie (later he was more casual), his first connection with the audience was his broad, boyish smile. While he claimed always to be nervous before doing a show, it was the adrenalin charge of speaking to a large audience, not stage fright, for he had a natural ease on stage. He quite simply – unlike most writers – loved telling stories to an audience. By 1967 he was being sought after in the banquet and conference circuit and was charging $300 plus expenses for those appearances. He was also giving lectures and seminars on the craft of writing, most of which included performances of his own work to illustrate his points. In the spring of 1968 he gave an address to Alberta teachers called "Grace and Illusion: The Writer's Task"[72] in which he set forth his philosophy of creating the illusion of reality through appeal to the senses and of employing the art that conceals art through the use of restraint and grace. He compared the writer to a magician or a trapeze performer: "The thing is that each of these people does his work so that it looks very easy. Yet each is in danger, in mortal danger, each time he gets up to perform. The trapeze performer is only in danger of losing his life; the writer or the magician is in danger of being found out."[73] In this talk he also compared the work of art to a pebble being tossed into a pond, the reader's imagination and mind. These ideas formed the core of a three-part television program, *Magicians, Acrobats and Writers*, which was produced by the Department of Education in Alberta in conjunction with the CBC,[74] and became the foundation for future talks to teachers for the next twenty years.

Mitchell had a psychological need to perform his work. He had always read drafts to Merna as they were completed, and in High River he was lucky enough to have neighbours who would kindly indulge him, indeed enjoyed listening to him, but beginning in the 1960s he got an even bigger thrill out of reading to large public audiences. In the "preface" to *An Evening With W.O. Mitchell* (1997), a collection of his performance pieces, he describes the importance an audience had for him:

> . . . writing is an intensely private and lonely act. Writing is like playing a dart game with the lights out so that the writer has no way of knowing whether his darts are coming anywhere near the bull's eye or are missing the board entirely.
>
> Early on I was lucky enough to find two creative partners who helped to dilute that lonely darkness for me, who acted as caring, honest, and perceptive sounding-boards for draft after draft of my stories – Professor F.M. Salter, for the six years I spent writing *Who Has Seen the Wind*, and my wife, Merna, for almost everything I have ever written.
>
> Then, later on in my career, I discovered another way to help dilute the writer's darkness – reading performances. My one-man shows over the years have given me what all stage performers love – the immediate thrust of a live audience as it responds

to story magic. Here, on stage, is no *illusion* of bridging between story-teller and audience. And I know immediately when the darts hit the centre, when we are really flying together. (ix-x)

It is interesting that Mitchell's performance career began to flourish in the midst of his period of depression. To some degree, the sense of worthlessness he experienced, as well as his loneliness as a writer, was allayed by the immediate response of a live audience.

9

CALGARY

– 1967 to 1971 –

ERB ARMSTRONG, president of the University of Calgary, had approached Mitchell in the fall of 1966 about a writer-in-residency. At the same time the University of Victoria offered him a position, and he made two trips out there to consider that possibility because he thought it would be helpful for Merna to be closer to her mother, who had come through a difficult brain operation in September 1965. However, Mitchell did not feel at home, either in the department or with the idea of becoming an island dweller, and he accepted a residency to begin at Calgary in the fall of 1968.

Becoming a writer-in-residence was an exciting proposition for Mitchell: "That umbrella of an artist-in-residence is probably one of the finest things to come out of the Massey commission on the arts and make it possible for people to do the silly and impractical thing of devoting all of their energies to the writing of fiction or of poetry or play writing. I shall never forget at first the invitation, saying fine, and then just simply being acquainted with the fact that the honorarium was to be $17,000!" This figure was double his book royalties, and it freed him from the applied art projects like magazine work and documentary films that he had just spent five years doing.[1] He was appointed "Resident Writer at the rank of Professor" for "a twenty-two-month probationary period" beginning in September 1968.[2] Even though this was a probationary appointment (meaning that after the probationary period his position would be reviewed for permanent tenure), Mitchell made it clear that he did not want tenure because he "did not believe in it for artists." However, his understanding was that his appointment would be renewable for a further few years.[3] Merna felt "a tremendous relief" because Bill would now "be able to do the two things he loved the most, have a select group that he felt had talent and teach them, help them, guide them, and write without any financial worries."[4]

In the midst of all the excitement about the writer-in-residency, Merna was worried about her mother, who was in hospital and deteriorating. On February 16, 1968, at the age of seventy, Mrs. Hirtle died. Her death stirred up old feelings of guilt in Merna that she had not been a loving daughter. She and Bill immediately left for Vancouver to make funeral arrangements and to sort out Spud's future. For a short time after his mother's death, Spud seemed to improve. He lived in a boarding house, returning to the Veterans' Hospital when he felt he was about to have one of his spells.

Merna was usually the one who initiated moves in their lives. With the university position coming up, she decided that it was logical to move to Calgary, although Bill protested that he could commute the thirty-five miles. She wrote to Orm and Barbara, "It took three months and histrionics on my part to get [Bill] to see the logic of the move. Now he's taken over. . . . As we want an old run-down place in Mount Royal or Elbow Park it takes a lot of looking and also [Bill] looks ahead to all kinds of buys at the Unclaimed and Damaged Freight to use in rebuilding. He's in his element."[5]

Bill noted a pattern of behaviour in Merna that was to become more obvious as time went on. There was more than simple "logic" behind her plans, and their "real cause or reason," he said, "is pretty well camouflaged."[6] One overt reason she gave for moving was that Willa, now fourteen, would benefit from attending a larger, more challenging school in Calgary. This did not work out quite as she expected, for Willa was ostracized for the first part of the year by elitist neighbourhood schoolgirls and ended up hanging out with what her father called "the greasers." The camouflaged reason for Merna's decision to move was her disenchantment with the High River community's conservatism, particularly its resistance to the idea of a recreation park and its stand on the Hutterite issue. She was also keen to take some courses at the university.

After about six months searching, Merna found a two-storeyed Colonial-style house, with an attached greenhouse, beautifully situated in an older, small community enclave. It was sheltered from noise and city life by a natural bluff that was part of the valley carved out by the Elbow River. The park and river, just half a block from their house, not only provided a natural wooded area in which to walk their dogs, now a French poodle (Demi-tasse) and a golden retriever (Plato), but gave them the illusion of living in a small town. It was truly a green retreat in the middle of the city's asphalt jungle, a wild sanctuary that even harboured coyotes, rabbits, and pheasants.

In June, just as they were thinking of Mabel Lake again, Bill's brother, Bob, had emergency surgery for a gall bladder problem, and Bill went to Brandon for a few days to be with him. On June 30 Bob had another operation and everything looked positive, so Bill and Merna headed out to the lake on July 12. Sadly, Bob died two days later and Bill returned to attend the funeral and spend a week with Bob's widow, Molly.

Bill had August to spend at his beloved Mabel Lake. That month the NFB shot a documentary of the Mitchell family enjoying themselves at their quiet retreat – fishing, sailing, water skiing. As son Hugh commented, the documentary was all "fairy land." Hugh Webster, the director, set up shots of Bill taking Hugh and Willa up water skiing, but the truth was they never trusted their father to do that because he was such an erratic driver. One scene, says Hugh, "finally got to me":

Here's Dad, trotting down the steps. He's got his fishing rod over his shoulder. Mum is leaning on the balcony saying, "Catch lots of fish, dear." "O.K. sweetheart." A *typical* morning with W.O. Mitchell! And I am sitting there saying, "I can't believe this." I said to Hugh Webster, "Do you want to know what it is really like? I'll show you what it is like:" "WHERE ARE MY GODDAMN SOCKS? JESUS CHRIST, MERNA, YOU HAVE LOST THEM AGAIN!" Every morning it was like this.

Webster also captured Bill in the kitchen, calmly, quietly, generously, stirring up his famous pancake batter. That, too, was far from the truth: "Dad used to come back from fishing and make his pancakes. What a sweetheart! Right? You think he washed his hands? He's got fish slime all over them! Have you ever eaten pancakes that smelled like fish. He's the only guy I knew ever served fishy pancakes."7

— "A COMPLETELY NEW NOVEL" —

Over the previous fourteen years Mitchell had occasionally pulled out "The Alien" to begin a major rewrite, but each time he was overwhelmed by it, and his efforts ended in defeat. In retrospect he realized, "[I had] put a finish on it that was good enough that it tyrannized me and I couldn't take liberties with it."8 By the fall of 1968, however, he was well underway turning "The Alien" into a new novel.

A number of elements coalesced to set in motion a five-year process that would see *The Vanishing Point* rise out of the wreck of "The Alien." In the summer of 1967 Mitchell read Orm's M.A. thesis on John Steinbeck, which "broke the dam"9 for him by reaffirming and clarifying some thematic and formal issues:

> It had quite an impact on me and believe it or not pulled my understanding to a better view of novel structure – as achieved through symbolism particularly. Result – for the last two months I have been working on THE ALIEN. . . . Particularly Orme's reference to Steinbeck's GRAPES OF WRATH thesis: man goes forward four steps and slips back three – his faith in

the flow of the life force – is precisely what I needed my attention called to. I knew that the inevitable tragedy of Victoria's failure wasn't right for me as a person and as a writer, but I was held helpless by it until I realized that her failure was not failure.[10]

Mitchell also made a very liberating decision – *not* to look at his original manuscript. He wrote John Gray, "I have wanted to keep quite free of commitment to it and to work as though I were doing a completely new novel." Mitchell was not revising; he was doing "that careless, sloppy, undisciplined, inspirational recall writing, hoping that the critical, censoring half of your mind sleeps while invention goes on."[11] Also, as well as the financial stability afforded by the University of Calgary appointment, the move to Calgary inspired him to use the city landscape to counterpoise the Eden Valley Native milieu. As a result, Mitchell's new novel was becoming as much a critique of white puritan civilization itself as it was a portrayal of Native culture and the damage it has suffered from white culture.

Mitchell knew he would use much of the material from Part III of "The Alien," but he did not look at it until *The Vanishing Point* had developed its own critical mass, at least three years after beginning the rewrite. The result of Mitchell's final attack on "The Alien" would result in a radically different novel with a more complex and engaging Carlyle (now a white struggling with his Scots puritan and "civilized" blood rather than a half-breed struggling with self-loathing about his mixed blood), along with new secondary characters who play key roles in Carlyle's quest for self-discovery, new "proliferating"[12] images and symbols, a tighter organic structure, and a more "comic" vision that is open-ended and richer in its scope and depth. There is still a dark side to this novel, but its vision is essentially existentialist. Unlike the old Carlyle who was a quitter, the new Carlyle, while squarely facing human limitations, finally refuses to give up.

Macmillan continued to show the same confidence in Mitchell. With his usual optimism, Mitchell wrote Gray in February 1968, saying, "I've been working at THE ALIEN since August and shall be with it until June, I trust. Therefore – is it possible that MACMILLANS

W.O. Mitchell, fiction editor at *Maclean's*, with a cartoon illustrating his *Jake and the Kid* radio program (1950).

Jake and the Kid, live on radio. Left to right: John Drainie, Jack Mather, Frank Peddie.

Bill and Hugh, Bon Echo (July 1949).

High River New Year's party (about 1952). Bill in forefront and Merna in the centre.

Bill and Hughena McCorquodale (about 1952).

Bill interviewing writing student Norma (Beck) Hawkins at Fort Qu'Appelle Creative Writing Workshop (August 1953).

KAY PARLEY

Florence James doing Bill's makeup for *The Devil and Daniel Webster.* (Qu'Appelle Valley Centre, August 1953).

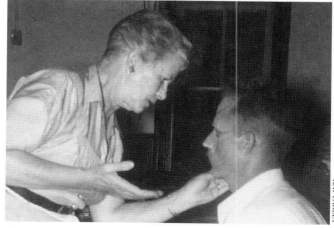

KAY PARLEY

Bill and Orm tying flies (about 1958).

Bill hunting with Beau (1958).

The Mitchells
out for a ride
(about 1958).

Bill making his
famous pancakes for
the neighbourhood
(about 1958).

Bill and Merna in
the High River
office (1958).

*The Devil's
Instrument*
(1956), CBC
Television. Left to
right: Jack Creley,
Douglas Rain.

*The Black
Bonspiel of Wullie
MacCrimmon*
(1962), CBC
Television. Left to
right: John Drainie,
Ed McNamara.

The Kite (1965), CBC Television. Left to right: Leslie Barringer, John Vernon, Jack Creley.

Royal Command performance of *Wild Rose*, May 24, 1967, in Calgary. The Honourable Angus J.B. Ogilvy and Princess Alexandra speaking with W.O. Mitchell and Merna.

Calgary house (around 1968).

W.O. in his orchid greenhouse (1975).

The Mitchells'
living room looking
into solarium.

W.O.'s office

Back to Beulah (1974), CBC Television. Directed by Eric Till. Left to right: Norma Renault, Barbara Bryne, Jayne Eastwood, Martha Henry.

Mitchell's "Pied Piper Caper" in Winnipeg schools (December 1974).

care to gamble $2000.00 advance against it on the basis of the old story?" After some negotiation, John Gray came through with the advance, and Mitchell wrote, "Thanks for your help in time of need; because of it partly I was able to complete my house deal in Calgary, and you shall see on your next trip out – what a lovely green corner we have found."[13]

— "ARTIST WHO LEAPED THE CONVENT WALL" —

Mitchell was not affiliated with any particular department at the University of Calgary. He was responsible to the president and had been appointed to do his own writing and to establish a creative-writing seminar, but he was happy to give readings and lectures to the English or Education departments. He also hoped to work with the Drama department on some of his own projects that "would in some degree re-pay the university for this marvellous thing that freed me . . . to only write."[14]

However, Mitchell's position as "an artist, who leaped the convent wall, and . . . seemed to float above the structure"[15] did not sit well with the Drama department: "That is when I ran in to the head of the drama department. Victor Mitchell called me over. I shall never forget that meeting. He said, 'The way I see it, you will teach theatre of the absurd, theatre of the cruel. Of course there is no place for you in improv.' And I said, 'I don't even know what theatre of the absurd or theatre of the cruel are.' I did, as a matter of fact, but I chose to live up to what he thought I was."[16] When Mitchell explained that he was not assigned to the Drama department for regular teaching, Victor Mitchell phoned the president's office to check. When he hung up the phone, "his face was quite forbidding." In his "innocence," Mitchell then described the play he was plan-ning to write (which later became *Back to Beulah*), and spoke of the work he was doing with Fred Diehl and Esse Ljungh on a revival of the *Jake and the Kid* radio series, which, he suggested, could be broadcast under the auspices of the Drama department from the University of Calgary.[17] Such projects, he enthused, would provide the Drama department students and faculty with a wonderful opportunity to work with professional actors, directors, and producers, and would give the university national exposure in the media. Victor Mitchell was not impressed, and said that the theatre was booked for two years in advance. Mitchell claimed he later got a list of the theatre bookings and discovered that one booking was for the Manchester Rotary Club's annual drag fashion show.

This was Mitchell's first run-in with university politics and the territorial imperative of academic departments, which jealously guard their facilities from outsiders. He was both disappointed and angered by the way he was treated by the Drama department ‒ and to a lesser extent by the English department. About this time he met Tyrone Guthrie, and they compared notes on the state of theatre in Canada. Guthrie observed that the development of theatre in Canada had been stunted in part by its lack of professional drama schools, such as those in England. As Mitchell recalled, Guthrie argued that schooling in drama had been co-opted by departments of drama in Canadian universities that attracted, for the most part, third-raters who did not have to compete in the real world of professional drama because they had tenured faculty positions, and who camouflaged their mediocre talents by dabbling in experimental or avant-garde productions.

Later that year Mitchell watched in amazement as an outside production of Bertolt Brecht's *The Resistible Rise of Arturo Ui* was virtually sabotaged by the props and sound departments of the university's theatre. He realized that he had run into a bureaucratic system that was very insecure about outside people, and he gave up on any hope of collaborative projects. The university's beautiful theatre, "like the Huston Astrodome," would continue to have "no goddamned football team to play in it." In the end, this was probably a good thing, for he said to himself, "I'm off the hook now"[18] for getting involved in a stage project. He shelved his play and turned his attention to working on "The Alien."

Mitchell loved teaching because it had the performer element that he thrived on. As well, though, he strongly believed that it was his responsibility to discharge the debt of mentorship he owed his previous teachers (Emily Murray and F.M Salter, in particular). He believed that writing workshops could help to shorten a writer's apprenticeship from five to ten years. At the university he conducted a two-hour weekly workshop and held individual interviews with each writer once a week. His students nicknamed his approach to teaching "Mitchell's Messy Method," and a few of the more advanced students (who also met on their own) called themselves the Mission Band, since Mitchell had said they were missionaries of the word. As one student said of the workshop, "There is no formal approach to our creative writing, there are no lectures, no analytical study of plot or storyline, conflict, crisis or character,"[19] and another student explained, "He was trying to teach us a process rather than get us to write a short story."[20]

Finding sensuous fragments and telling details of place, event, character, and dialogue from the writer's "stored past" was at the heart of Mitchell's "messy method." Through this process he encouraged writers to abandon their critical and reasoning side and retrieve from their subconscious the sensations of smell, taste, touch, and sound in all the freshness of their first encounter, which was often in childhood. During this finding process, he encouraged students to forget grammar, punctuation, discipline, refinement, and simply to write down whatever floated to the top of their consciousness. Developing a plot, a theme, and characters without the sensuous bits was like having, he said, a harness, but no horse. After this initial stage of rough writing, however, the writer must employ his critical faculties to shape the chaos of rough material he has discovered, at which point Mitchell's job as mentor was to comment on whether the organizing machinery was clanking: "With a good piece of art or a magician's illusion the machinery mustn't show. It would spoil the trick. Art must conceal art or in other words possess grace."[21]

Bill was exhilarated by the group and by progress on his own writing. He had a small setback in February 1969 when he became ill and had to have an emergency gall bladder operation. Given that his brother had died just seven months earlier as a result of the same operation, Bill and Merna were tense, but, as Merna wrote on her Christmas card to the Grays, "Bill came through a bad gall bladder operation beautifully," and furthermore, there was "no evidence of the ulcer he's been babying 15 years."[22]

— LIFE IN CALGARY —

Calgary was a mixed blessing. Ironically it was probably more difficult, initially, for Merna than for Bill. Bill was motivated by both his own writing and the Mission Band and spent much of the day at his university office, away from Merna. Merna had been excited about enrolling in some sociology courses, but Bill's response squelched that: "Why the Christ would you take sociology courses!? Take some real courses – history or philosophy!" He dismissed sociology as a "pseudo" discipline, viewing it as jargon-ridden and dealing in superficial generalities, diametrically opposed to what was, for him, the sacrosanct principle of the unique individual (his portrait of June Melquist in *Roses Are Difficult Here* is in part an attack on sociology). If Merna's heart had really been in it, she would have pursued her plan in spite of Bill's response, but, at forty-eight, she felt she had more than enough to look after with W.O. Mitchell Ltd. and organizing the details of Bill's three-ring circus life as writer, teacher, and performer/celebrity.

Orm, Barbara, and their two children moved to Calgary in the fall of 1969 so, with Hugh now teaching and Willa still at high school, all the Mitchells were together, which Merna and Bill enjoyed. Willa was causing some worry not just because she was not doing well in some classes at school but because she had begun hanging out with what her parents considered to be the wrong crowd. Willa, however, was feeling ignored. Some years later she observed, "I am speculating that the kind of parenting they did with Orm and Hughie was different than the kind of parenting they did with me. I know for certain that they knew nothing of my life outside of the house and that they were preoccupied. Now maybe that is a common thing with parents."[23] Merna and Bill did more socializing in Calgary because of Bill's university connection, and Merna enjoyed having dinner parties, which accounted for some of the preoccupation that Willa felt. From his early years Bill had respected people's personal boundaries. Thus, with Merna, with his children when they grew into adolescence, and with his friends, he did not pry into private areas. He was more aware of Willa's rebellious actions than she realized, but he allowed her room to manage her own life. Merna, as always, tried to preserve the peace between Bill and Willa.

A significant element in this change was Merna's drinking. Drinking had been a part of the social culture in High River and Merna had fallen into a regular pattern of a few drinks before and after dinner. Willa recalled how this affected their relationship: "I would confront Dad in the Calgary years and say that Mum is drinking too much and he would say things like, 'Well, there was a time in High River when she would go down and fall asleep in front of the television.' That clarified for me an image from the past of what that was tied up with. I was not aware specifically that that had to do with drinking, but I was aware that when she parked herself in the basement I could get away with a lot more. I could stay up later."[24]

Merna was not as happy as she had anticipated during these early years in Calgary. Two or three of the most promising of Bill's students demanded time outside of class, which Bill was happy to provide, but which Merna grew to resent. Partly this was protectiveness of his writing time, but she may have felt displaced as the prime listener of Bill's work. While the stimulation of the university and cultural events excited her, she was lonelier during the daytime when she no longer had friends to visit just down the street, and she did not have her volunteer work.

Bill had been asked to give a two-week writing workshop in Halifax at Mount Saint Vincent in the summer of 1969, an offer he eagerly accepted so that Merna could return to her native Nova Scotia. She had always wanted to visit her birthplace, Mahone Bay, which she had left when she was five years old. It was also on this trip that Bill and Merna visited Bridgetown and finally met Ernest

Buckler. They had not had much contact with Buckler since his 1953 letter, but had promised that they would someday visit him in Nova Scotia. Merna found Buckler painfully shy, but they all clicked just as they had through their letters. Bill recalled a conversation he and Buckler had about the nature of the type of writing they both engaged in, an apolitical writing geared "towards the individual interior":

> There have been several times when I have regretted not being enticed into this area [the political]. And the same goes for Ernest Buckler. As I walked down the railroad track with him, he just burst out one time (he'd had too much Cinzano), and he said, "Any god damned turnip farmer with one crop, or one vegetable from his whole crop, has done something more important than I have done with my life." I knew what he meant. And then I remembered when Mother and I and Willa saw Z – and I cried. We came outside and I said, "I've wasted my life." I was so moved by that thing. I could not deny the impact for good upon the attitudes of people once they had seen that.[25]

No doubt he shared with Buckler his excitement about the growth of "The Alien" into a very different novel that would be, in fact, his most successful novel in terms of blending a "political" vision with the exploration of individual interiors.

‑ "OLD KACKY AND THE VANISHING POINT" ‑

Mitchell now had been free-fall writing on the new book for two years and a great deal of this writing focused on remaking Carlyle's interior world. He decided to give Carlyle a childhood past, and he began to draw on memories of his own childhood to do this. Free-fall memories of the aunt he stayed with when his mother went with his father to Rochester for his gall bladder operation were the seeds for Aunt Pearl and little dead Willis's toy room. He also ascribed to Carlyle his childhood experience of selling lingerie in a "prairie whorehouse."[26] As Mitchell began to explore new thematic territory

successful as perspective drawings ---- you couldn't tell how it

would come out the way that perspective drawings could be predicted.....

it was hard to guess how wet or how not wet to get your paper ---

xxxldxx amd generally he got his too wet and it ---- as it dried it

shrankx and pulled unevenly so that it rippled and ended up all a mess.....

The smell of paints --- and the squares like tofee --- in their little

tin dishes --- and the squares of paint were like brilliant peices

of toffee in bright tin dishes ..... and it was a shame to take the

paint brush actually and

and besides it didn't look like a God damned sunset ......

XXXXXX PAINT
.... the paint had a subtle smell --- a flat smell ---- a flatly

xxxxxxx curved smell -----the loveliest one of course being the

red or possobly the blue and as soon as he saw the blue -- his

heart flipped and he thought of poor little dead Willis's

blue balls --- and then he thought of --- a blue baloon

that has been blown up tight and then exhaled and deflated ---

and a blue little scrotum bag .....

Going into --- the trip to Mr. MacKaye's room --- from plastacine

xxxxxxxxxxxxxxxxxxxxxxxxxx and the fragile smell of paste

to the flat tin box with protractor and compass and a tiny

geometry pencil which must be needle sharp so that it would

make points and measrement marks exact .... to geography and

atlas .... a new world --- and the kidney bean yellow spots in Africa

and California and Australia where gold was --- and like a miser going

over the bean shaped yellow spots that meant gold ---- and finding

them in British Columbia and in North West Territories and

in Northern ONtario .....

Example of W.O. Mitchell's "free-fall," in this case for The Vanishing Point

here, he was also in some ways coming to terms with his own Presbyterian and Victorian upbringing and the emotional and psychological damage that culture could have on the child's world, damage that comes to roost in adulthood. In *Wind, The Devil's Instrument,* and the *Jake and the Kid* stories he had explored the education of the child's imagination and how that process is nourished or thwarted by adult guardians, culture, religion, and place. But he was now broadening and deepening his exploration of these issues.

As well as free-fall writing, Mitchell was doing a great deal of free-fall talking about his developing novel. Just as his pores were wide open for usable fragments of life experience for his characters and stories, he was adept at picking up and building on ideas and insights gleaned from conversation.

During my two years at the University of Calgary, my father and I frequently used each other as sounding boards – he for his novel and I for my work on William Blake. He was fascinated by my work on Blake's depiction of the child's world in his poetry and art. We talked of Blake's ironic exploration of children and adults being lost and found, his concepts of innocence, experience, and Beulah, and how the adult's rational and materialistic world stunted the child's innate imaginative capacity. My father soaked up Blake's vision, which ended up playing a significant role in his developing novel and, later, his television play, Back to Beulah.[27]

In writing about my father's work, it hit me how deeply and indelibly he has "stained" me in my outlook on life and on my aesthetic predilections. But our relationship was, to use one of his favourite phrases, one of "creative partners" and the flow of influence ran both ways. We learn from our children as they learn from us, and what they return is inevitably tinged with what we taught them. He gave me Steinbeck when I was an "illiterate" teenager, and I gave Steinbeck back to him at a crucial point in the development of The Vanishing Point. *I also gave him a window into Blake's exploration of the education of the imagination. But I also sense that in some profound way my father's influence had pointed me toward Blake, or at least made me predisposed to Blake's vision, long before I had ever heard of him.*

Mitchell had been feeling more and more uneasy about his title, "The Alien," which had marked the essential characteristic of his original tragic anti-hero. One afternoon in the fall of 1969, he experienced a free-fall epiphany that crystallized for him the thematic and character arcs of the new novel and also gave him his title:[28]

My room was in the Student Union Building. I looked out the window, as I often do sometimes. I couldn't on that particular day get going. I said, "Okay forget it, let's just find, let's just write, say yes to whatever floats to the surface whether it's relevant to this piece of work or not." It's a little like taking a holiday. A holiday from artistic responsibility is what it is. And what floated up for me was a schoolteacher of mine in Haig school of whom I was extremely frightened. I'd always loved the art class, which was only for an hour at the end of the day, on a Friday I think. It wasn't nearly so important as Geography or Arithmetic or Civics. I remembered the vanishing point, how we had taken it up, and the delight and the joy of doing this essentially mechanistic thing of drawing a line across a sheet of paper and putting a dot and then drawing lines for the trees, the telephone poles, until you had a whole funnel of lines scaling to this vanishing point. And I pulled over a fresh sheet of paper and I proceeded to draw a line, and then I did it. I didn't have a ruler as we had in Mr. McKay's room, but I did the vanishing point, and then I did the fence, telephone poles, everything else.

That was quite irrelevant to the novel – I was really goofing off. I was fidgeting around, doodling, doing the vanishing point and – BANGO! I guess it must have been implicit in everything else. I suddenly then came upon the thematic idea of the vanishing point and saw it as applicable to man in his history. I realized that culture, communities, races seemed to shine and then seemed to be sucked down the vanishing point. I realized how relevant this silly thing was to my concern about the red segment of society, which is now in a state of despair and about to be sucked down the vanishing point. I also realized that individual humans in middle age can reach a very tricky part of their journey when they are about to be sucked down the vanishing point, or wish that they might be sucked down the vanishing point. The result was a complete re-writing and recasting of the whole bloody thing. This was when Aunt Pearl began to show up with such importance. It meant that I had to, and quite willingly, go back over it — work over it again and take outrageous liberties and discard and re-find again what would be necessary for this new meaning web.[29]

Mitchell speculated that this memory, which had no logical relation to "what so far had grown in the novel," floated up because of "the torque subconsciously exerted upon me by what was growing structurally about the novel I was committed to."[30]

The interior action of the new novel now involved Carlyle's self-examination, which is triggered by Victoria's disappearance in the city. In the midst of his emotional and psychological crisis, Carlyle is visited by vivid memories from his childhood, one of which is Old Kacky's vanishing-point class. At first Carlyle is fascinated by this geometrical exercise, but before the art period is over, "his drawing didn't satisfy him. Empty. It needed something" (*VP* 319). When Old Kacky discovers that Carlyle has added a poplar and a pine to his drawing, he demands, "'All right. Why did you do that?'" Carlyle hesitantly responds, ". . . it . . . just happened." Old Kacky insists that he has been guilty of "deliberate disobedience" and straps him. Spontaneous, artistic impulses, whose products accidentally "just happen," have no place in Old Kacky's world.

Old Kacky is based to a large extent on one of Mitchell's teachers in Weyburn who, he recalls, "scared the shit out of us."[31] And this is, literally, what Old Kacky succeeds in doing to the eleven-year-old Carlyle. After the painful strapping, he gives Carlyle five minutes alone in his office to compose himself before returning to class. Alone, Carlyle is overcome with a feeling that Old Kacky has "vanished" him from his classmates and, more terrifying, he was "being vanished from himself" (*VP* 322). His bowels cramp, he realizes his time is up, and he is guilty of another spontaneous "accident." He takes the neat stack of file folders out of Old Kacky's bottom desk drawer, relieves himself there, and puts the folders back. The implicit message here is that Old Kacky's puritanical, rule-dominated vision of "how to be" is, as his nickname suggests, "crap."

Mitchell's looking out the window and doodling was the seed for this key chapter in the last section of the novel. By May 1970 he had worked this episode into a short story, "Old Kacky and the Vanishing Point," and sent it to *Atlantic Monthly*, hoping that Dudley Cloud was still there. Cloud, however, had retired and *Atlantic Monthly* turned it down. He then sent it to *Canadian Forum*, which accepted it. When it came out in the October 1971 issue, two pink flamingos mysteriously appeared on Mitchell's front lawn. They had been secretly delivered (and suggestively positioned) in the middle of the night. The previous year he had delighted his writing class with descriptions from his new novel of Luton and his menagerie of cast garden ornaments, which included a flock of flamingos. In one of his fantasy escapes, Carlyle imagines the cast ornaments fornicating and multiplying at night and putting the world in danger of being "up to its arse in fluorescent flamingos!" (*VP* 41). When Mitchell verified that members of his Mission Band had delivered the flamingos, he proclaimed the establishment of the Order of the Pink Flamingo. Whenever a Mission Band member published a piece, the pink flamingos would appear on his or her front lawn.

~ FINAL YEAR AT UNIVERSITY OF CALGARY ~

Work on the new novel was "going fine," as Mitchell reported to John Gray in the spring of 1970. He felt it was "a unique novel" with "carefully worked out thematic webbing" and "petit point of symbol."[32] But on May 4 he was jolted out of this writing paradise by "a xeroxed copy of a letter to the MacEwan Hall space committee, saying that . . . the University have no need for a space for me as the appointment ends after August 31st." His original contract had been for a two-year probationary period, but he had had no indication in April, when speaking to one of the administrators, that his appointment would be terminated.[33]

Merna burst into tears when Bill brought this devastating news home.[34] They had moved from High River and taken out a large mortgage on a new house, assuming that Bill would be at the university for a number of years. Merna was frightened: "I went through a very bad time for a few years. I felt that we had been let down and there was a lot of anger in me at the time." Merna had "a tremendous fear" of not having financial security, and she was sure that Bill felt the same pressure "though he never, never showed it or expressed it to me. I think probably it was very hard on him, that it was so hard on me at that time. And it was, it was."[35]

Mitchell wrote President A.W.R. Carrothers and attached a report on his work for the past two years in which he listed his many lectures and speaking engagements (eighteen addresses in 1969 and more than thirty in 1970), which he felt, by association, reflected attention on the university. He pointed out his hope that the revival of *Jake and the Kid* on CBC Radio could have been done at the university and that, on the frontispiece of the new novel, *The Vanishing Point*, he would be identified as the university's writer-in-residence.[36] As Dr. Jim Black, a friend and supporter from the English Department, said, "If we had been more hospitable to W.O. and if we had been more energetic and imaginative in curriculum, both credit and non-credit, we could probably have kept him and used him optimally and basked in the glow of the quite rapid issuing of the books that came out afterwards. And then we could have said that he wrote *The Vanishing Point* at the University of Calgary."[37]

Jim Black and Dr. Gordon Swan, a member of the board of governors and a neighbour, attempted to speak on Mitchell's behalf, but with limited success. At a board meeting Swan pointed out that the letter of appointment stated Mitchell had expectation of tenure. President Carrothers ignored this and, with the support of the board chair, argued that they give Mitchell only a one-year renewal.[38] On June 8 he wrote Mitchell, saying that, as there was some element of doubt as to the interpretation of the phrase "twenty-two month probationary period," he would recommend renewing the appointment for one more final year.[39]

Mitchell was shuffled from his grand office among the students in MacEwan Hall to a small office in the Arts and Administration Building, and Jim Black scrambled to find difficult-to-come-by space for him to meet his students in a coffee room in the English Department. The glow of what had been such a "beautiful" appointment was irreparably extinguished.

Mitchell had established himself as a high-profile writer-in-residence, not simply speaking to students at the University of Calgary but to students in universities and in high schools throughout the province and country. Attesting to his growing reputation as a leading Canadian writer, he was invited by David Silcox, senior arts officer at the Canada Council, to join a week-long discussion at the end of July on the arts, humanities, and social sciences at Stanley House, a country retreat, on the Gaspé Peninsula. Among those invited were the architects Raymond Affleck and Raymond Moriyama, Les Levine, the avant-garde artist now living in New York, and Patrick Watson, television producer and host of *Close-Up* and *This Hour Has Seven Days*. The creative energy and circulation of ideas at the "Silcox Bids Us Shine Week," as Mitchell called it, made quite an impact on Mitchell, as did one of the extracurricular shenanigans.

When W.O. came back from this trip, he regaled the family with how he accepted a dare from Patrick Watson. During the afternoon breaks the guests swam in the Grande-Cascapédia River and Watson, who had flown his own plane to Stanley House, took guests up for sightseeing flights. W.O. declined the offer, and when Watson pressed and asked if he was afraid of flying, W.O. responded, "Only with amateur pilots." Miffed, Watson retorted that he was not an amateur pilot and that W.O. was a chicken. W.O., mercilessly teased by the others, spent the rest of the afternoon sunning and doing laps out to the centre of the river under the railway bridge. He noted the depth of the water and estimated the height of the bridge to be about forty feet. When Watson came back from his last flight, both he and his passenger pointedly exclaiming about how beautiful the Gaspé looked from the plane, W.O. said, "Okay, you think I'm chickenshit? Well, Patrick, I'll tell you what. If I jump off the railway bridge into the river, will you?" Watson said he must be crazy. There was no way he would jump off the bridge – and he dared W.O. to do it. W.O. climbed up to the bridge, walked along the rails to the centre, waved, and executed a graceful swan dive. When he came out of the water to general applause, Watson admitted that it was a pretty impressive dive. He added that neither he nor W.O. were chicken – nor amateurs – at whatever they did.

In the fall of 1970 a political crisis occurred that deeply upset Bill and Merna. On October 5, 1970, James Cross, the British trade commissioner, was kidnapped by the FLQ (Front de Libération du Québec). Five days later Pierre Laporte, the minister of labour in Robert Bourassa's Liberal Quebec government, was kidnapped. These acts galvanized crowds of Quebec nationalists who rallied and proclaimed their antagonism toward Bourassa's federalist Liberal government. On October 16, Prime Minister Pierre Trudeau proclaimed the War Measures Act, sent in troops, and ordered suspects to be brought into custody. The next day the body of Pierre Laporte was found in the trunk of a car. Feelings of panic, confusion, and horror descended on the entire nation. The CBC asked Mitchell to comment on the murder of Laporte, and on the evening of October 18 his address was telecast on *Weekend* just before a panel convened to address the political consequences of Laporte's murder.[40] Mitchell's address was moving and effective; it cut across French-English antagonisms and appealed to man's humanity. He began very simply, "There's been a death in my family." His theme was, as always, the necessity of a family, personal or national, to bridge with the other "<u>against</u> the heart of darkness." The death of Laporte had been "the destruction of a bridge – of a pattern" and man's life patterns must somehow reassert themselves against the "<u>game</u>" of "destruction" and of "terror." He concluded, "I know one thing – the death of Mr. Laporte is a death in my family – our family."[41] The following comment appears on the CBC script of Mitchell's address: "The passage was written at two hours' notice and was prepared solely to be read aloud. The words, the rhythms, and the punctuation suggest the author's sense of urgency and the intensity of his feeling. But he spoke his words without haste, his controlled delivery emphasizing his emotion and his concern for human values."

Barry Callaghan, who moderated the following panel, recalled being in the studio and watching Mitchell give his address:

> My executive producer flew Mitchell in to make a commentary about this, to say something to the nation. And I was flabbergasted. I'm seldom at a loss for words and many of the people I know are not at a loss for words. But to somehow take upon yourself the pain and the emotion that a nation could be feeling at such a moment, and tunnel that pain and that emotion – and at the same time the necessary triumph of the spirit that must take place – through yourself, is an extraordinary act of generosity. And I have never forgotten the way Mitchell did that, and saying to myself, "Whatever I do in my life, there is no way I would ever be able to do *that*." That was too generous, too vulnerable, too open.[42]

The speech was not politically motivated in the least, though both Bill and Merna were proud to be Liberals (in the Conservative West), approving, particularly, the Liberal support for the arts, the CBC, the NFB, and the Canada Council. In fact, a few years earlier in 1962 when they were still in High River, Mitchell had actively supported the Liberal candidate, Jim Coutts. As Coutts explained, "He introduced me on a wonderful night in May in the High River Memorial Centre with seventy-one people in the audience, and he chose as his text the story of David and Goliath, likening Coutts to David and the old Diefenbaker giant to Goliath. I am afraid that the comparison ended that night, for on election day, the giant won, David lost his $200 deposit and the great Liberal crusade bit the prairie dust."[43] Bill admired Trudeau more than any other prime minister he had lived under because Trudeau was a federalist and had succeeded in broadening Diefenbaker's Bill of Rights (1960) into the Charter of Rights (1982), binding on all levels of government.

A few years later they were very excited to meet Trudeau at a dinner held in Calgary in honour of Queen Elizabeth during her royal tour in the summer of 1973. When Merna and Bill had an opportunity to shake hands with Trudeau and talk to him, Bill chose to talk about their common love, springboard diving. Once again, on April 9, 1974, when Bill was a guest panelist on *Front Page Challenge*, he was able to speak with Trudeau when he was the mystery guest. He had two questions for Trudeau: What was your highest degree difficulty dive, and would you consider yourself a Platonist?

Bill and Merna lamented the parochial and self-serving politics of various premiers and their governments that, they felt, were more prone than the federal government to run roughshod over the rights of individuals and minority groups. They were particularly outraged by Alberta's "Let the eastern bastards freeze in the dark" campaign, its response to the National Energy Program. This inspired Mitchell to add some overt political satire to the stage-play version of *The Black Bonspiel of Wullie McCrimmon*. The Devil explains to Wullie that, although "sin is an infinitely renewable commodity," he has problems with Hell's non-renewable energy ("Deep thermal energy – mine! It is all mine!"). He ends his speech with, "We have an expression down below: 'Let those upper bastards freeze in the dark'" (*DWO* 118), a line that echoes Calgary mayor Ralph Klein's notorious comment about "eastern bastards."

In the early 1970s Mitchell's reputation, both as a serious writer and as a public personality, grew tremendously. Canadian literature in general was rising rapidly in popularity in schools and universities. After a decade of debate on the topic of whether Canada had an identity, writers such as Laurence, Atwood, Richler, Davies, and Mitchell were demonstrating clearly that it did. An unofficial calculation from Macmillan showed that 2,863 copies of *Who Has Seen the Wind* were sold to twenty-two universities and colleges in 1970, and this did not take into account numbers used in high schools. Based on those figures, both *Wind* and *Jake and the Kid* were reprinted in the paperback Laurentian Library series in 1972.[44]

Mitchell's three years at the University of Calgary were busy and productive. He had been able to devote much more of his time to serious fiction writing and had completed the first two parts of *The Vanishing Point*, which he sent to Gray in July 1971. In his covering letter he wrote, "Here's *The Vanishing Point* – the hundred or so pages from part three, I am doing – I hope by mid-August – a matter of last draft. I thought it might be a good idea to show you I have actually been a novelist over the past four years."[45] Gray responded, "I haven't doubted that you have actually been a novelist for the past four years – not for a minute."[46]

IO

THE VANISHING POINT

~ 1971 to 1973 ~

MITCHELL WAS offered a ten-month position at the University of Alberta (for $17,000), beginning in September 1971, which was then extended for the next term (until June 1973). This was not a writer-in-residency position, for he had three courses to teach: a first-year course (Literature in Progress); an introduction to creative writing (which he shared with Douglas Barbour, who taught the poetry segment); and the senior Creative Writing Fiction course (customarily taught by Rudy Wiebe, who was on sabbatical).

The literature course dealt with recent works that had not yet been canonized such as Robert Kroetsch's *Studhorse Man* (1969) and George Ryga's play *The Ecstasy of Rita Joe* (1967, pub. 1971). Mitchell chose Margaret Laurence's *A Jest of God* (1966) as an optional text and added, as one of his personal favourites, Alice Munro's *Dance of the Happy Shades* (1968). Ruth Fraser, one of his first-year students and the McClelland & Stewart agent for northern Alberta, said she learned more about "appreciating the art of writing and the love of words from Bill than [she] did from anyone else." In particular, she recalled how Mitchell taught Alice Munro's *Dance of the Happy Shades*:

He had a wonderful way of showing you where a scene was that you would think was seamless. He used to say that she wrote as if it was effortless because you could never tell where the energy had been increased or decreased because there was the same lovely follow through. But then he would say, "I'll bet she had a bitch of a time right here." And he taught me to look that way. So that when I became a full time book editor [working with first-time writers], that was something I was able to do – even with non-fiction. I couldn't have done that without Bill. But teaching Alice Munro, I think, was a joy for him because he loved her work so much.[1]

His creative-writing seminars were conducted much as they had been in Calgary, with the focus on process rather than product. Candas Dorsey, now a speculative fiction writer, was nineteen years old when she enrolled in Mitchell's class. She found that "the sense of freedom and permission that you have with that process is invaluable." Dorsey also recalled how he regaled the students with scenes from *The Vanishing Point*: "He was going to the faith healing temples, and he would take a pinch of snuff and wave his hand around wildly as he was reciting. And he basically did these faith healers for us – like stand-up comedy."[2]

The next term Frances Itani was in his writing class. She handed in some of her writing, and in the second class she thought he kept looking at her in a curious way: "At the break we went up the hall to a dumpy little kitchen to make a cup of tea and he was standing in a room on the way there and he hauled me in by one arm. And he said, 'Jesus, you're good.' I thought he was going to tell me I was out. And that is when I started to write." Very impressed with her work during the term, Mitchell encouraged her to take Rudy Wiebe's senior writing class the next fall, and in preparation she wrote a short story: "Bill looked at it for me. It was my first short story and he wrote to Bob Weaver and Weaver bought it – he bought my first story. It is a nice way to start!"[3] Itani went on to become an accomplished poet, short story writer, and novelist.[4]

Classes were arranged so that Bill could commute by airbus, teaching Tuesday to Thursday, then return home to Calgary for four days of work on his own writing. It was a taxing schedule for him, and Merna was lonely, but he could not count on freelancing to pay his mortgage. As always, though, he settled quickly into his new environment, made friends easily, and was energized by his writing students. Wiebe recalled when he and his wife, Tina, had Mitchell for dinner:

> We were absolutely dazzled because it was one of those evenings where he was in unbelievable form and he told stories . . . the entire evening. . . . I'd just been reading a book by Joseph Gold – *Story Species: Our Life Literature Connection* – his theory is that the thing that distinguishes humans as a species is that they tell stories. Well, Bill Mitchell was, I think – if that's true – one of the most developed of the species! Supremely developed of the species! Everything was a story to him.[5]

A few years later, when Mitchell received a Doctor of Letters from the University of Alberta, Rudy Wiebe gave the citation, describing Mitchell as "Canada's most marvelous word-spinner."[6]

— ARCHIE NICOTINE AND HEALLY RICHARDS —

Both Mitchell and Wiebe were working on novels that focused on Native culture; Wiebe shared parts of *The Temptation of Big Bear* with Mitchell, who, in turn, talked about *The Vanishing Point*. Wiebe was also working on a collection of short stories by western writers[7] and asked Bill to contribute. The story "Hercules Salvage" drew on material from the first two sections of *The Vanishing Point* dealing with Archie Nicotine's aborted attempt to buy rings and a rebuilt carburetor for his truck, and having to be bailed out of jail by the evangelist Heally Richards. Archie Nicotine and Heally Richards, two new major characters, were by now firmly entrenched in the novel.

Archie began taking shape in Mitchell's first year at the University of Calgary: "He was a character that threatened to take over *The Vanishing Point.* He's an amalgam of an Indian I knew, my second son, and a Hungarian guy [who helped Bill mould his boat hulls]. . . . That Hungarian and I would be working and he'd say, 'Beel, Beel, ah gypsy Beel. You sweet, kindly, gentle, generous Beel. The one trouble, you're focking stupid!' Then he would always end up saying, just like Archie, 'And that is de whole situation. Whole situation!'"[8]

The Vanishing Point explores the difficulty of humans "bridging." Carlyle wonders if the desire to get "out of my skin and into yours" is only a "love illusion" (*VP* 216). Interestingly, bridging became, for Mitchell, a technical question as well. His third-person omniscient narrator often slips into the stream of consciousness of Carlyle, Heally Richards, and Fyfe – all white characters. However, he was uneasy about directly entering the "envelope of consciousness" of his Stoney characters even though he had become very close to them and felt he had subconsciously absorbed enough of their culture to write about them. He felt particularly vulnerable when it came to Victoria, who was not only Stoney, but also female – two barriers for him to bridge.

Mitchell felt Wiebe's attempt to portray Big Bear from the inside was daring but not completely successful. However, there is one instance in which Mitchell does slip into Archie Nicotine's stream of consciousness, perhaps because of his discussions with Wiebe. Although Wiebe recalls that they talked a lot about this issue, they talked about it as a technical problem, not as an issue of "appropriation of voice:"

> We both just naturally assumed they're human beings and you
> understand their particular problems, and he had worked on
> a reserve and I had done a lot of research and talked to quite a
> number of native people and done a lot of research on Big Bear.
> I can't remember ever thinking that these people are so unique
> that we can't possibly imagine what they're thinking. Never
> entered our heads, I don't think. You see, neither of us –

certainly I – never dared to write about them until I had really tried to understand their beliefs and their basic fundamental humanity – the way they looked at the world.⁹

As part of his research for Heally Richards, Mitchell attended the Emanuel Chapel of the Free Assembly of God (Pentecost), where he listened to evangelists from Australia, Alabama, and California. One proved the existence and efficacy of Jesus Christ through a reading of *Snow White and the Seven Dwarfs*, and another claimed his laying on of hands moved God to miraculously fill the cavity of a woman's tooth with gold (but because of her fear, the next morning it had turned to brass and then to nothing at all).¹⁰ He had gone twice every Sunday "until I blew my cover and people started recognizing me."¹¹ In the last meeting he attended, the preacher began his sermon by exhorting the congregation to beware of Satan visiting in the guise of a follower and looked directly at Mitchell, who was sitting in the back pew. Having found plenty of rich material for his character, and sensing that he had outworn his welcome, Mitchell, as he put it, "arose and departed in peace."

Mitchell ascribed much of what he heard at these meetings to his American faith healer, Heally Richards. Richards meets his nemesis in Archie Nicotine, who is "a religious joiner" and "had been in turn: original Methodist, Presbyterian, United, Baptist, Pentecost, Mormon" (*VP* 17). Archie's anarchic and pagan existentialism disrupts the evangelist's world as well as Carlyle's puritan, civilized world. It is Archie who persuades Richards to try to heal Old Esau Rider, who is dying of TB.¹²

Mitchell delighted in performing his Heally Richards sermons. When he described on a Calgary television show how he had based Richards on life models, and performed one of his sermons, a woman wrote an angry letter to the *Calgary Herald* saying W.O. Mitchell "should be ashamed of himself" for "hold [ing] ministers of the Gospel up to public ridicule and scorn."¹³ The seeds for Mitchell's fascination with con characters, such as Heally Richards, Jake the rainmaker, and Professor Noble Winesinger the medicine man, go back to his encounters with Gypsy Smith and Aimee Semple McPherson in California when he was thirteen years old.[14] He often, humorously, referred to himself as a "phony" and a "con," for he was aware of the ironic similarities of his ham performances, which sold hidden truths in illusions for a fee, to the evangelist's rousing sermons, which sold faith for a fee.

Teaching and commuting were time-consuming and Mitchell was not carving out enough of his own time to finish *The Vanishing Point*. He wrote Gray at Macmillan, "It isn't good for it to lie around for long stages, and I have been quite unhappy since I left it last fall."[15] As well, a film opportunity turned up which, being too tempting a financial proposition to pass up, further delayed his completing the last hundred pages of the novel.

— *ALIEN THUNDER:* A GREEK TRAGEDY —

In October 1971, just as he had begun his term at the university, Mitchell was approached by Claude Fournier and Marie-Jose Raymond of Onyx Films in Montreal to write a feature film script based on an incident involving a clash between a young Cree, Almighty Voice, and the North West Mounted Police that took place in 1895 in the Duck Lake area of northern Saskatchewan. Mitchell was immediately interested in the project. He had become increasingly attracted to film as a serious medium for his work, and he saw that this story could have the same kind of emotional and political "impact for good upon the attitudes of people" that the film *Z* had on him a few years earlier when he had his moment of self-questioning about the usefulness of his own writing. Here was a similar drama that, by dramatizing both its political and human elements, he could treat as a universal Greek tragedy.

Fournier and Raymond came to Calgary to pitch the project, and Mitchell was immediately taken with them and with the story. Fournier had good credentials. He had been with the NFB in the 1960s, worked on more than 150 documentaries, and his first feature film, *Deux femmes en or*, had won the award for the best Canadian feature of 1970 with the biggest box-office success in Canadian film history to that date.[16] What Mitchell did not know, at first, was that *Deux femmes en or* was really soft porn, an erotic comedy – not a likely forerunner to the historic project on Almighty Voice with Mitchell as writer and the RCMP as resource and funding agents. However, at the time, with a budget of $1.5 million, apparently the first to exceed $1 million in Canada, and Donald Sutherland slated to play the lead, this project looked very promising.[17] The RCMP intended to premiere the movie during their centennial celebrations in May 1973. They helped with the reconstruction of the Duck Lake post, authenticated artillery and clothing, and even provided their mounted police from the celebrated Musical Ride (who, somewhat incongruously, performed the charge on the bluff near the end of the movie).

Historically, the incident began with a minor event when Almighty Voice shot a cow that had wandered on to the reserve. He was arrested and taken to the Duck Lake jail. During the night, however, he escaped, and over the next few days was pursued by Sergeant Colebrook of the NWMP, whom he shot. Because of the spectre of the Riel Rebellion only ten years before, this incident took on major implications and precipitated a nineteen-month search, one of the longest manhunts conducted by the NWMP in the Canadian West. On May 27, 1897, Almighty Voice and two companions were pinned down in a bluff. They repulsed two charges, killing three people and wounding a number of others. More forces and artillery were called in, including a seven- and nine-pound cannon. On May 29, with more than one hundred police and civilian volunteers surrounding the bluff, and Cree and townspeople watching, Almighty Voice and his two comrades were gunned down. When the shelling stopped, Almighty Voice's mother sang a death song for her son, and the bodies were retrieved to be handed back to their people. Almighty Voice had been seen as a "bad Indian" by the NWMP, but he was now a hero for his people.

Mitchell saw the story as a classical Greek tragedy in which "mortals are caught [and] they can only struggle."[18] He was most intrigued by the story that Almighty Voice escaped from prison out of fear for his life because he heard men hammering and sawing outside his jailhouse window and he mistakenly thought they were preparing a gallows for his hanging the next day. Mitchell, fascinated by how trivial and accidental events precipitated such a tragedy, did not see this as a "good guys, bad guys, the noble Indian, the villainous cop sort of thing,"[19] but as a human, existential drama in which "we perform our magnificent and graceful and humorous human trick of living to the best of our ability limited by fate." He envisioned the ending battle played out before "two Greek choruses," one voice belonging to the police and spectator settlers with the thunder of the canon, and the other the One Arrow band answering with the death chant.[20]

Mitchell saw the crucial issue as the clash of differing viewpoints. When Almighty Voice is taken to jail for shooting the cow, he cannot understand the white man's concepts of ownership and justice: "What is wrong! . . . I'll ride in with you and tell them the sufferin' in my people's heart! . . . I'll tell them they are wrong about what is wrong!" Colebrook, on the other hand, argues that civilization means "order – law," although his wife counters that "Civilization means – compassion."[21] Mitchell heightened the drama by creating a fictional character, Sergeant Dan Candy, a friend and colleague of the historical Sergeant Colebrook. Irreverent and freewheeling, but a decent man who mediates between the Native and the white views, Candy is modelled on Jake Trumper (indeed, he was called Jake Trumper in the early discussions).

Donald Sutherland was enticed into this project, to play Dan Candy, because of his admiration for Mitchell's *Jake and the Kid*, which he had heard on radio as a youngster in Bridgewater, Nova Scotia. As well, though, Sutherland said he "was obsessed with some kind of national pride" and "had a passionate desire" to make Canada "an integral part of my success," a desire that "affected my politics, it affected the women I married, it affected the books that I read, the humor that I felt."[22] Mitchell's and Sutherland's names gave this movie tremendous credibility as did that of Chief Dan George, who had become a major star two years earlier with his role in *Little Big Man* (1970). Chief Dan George played Sounding Sky, Almighty Voice's father, and Gordon Tootoosis, a native Cree in his first film role, played Almighty Voice.

The pressure was on Mitchell to prepare a treatment by the end of January 1972, with a final script to be submitted by the end of March. That was just five months to write a script, during which time he had to commute to Edmonton to teach, chair a workshop at a three-day national law convention in Ottawa, and give four or five addresses across Canada. Clearly Mitchell was rushed, but by the end of February he had a first full draft ready. He asked one of his creative-writing students, Alberta ombudsman George McClellan (a former RCMP commissioner), to comment on whether he had captured the authentic feel in his dialogue and characters. McClellan wrote on March 8 to say he had enjoyed it and had shown the script to the RCMP commissioner, who, he hoped, would not mind the cussing in it. From mid-April Mitchell was in Montreal for four weeks doing further work on the script.

At the same time that he was writing furiously on *Alien Thunder,* he was surprised by an offer from Allan King to make a feature film of *Who Has Seen the Wind.* Mitchell always thought *Wind* had the potential to be a major film, but previous propositions had come to naught. It is the nature of the television and film business that there are many more false starts than winners, but it was Mitchell's nature to treat each venture with unconditional enthusiasm and hope. So, he was tremendously excited, all over again, when Allan King phoned with his offer of an option in January 1972.

King was primarily known for his two successful docudramas, *Warrendale* (1966) and *A Married Couple* (1969), but he had directed two short television dramas based on stories by Alice Munro and Margaret Laurence that his wife, Patricia Watson, had adapted. King explained to Mitchell that he wanted to do a five-part series for the CBC and, from them, cull a feature film. It was the feature film that stirred Mitchell's interest, and he said that he wanted to do the script for it. King confirmed by letter on January 28 an offer of $10,000 for the rights to the novel. In his letter he said it would be "extremely helpful" if Mitchell were involved in writing the screenplay, but he added that he "would not like to tie the two matters [rights and writing] together contractually."[23] Mitchell believed that he had a gentleman's agreement with King to write the feature film script, although he understood that Watson was writing the five-part television series. In April King paid $2,500 to option *Wind* for two years, and he sent a draft contract for Mitchell to look over. All was satisfactory, and for the next two years King set about arranging financing for the feature while Watson wrote the five scripts for television.

‒ "LITTLE GIRL LOST" ‒

Around the end of April, Willa, now seventeen and in grade twelve, dropped out of school and took off to Vancouver and then Victoria. Merna and Bill had encouraged Willa in her creative activities ‒ art, music, dance, and theatre ‒ and of the three children regarded her as the most creative. Willa felt "some pressure" from them to finish her education and pursue a degree of fine arts, but everything she did ‒ skipping school, experimenting with drugs, involving herself with troublesome friendships ‒ spelled out her disinclination to do the expected. Although she described feeling left out, not "a part of their lives" at that time, she also recognized that her running away was "more of a curiosity, a driven desire."[24] In Victoria she moved in with Merna's friend, Shirley Northey, for a while, and when that did not work out, she moved into a rundown apartment with a friend. Shirley passed on what little news about Willa she could to Merna and Bill, who were dreadfully worried about her.

On May 26, 1972, Mitchell was to receive his first Honorary Doctor of Laws degree from the University of Regina. He was delighted that it was his home province that was the first to pay him this honour ‒ even though the chancellor, former prime minister John Diefenbaker, was his least favourite politician. Willa came home for this grand event and with her mother and father and Hugh and his wife, Susan, they all planned to drive from Calgary to Regina the day before the convocation. At first, spirits were high in the

Mitchell household, but then tempers flared. Mitchell was very concerned about the kind of life and relationships Willa was involved in on the West Coast, and they had a major blowup. Bill was uncharacteristically silent on the long drive to Regina.

The next day he received his degree and gave the convocation address. He began with Mark Twain's observation that "A foreigner can photograph the exteriors of a nation, but I think that is as far as he can get," and expanded on how writers, drawing on a lifetime of "unconscious absorption" of their particular landscapes and communities, can effectively map the interior character of a country. He used specific examples of how his writing had been indelibly marked by his prairie and Weyburn roots.[25] Later that evening at the convocation banquet, Mitchell broke his silence with Willa: "So there we are at the honorary party. After the dinner Dad dances with me. The first time we've actually even looked at each other. And I'm in tears and he is loving, and embracing, and forgiving. And then that was it."[26]

Merna and Bill left the next day for another honorary degree ceremony on May 28 at the University of Ottawa. While there they received the news that Merna's brother, Spud, had died. Spud had generally improved after the death of Mrs. Hirtle, so much so that he was able to live in a halfway house for part of the time. He had experienced a couple of relapses, but just before his death he was remarkably stable, so this was unexpected. Merna and Bill turned right around and went out to Vancouver to look after the arrangements.

Willa returned to her hippie-style life on Vancouver Island. She was always to have a tumultuous, though loving, parent-daughter relationship. She later realized that she must have "terrified" her parents with her lack of communication and her unsavory relationships. Willa had her father's sense of adventure, his impetuousness and his wilfulness, so there was no coaxing her back to the security of the family until she was ready. During this period Merna conveyed to very few friends her anxiety about Willa, but Bill wrote many of his feelings into *The Vanishing Point*, ascribing his own anguish to Carlyle as he desperately searches for Victoria, the Stoney girl who becomes a "little girl lost" on the streets of the big city

(Calgary). Looking back on this trying time, Bill recalled, "I had an eighteen-year-old daughter who I thought was about to be destroyed, leading the hippie, Gypsy life – my daughter is Victoria Rider, the Indian girl who's lost."[27]

Sometime in June or July, Fournier and Raymond verbally informed Mitchell that not only were they having to reshuffle their financing but that they had hired another writer, George Malko, to revise Mitchell's script in order to please the distributors. As a consequence they were reducing Mitchell's fee from $30,000 to $20,000. Mitchell immediately protested, through his lawyer. A few weeks later he received the script revised by Malko along with a contract indicating the new financial terms. He was enraged with Malko's cliché-ridden script and to make his point would scornfully quote lines from it: "Don't pay me no nevermind,"[28] and "A man's gotta do what a man's gotta do."[29] In an interview Mitchell complained, "They don't want a writer, they want Pavlov's dog." He felt that Fournier and Malko were turning his script into a Hollywood Western with an overtly politicized message of, as he said, the "Red Christ against the White Devil."[30]

Mitchell had his lawyer immediately write to argue for the original fee of $30,000, for equal ownership of the screenplay, for the right to approve all alterations and condensations of his original script, and the right to withdraw his name from the credits if necessary. Filming started in September 1972 and, after threats of a court injunction, the legal matter was settled in November. Mitchell was paid the original fee, and he also won the right to withdraw his name from the film, a decision he decided to keep in abeyance until he could view the film.

Mitchell felt his work was "all thrown out."[31] That was not quite true, but all motivation and subtlety in the characters had been lost. Mitchell's script, though, had its own problems. It was overly long, the balance between the comic and the tragic elements needed refining, and his attempt to piece together material from his other writing (*Jake and the Kid*, *The Vanishing Point*, "The White Christmas of Archie Nicotine") was not entirely successful. However, he had a clearer and more nuanced vision of the historical incident, which Fournier had simplified into "good guys, bad guys."

— "BILLY, BILLY, BILLY" —

Christmas 1972 was a break in tradition. Merna and Bill were family-oriented and Merna, like a border collie as Bill would say, gathered the Mitchell flock each year. This year, however, with Spud dead and Willa on her own, family ties had altered, and they decided to go to Florida, which proved to be more than a warm retreat from Bill's heavy university teaching and the cold prairie winters. It was soul renewing as he nostalgically revisited the place of his formative high school years.[32] While they were in St. Petersburg, Merna prodded Bill to contact his former English teacher, Miss Emily Murray, who had inspired him to consider drama as a profession. In fact, it was Merna who located her in California. When he telephoned, Miss Murray did not immediately recognize his name, but he persevered:

> And I said, "I'm probably Canada's leading novelist now, and I'm also a playwright and still a performer, and I wanted to phone you and tell you that. I think had it not been for you I would not be today a novelist and playwright." She said, "Oh that's very nice," and I knew she was not recalling me. I said, "Look, I was a diver, springboard diver, I had a metal brace on my right arm and I played the Andy Hardy in the senior play *Skidding*." She said, "Oh Billy, Billy, Billy, Billy, Billy!" She remembered me then.[33]

When they returned home from St. Petersburg, Bill came down with pneumonia, which took the "sap" right out of him for two months. Merna thought of something to boost his spirits. Without telling Bill, she arranged for Miss Murray to fly up for a visit and to attend a reading-performance that Bill was giving at the Canadian Conference of Writers and Critics in Calgary and Banff.[34] Bill was still in bed, "savoring his convalescence," but as Merna anticipated, he got up and felt much better as soon as Miss Murray arrived: "We had breakfast together and talked and I was overcome. I said, 'Oh, Emily, God damn it, Emily!' And she said, 'Oh Billy, Billy, no, no.' Then was when I discovered that she was a passionate Christian Scientist, that she had always been, and I also realized that my language had become corrupted a great deal in the intervening years."[35]

Willa, who had now been away for eight months, had temporarily returned home from the coast. She had become involved in a difficult relationship and turned to her parents, who were very supportive. The Mitchell household was rarely a dull place, and Willa's presence multiplied the possibilities for excitement exponentially. While Bill was very pleased at Willa's return, he was now also concerned about her language and proneness to explosive outbursts. She had had, after all, an excellent role model in these departments. But it was Bill, galvanized by Willa, who embarrassed himself with the teacher who had taught him about artistic restraint and grace:

> I went upstairs to bed about four in the afternoon to take a rest and, as I was extremely thirsty, I had a pitcher of Coca-Cola with ice cubes in it, on the night table. In the meantime, Willa wanted after-dinner mints, and they were in a drawer, her mother told her, beside the bed. "But don't disturb your father." She sneaked the door open. I was sound asleep, and I guess it had been hot so I had put the covers down, and was sleeping in my underwear shorts. In the dark Willa reached her hand out to open the drawer – and she's such a bloody ring-a-ding she hit the pitcher and inundated me with about a quart of iced Coca-Cola. I knew instantly it had to be Willa. There could only be one bloody person who would come in, in the dark when I was asleep and dying of pneumonia, and tip a quart of iced Coke over me. I came rearing straight up, shouting at the top of my voice, "Oh sheeee — it!"

Emily had decided to come upstairs to get ready for dinner and Merna was accompanying her. Merna had Emily's arm and she was just about to put her hand on the newel post at the base of the stairs as I screeched this out, and her hand came away. It must have been, according to Merna, the shock of it and concern, and Emily said, "Do you think he's all right?" And Merna said, "Oh yes, I think he is." "Well," she said, "I don't know. I distinctly heard him cry out, 'Oh shoot.'"

As Bill said, there was only one other woman who would have responded that way – his mother. So, he was concerned: "I had to change my whole reading program for Banff. . . . I think it's probably been the only time that I have deliberately settled for slightly less and ended up with cleaned-up Mitchell, because there was no way I intended for Emily to hear me do, well, 'Old Kacky and The Vanishing Point' or 'The Day I Caught Syphilis.'"[36] In shaky handwriting Emily Murray wrote a letter of overflowing thanks: "My thought has been filled with you and your loving kindness to me every moment of my visit of recent days. I still marvel at Bill's persistence and dear effort to conclude the search. Thank you, My Darling, for filling my life with this new happiness of finding you and your precious and much-loved ones."[37]

A week after Emily left, Bill went down to High River to be interviewed by Peter Gzowski for an hour-long special for the CBC Radio program *This Country in the Morning*.[38] With their similar curiosity, spontaneity, and sense of humour, they had established a fondness for one another. Gzowski found Bill an easy and entertaining, if somewhat unpredictable, interview. On this occasion he began by asking Bill why High River had been so special for him, and asked if he used High River people in his stories. He kidded Bill that now these people could tell stories on him and, to Bill's surprise, a whole group of his High River friends appeared from behind the stacks of books in the library where the interview was being staged. They spent the hour telling W.O. Mitchell anecdotes, the funniest, perhaps, being Merna's story, with Bill's usual interruptions, about Bill, in the La Guardia airport washroom, accidentally splashing water on the crotch of his new seersucker suit and trying to dry himself off by standing up on the sink and hoisting his leg over the hand dryer.[39]

~ "I FINISHED IT! I FINISHED IT!" ~

Over the next six weeks, working late into the evenings, Mitchell made the final push on *The Vanishing Point*. Now, however, just as he had had difficulties with the ending of "The Alien," he ran into major difficulties with *The Vanishing Point*'s ending. But finally, one late March afternoon, he "typed the last word, period, exclamation mark of *The Vanishing Point*. I let out a banshee Ya-hee! and startled the ass off Rudy Wiebe and his graduate seminar across the hall and went out, and with my usual restraint, said, 'Do you buggers realize I've finished this god damned book that I started back twenty years ago?!'"[40]

When interviewed, Rudy Wiebe proudly displayed his battered and dog-eared copy of *The Vanishing Point*, saying, "I really like this novel." He explained that it was falling apart because he had taught it in his Canadian literature course at the University of Alberta for years. He said it was "the substantial novel of the mature Mitchell output – it deals with very serious things and deals with them in a very searching and not quickly resolved way. I liked this. Partly because I guess I had some sense of him working in the office across from me and the way he struggled with it, especially with the ending. I think he had a real problem with the ending and that's why he was so ecstatically happy when he felt he had mastered it, when he finally found the way to end this novel."[41]

Hugh Kane, Mitchell's editor since John Gray's recent retirement, received part three of the manuscript on April 6, 1973, and was very impressed with it. In a memo to his production team, Kane wrote, "Bill has succeeded in tying up the ends pretty skillfully. It is, in my opinion, a good novel, and one which should sell well."[42] Although it was late to get things underway for fall publication, Macmillan needed the book for their fall list and Mitchell was anxious to get it out, so anxious he was willing to sacrifice American publication in order to speed up the process. Mitchell asked Macmillan to act as his agent in arranging publication in the United States. Kane was to send out copies first to Viking, then to Little, Brown or Farrar Straus if Viking declined.

When *The Vanishing Point* opens, Carlyle has been teaching on the reserve for almost nine years, hibernating from the experience of losing his child and his wife. He has been living on a reserve in a number of senses, for he has avoided forming any emotional attachments. Without realizing it, his parent-to-child and teacher-to-student relationship with Victoria has been developing into something else (just as the paternalistic attitude of the whites toward the Natives should have developed into something else). When she disappears in the city and Carlyle searches for his "little girl lost," he also embarks on a quest for a "little boy lost," which ends in self-discovery.

In Heally Richards, Carlyle discovers a distorted mirror image of his own well-intentioned but blind, and ultimately self-serving, egotism. While Archie's needling upsets Carlyle's puritan, civilized attitudes, Carlyle dismissively stereotypes Archie, assuming that he will always have to bail him out of jail for being drunk, and that he will never get his truck going again. But when Carlyle abandons Victoria on the city street after she tells him that she is pregnant, it is Archie who refuses to quit and who, by example, bails Carlyle out of his despairing defeatism. Archie, by bringing Victoria back to Paradise Valley, makes sure that she will not vanish in the city streets as a prostitute

Mitchell sets the climactic Prairie Chicken Dance scene against the "Rally for Jesus" scene in which Heally Richards attempts to heal Old Esau, Victoria's grandfather. As Richards lays on hands to heal Old Esau, emaciated to skin and bones by tuberculosis, the old man rises up momentarily from the stretcher and then falls back dead.[43] Just as Archie is directly responsible for Richards's sudden fall from "glory," he is partially responsible for a parallel but successful raising of the dead when he urges Carlyle to go to the dance because Victoria is going to be there. When Victoria offers the ritual dance bone to Carlyle, she releases him from the "bony spectre" of his white puritan imprinting, prompting him to join the dance of the living whole, the dance from which he had angrily pulled her away when she was a child. He thought he was the white knight in shining armour who could kiss awake Victoria and the Stoneys from their primitive reserve sleep when, in fact, this mission was a camouflage for his own problems. Archie and Victoria save him when they help him realize that he and his white culture are in just as much trouble as the Stoneys, that the city itself is a kind of reserve that leads to enervation and alienation, and that the only game in town is the human one of individuals bridging with one another. When Carlyle awakes from his blanket marriage[44] with Victoria, exulting in his finally expressed love for her, he slips out in the early morning to discover that Beulah Creek is flowing again. As he watches Ezra's grandson making miniature canal systems in the water, he pledges a new reciprocal approach to his Stoney children: "Let's you and I conjure together. You watch me and I'll watch you and I will show you how to show me how to show you how to do our marvelous human tricks together!" (*VP* 389).

Mitchell freed himself from "The Alien"'s various closures (character, structure, theme) by starting with a blank page. Like Carlyle in Old Kacky's art class on the vanishing point, Mitchell was originally fascinated by the neat and rigid closure of the lines of road, fenceposts, and telephone posts funnelling toward the vanishing point of Mount Lookout in the original blueprint of "The Alien." And also like Carlyle, who finally is not satisfied with his picture because it is "empty" and needs a gopher or a tree (*VP* 319), Mitchell opened up and enriched the original lines on the pages of "The Alien" with many new spontaneous finds, the most important of these being his Stoney character, Archie Nicotine. "The Alien" began with Mitchell's fascination with and concern for the Eden Valley Stoneys and, thirty years later, *The Vanishing Point* ends in a scene in which Archie Nicotine gets his truck going again. Carlyle has the last word in the novel, and significantly it is Archie's, "Hey-up!", now an affirming "Yes!"

As well as finishing *The Vanishing Point*, his first novel in eleven years, 1973 was a hallmark year for Mitchell in other ways. In June he was notified of his appointment as an Officer of the Order of Canada, with the investiture to be held at Rideau Hall in October where he would receive the award from Governor General Roland Michener. Also, the University of Toronto invited him to become writer-in-residence for the academic term 1973–74. Throughout the summer, though, Bill was busy adding a two-storey solarium onto their house, in which he could grow bamboo palms, staghorn ferns, flaming red hibiscus, banana plants, pink cascading bougainvillea, orange trees, and, of course, orchids, all of which he could look down on through the windows of his study on the second floor: "The neat thing about this office is when I take a break . . . when it doesn't flow like a meadowlark's song — I like to . . . just look down on the solarium below and . . . kid myself that I'm in the Caribbean."[45]

There was a cloud overhanging this excitement. Merna and Bill had not heard from Willa for some months. Mitchell was interviewed in August about his soon-to-be published novel and, although he does not mention Willa, he has her very much on his mind as he describes Carlyle's search for Victoria: "He has to find her before she is destroyed and I would think there are today a hell of a lot of parents of teen-agers who have left home and they don't know where they are."[46]

II

BACK TO BEULAH

~ 1973 to 1975 ~

I N SEPTEMBER 1973, Bill and Merna once again moved east, and
they were pleasantly surprised with Toronto: "The Toronto we
had known had been not really a city. It was a conglomerate,
and an uneasy one, of small Ontario towns. It was as though you
plocked together Lindsay and Peterborough and Waterdown and
then when we came back we suddenly realized it had truly become
a lovely sophisticated, large North American city. I don't know what
happened in that time. . . . Some people say the influx of European
people who leavened that WASP Toronto thing – I don't think it is
that simple."[1] However, in social terms, Toronto was less fun than it
had been in the 1950s when they were younger, more adaptable, and
caught up in the excitement of a new job and the *Maclean's* crowd.
Merna looked forward to the cultural opportunities, but, in fact, she
could seldom persuade Bill to attend the theatre, the symphony, or
ballet, and never the opera. Their apartment on MacPherson
Avenue, north of Bloor and just off Yonge Street, was spartan, but
Merna enjoyed this older, treed area, lined with imposing three-
storeyed brick homes. As she was the one who walked Plato, their
golden retriever, she met a good many of the pet-owning neighbours. The added bonus of being in Toronto was its proximity to

Peterborough, where they could visit Barbara and Orm, now teaching at Trent University, and their family.

Mitchell followed upon the heels of Margaret Atwood as writer-in-residence at the University of Toronto. He claimed, with much amusement, that he overheard her, on a phone call in the Massey College office, retort to one of the many claimants upon her time that if they wanted a tap dance, they should hire a tap-dancer. Mitchell was perhaps more tolerant of being, as he put it, a "performing literary seal,"[2] but he soon discovered that he was not able to do much of his own writing. However, he truly enjoyed students, and when one requester apologetically wrote that visiting schools must be a bore for him, he replied, "Speaking engagements with young people in schools have never yet bored me."[3] In the spring he happily judged the Canada Permanent Student Writing Contest in which first, second, and third prizes were awarded to a student in each province, as well as to an overall winner.

He was given an office in Massey College where Robertson Davies was master, and he was very thankful for "a beautiful and quiet eye in the middle of the urban storm."[4] He was too much of an egalitarian and a westerner, however, to enjoy the trappings of the Oxford-style college with its high table, sherry parties, and generally formal atmosphere, all of which he later lampooned in *Since Daisy Creek*. The story about the students from a rival college who threw detergent into the college fountains appealed to Mitchell's satiric sense of humour. In *Since Daisy Creek* he describes a scene of pandemonium as suds spew all over the courtyard during a sherry party, and the master and fellows of Kathleen McNair College try to rescue hundreds of goldfish from "Death by detergent" (*SD* 141).

— "YOUR WRITING HAS GUTS AND HEART AND POWER" —

Mitchell had some qualms about what the reaction to *The Vanishing Point* would be and in an interview earlier in the summer he said, "I'm glad I'll be in Toronto when the novel is published. . . . There's bound to be some flak here. I know it's going to hurt some people.

It's loving, in a way, but in another way, it ain't so loving."[5] However, when it was published in October, it was immediately a hit, selling 7,000 copies before Christmas, by May going into its third printing, and remaining on the best-seller lists for six months. Some reviewers judged it to be Mitchell's best novel and one of the finest Canadian novels in recent years. Of thirty reviews, only four were outright pans.

Most reviewers focused on Mitchell's treatment of the Stoneys. *TIME* magazine described the novel as a "painfully explicit and bitingly honest observation of life on Indian reserves across the Prairies and in the red ghettos of Western cities,"[6] and Robert Fulford wrote that "some people will hate Mitchell" because "no writer has ever before set it all down so graphically, and in such dismaying detail."[7] Heather Robertson's view was more balanced, pointing out that Mitchell "peels the layers of hypocrisy off both Indian and white with ruthless tenderness, mirroring one with the other, counter pointing the filth and fornication, the blood and boozing and fecundity of reserve life with the sterility of white society where everything has turned to stone and even our shit is white. It's a surprisingly serious novel, at least for those of us who grew up with *Jake and the Kid*, a salvation novel, a Canadian pilgrim's progress."[8]

Others responded to the "loving" part of the book's vision, among them Myron Galloway, who felt that the novel treated the Stoneys "with a compassion entirely unalloyed by sentimentality."[9] Beth Perrott, the only Native reviewer, argued that many of the other reviewers missed the novel's central theme by viewing it "as a social commentary on Indian life." Unable to free themselves from their "stereotyped image[s] of Native people," they made "value judgements when Mitchell's whole point is to view other individuals with tolerance, respect, understanding and compassion."[10] When Mitchell read Perrott's review, he broke one of his cardinal rules – ignore all reviewers – and wrote her a one-line letter: "Dear Beth, I have read your review and I love you."[11]

Reviewers admired the novel's authentic dialogue, layered structure, elliptical humour, and its sensuously descriptive prose that strikingly evoked both the foothills and urban landscapes. Many were impressed by the novel's rich cast of characters – particularly Archie Nicotine and Heally Richards. A few, however, were critical of Victoria. Heather Robertson observed that "Mitchell does not write well about women. He seems unable to get inside them, to present them with the same authenticity and wealth of language he brings to his salty male characters; Victoria remains vague, undefined, a cliché."[12] Because Mitchell felt uneasy about directly entering the consciousness of Victoria, and because she is very shy, he was unable to flesh out her character through dialogue exchanges. Although she is a catalyst in Carlyle's birth to awareness, she is more a symbol than a character (indeed, she is to Carlyle until the final scenes).

The Vanishing Point is Mitchell's most ambitious novel and shows the kind of maturity F.M. Salter said *Who Has Seen the Wind* promised. With this novel, the academic community began to take Mitchell more seriously as a novelist. It was reviewed for the most part favourably by seven academic journals and in the thirty-two years since its publication has been the subject of a dozen critical essays in journals and books. It has also been taught on Canadian literature and Native studies courses in universities across Canada.

The Mitchells had been keeping in touch with Ernest Buckler through Christmas notes, and Bill arranged for a copy of *The Vanishing Point* to be sent to him. Buckler, with his characteristic humour, wrote,

> It's a corker. Your truly inimitable humor is as fresh as ever. And your marvelous talent for evocative description. And your remarkable gift for seeing beneath the surface of things. Your writing has guts and heart and power. (So different from the work of some modern writers – which is either a sort of rarified nightingale's piss or else deliberately and tiresomely obscurantist or else a sickly preoccupation with their own scabs.) I've always saluted your exceptional talents, and I do so again.[13]

Buckler's letter meant a great deal more to Bill than all the positive reviews he had been receiving.

The promotion tour for *The Vanishing Point* began in October and ended, eighteen months later, with an intensive ten-day reading tour of all the universities in the Atlantic provinces. Nora Clark, his publicist at Macmillan, orchestrated his schedule, virtually becoming Mitchell's performance agent. She arranged the usual book promotion media interviews and appearances, but also set up many of his one-man shows, banquet addresses, and keynote speeches at conferences across the country. His standard reading fee was now $500, and Nora looked after collecting his payments and travel expenses. She played a significant role in boosting Mitchell's performance career and set the template for his subsequent book promotion tours. Probably because he enjoyed it, Mitchell proved to be the best promoter among all Canada's authors. On *This Country in the Morning*, he told Peter Gzowski, "I'd stand on my head on city hall steps – any city – anywhere – with nothing on —— to sell a copy of the book. My wife says this is undignified – I guess I'm not a dignified man." Although a book tour was not agony for him as it was for others, it still took its toll: "You wake up in the morning and you don't know for several seconds whether you're in Toronto – or Winnipeg – or Calgary or Vancouver. . . . . . . what time it is —— who you are —— the title of your own book —— A day can involve – seven shows – interviews —— and you run from the last to grab a plane. It is murder."[14]

— "HE'S AN ORNAMENT TO ANY INSTITUTION" —

Mitchell's nine months at the University of Toronto were very busy, though not entirely satisfactory. In his letter to President John Evans at the end of term, he described what he felt were the three responsibilities of a writer-in-residence. The first he noted was "to himself as an artist," and in this he felt he had failed: "I have written only about 30 pages on a new novel to which I had been committed for almost a year before I came to the University of Toronto last fall, and in finished work wrote only an hour drama, BACK TO BEULAH, which was broadcast in the C.B.C.'s series THE PLAY'S THE THING."[15] He said to an interviewer a few months later that he thought he had four more novels in him, but "not with this kind of year."[16]

The second responsibility he commented on was helping young writers, "the most important of the three [responsibilities]." Although he claimed he had discovered three promising writers at the University of Toronto, he felt this did not compare favourably with the work he was able to do in his three-year writer-in-residency at the University of Calgary. He urged Evans to consider a minimum two-year appointment for the writer-in-residence program so that the "annual academic game of musical chairs" would more effectively benefit both students and teacher-artist.

The third responsibility was to "accomplish a sort of public relations prestige" for the university, and in that regard, as he wrote President Evans, "I have done famously for the University." He appended a list of engagements he had undertaken that would reflect glory upon the University of Toronto. From September 1973 to May 1974, he had given close to fifty performances, interviews, speeches, conference addresses, and television and radio appearances. Of course, much of this attention arose from the publication of *The Vanishing Point*, but certainly the university benefited from his exposure in the media. In the *Toronto Star*, Robert Fulford noted, "If Mitchell did nothing but turn up on campus and he does a great deal more – he would personally justify the writer-in-residence system. He's an ornament to any institution: his personality itself a kind of artistic expression. His conversation is expansive and generous, his views are offered frankly but with a genuine kindness. To know him, even slightly, is to sense some of the larger possibilities of creative life."[17]

In March, while at Massey College, Mitchell had a meeting with a student of a different order – William Kurelek. Kurelek had established himself as a naive realist painter of prairie scenes, and that year there was an exhibition of his newest work, which appeared in *A Prairie Boy's Winter* (1973), at the Av Isaacs Gallery. Mitchell attended the show and very much wanted to purchase a painting, but they were all sold. Shortly after Mitchell received a phone call from Kurelek, who asked Mitchell if he could help him with his writing. Mitchell "looked over Kurelek's shoulder" for that year while Kurelek was working on *Lumberjack* (1974) and *A Prairie Boy's Summer* (1975).

Early on in their association, Mitchell suggested to Kurelek that he do some paintings for a deluxe illustrated edition of *Who Has Seen the Wind*. Kurelek agreed, and Mitchell wrote Hugh Kane pitching the idea, saying Kurelek wanted to do five paintings. Kane was very enthusiastic about this project. On June 16 when Kurelek sent Bill the manuscript for *A Prairie Boy's Summer* he added a P.S.: "I'm now about ⅔ through 'Who Has Seen the Wind'. The more I read the more I'm impressed. You certainly captured the prairies but even more important the very stuff of human life. Your prose is like a beautiful poem. . . . It's an honor to illustrate a book like that."[18]

Mitchell had heard nothing about *Alien Thunder* from Fournier and Raymond since May 1973 when they assured his lawyer that they would give him an advance screening. After a couple of requests he finally saw *Alien Thunder* in January 1974 and was decidedly unhappy. The main thrust of the movie had been twisted from the original intention, and Mitchell did not want to be associated with it. He withdrew his name from the credits, joking with Sutherland, "unfortunately you can't withdraw your face," and he felt "very guilty for having got this caring, compassionate, responsible friend into this historically inaccurate and badly done movie."[19] The previous spring the RCMP, with good reason, had objected to the film being a part of their centennial celebrations, for as one reviewer put it, "It shows the North West Mounted Police as the insensitive agents of an insensitive conquering race."[20]

Alien Thunder "had inauspicious world premieres in five Saskatchewan centres" on February 23, 1974.[21] Over a year later, when Sutherland and Mitchell did an interview together on *This Country in the Morning*,[22] Sutherland said "it was a beautiful story" that "went wrong in the cutting room." Mitchell less graciously added that there was "no foundation all down the line," suggesting there was nothing good about the production – not the directing, the cinematography, the continuity, or the narrative line. Although Sutherland felt that Fournier was "inadequate" both as a director and a cinematographer, he thought that there was still a good film to be had from the rushes. Sutherland also claimed that they had missed a marvellous opportunity to initiate a Canadian film tradition: "If they had had a good director like some of the directors who did Australian film it could have done for Canada what they did for Australia. It could have started a whole industry – funded by Canadian investors."[23] There was only one consolation for Bill in this whole mess – he used the money he received for the screenplay to pay for his solarium.

~ *BACK TO BEULAH:* "A CURIOUS KIND OF HORROR STORY" ~

Back to Beulah, directed by Eric Till, produced by George Jonas, and telecast on *The Play's the Thing* on March 21, 1974, was Mitchell's most complex and powerful television drama. It deals with three mad women living in a halfway house who take their psychiatrist hostage. Mitchell's interest in eccentrics and madness had been established early in his life. As a child he had become quite accustomed to seeing patients from the Weyburn Provincial Mental Hospital out on the prairie, or in town, or at functions at the hospital that he and his mother attended.[24] Two of his sisters-in-law, Molly and Mary, worked at the Weyburn Hospital, and through them he was introduced to Mildred, Betty, and Agnes. Mildred worked for and lived with Molly. Agnes worked for Bill's mother, and she and Betty eventually rented a place together. Later, when Bill came to town to give readings, he and his brother Dick would visit the three women. Molly recalled that Bill was intrigued by these girls, "they were so simple and plain . . . what they thought, they just said it." He made a big fuss over them and "they just loved W.O."[25] He invited them to his readings, and they would be "right down in the front row looking up at Bill."[26] These three women became partial models for Harriet, Agnes, and Betty in *Back to Beulah*.

Mitchell also drew on his experience with his brother-in-law's mental illness. Although Spud had been diagnosed with schizophrenia in 1942 when he was discharged from the army, Merna and Bill had never used this clinical term with the family and Bill never referred publicly to Spud's problem.[27] But for years he had observed close-up, and ascribed to his three women characters, Spud's pill-taking rituals, his shakiness and disorientation, talking at cross-purposes, obsession with tidiness and cleanliness, mood swings and violence, and his visits back to the hospital for stabilization. Mitchell was also aware of the thin line between the comic and the serious (even violent) in Spud's life, and this unsettling mixture became a part of *Back to Beulah*.

Back to Beulah, as Eric Till said, is "a curious kind of horror story."[28] The "biggest difficulty that other people had with the piece was not knowing what it is – is it a comedy? Is it a piece of macabre drama?" Betty, Agnes, and Harriet, who have been released from the Beulah Mental Institute to live in a halfway house, are watched over by their psychologist, Dr. Anders, who lives in the first-floor suite in the same building. Harriet, a manic-depressive personality, is a God-fearing woman for whom "power and ascendancy are paramount." The comic material revolves around Betty, who is schizophrenic and takes "frequent flights to a nicer world within herself" (*DWO* 41), and around Agnes, who is a nympho/kleptomaniac. Dr. Anders, one of a new wave of psychiatrists in the 1970s, believes, as did Mitchell, that neither institutionalization nor drugs is the best route to rehabilitation. Rather, the halfway house concept, "a dynamic life situation" (*DWO* 48), was believed to accomplish lasting gains, and Mitchell had personal experience with this as he observed Spud's situation. However, Dr. Anders believes so fervently in her "parable of hope" project that she forgets that her patients are human beings. The play becomes darkly dramatic when the tables are turned. Anders is imprisoned by her patients and accused, herself, of being delusional: "Go and get yourself another set of dolls. We are not your dolls – we are humans! That's your big mistake – you think our baby's a doll and we are your dolls." The final scene is of the four women walking Agnes back to Beulah. Their solidarity suggests success, however small, and Anders has had her moment of awareness as well: "I – have a feeling – now – that you've been entitled to do – what you've done – partly."[29]

Beulah had something serious and topical to say about the attitudes toward and treatment of the mentally ill. Mitchell's reading of R.D. Laing's *The Politics of Experience & The Bird of Paradise* (1967), Erich Fromm's *The Art of Loving* (1956), and Martin Buber's *I and Thou* (1923) fed into the vision behind both *The Vanishing Point* and *Beulah*. Mitchell felt that the healing of the psyche begins on a personal level, and doctors like Anders can make a difference if they can put themselves in the skins of those they treat. He told one interviewer, "What I disapprove of is the way drugs are used to simplify minding the shop by keeping people zapped out."[30] At the same time, this play explores a larger universal theme that haunts much of Mitchell's work: the danger of the overly proscriptive guardian (teacher, parent, lover, psychiatrist) who, with the best of intentions, attempts to control and make over his charges and in the process limits or cripples their ability to live full lives.

A week after the television show Mitchell met with Bill Glassco, artistic director of the Tarragon Theatre, to talk about putting the drama on stage, and he set to work in May adapting it. *Beulah* was one of the highlights of Mitchell's writing career. Although he never wrote to please his critics, after the fact he felt he could brag that *Back to Beulah* answered them in a number of ways. He proved that he could create strong female characters, a criticism that had hounded him ever since *Jake and the Kid*. Now, he would say with delight, he had not simply created one strong female role, he had created four in one play. Furthermore, it was a play about tough issues, and he had set it in the city, breaking the mould in which he had been cast of the "homespun, folksy old so-and-so."[31] *Back to Beulah* earned Mitchell two ACTRA nominations, one for Best Writer in the Dramatic Mode in Visual Media and one, which he won, for Best Writer in Dramatic Mode in Radio.[32]

Mitchell had heard little from King about the *Who Has Seen the Wind* movie project since 1972, but in May he met with him in Regina. It may have been then that Mitchell was presented with Patricia Watson's five television scripts. She recalled his exuberant response: "I picked up the phone, and it was W.O. at the other end saying, 'I love you, I love you, I love you' five times [once for each episode]."[33] There was no discussion, however, about his beginning to work on the screenplay.

— "I LIKE TO TEACH ONLY SLIGHTLY
LESS THAN TO WRITE"[34] —

With the completion of his term at the University of Toronto at the end of June, Mitchell decided to leave teaching for a while and devote his time to his next novel. Although he had not been happy with the short nine-month appointment, he recognized the value of the writer-in-residence program. In a convocation address given at the University of Alberta a few months later he spoke of the importance of universities providing good guardianship to their students by maintaining a balance between spontaneity and discipline. In both teaching and writing, he said, he was "concerned about the corruption of the living thing by the patterning and forming mind." Within the huge institutional machine of the university, there is a danger of such corruption, and he believed that the teacher-artist played a role in promoting spontaneity, excitement, passion, and insight: "I would like to discover more of this in our Universities, particularly in the last one [Toronto] where I served."[35] He was upset to hear that the University of Toronto was no longer contemplating hiring a writer, even for a year, let alone the two-year term he had advocated in his letter to the president.

He returned to work on the new grizzly novel, which he had started in the spring of 1973 after completing *The Vanishing Point*. The book was to be a study in various kinds of corruption, but he now decided to replace the milieu of a small foothills town with a university community, and his trophy hunter began to take shape as a university professor of creative writing. However, Mitchell's love of teaching interrupted the writing when two projects came his way that he simply could not turn down.

The Banff School of Fine Arts invited him to head its writing program and to introduce a summer workshop based on his writing philosophy. Alternately known as Mitchell's Messy Method or "How to find in the dark all by yourself,"[36] it soon was christened free-fall writing, a term that described well Mitchell's emphasis on the "sort of rough, and quite uncritical, capturing of whatever floated to the top of consciousness."[37] Rather than teaching in the usual sense of the word, he preferred to think of himself as conducting workshops that would provide "caring and honest attention from listeners who can be trusted."[38] He did not believe that writing workshops could teach a writer how to write: "The didact, with lectures on craft and technique, can accomplish really very little for the young artist whose creation must begin always in very private sea caves, which make very poor lecture theatres."[39] The Banff program was a very intensive six weeks with students writing daily. Mitchell knew he needed help in looking over all the material that would be coming in, so he asked Sandra Jones, one of his Calgary Mission Band students, to co-ordinate the program and to lead writing workshops along with him, and he asked Ruth Fraser, a student from his Canadian literature course at the University of Alberta, and also a field editor for McClelland & Stewart, to be the editorial guide and to produce the *Free-Fall* magazine. In 1979, Richard Lemm, a poet who had been in Mitchell's 1976 workshop, was asked to run the poetry workshops. David Leighton, director of the Banff Centre, wrote that this team "took Banff by storm" and by the mid-1980s "Mitchell's style of instruction had established its credentials beyond any doubt."[40]

From the free-fall material the students submitted each day, the instructors selected certain passages to be read aloud to fuel discussions in the morning workshops on such topics as character, voice, story, point of view, dialogue, and language. When Richard Lemm arrived at the 1976 workshop, he was filled with distrust about "the whole notion of writing groups," but he soon discovered a different kind of course here, not the usual cozy, cultish type of seminar. Although Mitchell was humorous, charming, and kind, he also had a tough, critical side and took very seriously his job of helping promising writers perfect their craft. Lemm, who had already published stories and poems, recalled his first day in the 1976 workshop, a large class of thirty-three impressive beginning writers:

> I was singled out the first day. They used my piece and they read the whole twenty pages. Then there was silence in the room. I remember thinking that people seem to be impressed by this. W.O. was the first to speak. He said, "That impressed you didn't it?" He asked what impressed people. "Oh the metaphors, the character comes to life, and the setting, the skid row of Seattle is vivid. It is very accomplished and this writer could be published quite clearly." And then his voice raised, his eyes flared and he said, "But it is one cell deep. It's easy. It's cheesy. It's performance. This writer went off to perform." And he emphasized how the writer was trying to show how good he was. To me, [this] was very useful. W.O. is a spontaneous and instinctive person to a certain extent. He is also a very calculating person. It worked, it worked with me. Now I was mad; I was upset. But I didn't go home. And I think I knew that I was singled out. They wouldn't do that to somebody who was bad, or who was fragile. They did this to somebody who could take it and who had merit.[41]

The writing program at Banff was an exhilarating experience for most writers. They were surrounded by creative energy not simply from their companion writers but from musicians, dancers, painters, photographers, potters, and many other artists. Mitchell usually came for a two-week period, one at the beginning and one at the end. His name and presence gave prestige to the program, and he was able to convince top Canadian writers to come in for a week or two to give readings and provide other perspectives in the workshops. Among those who came between the years 1974 and 1986 when Mitchell was head were Irving Layton, Alice Munro, Margaret Atwood, Sylvia Fraser, Dale Zieroth, Eli Mandel, Tim Wynne-Jones, Robert Kroetsch, and Alistair MacLeod. MacLeod, in fact, became a regular and usually stayed for two weeks, eventually taking over the advanced studio. A number of students from these classes went on to become published authors, such as Diane Schoemperlen, L.R. "Bunny" Wright, Joan Clark, and Sylvia Gunnery.[42] But students benefited in other ways. Gordon Morash, who became a literary journalist, commented that Mitchell's influence "wasn't just a matter of trying to teach you how to write or another way of trying to express yourself. He altered your experience of how you viewed life."[43]

– THE "PIED PIPER CAPER" –

Although Mitchell had promised himself time to devote to his grizzly novel, he was again seduced by a teaching appointment. Agnes (Nan) Florence, chief librarian of the Winnipeg School Division, invited him to conduct a roving writer-in-residence program in the fall of 1974. As part of the Manitoba School Board's centennial project, he was set up to visit about thirty-five schools, over two and a half months, three days a week (commuting from Calgary). He specified that he would like to address large groups of children in the gym or auditorium rather than small groups in a classroom setting. One vice-principal was not impressed with that idea: "We were horrified when he said he wanted to talk to groups of one hundred to four hundred. We wanted to give him sixty. Now we are sorry we did not include more. He kept two hundred youngsters sitting on a hard floor for two hours, entranced!"[44]

With the young students he would wander among them with his microphone, inviting them to be aware of the world inside themselves and around them: "What are you thinking about?" he would ask. Then he would take all their bits and pieces and weave a story.

He encouraged them to continue writing in this way. At one school a teacher reported that Mitchell's "effect on 640 kids was sensational. I've never seen anyone who could get their attention and hold it and entertain them that way."[45] He fascinated them with stories from his own life, of playing hockey, for instance, with "hockey sticks that were worn and shredded down and bleached with snow and melting water – and the skipping puck substitute of frozen horse manure – a road apple."[46] To make a story, he said, you take such memories and you ask, what if?: "What if a schoolboy had thrown this frozen puck at him in the long-ago streets of Weyburn, Saskatchewan, and then run home and slammed the door on his nose – 'what if I had kicked the door in, run into the parlor after him, turned the chesterfield over when he was hiding behind it, pushed the piano over on top of him?'"[47]

He had to be more didactic with the older students who had lost some of their childish spontaneity; with them he shared his own free-fall material and read to them from his novels to show how bits of random writing can be used to create a story. He also conducted a series of twelve seminars for teachers of creative writing. About thirty teachers were expected, but on the first night 185 showed up. Teachers themselves submitted free-fall and brought writing from their students.

Mitchell's "pied piper caper" was tremendously successful.[48] He spoke to about 10,000 young students over his eleven weeks in Winnipeg, and felt tremendously charged up by their spontaneous excitement and by what he hoped would be a "ripple" effect, with the teachers he had inspired with his "messy method" continuing to engage new generations of students.

Once again, as in the Edmonton commuting years, Merna was alone for much of each week, although, with special pleasure, she accompanied him to Halifax, where he was giving an address on November 7. Here she had time to meet with her cousin, Curtis Hirtle, at Mahone Bay. Immediately after that mini-holiday Mitchell flew to Brandon to receive an honorary degree. As a part of Brandon University's seventy-fifth anniversary convocation exercises,

Chancellor Stanley Knowles awarded honorary degrees to three fellow prairie authors: Mitchell, Paul Hiebert, and James Gray. Mitchell gave the convocation address in which he urged educators, parents, and graduates to listen for the poetry of earth and to nurture the imagination.

Most often Merna chose not to travel with Bill because of the cost and because it was exhausting and stressful looking after him. On one occasion when Bill had to speak in Nanaimo, British Columbia, to one of Jack Hodgins's classes, he stayed with his friend, Shirley Northey, in Victoria. Merna sent a note to Shirley with a number of questions that must be asked of Bill before he left for his engagement: did he have his snuff, the first and most important question; did he have his glasses; his reading material; phone numbers, travel instructions? All this was her constant worry, and it was a relief to turn Bill over to someone else.

Merna ran every aspect of the household, managed Bill's appointments, prepared the company books (a job she loathed), and answered his mail. It was often impossible to get his attention for mundane matters like bills, clothes, appointments, and household tasks. Because she did not like letter-writing, she frequently accepted or rejected engagements by telephone; consequently the amusing letters that Bill was known for disappeared from about the mid-1970s. When Bill took the telephone calls he often muddled up Merna's well-formed plans, and often responded impatiently to Merna's organizational attempts. One of his most frequent expletives was, "Jesus Christ, Merna!" and Luigi Zaninelli, a friend, a composer, and a music professor at the University of Calgary, claimed he was going to write a rock opera about them called "Jesus Christ, Merna!"

When Bill was at home everything moved to his tune. Merna enjoyed the quiet time before he arose. Because of him, she had become almost fanatically organized in the morning: she would tend to the dogs, get Bill's porridge ready to go, then sit down with her coffee and the Globe and Mail *cryptic crossword puzzle. Soon after he got up, the quiet ended; it was as if someone had turned on the radio full blast. If it was a good day he was off and running from the start. If it was a bad day and he needed time to surface, Merna would quietly point out various articles of interest for him to read in the newspaper while he breakfasted.*

By the mid-1970s Bill's hearing was deteriorating, but rather than admit it, he accused others of not articulating. Thus, voices were necessarily raised. He constantly bombarded Merna with questions: "Merna, am I busy on . . . ?"; "Merna, when are we going to the lake?"; "Merna, where is my snuff box?"; "Merna, what's the name of . . . ? Dammit, you know who I mean!"; "Merna, can you drive me now to check out the Unclaimed and Damaged Freight Sale" (this was not a question); "Merna, CBC needs me to record at 7:00 a.m. tomorrow." She would begin patiently, "Now, Bill, I have explained all that" or "Just a minute, Bill," or she would come up with the name or item he was anxiously looking for. Pushed to her limits, she could become snappish and authoritarian. Over the years they developed defensive and offensive plays against one another. Bill's method was dramatically offensive or sullenly defensive. He simply expressed his wishes – loudly – or withdrew sulking. Merna, knowing that Bill would often resist her suggestions, either camouflaged her true desires, or informed him at the last minute when it was too late to change.

All this was exhausting to orchestrate, and Merna more and more chose to stay at home while Bill travelled. But, while she revelled in her own time, she missed her daily dose of Bill-ness. He would phone her nightly from wherever he was, announcing, "I have to check in with Merna." He would embellish and exaggerate and reperform and brag about his day's accomplishments and Merna would laugh and enjoy, vicariously, all the excitement – without the frustration. "I love you, Merna," he would conclude. And she would say, "I love you, Billie."

– DISAPPOINTMENTS –

In November 1974, Allan King sent Mitchell the promotional brochure he had prepared for the *Who Has Seen the Wind* film project, which outlined the story, the budget, and the key players in the project. The executive producer was Budge Crawley, the much celebrated and colourful entrepreneur of independent Canadian film who, besides producing commercial documentary films, had made his reputation on such artistically renowned films as *The Loon's Necklace* (1948) and the movie version of Brian Moore's *The Luck of Ginger Coffey* (1964). Richard Leiterman, the brilliant Canadian film cinematographer, was the director of photography. Patricia Watson was listed as film adapter. Mitchell was cited simply as author of the novel. The financing had been difficult, but King thought he had commitments from the Saskatchewan government, the CBC, the Canadian Film Development Corporation (CFDC), and private investors. In the accompanying letter, King made no mention to Mitchell of the screenplay, and Mitchell was unaware that it was already in first-draft form. Mitchell had been away much of the fall conducting sessions for the Winnipeg School Project and was caught up in his own activities. Apparently it did not register with him that the *Wind* project was this far advanced, for he did nothing to protest King's lack of collaboration with him on the film script.

In January 1975, Merna and Bill eagerly accepted an invitation to Grand Cayman for about three weeks as guests of their friends Shirley (Northey) and Ferd Missiaen, who had bought a house there and were honeymooning. Typical of the Mitchells they had befriended Shirley through a difficult marriage breakup in the late 1960s and then had offered their house for Shirley's wedding in December 1974. The newly finished solarium, with slate-black floor and abundant lush greenery opened, through wide French doors, into the living room decorated in soft rose and green colours. Bill decided that more vivid colour was required for the occasion. He went to his favourite plant supplier to borrow – not buy – all the white and red poinsettias they had in stock. As usual his charm worked, and the total effect was a blaze of colour, ideally suitable for a Christmas wedding.

The Mitchells spent about three weeks on the island. Bill used the time to adapt the television version of *Back to Beulah* for stage, working as usual late into the night. During the day, though, he was like a kid in Florida all over again, and on one special occasion he went snorkelling for the first time. He had not done this in Florida and was reluctant to try, but Shirley insisted: "Once we got him into the water he wouldn't get out. He looked like King Neptune when he would rear up out of the water with his mask and snorkel. 'Merna!' he shouted, 'there's a whole new world down here.' Merna, too, went out to snorkel and there they were until almost dark. We couldn't even get them back to eat."[49]

After warming his corpuscles, as Mitchell described it, in Grand Cayman, he returned to a busy agenda of winter and spring speaking engagements. He toured the Atlantic provinces in March, speaking at nine different universities and colleges from Memorial to Acadia to Truro. Then he flew back and forth across Canada speaking to engineers, geophysicists, teachers, chambers of commerce, and women's clubs – the type of frenetic activity that he continued for another fifteen years and which accounted for his being the most publicly recognized author in Canada. He became almost a regular feature on Gzowski's *This Country in the Morning*, reminiscing about his past: the perils of speaking French when he was in France in 1933; or of transporting Grandma across the U.S. border; or importing bananas from Hawaii – all pieces he was thinking about for his memoir book.

The *Wind* feature film had been stalled in January 1975 when the CBC withdrew their support and the miniseries was abandoned. Then the Saskatchewan government, which in King's view was pivotal, postponed their commitment due to an upcoming provincial election so the feature film, as well, was put on hold. Behind the scenes, and unbeknownst to Mitchell, there were difficulties getting a workable and interesting film script. King and Watson disagreed about what should be the focus of the screenplay: the community (King's view) or Brian and the prairie (Watson's view). One of King's decisions, which upset Mitchell when he eventually saw a script, was to shoot the film in one season only (late summer). By March 1975 Watson had completed a third draft without any collaboration with Mitchell. Although King claimed that Mitchell saw this draft, Mitchell neither mentioned receiving it nor is it in his papers at the University of Calgary.[50]

The deluxe edition of *Who Has Seen The Wind* illustrated by William Kurelek, which Mitchell thought was coming out in the fall, was also experiencing problems. He was very disappointed when Hugh Kane wrote in June to say that it would not fly this year. Kane said that everything was against it: coffee-table books had been a disaster the previous fall (including Hugh MacLennan's *Rivers of Canada*); the large format size was a pricey venture; *Wind*, Kane felt, was not a coffee-table sort of book; and, most importantly, he felt that more work from Kurelek was required to make this a saleable illustrated edition. He had tried to get Houghton Mifflin interested in publishing an American edition, but they found the book old-fashioned. Kane had countered, "So is *Huckleberry Finn*," but to no avail.[51]

Mitchell was already angry with Macmillan because of their failure to have his books on hand for his readings. On his Maritime tour earlier that year ten bookstores where he was reading had placed orders and not one of them received the books in time for his reading. Kane's letter was the last straw, and he now considered leaving Macmillan and taking the Kurelek project to another publisher. In an effort at damage control, Nora Clark wrote a personal letter to Merna saying she understood how upset Bill was, that he should let Kane know that, but it was important for him to just keep on with his writing. She also told Merna that Kane was disappointed Bill did not have his book of reminiscential pieces ready for publication that fall.

In the spring Mitchell began writing a television script for Philip Keatley, a CBC director/producer, and by fall it was ready for filming. *Sacrament* had an interesting genesis. In May 1974, soon after Mitchell met with Bill Glassco at Toronto's Tarragon Theatre to discuss doing *Back to Beulah* as a stage play, he was invited to attend a Tarragon production of *Hosanna*, a play by Michel Tremblay that boldly dealt with issues of homosexuality and identity through the eyes of a transvestite and his lover. Mitchell did not like the play: "I considered it a freak show."[52] He told Glassco that he felt he could create a more realistic homosexual character. Mitchell had no phobias about homosexuality, and he claimed that he was "much earlier aware than most kids were of this facet of

Back to Beulah *stage play program*

human behaviour."[53] Nevertheless, his remark about *Hosanna* indicated that he was not open to the more extreme gay culture explored by Tremblay.

Glassco dared Mitchell to do it, and Mitchell created Norman Hooper, a homosexual character, who, Mitchell felt, was "one of the most compassionate and understanding characterizations of loneliness that I can think of."[54] Norman, a hairdresser with an artistic inclination, was one of eight single, lonely characters he created to populate his boarding house setting for *Sacrament*. Norman is a sympathetic character but, like the characters in this drama, he is largely stereotypical, apart from his moving speech at the end of the play, which adds depth to his character.

The boarding house story originated in "Sacrament," a *Foothill Fables* episode,[55] which, in turn, evolved from a section near the beginning of *The Kite* in which David Lang recalls a bittersweet time when he was about twelve and made a kite with one of his mother's boarders. It is a beautifully simple and touching story about mortality and human connectedness. In the television version, Margaret (a widow), Keith (her eleven-year-old son), and Lon (a retired B.C. ferryman and father figure to Keith) are the main characters, expanded from the original story. Instead of a kite, they begin constructing a sailboat, and dream about sailing her around the world. Keith's faith in this dream and in friendship are nearly destroyed when Lon dies, but the rest of the boarders, emotionally moved by Margaret and then Norman, come to his rescue.

Sacrament was the first drama production for Vancouver's new CBC studio. The boarding house location of the story was exactly the setting that allowed Mitchell to create the unique marginalized characters that he was so adept at imagining. In fact, he had in mind an actual boarding house in Vancouver, the one in which Spud, his brother-in-law, had lived when he was not hospitalized, so he had first-hand knowledge of various tensions and petty arguments among boarders. Keith is an interesting character study, and a precursor, in terms of adolescent personality, to Hugh in *How I Spent My Summer Holidays*. Unlike Hugh, though, and Brian in *Wind*, he reflects the effects of an urban and single-parent upbringing. In cinematic terms, the film was an interesting attempt to find external equivalents for the boy's terrible sadness and helplessness.

Mitchell worked with Keatley throughout the fall. A script was sent to executive producer John Hirsch near the beginning of November 1975, and it was filmed soon after. However, according to Mitchell, John Hirsch "blew up" when he saw the rough cut.[56] He was upset about the character of Norman and asked that the script be rewritten and reshot. Keatley refused, and the film was shelved.

There was good news, though, with the illustrated *Wind*. By the end of the year Kane reported that he had finally had a talk with Bill and Merna, who "appear to be very friendly and kindly disposed toward Macmillan and even me." Kane decided to ask Kurelek to redo two of the paintings and create two new ones along with about fifty black-and-white pieces.[57] The illustrated *Wind* was back on the rails, to be published in the fall of 1976.

12

DRAMATIST AND FILM WRITER

~ 1976 to 1979 ~

*B*ACK TO BEULAH was given a two-theatre run in 1976, first at Theatre Calgary in January and then at Toronto's Tarragon Theatre in February. Initially, Mitchell had wanted Bill Glassco to direct it at Tarragon, but he declined for budgetary reasons and, perhaps, artistic reasons, since he did not think the third act was quite resolved.[1] However, Glassco suggested Guy Sprung, a young director who was fresh from working in England, and Sprung came out to meet Mitchell in the summer of 1975: "He stayed with us in the house and we talked, and then I phoned Bill and I said I'm optimistic about him and I'll work with him."[2] Mitchell had expanded the television version into a three-act play, adding more humour and more horror, enlarging the role of Dr. Anders and introducing her colleague and lover, Dr. Wilson. The humour achieved in the television version by Agnes's and Betty's activities outside the apartment could not be handled on stage so Mitchell devised another vehicle for humour. Using his own child-hood home in Weyburn as a visual model for the halfway house, he realized that the dumbwaiter, in which his mother had their meals transported from the basement kitchen to the dining room, would be the ideal prop for moving the drugged Dr. Anders from floor to floor to keep her out of sight and that this would create a kind of mad confusion and visual humour perfectly suited to his play. In a preproduction interview he commented about one of the dumb-waiter scenes: "It's funnier than hell. . . . better than any goddamn French bedroom farce."[3]

The world premiere in Calgary on January 9, 1976, was brilliantly successful in Mitchell's eyes, and he was impressed with the performances of the four women with whom he had established a warm rapport throughout rehearsals.[4] The play opens starkly with Harriet in a rocking chair, humming "Amazing Grace." It is very quickly evident that she has been unable to control the delusional behaviour of her two companions, Agnes and Betty. In Act II Mitchell deliberately blends humour and horror as Dr. Anders is taken hostage, medicated, and shuttled back and forth in the dumb-waiter. In Act III, Anders is interrogated by the three women much as they have been in the psychiatric ward. From the psychological battering Anders receives at this inquisition to the climax when Harriet threatens to kill her with a kitchen knife, the harrowing tension is broken only once or twice by the innocently humorous interjections of Betty and Agnes. At the conclusion, Dr. Anders breaks down crying as she prepares to take Agnes back to Beulah. Mitchell wrote in the stage directions, "She has truly reached as a result of her experience – a compassion destination she had never known before."[5]

The ending, however, is not entirely satisfactory. Anders's precipitous moment of recognition and the pull of attention away from the three mad women, who are the emotional centre of the play, are not prepared for. In an effort to shift the focus more toward Anders, Mitchell wrote another ending that appeared in the published version of the play in *Dramatic W.O. Mitchell* (1982). In this ending Anders reveals, under Harriet's questioning, something of her own interior, of her love for her father and her hatred of her mother, which have made her distrustful of human compassion. While Anders's character needed to be developed, the writing itself is not Mitchell's best and the scene is structurally wrong. Mitchell recognized this when he saw that ending performed in Windsor in 1987: "I agreed with Merna I had made a mistake so this [ending] has changed back to the old ending."[6]

The audiences in Calgary responded deeply to the play's movement from the hilarious to the harrowing. Carol Hogg, writing the review for the *Calgary Herald*, reported that "it is a tribute to the success of both the play and the production that the audience is led, firstly, to cheer the revolt and the revolutionists" and then in the last act to yearn "for a return to order that is at least more conventional and comfortable, if no more 'sane.'"[7] Mitchell personally felt that the play had achieved what he had hoped for in emotionally engaging the audience in the distressingly confused world of his three mad women.

However, the strange mix of comedy and horror was a problem for one Calgary reviewer, who found the play "a repellent farce." He was angered, rather than moved, by Mitchell's attempts to unsettle his audience, and he betrayed the kind of unfortunate attitude toward mental patients that Mitchell was attacking, when he wrote that the play "is not for any audiences at all – unless large collections of hopeless schizophrenics with sadistic impulses can be transported to Calgary to see their homicidal dreams acted out." He dismissed the three women as a nymphomaniac ("a male sexist creation"), a "hysterical type," and "a fat zero with maternal impulses."[8]

Opening night at Toronto's Tarragon Theatre on January 31 was filled with expectation and nervousness. Mitchell wanted to make an impression, and, at least on opening night, he did. The performances were stellar and the audience was very moved, giving a standing ovation and calling out "Author! Author!" However, as Guy Sprung wrote, "Toronto, then as now, was a cold and judgmental beast" (*ML* 311), and the critics gave it mixed reviews. The *Globe and Mail* reviewer, who admired the acting and "the author's characters and dialogue," criticized Act II with the dumbwaiter sequences as "a bizarre series of Three Stooges-style hide-and-seek games" and felt that Mitchell did not quite move to a meaningful resolution from the "slapstick foundation."[9] The *Toronto Star* reviewer commented that the "inter-action" between the three mad women should have remained the core of the play, and that the attempted transformation of Dr. Anders was "weakly executed."[10] Perhaps Mitchell tipped too far toward farce in some of these scenes, sacrificing theme and character for entertainment value and plot. The play had flaws, but overall, as Martin Knelman commented, it was "one of the few original dramas of consequence in English Canada" in the 1976 season.[11] He also noted, which pleased Mitchell immensely, that here was an occasion in which regional theatre was ahead of Toronto. In January 1977, Mitchell was presented with the Chalmers Award (shared with Larry Fineberg) for the best play of the season.

Back to Beulah is Mitchell's most complex stage play in terms of character and theme. Sprung described the play as "very close to being a major play" (*ML* 311). Although it is not his most performed play (both *The Black Bonspiel* and *The Kite* have proven to be more popular over the years), Mitchell considered it one of his top achievements as a writer. Over the years, he talked more about, and expended more energy on, *Back to Beulah* than he did on any of his other work. It seemed, on the surface, to be a striking departure from his other writing such as his universally admired *Jake and the Kid* stories. But the dark notes of alienation and despair are akin to those in *The Devil's Instrument* and can be found in *Who Has Seen the Wind* as well, not to mention the unpublished "The Alien" and *The Vanishing Point*. Mitchell, himself, did not see it as entering new territory, although he knew he was more obviously manifesting a side of his vision that the general public overlooked.

– "HOW INCREDIBLE AND SAD FOR ME" –

Mitchell was having great success with his drama. A production of *Back to Beulah* was scheduled for March in Vancouver, and first professional productions of "The Day Jake Made Her Rain" and of *The Black Bonspiel* were set up for Calgary and Regina respectively. Busy with plans for a television series of educational programs for children on reading and the creative process called *The Magic Lie*, and then another trip to Grand Cayman, Mitchell was not keeping tabs on the *Wind* project.

King had secured the financing from the CFDC, Famous Players, private investors, and from the newly returned NDP Saskatchewan government. Casting had commenced, and a new draft of *Wind* was in the works. In March 1976, Mitchell received from King a contract to be signed along with a cheque for $6,000 – the final amount owing on the agreement of $10,000 for the rights to *Who Has Seen the Wind* plus the option payment of $1,000. This was a small amount by the day's standards for film rights to a novel of *Wind's* stature, but, as with *Alien Thunder*, Mitchell thought more would be forthcoming from the screenwriting and from the 5 per cent of net revenues clause.[12] Without running it by his lawyer, and apparently without reading it carefully himself, Mitchell signed the document. In so doing he gave away cinematography and television rights throughout the world "in perpetuity."[13]

Suddenly, at the end of March, the whole project was put in jeopardy. King blamed Budge Crawley for stirring things up. On his way back from Hollywood, where he had just won the Oscar for *The Man Who Skied Down Everest*, Crawley stopped off in Calgary to talk to Mitchell about the screenplay. He told Mitchell that he had serious reservations about the commercial viability of Watson's script and about King's ability to direct a feature film. Mitchell was stunned. He had no idea production was this far along, and, furthermore, he was now very concerned about the script. He immediately telephoned Laurence Arnold, his Toronto lawyer, and arranged to meet him in a few weeks.

Mitchell came to Toronto to present the award for the best radio drama at the ACTRA Awards on April 21. Apparently he was "a humorous delight,"[14] but behind the scenes, over drinks and dinner with Crawley and King, he was an angry man. As King reported, it was "an incredibly painful, difficult conversation."[15] Mitchell told King that he had thought all along that he would be writing the script – and he wanted to do so now. It was agreed that they would meet at Arnold's office in four days to discuss Mitchell's formal request to write the screenplay.

At the same time there was a smaller problem Mitchell had to deal with regarding the Kurelek illustrated edition of *Wind*. Av Isaacs, of Isaacs Gallery, who represented Kurelek's interest in the book venture, had asked a prohibitive amount for the use of Kurelek's paintings, and Kane explained to Bill that his counteroffer to Kurelek would only work if Bill were to agree to a reduced royalty. Bill agreed, and the book was to be typeset by the end of June. Kurelek brought in two new superb paintings and was working on thirty-two chapter headings in black and white. It looked as if it would be a fine edition.

The film project, though, was on the verge of collapse. King felt it was life or death for the project: "If we had got into a row we would have destroyed the project. There would be no film because nobody would have gone with Budge on that film at that point. You would have had to wait for another year and by that time –"[16] When they met at the lawyer's office on April 26, Mitchell insisted on writing the film script. As Arnold recalled, "He made it very clear to me that his concern had nothing to do with money; it had only to do with the artistic use of the book. And that was his only concern with anything he had – with 'Burmese' and 'Back to Beulah' and *Jake and the Kid* – he had to maintain artistic control. And that's very difficult. And the film makers didn't want that to be in anyone's hands but their own."[17] Arnold drafted an amendment to what he called the "unfortunate document,"[18] but it was not acceptable to King. However, after some negotiation King agreed, in an unbinding letter of understanding,[19] to give Mitchell the opportunity to prepare a script, with dates set forth for delivery.

There were accusations flying from all quarters. King called Crawley a garbage collector (implying that Crawley scavenged film projects such as *The Man Who Skied Down Everest* and *Janis* from the waste heap of bankruptcy); Crawley called King an incompetent director; King called Mitchell "dishonourable";[20] Mitchell felt King had betrayed him, believing that he and King had, as he referred to it, a "gentleman's agreement" for him to do the screenplay. He claimed he had been assured by King that, in spite of the lack of mention of this in the formalities of contracts and promotional literature, "You and I know what's what, Bill."[21] However, King said that he had been warned that Mitchell had difficulty delivering scripts: "I was clear that I didn't want Bill to write the script – for that reason. Also to collaborate at that distance would have been extremely difficult . . . it would have been foolhardy from my perspective to get involved with that."[22]

King had kept Bill at arm's length regarding the script from the beginning, and Crawley, perhaps deviously, had left his concerns until the last minute. From what Crawley had told him, Mitchell believed that the project was doomed. Mitchell, though slow to suspect such machinations (much to his continual detriment), was now angry, determined, and unpredictable. King, from the beginning, had been worried about Mitchell's volatility and now he met it face to face. As with the CBC/NFB fiasco, Mitchell had again run into the nasty side of the film business and had obviously failed to recognize the necessity of retaining a good agent or lawyer. Now he said, "Never again. From now on I won't even go to the can without calling my lawyer and getting it in writing. I don't ever want to be caught in this."[23]

Faced with Mitchell's hostility, King said that he had felt bound to save his project for the sake of the crew, and admitted, "There was a point where I was less than candid" with Mitchell.[24] That is, he had no intention of using the script Mitchell was now writing. Mitchell, however, proceeded as if there was a formal agreement and worked toward a deadline of June 1 for the first submission of his script.

Considering he had been left out of the process for so long, this deadline was unrealistic. He worked frantically throughout May on a film treatment, in the midst of preparations for his daughter's wedding on May 22. He felt that a new, dramatic direction was required to address the structural weaknesses of Watson's screenplay. Aside from his disappointment that all events were to be condensed into one season, instead of three as originally planned, he felt that

Brian's internal search and his "feeling" had not been translated into cinematic equivalents, both visual and aural – of wind, prairie landscape, sky, and seasons. Twenty years earlier when a young filmmaker had approached him about making a film of *Wind*, Mitchell had said, "Some day I am going to do a film treatment – atmospheric as all hell with wind in wheat and far spreading horizons – about a boy and his prairie search."[25] King and Watson had turned the focus away from prairie, away from Brian's search. When he heard that King had described the novel as "a celebration of the family" he retorted, "My God, they're Waltonizing it."[26]

Bill and Merna hosted Willa and Ben McLeod's wedding in their living room and conservatory. Bill's phalaenopsis orchids were in bloom in the greenhouse, and Willa carried an orchid corsage. She had asked her father to write her wedding vows as she wanted something special, original, and personal, but when it came time to rehearse the speech, she was aghast: "I hated it. It was so inauthentic, so artificial, so lofty. This was my wedding – and he was being W.O. Mitchell. He wasn't being my father."[27] When she told him that it wouldn't do, he was terribly hurt, but, as usual with Mitchell and his daughter, the tempest was soon resolved.

When the wedding celebrations were over, Mitchell went back to the film script and, by June 16, he had sent King 110 pages. Crawley had become increasingly uneasy about Watson's script and about King's ability to direct. In fact, in May, he had approached Kelly Neal at Cinemaworld in Seattle for a formal opinion about the potential for success of *Wind* in the States. Although Neal was impressed with the concept, she advised Crawley that it required considerable revision. Crawley was unable to convince King that there was time to rewrite the script using Mitchell's ideas so, on June 22, he withdrew from the project. King was livid: "We were about to sign the contract. Budge's only real function was to be completion guarantor because I had raised the money . . . but an hour before the signing of the contract with the Saskatchewan government, with the CFDC, with Famous Players and all of the money from Souris Films that we had raised, Budge phoned up . . . and said,

'I am sorry, I am not in' and the whole thing collapsed."[28] King now had to scramble to find someone to replace Budge as completion guarantor – with only two months before shooting was to begin. He managed to keep the project alive by securing Pierre Lamy.

On July 6, Mitchell mailed King another sixty to seventy detailed pages. His final submission, 109 pages (completing his 240-page script), was ready by August 18, and that day he telephoned King. During the conversation it became clear to him, as he wrote in his letter the next day, that King "had worked only with the Watson script." Working against time all summer, he had "kept reassuring" himself that King was actually looking at his submissions. Now he knew that was not true. It was a sad conclusion to what Mitchell originally had hoped would be a wonderful collaboration: "How incredible and sad for me and for the film if there had been no real intention at all of considering the script we agreed for me to do."[29]

King thanked Mitchell for his script and said he would attempt to use some of his material. Although a few of Mitchell's suggestions for landscape shots from his June 16 submission were incorporated, none of his plot or structural ideas were used. Filming started on Monday, August 30. King obviously did not understand how upset Mitchell was over the script and attempted to placate him by offering him a small role as Judge Mortimer. Mitchell declined. He also refused to attend the premiere, a year later, in Arcola, Saskatchewan, where the movie had been shot, and he claimed never to have seen it.

Officially King told reporters that, although there was much material that he "would have liked to have used," Mitchell's script had arrived too late.[30] Privately, though, King and Watson complained that Mitchell's script was "full of 'slapstick' elements, 'people falling into cow flops'" (*ML* 293). Watson thought it was "broad" and "corny;"[31] King commented that it was "simply and totally unworkable."[32] Both recalled extended passages of boring dialogue that simply were not cinematic. Budge Crawley, on the other hand, after reading the first two submissions felt that "Mitchell [was] the hope of that project."[33]

With good reason King and Watson were put off by a silly sequence (of about twelve script pages) in which the minister and the teacher chase after the young Ben across fields and farmyards, ending in a pratfall in cow manure. Mitchell's script was not perfect. However, in one aspect he was absolutely right. There should have been more wind and prairie in this film. Mitchell's script called for landscape shots and sound effects to act as cinematic equivalents for Brian's interior feeling of wonderment, his search for meaning. King, instead, opted to focus on the tame element, with about two-thirds of the scenes taking place in town. Although King's film begins on the prairie as the credits roll, and although he did manage to film a spectacular storm for a key scene in the script, the main locale of King's film is the town rather than the prairie.

Mitchell had clearly foreseen the problems of adapting his episodic novel for film and had come up with innovative solutions. He felt the story could be unified around the relationship between Brian and the Young Ben. Mitchell planned to make the Young Ben even more mysterious in the film than in his book. In his first draft Mitchell wrote, "As long as possible, [Brian's] parents and the audience are not sure whether or not the wild Young Ben is not [sic] a creature of Brian's imagination. Real or not he is Brian's alter ego, was so intended in the novel — what Brian might have been had he not been influenced by civilization."[34] Mitchell also wanted to emphasize the darker aspects of Brian, which must have been unsettling to King and Watson. Their civilizing of the novel resulted in what critic Martin Knelman (who praised the movie overall) called "the Sunday school cleanness of it all."[35]

With great restraint Mitchell refrained from bad-mouthing the movie (except for humorously calling it "Who Has Seen the Waltons") and when asked if he was angry he replied that he was "disappointed" and that King was "the boss."[36] Unlike *Alien Thunder* this movie was competent, professional, and relatively well received. Some critics applauded it because it adhered to the book;[37] others were dismayed that it stayed too close to the book.[38] Some reviewers criticized those very aspects that had worried Mitchell, that there was no "real dramatic unity to hold it together."[39] However, it "became Canada's highest grossing film for 1977" (*ML* 295) and won the *Prix Grand* at the Paris Film Festival in November 1977. It received little attention in the United States, opening at first in the northwestern states only, and moving to New York in April 1982, where it was reviewed by Vincent Canby of the *New York Times* as a "sweet, generous reverie of a movie" with a "lack of narrative sophistication."[40] Generally given a three-star rating, it was sold around the world on video, and was considered a Canadian success.[41]

Meantime, another visual adaptation of *Who Has Seen the Wind* was going very well. Kurelek had now completed eight full-page colour illustrations and thirty-two black-and-white chapter headings. Later that fall, when Mitchell met with Kane and Kurelek to sign the contract, he met Douglas Gibson, who would become his editor for the rest of his writing life. Gibson recalled this meeting when he and Kane took Mitchell and Kurelek out to dinner at the Westbury Hotel's top-level dining room, and he got the "full benefit of the W.O. experience":

> W.O. did his Reverend Healy Richards act, and he did it so enthusiastically and loudly that Konrad, the maitre d', had to come along and have a quiet stooped-over word with Hugh Kane. Hugh Kane, and I had never seen this before, reached in his pocket and handed five dollars over to Konrad and Konrad went away. It was also suggested to Bill that he tone down his Reverend Healy because he was actually rising from his chair doing, "BROTHERS AND SISTERS!!" It was wonderful. I was sitting there thrilled. Kurelek, who was a shy and retiring guy, was just sitting there with his eyes like saucers. I loved every moment of it. And I don't think since then there has ever been a dull moment in my relationship with W.O.[42]

Mitchell was especially pleased with the illustrated edition of *Who Has Seen the Wind* and the way his and Kurelek's visions of prairie life complemented one another. Mitchell loved the chunky Ukrainian children who had been inspired by Kurelek's own unique stored past of prairie life, though one reviewer was disappointed for exactly that reason: "Mitchell's characters, save one, are not Ukrainian."[43] Mitchell's instinct that the illustrated *Who Has Seen the Wind* would do well proved correct. It sold 9,280 copies in its first two years.

— *BACK TO BEULAH:* FILM PROJECT —

During the past four or five years Mitchell had felt more like a playwright and screenwriter than a novelist: "I would say that four-fifths of my writing has been exterior, visual playwriting rather than prose writing."[44] To this point in his career, he had published only four novels, but had to his credit – aside from the 175 or so radio dramas – more than thirty-five stage, film, television, and docudramas (some of which were derived from early short stories). In one year alone, 1976 to 1977, there were five stage productions of *Back to Beulah*, two of *The Black Bonspiel* and one of *The Day Jake Made Her Rain*. During this period he claimed that he had been "more productive than I have been in any five year period in my life."[45] He did not add, however, that a number of these projects (*Sacrament* and *Who Has Seen the Wind*) were hard writing with little satisfaction. With his film and stage work and his public speaking, he was now making a good salary, on average $43,000 per year between 1974 and 1977.

He had been burned twice with film ventures and felt that, given the nasty business of it, film was no place "for an innovative artist to be." Yet he recognized that "film as an art form is tremendously elastic and exciting,"[46] and the visual possibilities drew him once more to consider another film project, *Back to Beulah*. This time, however, because of the betrayal with *Alien Thunder* and *Wind*, Mitchell was determined to retain control. He had a good working relationship with Eric Till, so he entrusted him with the director's role and, later, even with a co-writer's role.

Through Ruth Fraser, who was working with him at the Banff Summer School, Bill met her husband, movie producer Fil Fraser. Fraser had been involved in radio and in educational television in

Edmonton but was now excited about the prospects of producing Canadian films. He had very good success with Max Braithwaite's *Why Shoot the Teacher* in 1977, and when he saw Theatre Calgary's production of *Back to Beulah* he asked to option it for a movie. Mitchell began working on the film script in the fall of 1976 and, before he flew off to Hawaii in December, he had a first draft of two hundred and forty pages completed.

Over Christmas and New Year's, Merna and W.O. went to Hawaii with us and our family. It was quite an adventure. For W.O. any time in the tropics brought back memories of his teen years in Florida, and he thrilled to see the waves and smell the tropical air, rich with earth and flower scent. He told us more times than we cared to hear the Latin names of all the tropical plants. We visited an orchid nursery, and, like a kid in a toy shop, he moved up and down the benches selecting plants to be shipped home.

*   W.O. had a solution for sunburn prevention that embarrassed us all. He spread milk of magnesia over his nose, cheeks, and forehead, saying it was a remedy he had used as a kid in Florida in the 1930s. One day we were sunning with about sixty other hotel guests around the pool when W.O. said to his grandchildren, Geoff and Sara, "Watch this." He walked over to the springboard tower and started up the ladder. By this time he was white-haired, and, while still quite sturdy, he had developed a "bum" hip as he called it, which gave his walk a slight hitch. Astonished, people nudged each other, sat up on their lounges, and stared at this grandfather climbing up to the three-metre springboard. His white hair, white bathing suit, the matching milk of magnesia on his face, and his exaggerated gestures made him look like Marcel Marceau about to begin a mime act. He pranced to the end of the board and looked down, windmilling his arms as he almost lost his balance. Shaking his head he backed off, but then came forward to look again. He now had everybody's attention. From his starting position at the back of the board, he took three strides, jumped up to hit the end of the board, only to have one foot completely miss it. With a yodelling yell he went off the side of the board and into the pool. A gasp went up. Two sunbathers*

went to help him as he climbed out of the pool. Sputtering, he motioned them away, walked over to the ladder, and started up again. People were now standing, and one woman muttered, "The old fool's going to kill himself." No one knew what to do. Again he took his starting position at the back of the board, his arms stretched out in front of him. He took three strides, sprang up — everyone held their breath — and executed a lovely swan dive. He emerged grinning — and to applause. As he towelled off, he said to Geoff and Sara, "The first one was a slip dive — and it's a hell of a lot tougher to do than it looks!"

Soon after we went body surfing at Waimea Bay. W.O. professed to know the technique. When we arrived there were only a few natives surfing in eight-foot waves, which came into shore in a curling roar of white. W.O. watched for a few minutes, commenting that the bodies looked like raisins in the emerald-green waves. He swam out, watched for the right wave, and, not quite expertly, surfed in and disappeared into a froth of white as the tail end of the wave slammed him full force onto shore. He staggered up out of the receding wave, pulling up his white trunks, which had been dragged down almost to his ankles. Naturally he encouraged the rest of us to join in, including his eight- and twelve-year-old grandchildren. It was exhilarating and even being thrown up on the beach did not deter us. We soon realized that the experienced Hawaiians were not riding a wave to its finish but, at the last minute, dove under the wave and swam back out to catch another one.

We were lucky. The worst we experienced were scraped noses and Waimean sand ground into every hem of our bathing suits, not to mention every crevice of our bodies. The next day we were told that Waimea was a championship beach and no place for amateurs. The day before we had gone, a novice body surfer had had his neck broken.

W.O. was sixty-two, and as he aged he became more like his eccentric character Daddy Sherry — a daring old man on the flying trapeze who lived his life in extremes. Inhibition no longer held him back from openly showing his disapproval of anything that annoyed him — which often embarrassed Merna and the rest of the family. He made amusingly rude comments to the tour guides when we visited the Polynesian Cultural Center, which purported to have created authentic Polynesian villages and exhibits. W.O. disputed the authenticity of the dances, the long boats, and the food. At our New Year's Eve dinner at the Royal Hawaiian, W.O. took an instant dislike to the waitress when she delivered her introduction by rote with the phoney exuberance of a summer camp counsellor. When she brought our hors d'oeuvres and ingratiatingly asked, "Is there anything else I can get for you?" W.O. brusquely retorted, "Yes, another waitress." This was a mistake. It was an hour before she reappeared with our entrees. When she asked, "Now, how were your hors d'oeuvres?" we all politely mumbled fine, but W.O. in a clipped and stern voice said, "I don't know – [long pause] – it's been so long I've forgotten."

Mitchell had been appearing regularly on Peter Gzowski's CBC-TV show *90 Minutes Live* and on January 15, 1977, he amused the audience with his stories of body surfing in Hawaii and peeled off his shirt to show his tan. He was also now appearing in a television miniseries about reading for young people, *The Magic Lie*, which he had taped in December. Mitchell was the host and narrator for these shows, in which various children's books were selected by librarians for children ages six to twelve. Mitchell would introduce a book and, following a dramatized "cliff-hanger" scene from it, would conclude by telling his audience that if they wanted to know what happened they should get the book from their library and read it. It was an innovative way to use television to encourage children to read.

Mitchell now launched into a full agenda of talks and readings, and the writing of the film script for *Back to Beulah*. Also, in March, at the request of Larry Fineberg, the playwright with whom he had just shared the Chalmers Award, he agreed to chair the steering committee to form a Guild of Canadian Playwrights, to open the group's inaugural conference later in July, and to speak at a fundraising benefit in September.

Just before the Hawaii trip, Eli Mandel, poet and professor of English at York University in Toronto, telephoned urging Mitchell to consider taking a writer-in-residency at York. In February Mitchell spoke at York and met with Joe Green, the dean of Fine Arts, and soon after agreed to be the writer-in-residence for the

1977–78 term. In March when he and Merna were again in Toronto, Merna met Doug Gibson for the first time. By now Bill and Doug had established a warm friendship as well as a lively, mutually admiring, professional relationship. Gibson was a Scotsman from Dunlop, Ayrshire, the very area from which Mitchell's great-grandfather and grandmother had originated. Merna and Doug immediately clicked, Doug writing later that he was very pleased to have finally met "the Myrna of so many legends" and that Toronto was going to be all the more interesting next year with the two of them in town.[47]

In the meantime Mitchell continued to work on both the film script for *Back to Beulah*, for which he had completed a fifty-two-page story outline for Eric Till, and on the stage-play version of *Sacrament*, now called *For Those in Peril on the Sea* for Tarragon Theatre. He met regularly throughout the spring with Fil Fraser to discuss progress on the *Beulah* script and trumpeted around that Colleen Dewhurst was going to play Harriet and that shooting would begin in the fall although, as yet, these were simply dreams. Now that he was getting close to finishing the stage version of *For Those in Peril*, he formally requested through his lawyer that the CBC not televise it until after Tarragon Theatre's Fall 1977 production (*Sacrament* had been shelved by the CBC for close to fifteen months now).

~ "THE SERPENT AND THE CAVE" ~

In the fall of 1976, Mitchell had again turned his attention to the collection of reminiscential stories about his childhood that he had written in the 1960s. Macmillan asked him to submit the stories by mid-February for an early fall 1977 publication. However, by March he was well into free-falling childhood memories of Weyburn for a new novel: "I had a thing about a boy digging a cave and blowing up his grandfather, and that boy becoming a psychiatrist, and as I looked at that it sort of teed me off – I got to thinking how an important part of our community was the Weyburn Mental Hospital, and there was a guy called Bill the Barber, whom I call Bill the Sheepherder, who was an escape artist."[48]

Free-fall material from about this time indicates he had worked out "several societies distinct within the larger constellation" of his prairie community – those of the adult, the child, the mental hospital, and "Sadie Rossdance's three little cottages" (*SH* 6), and he had also written a first draft of the campfire scene in which a hot rock explodes and Bill the Sheepherder has a fit. By the fall of 1977 he had written a large amount of free-fall about digging caves and their potential symbolic resonances (the cave as womb, grave, sanctuary, and the mind), about the mental hospital inmates (Bill the Barber, Buffalo Bill, Blind Jesus, Horny Harold), and about the Souris River swimming holes. In one page of free-fall titled "<u>THE RIVER,</u>" he wrote,

> Actually there are two symbol[s] – re[s]onant meaning things that have floated up ,out of this stuff . the cave of course —— but also the river – the river as a cleansing place – fluid – medium – a gathering place – a magnetic center – for: the children – it was the center of our world and our society. but only of course – from May 24th to October —— in a sense we were like the Metis and the Indians —— we were seasonally influenced. . . . .
>
> The river – the river —— this silty artery —— it was an artery and not – it was not an artery actually this was a prairie vein – for it was dark – it carried the suspended earth flour – there was at all times and seasons earth flour suspended in it —— because when you came out of it and into the sun – the alkaline clay flour – our bodies were floured with it and by it —— we were like young and naked holy men —— LOOK UP: the holy men who daub and paint themselves with ash and clay – looks like anyway . . . ——
>
> Not bad, Mitchell[49]

In the final manuscript, the river description was distilled to "the Little Souris River, a wandering prairie vein, dark with earth flower." (*SH* 5) This free-fall was the seed for the scene in which Hugh and Peter paint themselves with white alkali silt and sneak up on the boys in the swimming hole.

Mitchell also recalled fragments of his childhood heroes, particularly Roy Murray, one of the models for his main character.[50] In October 1977 he optimistically said he was completing a new novel that would be published in a year: "It is a story of a man in the 1920s. . . . He is a First World War hero living in a small prairie town. He goes through three different 'communities' . . . before he ends up in a mental hospital."[51] But at this stage, although he had worked out some of the plot (the man beats his wife to death in a rage and ends up hanging himself in the mental hospital), the "man" is still taking shape and has not yet found his name. In one piece of early free-fall, Mitchell recalled images of death from his childhood that find their way into the scene in which young Hugh discovers the wife's body in his cave:

> And I thought of the eyes on a gopher that's been clubbed – the bulging blue eyes ——— they were like some marbles . . . . . . a great deal like them ——— only not beautiful ——— so perhaps the mental marking most vivid to me as a child were the cadavers of dead things ——— cats and dogs and cows – and the cigarish rottenness of decay and of death ——— and the maggots ——— always the maggots. . . . . So: there must be something to indicate the rages that Gizzy is capable of ——— x ——— these might come when there are fights on the ice and Gizzy is always into them ——— and indeed frequently starts them himself. . . . .
>
> Aw shit, Mitchell you're making it all up![52]

We noticed a pattern to the way W.O.'s characters developed. In the initial stages he would refer to them in neutral terms, as "he" or as "my guy," but as they gained a critical mass and found their names, he would talk to us about them as if they were actual people – indeed, he would talk with *them when working out their dialogue – and argue with himself about their motivation. His hero at this stage was growing into King Motherwell and was resisting some of the things W.O. tried to ascribe to him – including the name "Gizzy." King did end up being the goalie for the Trojans, but he did not get into fights on the ice.*

Margaret Laurence once described Hagar in The Stone Angel *reaching this stage for her, and how she decided to have Hagar do something but "heard" Hagar say, "No, Margaret, I won't do that." This sense that some writers have of a character talking back, of a character taking on a life of his own, was particularly felt by W.O. as King's character grew. On the one hand, he loved this hero character who was a strange mix of Socrates and Holden Caulfield in his desire to teach and to save young boys from the horrors of the adult world. But at one point he was upset about where King was taking him and, almost plaintively, asked us, "Why in God's name — why am I compelled to create such a dark and destructive character?" Perhaps W.O.'s Presbyterian moral streak was conflicting with the "larger" amoral code of the artist's "negative capability" which goes beyond moral imperatives and rules, and which delights in creating both an Iago and an Imogen.*[53]

Reviewing his reminiscential pieces loosened more childhood memory-lumber for this new novel, and "Melvin Arbuckle" and "Take a Giant Step" become central scenes in it. But there is a striking difference in how this material is reused. In the original pieces, childhood experience and the initiation into the adult world have no dark undertones and are treated humorously, nostalgically, at times sentimentally (but they are not maudlin). In "Take a Giant Step" and "The Day I Sold Lingerie" there are only hints of the domineering female (mother and grandmother), and the conflicts between the child's world and the adult world are resolved in a positive way. Some of the most painful material Mitchell ever encountered through free-fall was now surfacing and it involved his mother. He disliked what he called her "Victorian hypocrisy" and resented her power over him as a child and adolescent. He found it "very hurtful" to think of his frustrations with and distaste for her and would compensate by thinking of the "good things about her."[54] When his mother died in 1960 and he experienced his creative drought, he began to mine his childhood past but blocked out the less pleasant aspects. But now, with a time-lag of twenty years, he tapped this material without evasion, and the relationship he created between Hugh and his mother grew directly out of this more painful free-fall. He recalled how he defended his "interior" from his mother because she "came on too strong, right through neutral territory and into my own" (*SH* 125). In the opening pages of the novel, Hugh thinks of Hesiod, who "could compare us to pre-Aryan silver age heroes: '. . . eaters of bread, utterly subject to our mothers, however long they lived'" (*SH* 3).

Billy in "The Day I Sold Lingerie in a Prairie Whorehouse" is completely innocent, and Mitchell looks back on his first uncon-scious contact with adult sexuality in a light-hearted and humorous way. Unlike the children in these pieces, the children in "The Serpent and the Cave" are playing with various kinds of dynamite that detonate real horror, which wound and scar emotionally and psychologically "for keeps." One of the central themes in the new novel is the realization that "adult guardians have printed more than we in later life realize" and "the real damage is in the id not yet rec-ognized."[55] Mitchell was continuing his exploration of the lower layers of self and reality that he had begun in *The Vanishing Point* and *Back to Beulah*.

～ TENSIONS ～

Although the new novel was beginning to firmly declare itself, Mitchell's attention was diverted to the film script for *Back to Beulah* and the new play for Bill Glassco at Tarragon Theatre. Once again his work was prominent on the drama scene, though it did not always bring in much money. During 1977, five of his plays were staged, three specifically for younger audiences. "The Day Jake Made Her Rain" played in Vancouver in April for a children's theatre. In October, Alberta Theatre Projects put on thirty-eight performances of *The Devil's Instrument* for Calgary schools, and, at the same time, "Cabin Fever" (a *Jake* radio play) was performed by Young People's Theatre in Ontario schools. In June he went to Peterborough to consult with Guy Sprung, who was directing *The Black Bonspiel* for the Peterborough Summer Theatre, a promising production with Hugh Webster as Wullie MacCrimmon. The play was performed in July, but unfortunately the theatre company went bankrupt and Mitchell was never paid his royalties. A powerful production of *Back to Beulah*, directed by John Wood, was put on in August at Neptune Theatre in Halifax, and that production travelled with much success to the National Arts Centre in Ottawa and to Montreal in the fall.

But there was disappointing news about *For Those in Peril on the Sea*. At the beginning of July, Bill Glassco wrote, "I don't feel this makes a play; and I think it would be disastrous at this stage if we were to go ahead with it."[56] He had been lukewarm about the television script that Mitchell had shown him and felt that Mitchell's reworking of it for the stage had not worked – particularly the transformation of Keith into Howard, "a twelve-year-old boy trapped within a seventeen-year-old body" who, after taking Lon's pills, attempts suicide (*DWO* 219). Although *For Those in Peril on the Sea* never made it onto the stage in Toronto, it was produced in Ottawa in October 1981 and at Theatre Calgary in February 1982. However, it has only been staged three times. With its lack of theatrical action, its largely one-dimensional characters, and its abrupt ending, it was, in the words of one reviewer, an "unremarkable" play although still a "song" worth "hearing."[57]

Mitchell began his eight-month creative-writing position at York University in September 1977, teaching both a first-year and an advanced workshop. Bill and Merna rented the main floor of a house in Cabbagetown, but that was short-lived when the landlord, who lived upstairs, objected to Merna's smoking, to the dog, and to the general Mitchell messiness and gave them a few weeks' notice to move out. This was an upsetting situation for Merna, who had to find a new place by November 1. Although she located a more suitable place for them in Leaside, the tension arising from this situation and the move in general probably contributed to her bout with shingles that began soon after Christmas. As the year wound down, Mitchell completed the first draft of the screenplay for *Back to Beulah* and announced that shooting was to begin in the winter with Katherine

Hepburn and Maggie Smith playing two of the mad women. In November he taped thirteen shows for the second season of *The Magic Lie* series, which began broadcasting on January 4, 1978.

Back in Calgary for Christmas, Mitchell was finally able to watch his television drama, *Sacrament,* which had been shelved since the fall of 1975. Without any advance warning, the CBC slotted it into the most unpopular time they could find – midnight on New Year's Day. Mitchell, however, felt it was a good production, and he especially enjoyed the irony that, because of the title *Sacrament,* some people thought they would be tuning in to a religious program. Bill Musselwhite of the *Calgary Herald* considered it not Mitchell's best, but "better than most of the CBC drama shown last year," and he thought it was dreadful that Mitchell, "who is . . . perhaps the best-known playwright in Canada," had not been treated better.[58] Mary Jane Miller, in her book on CBC-TV drama, commented that it was one of the best dramas to come out of Vancouver, and that "its best moments are very good indeed."[59]

The stage version of *Beulah* continued its success with a new production at Centaur 2 in Montreal in March and a French version planned for the fall of 1978 at Place des Arts in Montreal.[60] Between teaching at York and the *Beulah* film script, Mitchell found little time to work on his fictive memoir stories or his new novel. He knew well his vulnerabilities in regard to the writer-in-residence programs: "I have always been in danger of that, of spending more time teaching than writing, because it is a valuable pursuit and [you can] quite honestly convince yourself [that you are] using your days well. The same as performing. I have to worry about that too."[61] Merna was still suffering from shingles and that, along with his own frustrations with the *Beulah* script and his teaching, seemed to have put Bill on edge. Indeed, in March 1978 he explained: ". . . ten years ago I was a lot more elastic than I am now. Today I find I can't turn from one thing to another quite so effortlessly. I get tripped up easier."[62] Bill had just turned sixty-four. He was still the most active Canadian author on the speaking and media circuit. The high from these interactive engagements was addictive, as well as financially satisfying, but recovering from the travel and the post-performance low was becoming more and more difficult to deal with.

Around this time family and very close friends noticed that the active life of Merna and W.O. was taking its toll. They had less patience with one another and the shouting would sometimes have an unpleasant edge to it. Publicly W.O. was the same genial, enthusiastic person, who travelled coast to coast giving very amusing performances and causing interviewers like Peter Gzowski delightfully anxious moments when he uttered his usual irreverent remarks on radio or television. He was doing even more banquet and convention addresses, now charging $1,500. He was also giving, gratis, performances to raise money for ventures like Nellie's Hostel (March 1978) or to help struggling theatre companies like Centaur (May 1978). Less able to handle the stress of travelling and multiple assignments, he took out his frustrations on Merna as he became crankier, more impatient, and less considerate. Being on call to perform almost constantly accounted for, but did not excuse, a great deal of the stress he caused her.

Always talkative and accustomed to being the star attraction even at home, Bill began to monopolize conversations: "Let me finish, Merna," he would snap, not allowing anyone to interrupt for the next five minutes. Merna was feeling more assailed by his constant talk and demands on her time. Sometimes she humoured him ("Quiet time, Bill!"); sometimes she retaliated ("Shut up, Bill. Let others speak"); often she retreated in silence. His responses to Merna's suggestions regarding his work were more impatient, often explosive: "Don't interfere, Merna"; "You are invading my territory"; "No, Merna, for Christ's sake you have it wrong!" Some of her opinions were misguided, but oftentimes she was intuitively correct.

She confided in a few of her close friends about Bill's verbal attacks: "I forget about it, or rather I wish I could forget about it. I'm like fresh clay waiting for Bill's imprint. I am submissive. Being shit on gives me real physical pain — knots in my stomach and the runs. He can't work when I'm not around."[63] *It is telling of Merna's character that she twinned her personal pain with her statement that Bill needed her. She often excused his behaviour because he was a great writer.*

Merna's stress at this time was probably what triggered the shingles, causing her considerable pain for a couple of months. She stoically kept on with most of her regular duties, but she also began to drink more in the evenings, which exacerbated the situation with Bill. Able to battle it out, both lovingly and assertively, about intellectual and aesthetic topics, they were not good at discussing their own injured feelings and in their separateness they did not see what they were doing to one another. While there was, without a doubt, a deep love, happiness, and respect at the foundation of their relationship, it was a complicated one. Because of Bill's disorderliness, he needed her assistance in all the mundane details of his life, but he simultaneously resented her interference. In fact, she did interrupt Bill and she did give him orders about everything from what he should wear to where he should be. Much of this was necessary. But they ended up foisting unsatisfactory roles on each other: she created a reliant, helpless individual who was angry about his own loss of dependence; he created a self-sacrificing martyr who was depressed about her status. Though they invariably recognized the value of each other (he often used the first person plural as in "we went free-lancing"), the tensions became more pronounced as the demands of Bill's career grew and his elasticity lessened.

W.O. began to complain that people were treating him like an OLD person. In some hand-written free-fall material for Since Daisy Creek *he mused, "So much of aging is the result of conspiracy. It is others who give you a sense of being old. Whether you want them to or not, they are going to help you do such intricately difficult things as putting on your coat. They pull out chairs for you, grab your elbow helpfully at stairs. They even use a different voice for you — more solicitous — or — impatient. . . . Got your wallet? Credit cards? Your speech? Your reading glasses? Don't forget your snuff – your fly zipper. It is an insidious and imperceptible conspiracy, starting just before you've reached sixty." Following this is a list of five "signs of age": "They are making the print smaller on medicine bottles. . . . Your immediate family has very bad speech habits. They do not project. . . . they mumble. . . . They claim you have the TV turned*

up so high it is blasting them out of the family room. . . . They say you
have turned the thermostat up to ninety. . . . They tell you that's the tenth
time you have told about how the municipal office paid three cents a tail
for gophers. . . ."[64]

— "IT WAS ALMOST THERE" —

The Mitchells returned to Calgary in June 1978. Doug Gibson continued his pleas for the reminiscential pieces, but Mitchell was
underway on his new novel. He taught at Banff and spent as much
time as he could in July and August at Mabel Lake. This was the year
of numerous book bannings, and Mitchell was enraged by them. He
appeared on the CBC's *Sunday Morning* in July[65] to rail about the
bannings in Ontario of Margaret Laurence's and Alice Munro's
books. Mitchell told Laurence to ignore the bigots ("Don't knock it,
kid, it will sell you a lot of books"), but Laurence was deeply hurt by
these attacks and could not ignore them. In August, at a general conference of the Pentecostal Assemblies of Canada, Rev. Gerald Morgan
had urged banning a number of books from school lists, including
Who Has Seen the Wind.[66] So Mitchell was fired up a few months later
when he was invited to appear on *Point Blank*, a Global Television
series hosted by Warner Troyer, to debate the issue of banning books
from schools.[67] One of the guests on the program was the Rev. Ken
Campbell, founder of Renaissance Canada, which was spearheading
many of the book-banning initiatives across Canada. The debate was
lively. Mitchell recalled that, after the show, Campbell approached
him, all friendly and with a big smile: "Bill, I bear you no animus."
Mitchell, refusing to shake his hand, said, "Well, Reverend, I don't
bear you any animus either – but my animosity towards you has no
bounds."[68] Mitchell took every opportunity he could to attack publicly the book banners, Campbell in particular.[69] He also lent his
name to a letter for the Canadian Rights and Liberties Federation
appealing for funds to lobby against book banning.[70]

Without onerous commitments in the fall of 1978, Mitchell
turned his focus back to the *Beulah* movie script. There had been

numerous meetings about *Beulah* through the winter and spring, and a contract was finally drawn up in July that granted Fraser's company the option until December 31, 1979. It was announced that shooting was to begin on January 1, 1979, with Colleen Dewhurst signed on for the major role. Mitchell had ensured in the language of the contract that he would have artistic control, would write the script, and that Eric Till would direct it. Mitchell felt that Till understood his vision and his sense of humour, and he had more confidence in Till's abilities than in any other director of his film work. Till, likewise, found Mitchell "invigorating to work with . . . he likes to free-fall, he likes to push around ideas, he has a lot of energy and truly you have to keep up with him. Also . . . he will listen, he doesn't close his ears off . . . so it becomes a very, very collaborative affair, which is the best way a director and a writer can work together."[71]

In spite of Mitchell's optimism, the script was not moving along well. In fact, in late 1978 through 1979 Fraser became more and more anxious: "I would get drafts and semi-drafts and have long meetings with Eric Till and W.O. It was almost there, in many respects, but it wasn't complete. It wouldn't work as a movie. Eric Till messed with it. I messed with it. He [Mitchell] wasn't very happy with that." Shooting did not commence in January as predicted, and the drafts only got wilder rather than better. The success of the television version hinged on its subtlety and its compactness. The various film adaptations stretched it too far in both directions: the comedic line became slapstick; the tragic line became "B" grade horror. Fraser recalled that it was difficult to get Mitchell to focus on the project at times: "He was always performing. In fact, I found it hard to have a serious conversation with him. It was always jokes and laughs and stories."[72]

Till, too, acknowledged difficulties, but recognized the way in which Mitchell would free-fall a script: "I really sat beside him on it – in effect. And he did come up with some dumb ideas but gradually, gradually, gradually, one could have gone to something that would have been very interesting." Mitchell had a good visual sense, flexibility regarding narrative suggestions, and a facility for dialogue – all of which were important for the development of the script. Till felt, however, that until he worked with him on *Beulah* Mitchell had no firm recognition of how to economize on dialogue, how to "collapse ideas" and "collapse events," how to pare down and allow the visual scene to speak as much as the actual words.[73] In *Alien Thunder* Mitchell had overindulged in dialogue; in his film script for *Wind*, he overdid a couple of farcical scenes in attempting to let the visual speak. In *Beulah* he was learning a few more of the tricks of adaptation, although, encouraged by Till and Fraser, and indulging his own tendency to broad comedy, he began to excessively expand the comedic line. Perhaps the marketplace demanded broadness, but he was losing the delicate balance that he had achieved in the one-hour television drama by overloading the film script with scenes of action, horror, and humour involving Skilsaws, axes, a stolen ambulance, an escape from a Pentecostal revival meeting, and a confrontation with a bull. On top of that, his stage version ending was not "upbeat"[74] enough for the commercial producers, and he was having difficulty bringing the drama to what both he and they considered a satisfactory resolution.

A cheque for $10,000 for the option came through from Fraser in February 1979. Fraser was nervous, for he had committed a substantial sum and still had, in his opinion, no workable script. Mitchell was not working well – either on the film script or on the new novel. He had a bout with the flu that put him further behind, but he was looking forward to three weeks in Hawaii with Willa, Ben, and Brenna, their eight-month-old daughter. Merna and Bill had been strong supporters of the creative talents of both Willa and Ben, and, as Ben had recently decided to begin sculpting in wood and stone, the Mitchells made it one of their tasks to locate speciality hardwoods for his work. A great deal of their Hawaiian holiday was spent collecting and chainsawing logs of various tropical hardwoods that had been culled from a forest reserve, trucking them to the shipping yard, and arranging for them to be shipped to Calgary.

— MISADVENTURES —

The Mitchells arrived back from Hawaii in time to see the closing night of Theatre Calgary's production of *The Black Bonspiel of Wullie McCrimmon*. Although it had been staged before, this production firmly established its continuing success in major Canadian theatres. Directed by Guy Sprung and starring Hugh Webster as Wullie and Michael Ball as the Devil, it was a sellout hit. It has proven to be Mitchell's most popular play and, to date, has been performed nearly fifty times. Artistic director Rick McNair commented that "it has played in every major centre [in Canada], with the exception of Toronto," which, he adds, thinks itself too sophisticated for this play (*ML* 301).

For the stage-play version, Mitchell expanded Reverend Pringle's role and added more dialogue and action to the curling match. He also slightly expanded the minor role of "Woman 1" from the radio play (who represents religious fanaticism and gossiping hypocrisy) into Annie Brown, Malleable's wife. She is like Mrs. Abercrombie in *Who Has Seen the Wind*, and in her overly strident efforts to discover and stomp out sin in her community she has, herself, become marked by the Devil. Hers is a difficult character to play as she bears the heavy weight of that narrow-minded puritanical soul that Mitchell so despised. Guy Sprung commented, "If W.O. has a fault it is that his comic caricature encapsulations, which attempt to go deeper than mere wit, too often get sabotaged by brevity. . . . It was uncomfortable watching the actresses who had to play Annie Brown going through the agony of trying to give reality to that thinnest of roles" (*ML* 315).

On the final night of the play's extended run, Bill decided to present "Annie Brown" with an orchid from his own greenhouse. He took it to a florist to be arranged into a proper corsage to be picked up just before show time. Although Merna seldom allowed W.O. to drive on his own by this time, because he was so accident prone, she had other people to ferry to the theatre and let him go alone. He was to meet her in their seats at the theatre.

The orchid was beautiful and, as he drove toward the theatre, he glanced over to check it on the car dashboard – just in time to see it start to slip off. As he grabbed for it, the car swerved off the road up onto the sidewalk and mowed down three parking meters before coming to a stop against the wall of a building. When he tried to back away from the building, the last parking meter caught on the undercarriage of the car. Frantically he rocked the car back and forth, then gunned it, and managed to free the car and get back on the road. He did not look back, or under, to check the damage.

He went backstage and gave the orchid to Sharon Bakker, told her about his adventure of finding "a parking meter up (where the sun don't shine)," but asked her "not to tell Merna, because she was trying to stop him from driving at that point."[75] When he slid into his seat as the theatre darkened, Merna whispered, "Where were you, Bill?" No answer. Her antennae for his misadventures now alerted, she demanded, "Bill, what happened?" He innocently replied, "Nothing." "Billllll (her I-don't-believe-you tone)." "I ran down six parking meters." "Jesus, Bill! Did you call the police?" "Of course not," he replied, "Do you think I'm stupid!?" Furious she said, "That's it. You're not driving ever again." He never did drive again.

In June, shortly after doing another of his one-man shows as a benefit for Theatre Calgary (May 31, 1979), Bill and Merna visited with Orm and Barbara in Peterborough. Bill enjoyed showing off to his fourteen-year-old grandson with some springboard dives and then, in a moment of characteristic impetuosity, he decided to demonstrate a snap-up on the lawn. It was an impressive and agile snap-up, but at sixty-five his vertebrae were not as elastic as he thought. He paid dearly for his Daddy Sherry–like exuberance and was in great pain the next day. For the next while, he had to wear a neck brace (its pristine whiteness soon stained with brown snuff), take muscle relaxants, and do a series of therapeutic exercises. He contemplated, but finally refused to use, a contraption that would hang him upside down to stretch out his spine. Instead, he used what he called his medieval torture rack, a neck traction kit consisting of a canvas bag that fit under his chin, around his face, and laced up at the back of his head. This was attached to a rope that went through a pulley clamped to the top of a door jamb. He would sit in a chair, harness himself into the canvas bag, and get Merna to attach the weight to the end of the rope.

Later that fall, on a visit to Peterborough, he brought his neck-stretching contraption and we used a couple of bricks in a plastic pail for weight. He would do his daily twenty minutes of stretching, sitting bolt upright in a chair by the wood-burning stove — which he insisted on having turned up full blast because he was always cold. While we were all sympathetic, it was difficult to resist laughing at the picture he made, his cheeks bulged up over the edges of the canvas. He looked as if he was wearing a jockstrap around his chin and face. Although these traction sessions gave him relief from the pain, they were another kind of torture because he couldn't talk. He would glare if we spoke to him or continued with conversations to which he wanted to contribute. Later, he used this situation in Since Daisy Creek *when Annie takes advantage of her father's similar predicament and corners him when he cannot talk back.* (DC 106–07)

Over a year later Merna wrote to a friend that Bill was still experiencing pain from the whiplash injury and having regular physiotherapy and neck-stretching: "He's just now feeling some improvement and he's not a very cheerful patient!"[76] In fact, he had broken two cervical vertebrae, and the effects of the injury stayed with him for life — and he continued to jokingly blame his grandson for the injury.

— "I DID A GREATER VARIETY OF THINGS" —

In spite of the discomfort from his whiplash injury, Bill kept on with his regular agenda. In July, Robert Duncan began interviewing him for an hour-long National Film Board biography and came to the Banff Centre to film him teaching and giving a reading. In fact, Duncan opened his film with Mitchell (wearing his neck brace) giving one of his performances at Banff. Peter Gzowski, the narrator for the biography, introduces him, "His one-man show sells out across the country. Talk-show hosts beat a path to his door. Universities pursue him to be their writer-in-residence. At cocktail parties, guest line up to talk with, listen to, and be charmed by . . . William Ormond Mitchell."[77]

This was the first biography on Mitchell's life and the most extensive, in-depth interview process Mitchell had gone through. While some of his responses regarding his early life were well-rehearsed set pieces by this time, Duncan pushed Mitchell hard to think about the writing process, about the difficulty of writing novels, about regionalism, about whether or not the public knew him as a performer or a writer, and about how Mitchell wanted to be remembered when he was gone. This was interesting and revealing conversation. Soon, however, Bill recognized that Duncan had a thesis about him that was not very flattering: "He's trying to tell me I've squandered my career."[78]

When interviewing Kildare Dobbs (an editor at Macmillan), Duncan began, "Our thesis on this film is that Mitchell has wasted a lot of his life by being a performer instead of a serious novelist." Dobbs responded, "Bill Mitchell was finding a new way of being a storyteller. It wasn't in fact a step down from the position of 'serious novelist,' in quotes, it was a continuation of storytelling, which is what the novelists do. . . . There's no reason why a man shouldn't spend his life telling stories like the forerunners of the novelists, forerunners of the poets, like the bards."[79] Duncan, however, doggedly pursued his thesis, slanting his questions toward that end. Bill and Merna, and some of the interviewees, as is apparent from the interview transcripts, were annoyed by Duncan's line of questioning. Duncan suggested to one neighbour that Mitchell was a "fraud," to another that he spent too much time hunting and fishing, and to Mitchell himself that he "wasted a lot" of time on activities other than novel writing.[80] Mitchell patiently explained that between 1947 and 1979 he had published not just four novels but had produced two failed novels, and had been very productive as a playwright (radio, television, and stage): "You see, why I am lucky is [that] I made no compromises but I did a greater variety of things which I may not have done, so in a way who is to say [that I wasted time], because I love playwriting, I respect playwriting, and I had managed to do it."[81]

Doug Gibson and Robert Fulford, then editor of *Saturday Night*, pointed out that Mitchell's varied talents had allowed him to make a contribution in many areas other than novel writing. Gibson commented that "it would be churlish of us to try to lock the man up so that he could produce the next book."[82] Fulford pointed out that Mitchell felt an intense duty to teach creative writing, "not as a little frill and not as something you do every couple of years for a month, but as a duty, as a part of his life."[83] However, many of these comments were edited out because they contradicted Duncan's thesis. Dobbs later said, "I was cut, replaced by someone who gave the answer the producer wanted – that Mitchell wasted his gifts goofing off in the lecture hall, or words to that effect."[84] Duncan preferred to use footage containing a remark made by Mitchell's rancher friend, Dave Diebel: "If he could just use that enthusiasm in writing. What he could have did."[85]

Duncan's accusation that Mitchell had betrayed his own talents by failing to focus on being a serious writer hit a nerve with Mitchell. Throughout his career, he had to contend with the question of whether he was a "serious" writer, and certainly Duncan, and many others, assumed "serious" applied to novelists who wrote prolifically and solemnly. Mitchell argued that humour was his vehicle to deliver a deadly serious and universal message. However, he unintentionally contributed to his own dismissal by referring to himself as a "folksy old foothills fart." He was always peeved when this characterization was turned back on himself by his critics who missed the ironic humour with which he delivered it. He was compared to Stephen Leacock and to Mark Twain, who have also been categorized dismissively as humorists. More often than not, he felt, people considered him a "homegrown Mark Twain" because of his appearance, the white tousled hair and moustache. "I'd be extremely flattered," he said, if people meant the comparison in terms of style and subject matter: "Look, *Huckleberry Finn* was one of the earliest novels evoked out of the natural context of the New World. . . . I've never liked the simplistic link-up with him [Twain] based on our personalities, but I *would* approve a comparison of the way he and I have written things that are valid because they come out of the unconscious absorption of real life."[86]

Following the release of *Novelist in Hiding*, critics across the country zeroed in on the theme of laziness and irresponsibility, suggesting that "by his conscious decision to lead a normal life [he] is hiding from his primary responsibility of being a novelist,"[87] and many of them chose as their only quote the unfortunate remark made by Diebel. A popular myth was created that Mitchell was not engaged in serious art. Mitchell, who during the interview process was positive about the conversations, felt let down, then angry about the final biography. He exclaimed to an interviewer (who must have edited the language), "Buffalo chips! Think of what I *did* do. Think of what I *am* doing, what I *plan* to do."[88] And he did have plans: his new novel, *How I Spent My Summer Holidays*, was moving along well; he had another novel in the works; and he was still hot with plans for the movie *Back to Beulah*. Duncan's portrait is flawed because he failed to see the symbiotic relationship between Mitchell's "life art" and "art art,"[89] how the life he led fed into his multiple talents as performer, teacher, novelist, and playwright for radio, television, stage, and film.

13

HOW I SPENT MY SUMMER HOLIDAYS AND DRAMATIC W.O. MITCHELL

– 1979 to 1982 –

I N THE FALL of 1979, Mitchell became writer-in-residence at the University of Windsor, "the sweetest university creative writing department I know of."[1] Of all his university attachments this was the most emotional, the longest (eight years), and the one during which he accomplished the most creative work (three novels). It was a different appointment in that, except for one year, he did no formal teaching, although he frequently met with individual students to discuss their writing. Because of the length of time he spent there, he and Merna became more socially involved in the university and in the community than they had during his other residencies. In particular they became friends with Alistair and Anita MacLeod. MacLeod taught creative writing and romantics in the English Department, and had recently published his first collection of short stories, *The Lost Salt Gift of Blood* (1976), which Mitchell admired greatly.

MacLeod had suggested that Mitchell be considered as writer-in-residence when Joyce Carol Oates left in the spring of 1979. He had met Mitchell five years earlier:

The first time I remember being with him was when we brought him in for a reading. I was with him from about 10:00 until late afternoon. I was kind of in awe of him at the time because he was the legend that he was, and I was considerably younger. I remember saying, "Now we will go to the bookstore." Then the bookstore would phone and ask where he was. And so on. The photographer called up. Bill would say, "What time is it? I guess we have time for a drink." We got along well. Then I had the courage to tell him that we didn't have time. What had happened was that his watch was on Calgary time so he had spent the whole day being late for every single thing. People would phone up and say, "You are supposed to be here at 2:00," and I would tell him that and he would look at his watch and say, "Okay," but his watch was reading 12:00. . . . I had a whole campus furious with me.[2]

In September Merna and Bill found an apartment and settled in. Right from the start they both liked Windsor for its friendliness, its openness, its ethnic mix, and its core of blue-collar workers who understood and cared about people when they were down and out. Bill remembered an incident with a young university graduate who was given a jacket on credit and loaned $200 on faith by a shop-keeper, which reminded him of his own experiences in Calgary during the Depression. Surprisingly, they did not find Windsor Americanized: "In fact, Windsor is much more intensely Canadian in our view than Calgary is."[3]

Mitchell was immediately at home in the English department. He could be heard banging away on the electric typewriter (he destroyed three typewriters at Windsor alone) from about eleven to four every day, including Saturdays and Sundays. Quite soon his office took on the Mitchell ambience of brown snuff and tea stains. Pungent eucalyptus scent and brown smudges permeated everything, including his manuscript pages and, to the amusement of the secretaries, every part of Mitchell himself – shirt fronts, fingers, moustache, and hair. When he had to look presentable for an interview, he would take off his turtleneck and put it on back-wards, sporting a clean front. Beth Proctor, one of the English department secretaries, made him a bib, but that did not last long.

He made friends with a number of faculty members, and would burst from his office seeking the nearest colleague to read aloud a portion from his current novel. Tom Dilworth, professor of English and one of Bill's frequent captives, described him as an Ancient Mariner monologist – dramatic and compelling, but very time-demanding. He had a "huge ego," not an offensive one, but "very healthy" because "built into this is a kind of generosity and consideration and benevolence which is really rare."[4] At times, though, Dilworth and others would see Bill coming down the hall and would close their doors, because a promised ten-minute reading from him could easily turn into a two-hour session. Bev Stahlbrand, assistant to the chair of English, was in charge of Mitchell's secretarial and agenda needs. She nicknamed him "the human yo-yo" because of his cross-country book tours and reading schedules. As always, when he discovered someone he liked, professional boundaries disappeared. Bev became one of his most frequent listeners for whatever book he was working on, and she and her family became close friends with Merna and Bill.

— "I DIDN'T KNOW THERE WAS ANY FORNICATORS IN OUR TOWN" —

Like the Ancient Mariner's tale, the two novels Mitchell was working on at this time were about betrayal, guilt, loneliness, and quests for redemption. In one of the NFB September interviews, he described how his fictive memoir "got away" on him and became a novel about "different kinds of caves." While "very excited about this novel," he said it would not be completed for another three years and that his grizzly bear novel about corruption would be finished in April for fall 1980 publication.[5] However, during his first year at Windsor it was the cave novel that demanded his attention. He worked on fleshing out its main characters, themes, image patterns, narrative arc, and wrote the "Dionysian" scene in which Sadie Rossdance's whores come down to the swimming hole and "reed-pipe fun turned mean and rotten" (*SH* 186). Young Hugh, hiding in wolf-willow bushes, sees for the first time a naked female body and watches as Sadie's girls get into a vicious bulrush fight.

Brian's spiritual quest for "the feeling" in *Who Has Seen the Wind* has been replaced by Hugh's search for an "it" (*SH* 1), which has a disturbing and perverse sexual undercurrent. But there is a premonition of Hugh's darker quest in *Who Has Seen the Wind*. After Brian and Ike hear Saint Sammy's harangue against the town's wickedness, Brian asks, "What's a harlot?" and Ike responds, "A hoo-er. . . . They don't wear no pants. Fornicator's a new one on me. I didn't know there was any fornicators in our town" (*WW* 228).

As a child, when Mitchell and his brother Bobbie dropped by Jesse Hart's three cottages on their milk-and-cookies run, he did not know that there were "any fornicators in our town" either – nor that there was a bootlegging operation going on at the Dickson Hotel where he and Bobbie were given candy cigarettes.[6] He discovered all this years later in 1939 (he was twenty-five at the time) when he returned to Weyburn. An old family friend told him that the women who lived in the three little cottages on the edge of town were prostitutes, and that the owner suddenly left town as a result of a blackmailing scam involving some of Weyburn's "top-drawer" citizens and a coverup for an abortion: "It was an eye opener to me when he told it to me – of the hypocrisy. . . . I guess it's marked me all my life, really, and whether I like to believe it or not, in fact I'm not, but I was, innocent. I did not see below the Calvinist skin, the Victorian."[7]

In some free-fall about this time, Mitchell explored how children and adolescents are unsuspectingly programmed by their culture and how Hugh, "in his last days," will realize this as he re-examines what happened in the summer of 1924: "It is not so dreadful that one recognized and either resisted or complied with the moulding of the tabula rasa – the wicked thing is to be moulded and not be aware and therefore not to have been able to make an understanding decision about what was being done to one." Following this, Mitchell continued to talk to himself about how King, as well as Hugh, was betrayed and irreparably damaged by his puritan imprinting: "The hero [King] of course was victim of that – he was programmed into the war and into killing – he was programmed into but resisted the sex – no – not at all successfully – while he acted against the order of Victorian society – . . . he could escape the strictures that were outer but he could never escape the inner bonds of guilt."[8]

In exploring Hugh's growing awareness of the deep caves below the "Calvinist skin," Mitchell was drawing on his own Presbyterian upbringing. In a 1980 interview Mitchell said, "I've had to break puritanical bonds."[9] He felt he had been "moulded" to an unhealthy attitude toward sexuality, an attitude that kept him innocent in a way that, at least on hindsight, was embarrassing and which in some ways he felt betrayed by – especially in the context of looking back from the vantage point of the so-called sexually liberated 1960s and 1970s.[10] Sexuality in his earlier work is handled in a rather superficial way – partly because the focus in much of this work is the very young and the very old. *The Vanishing Point* and *Back to Beulah* treat sexuality in a much more direct and complex way, and "The Serpent and the Cave" explores the effects of a small prairie community's Victorian and puritan culture on adolescent and adult sexuality.

‑ DOCTORING – OF VARIOUS SORTS ‑

Mitchell had become more and more unhappy with the way Fil Fraser and others were "messing around" with the *Back to Beulah* film script behind his back. What angered and deflated him was the discovery that, in a last-ditch attempt to salvage the project, Fraser had sent the script to a "film doctor in Los Angeles who was going to try to find a through line and tie it together."[11] Mitchell claimed that this film writer had worked on the script for *Psycho* and that he turned *Beulah* into a Hollywood murder thriller. Fraser, of course, was trying to find a way out of the impasse, but Mitchell, as with *Wind* and *Alien Thunder*, felt betrayed by the surreptitious methods so common in the film business.

During the summer, Colleen Dewhurst, Carol Kane, and Carole Shelley had been cast, but there was still dissatisfaction with

Dr. Anders's characterization. However, Fraser said that Susan Sarandon "had read enough of what Bill had written and she was ready to do it." According to Fraser they were very close to making the film. But in October "the whole thing collapsed."[12] Mitchell and Fraser were barely speaking to one another. Fraser had run out of money, and there was still not a script that all parties were happy with. Fraser tried one last time to cobble together the first version with an ending from another version and sent it to Mitchell assuring him that it was all his work. However, nothing came of it and Fraser's option expired at the end of December.

During all this, Bill had not been feeling well. In September 1979 he found out that he had late-onset diabetes, and he now had to carefully monitor his diet. When Merna was around he was good about trading in his ice-cream desserts for bananas, his martinis for white-wine spritzers, and the brown sugar on his porridge for sugar substitute. However, he still experienced great blood sugar fluctuations that accounted in part for the fatigue, bouts of dizziness, and mood swings he experienced from this point on in his life.

In October he noticed numbness in his fingers and his right forearm and more problems with his knees and hips, particularly on the left side. He began complaining that his legs simply did not work properly. Finally, at the end of January 1980 he saw a neurologist, who diagnosed the hand numbness as a problem with the ulnar nerve in his right arm caused by his diabetes. In March he had surgery to transpose the ulnar nerve. A week after his release from the hospital, he and Merna flew to Barbados for ten days to recover.

On May 1, 1980, Mitchell attended the premiere of *Novelist in Hiding* in Calgary, giving a reading before the showing. There were various screenings of the film throughout the country, culminating in a CBC national airing that was followed by *Who Has Seen the Wind*.[13] His calendar was packed with readings and addresses during the spring and, as usual, he headed off to Banff in July to teach. While there, he was "flattered and moved" to be given the first Banff School of Fine Arts National Award (for substantial and continued contribution to arts in Canada). The theme of his short address was that "art, with a capital A" is a form of the "human need to bridge" and he expressed the hope that, during his writing career, he had "built some successful bridges," including those he had built through the writing program.[14] He was presented with a medal, specially designed and sculpted by Dora De Pedery-Hunt.[15]

As usual, W.O. and Merna went to Mabel Lake following his session at Banff. However, this summer's relaxation and fishing came to a painful end for W.O. The cottage was set on a bank about twenty feet above the lake, and flat stones had been used as steps down to the beach. Because the bank was eroding, a fifty-foot cement and stone retaining wall was under construction – and had been so for a number of years, earning the name "Hugh's Wall of China." Half-inch reinforcing iron bars stuck out of the bottom layer of cement like blunted pikes. Although Hugh and W.O. had started the project, others occasionally worked on it, including Paul Sveigard, a local handyman and Christian evangelist, who, on this fateful day, was mixing a batch of cement on the beach as W.O. started down the steps to go fishing. W.O. tripped, rolled into a somersault to save himself, and cursed and screamed his way down fifteen feet of steps. He just missed being impaled on the rebar at the bottom and landed on his back at the feet of Sveigard, who fell to his knees and began to fervently pray over W.O.

 W.O. had broken his elbow (the one that had been operated on six months earlier) and badly scraped and bruised himself. Because Merna had returned to Calgary the week before, he had to accept Sveigard's offer of a ride into Enderby to catch the bus home to Calgary. It was a ride he never forgot and he would say he wasn't sure which was worse – the pain in his elbow or Sveigard's proselytizing. As loudly as W.O. cursed and complained, Sveigard matched him with prayers, asking the Lord to forgive Bill Mitchell and look after his arm. Halfway into town, he even pulled off the road and knelt by the car to ask God's forgiveness for such a blaspheming devil of a man. For Bill, it was utter relief to get on the bus and try to sleep away the pain on the seven-hour journey. When he arrived in Calgary, he caught a cab to the house, and calmly announced to Merna that he had to be taken to emergency immediately

to have his broken elbow set. Two days after the accident, on August 29,
he was operated on, and a pin was inserted, but it was never pain-free,
acting as an internal barometer for cold-weather fronts for the rest of his
life. In spite of the pain, though, and just two days later, he went to Regina
to celebrate the city's seventy-fifth anniversary on September 1. Following
that he performed a Theatre Calgary benefit, "W.O. Mitchell and
Friends," on September 6. Although at home W.O. could be a whining,
demanding patient, he also had grit. He seldom cancelled engagements,
and when the adrenalin of performance was running he somewhere found
reserves of energy and stamina that were quite remarkable.

— BACK TO WINDSOR —

At the end of September 1980, Mitchell was back at Windsor for his
second year. He was "on a roll," as he liked to say, with the new
novel, which had now been set in the framework of a memory search
by an older narrator, Hugh, who "realises his days are numbered and
now his mortality is leaning on him with some real weight."

Mitchell, now sixty-six, was feeling his age too. The pain from
his elbow and from his neck continued to bother him so much that,
in October, he returned to his neurologist. He had also begun to have
difficulty walking because of an elastic quality in his left hip. However,
the doctor found him unusually supple and felt his complaints were
related to the aging process and the diabetes. But the hitch in his walk
became more noticeable, and Mitchell railed loudly against these
betrayals of his body that evoked darker thoughts on time, loneliness,
identity, and aging. He imagined his narrator to be, like himself,
involved in a university community although "perhaps . . . a master
of a college in a University being damaged by cut-back and threat" so
as to produce some crisis in his life that would toll the narrator back
to that horrific summer. In his free-fall Mitchell put himself in the
skin of his older narrator to muse about "the deep depressions – the
limbo feelings – the sadnesses – and in the end they all added up –
he guessed to loneliness." These free-fall explorations indicate that
Mitchell himself was experiencing a deepening sense of his own

```
Time --- why is it that time seems to speed up as one
grows older -- and it does --- I can remember waiting
and waiting for Christmas -- for summer holidays --
waiting to be ten -- for that would be an important
milestone age -- that seemed never to come --
waiting for a birthday -- waiting for Valentines
Day and for Ester --- and now the proportion seems to be
about -- a year is actually a month.....


And looking at the inside of my left elbow with the
purple freckle there and the yellow aureole -- where
the little girl uncertain from her training -- trying
to find the vein -- so -- the check-up medical
check-up ----
These have to be the winter years -- when the sunlight is
long and glancing and tepid  -- and the days are so short
and the dusk comes so early in the afternoon  ---
the actual days newxx now_  -- all seem short ---
and the ineffable sadness I felt in Grade Two and
Thr e and Four -- in Miss COldtart's room -- when we
sang "Now the Day is Over."   It is as though
I am filled now with that "Now the Day is Over"
Feeling."  I have truly entered the  society of the
old --- and it is not supposed to be good -- they
protest that these are good years and this is a good
society --- then why do they call the retirement homes
Sunset Lodge --- Golden Age ---
```

Free-fall for How I Spent My Summer Holidays

mortality: "These have to be the winter years – when the sunlight is
long and glancing and tepid – and the days are so short and the dusk
comes so early in the afternoon – the actual days now – all seem
short – and the ineffable sadness I felt in Grade Two and Three and
Four – in Miss Coldtart's room – when we sang 'Now the Day is
Over.' . . . I have truly entered the society of the old."[16]

In another piece of free-fall from this period, Mitchell muses about his sense of growing detachment:

> It's only in the past five or perhaps ten years that it has happened to me — but I lose a grasp on my self — my own selfness — the individual point within that says I think or I feel — therefore I am . . . . it is as though I've stood unknowingly aside and become a detached and quite uninvolved spectator of myself — uninvolved is too mild a word — uncaring — uninterested actually — That does not capture it —— I suppose a psychologist might mean this when he uses the word dissociated —— is that it — is it a primitive form of split personality — is that what the old term possession means?[17]

This mode of thinking was related to his creative process, which involved a negating of his own self as, chameleonlike, he took on the personalities of his characters. But this was shifting into something else, into uncaring withdrawal from, rather than intense identification with. Possibly the reason for this was that Mitchell had become fascinated by a character who was dissociated in an uncreative way, who had lived a wasted life. Other batches of his free-fall for the new novel contain reflections about the "fear of failure [that] corrupts love – and marriage and life," thoughts about death, and about the vulnerability of the self – all of which Mitchell ascribed to his narrator but which he was, to some degree, experiencing himself. Mitchell felt that *How I Spent My Summer Holidays* was the most autobiographical novel in terms of the emotion that underlay its creation. There is an intensity of emotion that is unique to this work, and which is heightened by his use, for the first time in a novel, of the first-person recall point of view.[18]

In November, Mitchell went to Banff for a two-day symposium. A six-week pilot project for a winter writing program had just finished, and the instructors and writers who had participated in the project met with "writers, publishers and book agents from across North America" to discuss establishing a winter writing program for advanced writers. The idea was to establish a program that would go beyond the summer free-fall sessions set up for beginning writers. Mitchell could see the necessity of this move, so advanced sections in fiction and poetry were introduced (led by Alistair MacLeod and Richard Lemm). However, at one point during the symposium Jack Ludwig, Rudy Wiebe, and Al Purdy "expressed anger at the way the [summer] course was treated as a 'near religion.'" Participants in the pilot project were alarmed at "such a 'passionately negative' discussion" and annoyed because it "did not deal with the focus of the symposium."[19] Mitchell was very upset by what he perceived to be an attack on his free-fall method and, even eighteen months later, recalled the event as a public humiliation.[20]

Considering he had the novel to complete for fall publication, Mitchell took on too many commitments for the spring. In March he did a reading and a panel discussion for the Canadian Images film conference in Peterborough, and then he was off on a tour of Saskatchewan libraries with seventy-five commitments in nine days. He felt "like the baton in a relay race:" "One library drops me off at a filling station half way and then the next one picks me up."[21] But he continued to perform well, or as one fellow from Cut Knife, Saskatchewan, put it, Mitchell was "better than television." Merna, as always protective of his writing time, wrote a friend that "with the extra financial burden" of helping their daughter through fine arts at the University of Calgary and their son-in-law through the College of Art, "Bill has taken on too many speaking engagements." However, she concluded that busyness had perhaps been "good" for him, for he submitted a large portion of the new novel on April 3, and he was able to "stop the traction on his neck."[22] By the end of April, Bill had submitted the remainder of the manuscript to Gibson.

At the same time that Mitchell was completing *How I Spent My Summer Holidays*, he was consulting with Rick McNair, who was staging *The Kite* at Theatre Calgary with Jack Creley playing the 117-year-old Daddy Sherry. The play premiered on April 30, and Mitchell was particularly pleased with Creley's performance. The play moved on to the Toronto Theatre Festival, opening on May 26.

As Martin Knelman noted in *Saturday Night, The Kite* was not only successful, it was in vogue: "Geriatrics are stealing the spotlight [with American and Canadian theatre productions such as *On Golden Pond* and *The Gin Game*], and W.O. Mitchell has created the most cantankerous daddy of them all." Knelman, zeroing in on the comic elements of the play, ended his article with the comment that "the character of Daddy Sherry is very close to the persona Mitchell has created for himself," that of the "artist as beloved old fart."[23] Part his own creation, part the media's mythmaking, Mitchell did not always like this tag and, as late as an interview in 1990, he showed his frustration with the image: "I always introduce myself as Bill Mitchell. A few moments go by and all of a sudden I see a look. What it says is, 'Don't be who you are, be who I think you to be and this is your writing facade.' It's flattering because it means my fictional character conned them. Most people associate me with [Jake] Trumper . . . they think I'm a rural hired man. Hell! I won the gold medal in philosophy. I've been a writer in residence at universities . . . I'm afraid I'm an urban sparrow."[24]

Doug Gibson had been "shaking [his] fist – metaphorically" for close to seven years to get Mitchell to deliver a manuscript. His first one arrived smelling of snuff. Gibson was not disappointed: "I can remember reading *Summer Holidays* with a sense of wonder because it seemed to me that this was a much darker, more serious version of small-town prairie life than what we had in *Who Has Seen the Wind.* This is really going to shake up people who see W.O. as nothing but a teller of comic stories and writer of cute stories about little kids growing up. I read *How I Spent My Summer Holidays* with great excitement. 'Wow! – This is a powerful piece of work!'"[25] According to Mitchell, right after Gibson had read the manuscript he phoned and began, "It's epic! It's bloody epic, Bill!"[26]

From mid-May through June Mitchell worked on the final editing for *How I Spent My Summer Holidays.* Gibson recalled, "You never know why you click instantly with someone else, but W.O. and I clicked and it was great fun." Gibson pencilled in suggestions on the margins of the manuscript and Mitchell replied "Yep" or

"Nope" or "Sure," sometimes with a justification. When Gibson wrote "Terrific!" on the manuscript description of the Rossdance girls' bulrush fight, W.O. responded, "Yeah!"[27] Gibson, like earlier editors, had problems with Mitchell's use of dashes and interrupted dialogue and said that the typesetter called him the "em-dash king": "I was always trying to cut that back a bit. It may be an accurate rendition of the way conversation goes, but it is tough on the eye . . . I lost most of [those battles]."[28]

Most of Gibson's editorial suggestions were minor, but two were substantial. He felt that something was needed to tie Bella and Mrs. Inspector Kidd together in the reader's mind. Mitchell responded with a new scene in which Hugh witnesses King and Bella arguing over a dress (which Hugh knows has been bought for Bella by Mrs. Inspector Kidd). Not only is this a significant piece in the gestalt puzzle that Hugh, and the reader, put together at the end of the novel, it effectively dramatizes King and Bella's volatile relationship. Gibson's second suggestion was to cut Hugh's opening nightmare, or at least move it to later on in the book, so that prospective buyers would not skim-read the first few pages and then reshelve it in disgust. Gibson recalled, "I thought – I still think – that if you are going to shock a portion of your traditional readership you should hook them into the story before shocking them. . . ." Mitchell, however, insisted that it stay because he felt it was crucial for his purposes to invade and shock the reader right at the beginning.

The editing process was relatively quick and the galley proofs were sent out in July with a covering note from Gibson saying, "No rewriting – it's just plain wonderful the way it is." At the end of the note he added, "P.S. Please show this letter to Myrna – I think I need her help here."[29] Gibson had already figured out that "it wasn't just his snuff boxes and his glasses that Merna had to keep track of; it was his life." He recalled their joint phone calls:

> The other side of the relationship that brought me endless joy was
> when I would phone the house and it was tag-team telephone
> conversation. I remember there was one wonderful incident that

went on for two, three minutes while I sat there looking at the ceiling while the phone was being passed from one to the other and they were having this spirited debate, grabbing the phone from one another, as to whether they were wasting my time by passing the phone. It was always two for the price of one. I always came away laughing and delighted.[30]

– CANADA'S MARK TWAIN ON THE PLATFORM –

In May, Mitchell went to Toronto to play the role of Stephen Leacock in Patrick Watson's new CBC series, *The Titans.*[31] As a humorist he was frequently compared to Leacock and his impersonation of Leacock was very good. However, physically, especially as he aged and his hair became whiter and more uncontrollable, Mitchell came to be known as Canada's Mark Twain. The similarities go beyond the physical. Like Twain, he had a streak of irreverence, a bawdiness (sometimes exaggerated), a wit, though not quite as sardonic as Twain's, and, finally and most significantly, an adult sensibility made keen, poignant, and exuberant by a sharp recall and empathy for childhood experience.

Like Twain on the stage, Mitchell perfected the technique of appearing *not* to be performing but to be spontaneously telling his stories for the first time. He would adeptly draw in his audience through deliberate mistakes and confusions, "Oh, I forgot to mention . . ." or "Did I tell you . . . ?" In his most popular piece, "Melvin Arbuckle's First Course in Shock Therapy," he slipped easily into its various voices, from Melvin's interrogative sentences to Peanut's English schoolboy accent. He imitated Melvin's grandfather's "saliva trouble" by shaking his jowls (as if "rattling dice") and dry-spitting into the microphone (*Eve* 19). While he appeared to be ad-libbing most of the time, and seemed to lose his way in the first half of this piece, it was all very carefully planned storytelling.

Mitchell's readings were dramatic performances. His shock of white hair, brown snuff-dusted moustache (and shirt front), gravelly voice, and dramatic gestures became trademarks of his storytelling. He brought the houses down with a well-timed pause, a grin, or a raised eyebrow. Over the years his snuff box and reading glasses became stage props. His glasses, usually damaged and held together at the bridge with white adhesive tape, would take on a perverse life of their own and refuse to behave. In the middle of a reading at the Banff Centre he was using a pair of glasses with only one arm and they clattered onto the lectern and bounced to the floor. As he retrieved them he explained, "I left my glasses in Prince Edward Island. This is my spare and one arm is gone. I get them at Woolworths. I get six at a time because I drop glasses all over North America." In "The Day I Spoke for Mister Lincoln," when describing Miss Finch's elocution lessons, he would give a seemingly impromptu performance of "The Fool." Pausing to look up at his audience over his glasses and holding up his original copy of "The Fool" given him in 1930, he would say, "Well, look – here's 'The Fool.' And here's Billy Mitchell performing it." He then stepped aside from the podium and microphone and punched out "The Fool" in classic elocution style using the various facial and hand gestures he had been taught half a century ago by Miss Finch.

Mitchell's career as a performer was now at its peak and continued through the 1980s and into the early 1990s. His sliding-fee scale ranged from no fee for charities and benefits up to $3,500 for well-heeled professional associations. Before returning to Windsor for his third year in the fall of 1981, Mitchell, for the third year in a row, was the kingpin for a benefit to raise money for Theatre Calgary. The performance held on September 11 in Calgary's Jubilee Auditorium was attended by more than 1,000 people.

Ken McGoogan, in his review of this event, asked, "How does he do it, get the whole crowd laughing at what many of them, you can bet the rent, would normally condemn as crude, vulgar, indecent – even blasphemous?"[32] Peter Gzowski and other television and radio hosts asked the same question, awaiting with both nervousness and amusement Mitchell's latest irreverent remarks. For the benefit Mitchell read a passage from *Summer Holidays* in which young Hugh, hidden behind some bushes, watches the Holy Rollers celebrate baptisms by immersion in the Souris River. It may have been the description of young Hugh noticing the "sculpted breasts" and "nipples standing at attention" of one female candidate and the "emotionally uplifting experience" (*SH* 83) of a male participant that caused McGoogan to wonder how the Calgary audience would respond. From *The Vanishing Point* Mitchell read the beautifully crafted story of Carlyle being strapped by Old Kacky and then defecating in his desk drawer (*VP* 266). McGoogan's answer to his own question was that Mitchell got away with it because of his "joy" in the language and his use of "superb images." This explanation was, in part, Mitchell's own answer to all censors – if the sexual, the scatological, the risqué have a foundation in reality and an integral purpose to the thematic thrust of the work, then they are not gratuitously titillating or shocking.

Perhaps twenty-odd years later it is surprising that those particular passages were considered risqué and that Mitchell was considered irreverent and shocking – but by 1980 rural prairie standards, and even by national CBC standards, he was. *Who Has Seen the Wind* was censored on a number of occasions for its blasphemy and, as Mitchell's career advanced, he became more, rather than less, risqué. Audiences grew to expect this from him, and, with an innocent twinkle in his eye, he happily obliged. Coming from an upright Presbyterian background he was, much of the time, exploring his own puritan hangups and revelling in his freedom to have shed those shackles.

– MOWAT AND MERNA –

In September 1981 the NFB's *In Search of Farley Mowat* was screened on CBC national television. Early on in the film, Mowat repeated the story about Mitchell's rejection of him: "[Mitchell's] going to hate me for saying this, for telling the story, but what the hell," and then he related how Bill had told him to write "boy meets girl, 5,000 words, happy ending" type stories if he wanted to be successful. Merna was so angry she immediately telephoned Mowat following the program and, according to Mowat, "She chewed my ass off like you wouldn't believe." He added, "It took me off balance, I must say. And I suddenly realized that this was a serious matter. That what I had been treating as sort of a little in-joke digging . . . we were both talented guys, we were both up there so, you know, you could do that. But it was not a joke any longer."[33] For Merna and Bill, it had always been a serious matter. Her telephone call did not squelch the story, for Mowat continued to tell it over the next twenty years.[34]

In our interview with Mowat, he said his story about Bill "became part of my act," and that he "wasn't holding anything against him. It just was a handy little needle to – you know, I'm a shit disturber, and if I can needle somebody, I frequently do. Sometimes it's a good thing."[35] Though Mitchell, too, could be a "shit disturber," needling was not his style. Mitchell mostly ignored Mowat's "act," but there was one occasion when Mitchell, as part of his own act, publicly proclaimed, "I taught him [Farley Mowat] how to write and I've encouraged a lot of others."[36] As we talked with Mowat, it was evident that he had some regret that he had publicly needled W.O. over the years and that he respected his work:

> I don't think there's any question that his popularity, which was enormous in that period, had a really positive effect in setting the scene for the rest of us. . . . He'd done it, he'd made it. He had an appeal to the Canadian audience which overmastered the conditioning we'd all got that anything from Canada was second rate. . . . The fact that he had stirred so much interest and readership opened a lot of people's eyes I'm sure – changed the atmosphere, changed the feeling. If he could do it, so could other people. I don't think there's any question that we all owe him a great debt, which is kind of a cold way of putting it. But I have no hesitation in saying that.

⁓ HOW I SPENT MY SUMMER HOLIDAYS ⁓

How I Spent My Summer Holidays is a novel about heroes and about the emotional and psychological "buggery" of children by their adult guardians. In the opening pages the narrator, seventy-year-old Hugh, is trying to capture something from his past, and he describes a recurring "brothel-ugly" dream he has been experiencing in which he sees "child anuses" opening like "mushrooms to reveal their chocolate gills" (*SH* 2). At this point he only remembers what he senses are significant fragments of a summer in 1924 when he was twelve. The novel then takes the form of "memory loops" as the narrator attempts to retrace and understand the events of that summer and King Motherwell's role in them. By the end of the novel Hugh realizes for the first time how adults had been "guardian trespassers" in their "child caves" and though they had "wanted only to make it safe for their vulnerable young," they "did not know, nor did we, that they could be carriers, unintentionally leaving serpents behind, coiled in a dark corner, later to bite and poison and destroy" (*SH* 222). Hugh, also for the first time, confronts and accepts his own implication and guilt in his loss of innocence and in the events of that summer. Unlike Carlyle in *The Vanishing Point*, however, Hugh's self-discovery is too late. He is, after all, seventy years old when he finally confronts his past, and Mitchell implies that he has led a wasted life as a result of his shocking coming of age when he was twelve.

Thirty years earlier Mitchell had written Dudley Cloud, saying that his main concern about "The Alien" was whether the reader would find sympathy for his tragic hero, Carlyle, because "you can't purge worth a damn if the central human is a heel."[37] In *How I Spent My Summer Holidays* Mitchell succeeded in creating two sympathetic tragic heroes – Hugh, the teller of the tale, and King, his hero. As one reviewer put it, "We hate the sin but love the sinner."[38] King is a wonderful creation and his relationship with Hugh is one of the most complex and compelling in Mitchell's work.

In September 1981, *How I Spent My Summer Holidays* was published to as much critical attention as, and certainly more financial success than, *Who Has Seen the Wind*. Gibson wrote, saying the book was a "sensational success."[39] A Book of the Month and Literary Guild selection, it was a national best-seller and sold more than 20,000 copies in three months. From November 1 to December 5 Mitchell criss-crossed the country, making more than twenty stops for readings and interviews.

As Gibson had feared, *How I Spent My Summer Holidays* did upset some of Mitchell's faithful readers. One wrote telling him that he had let down his image, that he was a nasty man and had written a nasty book.[40] However, of the thirty-some reviews, only a few were negative. George Woodcock, who had always been dismissive of Mitchell's work, grudgingly admitted that *How I Spent My Summer Holidays* "compels one's attention with a vision that seems to have stepped straight out of the Puritan nightmare."[41]

Many reviewers felt that this was Mitchell's best novel yet. Ted Allan wrote that it is "funnier and more powerful than *Who Has Seen the Wind*"; "a crafty, deceptive work, it disarms and seduces the reader with its casually achieved detail and easy humour before stunning him with its uncompromising, bleak conclusion."[42] The *Quill & Quire* reviewer described it as a "tightly plotted and morally complex book . . . surely among the best of the season." Robert Fulford said that King Motherwell "is the best representation of a boy-man that I've recently encountered in fiction" and that "Mitchell turns the pastoral myth of prairie boyhood inside out. What begins as a dream of innocence ends as a nightmare of corruption. It's as if Mitchell had become annoyed by his own reputation and set out to subvert it. The story he has to tell us this time is more complex and menacing than anything in his earlier books."[43] William French described it as "prairie Gothic" and admired the "powerfully evocative prose that brings the sights, sounds and scents of the prairies to life." He felt that the violence at the end was overdone, but "the novel would be worthwhile if only for the powerful feeling Mitchell is able to convey of what it was like to be a 12-year-old boy in a small prairie town in 1924. That talent owes more to magic than to memory."[44]

Jamie Portman's review places the novel in the context of the questions "Has the populist performer taken over from the serious artist?" and does Mitchell effectively integrate his penchant for anecdote into the novel's fabric? His answer is that the book, "for all its uninhibited comedy, is really a tale edged with darkness and ultimately a wrenching account of the death of innocence. . . . By the end, *How I Spent My Summer Holidays* has assumed real unity," and Mitchell has achieved "a new quality of tragic-comic grandeur."[45]

This was a particularly productive fall season for the top Canadian writers. The October *Maclean's* cover featured Mitchell (*Summer Holidays*), Timothy Findley (*Famous Last Words*), Margaret Atwood (*Bodily Harm*), and Robertson Davies (*The Rebel Angels*). Barbara Amiel wrote a three-page article discussing the maturing of the Canadian literary scene, pointing out that, in spite of this success, writers were still unable to make a living at writing, with an estimated average income of only $7,000. Even established writers like Mitchell could not depend solely on their fiction writing. Mitchell had received a $10,000 advance on *How I Spent My Summer Holidays*, but as he said, "I live on my free-lancing, stage productions, television and $3,000 a speech."[46]

In fact, his drama was now a major source of his income. In the fall of 1982 he reported that for the past year at least "the royalties from my novels do not come to any more than half the royalties my plays come to."[47] During this twelve-month period he had ten theatre productions: one of *For Those in Peril on the Sea*, four of *The Kite*, and five of *The Black Bonspiel*. Manitoba Theatre Company's production of *The Black Bonspiel* drew houses of 92 per cent capacity (the best-selling play in MTC's history to date) and grossed more than $180,000, of which Mitchell received 10 per cent, so he wasn't far wrong when he predicted that he would make more than $50,000 from these productions. As well, his writer-in-residency at Windsor made life easier (and helped buy a few of the antiques he was so fond of to furnish the apartment in Windsor). In December 1981, he got a terrific Christmas bonus, receiving half of the $125,000 deal that Macmillan made with Seal (to be paid between January 1982 and December 1983) for mass paperback rights to *Who Has Seen the Wind, Jake and the Kid, The Kite, The Vanishing Point,* and *How I Spent My Summer Holidays.*

These next few years were the pinnacle of Mitchell's writing career. He was sixty-seven years old, and although there were four more novels to come, he had now produced his three finest works, *Who Has Seen the Wind, The Vanishing Point,* and *How I Spent My Summer Holidays.* He was firmly established not simply as Canada's humorist and raconteur but as a serious novelist and playwright. He was, however, a decade too early to reap the benefits from a world-wide interest in Canadian books that grew rapidly in the 1990s. As Barbara Amiel noted in her *Maclean's* article, "International recognition remains the last stumbling block for Canadian writers." Mordecai Richler had made it to the American Book of the Month club, and Margaret Atwood and Alice Munro were riding the feminist surge in the States.[48] While Mitchell's *Who Has Seen the Wind* had been accepted and published first in the United States in 1947 and had been translated into French and Hebrew and sold to Canongate (Edinburgh) in 1980, he never achieved a substantial international success. *Summer Holidays* was not taken up by an American publisher.

Mitchell himself recognized that he might be out of step with the Canadian contemporary novel that, at present, focused on the urban setting. In fact, he commented humorously that, "If you really want to have the odds stacked in your favour and if you had the choice, you really should be no older than 45; you should be a woman; you should be suffering – and the suffering should be caused by males." Seriously, he added, he still thought "the good writing in this country comes from the female" such as Atwood, Munro, Engel, Laurence, Pollock, Bolt, and Gallant.[49] In an interview in 2003, Doug Gibson pointed out that when Mitchell was in his most productive years "it was a disadvantage in the international market to be a Canadian writer writing about Canada. That's changed in the last fifteen years – even for those who write with a very specific Canadian setting and a specific set of Canadian characters as W.O. did. But before that it was tough. And I would say that W.O. is the outstanding example of how tough it was. Because we know that *Wind* was published and did okay in the States."[50]

— BETWEEN NOVELS —

In February 1982, Bill and Merna took another trip to Florida where Mitchell worked on his book of stage plays for fall publication, an idea he came up with in response to requests from theatre groups for copies of his stage works. Macmillan knew it would not be a big money-maker but felt Mitchell's name would sell it. However, this was just a sideline, for his focus was on the grizzly hunt novel, except for continued forays into the *Back to Beulah* film project, which had been renamed "Listen to Me" to look like a new property. In mid-March Mitchell and Eric Till led a film workshop at the University of Lethbridge, which got them both fired up again. Till sent out a number of letters to film industry people attempting to raise interest and financing, still hoping for a Christmas 1982 release. They formed a film company, christened Meadowlark by Till in honour of Mitchell's frequent use of the meadowlark song as a symbol of hope. Mitchell was full of plans to produce a number of feature films based on his novels and *Jake and the Kid* stories.

For some time, the Mitchells and the Itanis had been talking of a trip to Germany. Frances Itani, Bill's former student and now a close family friend, was living near Heidelberg, where her husband, Ted, was working for NATO. Itani initiated arrangements with the Canadian Club to sponsor Mitchell's talks in Lahr and Baden. She organized an after-dinner address in Heidelberg, and set up discussions with Canadian students at schools in the area. When the cultural attachés to the Canadian embassies in Bonn and Paris heard of these plans, they arranged to have Mitchell's visit expanded into a month-long intensive speaking tour through Germany and France.

Merna and Bill flew out from the Canadian Forces air base at Trenton, Ontario, on May 2. After a few days' visit, Ted drove Bill to speak in Lahr and then Baden, dragging along with him the two hundred pounds of books that Bill had insisted on bringing, and which Ted sold for him out of the back of his station wagon. After a speech to the NATO community in Heidelberg on May 10, Bill and

Merna set off by train to Strasbourg and then on to seven more cities in France and Germany where Bill gave readings and talks at the universities. One story that absolutely delighted Merna was her encounter with a prostitute in a red-light district in one of the German cities, who angrily ordered Merna to get off her territory. Their guide from the Bonn embassy was embarrassed and hurried them along, but Merna roared with laughter as she told how she, at sixty-two, had been perceived as a threat to this woman. They had three days on their own in Paris, and Frances had arranged for a visit with Mavis Gallant, which pleased Bill immensely.

On the last couple of days of their trip, back at the Itani household, Bill was cranky and tired. It had been a demanding tour, and the comedown from the highs of performance often produced an irritability in him that was difficult for others to deal with. On this occasion it was exacerbated by the discovery that his newly purchased sterling-silver snuff box was missing. He threw one of his infamous yelling tantrums, blaming Merna. Frances attempted to intercede and offered to call the hotel where he had last been, but that produced no results:

> Merna was sitting in the chair and I started walking past. He is standing there after this mean performance and, as I passed the chair, I said, "I just want you to know that Merna is one of the finest people I have ever known." And I went out into the kitchen to make the tea. I saw Merna go, "Humpfh [so there]." And he followed me and he shouted, and he looked at Merna: "I want you to know all the years I have known her [Frances] she has never said that about me!"[51]

It was enough that Bill recognized his own nastiness; good feelings were quickly restored, though the snuff box, which Frances "tracked in at least three languages across two broad continents," was never recovered.[52]

Just three days after flying home Mitchell was in Calgary to receive an honorary degree at the university. During his convocation address, there was a disturbance that, he later learned, was caused when security guards escorted a man off stage: "Instead of waving hi to Mom and Pop and doing all the various things graduates do, this guy was going to flash." Mitchell was always amused by what life offered for his fiction, but commented that if he used this in a novel his critics would accuse him of going beyond reality: "Oh, there's that slapstick old farceur at it again."[53]

The next day, June 5, he received another honorary degree, this one from the University of Windsor where, unusually, he inserted a slight but pointed political reference into his address: "I am a Canadian, I'm not an Albertan or a westerner. I am a Canadian, and my wife and I feel very privileged and lucky that we have spent one half of our year here and one half of our year out in our home in the foothills. With all the east-west crap floating about in this nation, it gives one a marvellous perspective on what it is to be a Canadian."[54] Bill was a federalist and felt very strongly about the sense of alienation in both the west and Quebec, which was dividing the country.

There was division of a more personal nature in the Banff workshop that summer. For the first time Mitchell was put off kilter by a few of the writers, a small group of assertive feminists who challenged him at every opportunity. As one of his assistants described the situation, Mitchell was upset:

> People decided that he was this macho man who had very sexist ideas about men and women, and they took him on. It was interesting to see his reaction to that because he spent a lot of time thinking about it and fighting it. . . . These women were really feeding each other emotionally. . . . They were angry and W.O. responded with anger because they had put him into a very narrow category, and he was not comfortable with that at all. He found their focus narrow, and he was trying to help them beyond that and they misinterpreted his guidance.[55]

But there were more serious administrative problems facing him at Banff. In fact, for the past two years there had been rumblings of discontent. Mitchell felt he was being undermined by his staff, who did not keep him informed and who wanted to introduce new ideas of teaching. He felt that he had put his stamp on the program, and while he remained the head of it he wanted the emphasis to be on the free-fall finding process rather than on technique-driven workshops. Confrontations were highly distasteful to him, and it had been difficult for him to dismiss one of his assistants, so difficult that he declared that next year would be his last year at Banff.

In the meantime, Mitchell was back at the University of Windsor for his fourth term. *Dramatic W.O. Mitchell* came out in October, and he went on his usual reading tour. Macmillan printed only 5,000 rather than the usual 15,000 or 20,000 copies of his books, but Gibson wrote, "I'm sure we are going to sell the book on your name and face – hence the title, the jacket, and our promotional campaign, which will make the book – I think – the first successful hardcover collection of plays in twenty years." Mitchell, hair wild and snuff on his moustache, gestures dramatically on the "immodest" cover, as Gibson called it.[56] Unhappily though, after five months, Gibson wrote that "sales were tough" and they had only sold half the run.[57]

All of the stage plays included in *Dramatic W.O.* have their beginnings in a different medium from stage: in radio, television, or a novel, as in the case of *The Kite* (which had its beginnings in radio). He was hammered for this by reviewers, notably Urjo Kareda of the *Globe and Mail,* who commented that "like a feverishly frugal tailor, Mitchell keeps cutting and re-cutting his cloth to suit whatever needs he has" and the result is a book that is "threadbare and shabby."[58] However, in his defence, Mitchell had initiated this project simply to satisfy the many requests he had for scripts for his three major plays, not to create new work.

There are various staging difficulties in each of these plays that require the attention of a creative director, but Mitchell was always open to suggestions and revisions each time one was staged. *The Devil's Instrument,* written for radio and then television, contains a number of rapid short scenes not readily adaptable for stage, and it is seldom produced. For *Back to Beulah* Mitchell wrote a new ending, a nightmare sequence focusing on Dr. Anders, which he subsequently realized was melodramic and improbable. Nevertheless, *Back to Beulah,* especially with its original ending, is a deep and searching play.

The two plays most frequently staged, *The Kite* and *The Black Bonspiel of Wullie McCrimmon,* are very successful, entertaining works, though Mitchell could have enhanced their power had he sustained their intellectual depth. In *The Black Bonspiel,* for instance, the tension between Wullie and Reverend Pringle, between ambition and moral integrity, is dropped in the second act. However, Wullie is such a strong character and this play is so wittily entertaining that it has been regularly and enthusiastically staged throughout Mitchell's lifetime and after. *The Kite,* similarly, depends on a vivid, engaging character, Daddy Sherry, who carries the play. However, to enhance the entertainment value, Mitchell created a new comic character, Harold Motherwell, who is a bumbling television producer (unlike the more serious journalist, David Lang, of the novel) and, furthermore, he gave to Daddy, as well as Keith and his mother, spicier language that he thought would get a laugh. Lastly, *For Those in Peril on the Sea* is the weakest play of the collection. While having the potential for portraying a moving relationship between an old man and a young boy, it did not transcend the stereotypical, and it has only been staged twice professionally.

Though his novels were his supreme achievement, this collection of plays paid due attention to his notable career as a playwright, and at least three of them have a lasting vitality borne out by their continued performances over the next years.

14

SINCE DAISY CREEK AND
"THE GREAT MARK TWAIN NOVEL"

~ 1983 to 1987 ~

D URING THE WINTER and spring term at the university Mitchell was able to concentrate on the grizzly novel, which he anticipated being released in the fall of 1984. Once classes were finished in April, he started up on the reading circuit again. He was proud to have been asked to be part of the Stratford Celebrity Lecture Series, and on July 3 he gave a lecture and reading at the Festival Theatre to a large and appreciative audience. He began by speaking of his early occupations as encyclopedia salesman, oil royalties salesman, stunt diver, lifeguard, teacher, and went on to say that he was still a salesman:

> I don't sell stocks or bonds or take out people's gall bladders or do caesarian sections. I don't clothe or feed or shelter. In a way though I am still a salesman. I have very many fine lines. I sell emotions, feelings delicate and passions vivid, nobilities, intolerances, delights and disappointments, births, deaths, hungers. I am also a collector. I collect bits of people to sell, distinctive fragments of youth and age, faith and disillusionment, the denotative ways in which humans walk, or talk, or make love or make hate. I do all these things androgynously. It doesn't sound

332

very respectable, certainly not very useful, though possibly attractive to an undisciplined or lazy man or woman.[1]

He spoke about his way of writing, his absorption of the landscape of his childhood, his subconscious notebook, and then he delivered "The Day I Spoke For Mr. Lincoln," "Saint Sammy, Jehovah's Hired Man," "Old Kacky and the Vanishing Point," and passages about King Motherwell from *How I Spent My Summer Holidays*. It was a fine performance.

On July 5 he was back at Banff for a few weeks of teaching. After last year's crisis this session was uneventful, though Mitchell had lost some of his keenness for the program. However, most of the students were responsive and appreciative, thanking him for opening doors for them.[2]

W.O. and Merna again headed off for their annual "fix" of Mabel Lake, "a place where," W.O. wrote years earlier, "a man can knit together again his own sacred and individual self." After the previous summer's tumble down the stairs and two incidents this summer, he may have wanted to qualify that statement.

On their way through Enderby, twenty-three miles west of their cottage, Merna suddenly shrieked at Bill that there was a bee in the car. Unperturbed he said, "Jesus Christ, Merna! Just leave it alone. It won't hurt you." Moments later the bee flew up his shorts and stung him on the scrotum. Then the shrieking really began. Fortunately, they were right in front of the Enderby drugstore. W.O. bolted out of the car, into the drugstore, and up to the dispensing counter. In as quiet a voice as he could muster he asked for ammonia. Flabbergasted, the druggist and shoppers looked on as W.O. held open the top of his shorts and doused himself with half the bottle. Relieved, he casually asked the druggist, "How much is that?"

Later that summer, W.O.'s crotch attracted more attention. While salmon fishing, he got his fishing lines tangled in the propeller. To untangle them, he had to take the motor off. As he humped the motor into the boat, he spilled gasoline all over himself. While not as painful as a bee

sting, gasoline causes an unpleasant burning sensation on sensitive areas.
Cursing, he slipped off his swim shorts and used the bailer to slosh his
crotch with water. He untangled the lines and then, as he crouched over
the back seat engrossed in reattaching the motor, he heard a female voice
say, "What's he doing?" He looked up to see a sailboat, just twenty feet
away. Attempting to cover up, he abruptly sat down right in a puddle of
gasoline on the seat that he had neglected to clean up. More yells and
frantic washing. Then, as if everything was quite normal, he noncha-
lantly waved to the shocked couple, asking, "What class is your sailboat?"

Merna took particular pleasure in telling what came to be known
in the family as "W.O. crotch stories" and would always emphasize the
poetic justice of the bee story.

～ SINCE DAISY CREEK ～

Back for his fifth year at Windsor in September 1983, Mitchell kept
up the pace on his grizzly novel, which he was alternately calling
"Trophies" or "Ceremonies." The main character, Colin Dobbs, is a
creative-writing professor at Livingstone University.[3] When the
novel opens, Dobbs is in the hospital recovering from a grizzly bear
attack, and his daughter, Annie, has arrived to look after him. Badly
disfigured and angry, he is still obsessed with getting his trophy
grizzly hide dressed by the taxidermist. At the unveiling party,
instead of his grizzly, he unwraps a small brown bear hide. Enraged,
he takes Mr. Munro, the taxidermist, to court, and in the process
confronts his own destructive obsessions.

Mitchell believed that he was the first Canadian male writer to
focus on a father-daughter relationship. Both Munro and Laurence,
superbly adept at depicting family relationships, wrote father-
daughter scenes but their focus is on mother-daughter or grand-
parent-daughter relationships and their vantage points are the
daughter's, whereas Mitchell chose the father's perspective. Except
for the three mad women in *Back to Beulah*, Annie is Mitchell's first
attempt at a fully rounded female protagonist. She is Dobbs's
primary guide in helping him to come to terms with his past and

spurring him on to resume his writing. The grizzly bear's "embrace" (*SD* 5) initiates his journey from interior darkness to his re-emergence into the light of the world. On the way, he is taught about compassion not just by his daughter but also by Archie Nicotine, his Indian guide on the hunt, by Helen Sweeney, the woman in the sauna who temporarily pulls him out of his poison-ous self-absorption, and, finally, by Mr. Munro. At the end of the novel, when Dobbs realizes that his own corruption has corrupted others, he tells Annie that he is crying, "For a woman in a sauna and for a broken old man who asked me to give his love to my daugh-ter" (*SD* 277). Dobbs's obsession has forced Mr. Munro to perjure himself in court in order to protect his grandson, and Archie to break his "deal" with Master Bear in order to save Dobbs's life (*SD* 272–3). When he realizes that he has bent others to his own selfish will, he calls off his appeal case.

Alongside this exploration of personal corruption Mitchell also attacks university politics, where trophy hunting finds its parallel in the pursuit of academic fame – in degrees, positions, and publica-tions, rather than in the ideals of good teaching. The dean, the president with his bogus degree, and Liz Skeffington, who slept her way to the rank of assistant professor, are easy targets for Mitchell. Skeffington, Dobbs's colleague in the English department (deliber-ately named after Skeffington's Irons, a sixteenth-century torture device), plays the female seductress. Her seduction of Dobbs, on the floor of his office, amid a pile of midterm papers, and between wild "paroxysm[s] of sneezes due to his allergy to her perfume" (*SD* 67), is Mitchell's first sex scene and is wonderfully comic. He also sati-rizes the legal system, with its judges and lawyers who ratchet up huge fees playing with humans as if they are pawns in a chess game. Nor is creative writing itself exempt from his attack. Writing should not be done to win "High mark in English 319" or the "Nobel Prize for Literature" (*SD* 103). In an interview Mitchell later said, "You'd better know why you're writing. And it better not be to get pub-lished, and it better not be for money. It better be because you're loving-hearted, and for its own sake, and not to beat anybody else."[4]

As far back as 1974 he knew that his theme would be about "a certain type of corruption which man is subject to. A corruption which makes him take a real and living value and then, through an institution, a routine or a ritual turn it into something else which, while it looks like the real thing, isn't."[5]

The epigram Mitchell chose for his novel was intended to raise this issue of the egocentric pursuit of trophies of power and importance to a universal and moral level. At the core of all his novels is the concern with how to be an honourable human being, how to withstand succumbing to the heart of darkness either inside or outside oneself. The epigram he chose was Immanuel Kant's famous maxim, the categorical imperative: "Act as if the maxim of thy will were to become, by thy adopting it, a universal law of nature." Mitchell wanted to use it ironically, taking the view that such a rule could lead to corruption. At first he planned to list, after the epigram, the names of leaders who adopted the Kantian maxim as a justification for power, a rationalization for action that led to destructive and corrupt rather than good behaviour:

> I had come across the idea that corruption corrupts. It's a chain that must stop somewhere. Then my son, Orm, . . . reminded me of *Heart of Darkness* and the "whited sepulcher" – the idea that sticking with a simplistic principle can result in the ultimate in corruption. Witness Jamestown, Reverend Ian Paisley, Ayatollah Khomeini, the Spanish Inquisition. I had a whole list of these bastards! I realized that the categorical moral imperative is truly cant. . . . Finally I said to Doug [Gibson], "Am I trashing up the front of this book?" He said, "Not necessarily trashing it up, but being too didactic." So I didn't include the names.[6]

Dobbs is not a likeable protagonist. He is, as he says, "a self-pitying bugger. Insensitive to others' suffering, too" (*SD* 5). His daughter, Annie, loves him but wishes "it were as easy to like" him (*SD* 116). Like Hugh in *Summer Holidays*, Dobbs has been living with ghosts of the past (his dead mother, unknown father, a failed marriage), not to mention the recent one, the grizzly who mauled him, and he has developed a sarcastic wit to camouflage his feelings of frustration and guilt concerning his personal and work-related failures. Dobbs is someone, said Mitchell, who "enjoys setting up an adversarial relationship." He is "not like me."[7] Mitchell, in fact, compared Dobbs's adversarial, bad-boy routines to those of Harold Town, one of the group of Painters Eleven, whom Mitchell had met in 1975 and who was notorious for his verbal acerbity.

Though Mitchell did not share Dobbs's obsession with trophy hunting, his mean sarcasm, his quitting spirit, or his anti-socialism, there are some elements of this novel that cut close to home for Mitchell, primarily the father-daughter relationship and Dobbs's angry outbursts. Dobbs's relationship with Annie is modelled on Mitchell's with his daughter, Willa (to whom he dedicated the novel), which, while loving, was at times explosive. Willa, like Annie in the novel, had left home in her teens, but she, unlike Annie, was now settled with a husband and enrolled in the Faculty of Fine Arts at the University of Calgary. Willa's decision to paint her father for one of her class assignments in the spring of 1983 prompted the very significant painting scene between Annie and Dobbs. Mitchell went out to Willa's place in the foothills northwest of Calgary and spent about two weeks sitting for her. By mutual agreement he was supposed to write while she painted, and Willa insisted that he keep busy on the typewriter. Unlike Dobbs, Bill was not a blocked writer, so the chore for him was simply the difficulty of maintaining the pose and of working silently. Bill laughed about these sessions and said that he did more work in those two weeks than ever before, because Willa made sure he kept quiet and kept his hands on the typewriter.

But, as Willa explained, there was a resumption of "some of our battles," and it was not an easy time for her: "There was stuff coming up about what I was painting that wasn't very nice. He was turning to monsters on me — to an extent. Why all these different-looking men?" Mitchell pointed out to her how free-fall, in painting or in writing, unearths unsavoury bits. As Dobbs tells his students, "The seven deadly sins are just a good beginning. There are lots of dirty bits lying in the dark down there: shame, guilt, hypocrisy, hurt, greed, selfishness" (*SD* 103). Just as Willa was trying to unveil the various faces of her father, so he, in the novel, was attempting to track and understand his relationship with her. While Willa was a model for Annie, there was, as with all his characters, no direct equation. As Willa said, "Within the dialogue I sense there is a reality, but the whole person doesn't fit." One part that Willa took personal offence to was the ending: "I don't think that Annie would have decided to go to Teacher's College, necessarily, and Dad said to me, 'How do you like that little sneaky message in that book?' It was so obvious to me that that is what he was doing – giving me a message and tying up loose ends in an easy way."[8]

Mitchell, too, was free-falling some unpleasant bits. For the physical and mental disablement of Dobbs, he drew on his own fairly recent problems with his neck, arm, and hips. Mitchell found that "the mornings were awful," and he frequently went through a mini-version of the process he ascribes to Dobbs at the opening of the novel. The anger, the withdrawals, and the stubbornness of Dobbs bear resemblance to Mitchell's own darker self when he was dealing with his depression in the 1960s. Now sixty-nine, Mitchell had discovered that "age wounds fuelled the anger" (*SD* 233). Indeed, the following conversation between Annie and Dobbs about his traction exercises echoes the cranky tone Mitchell could adopt, particularly with Merna:

> "Done your traction?"
> "Not yet."
> "Exercises?"
> "Later." . . .
> "You'll just stiffen up if you don't. Your whole spine –"
> "It's *my* goddam spine!"
> "Exercise lubricates the joints."
> "Shut up!" (*SD* 233)

Aware of his own emotional outbursts, perhaps Mitchell was examining, through Dobbs, his own problems. As always, his writing depended on autobiographical detail for its texture and strength; but, in this case, it was not simply a matter of digesting and incorporating the usable past but of examining his emotionally charged present. With this book, his writing was revealing something more immediate of himself to himself.

For nearly two years Bill and Eric had been working with renewed energy on the "Listen to Me" ("Back to Beulah") feature film, and the new producer, Harry Gulkin, had managed to raise funding.[9] However, in the summer Mitchell had begun to feel uneasy about the amount of money he had personally put into this project, and in November he and Gulkin had a parting of the ways.[10] But Mitchell simply could not give up on this film project. Writing about obsession in connection with Colin Dobbs, Mitchell, surprisingly, failed to see his own obsession with, as Gibson called it, "the Hollywood Grail:"

> There was clear approval, a hungry market for "the latest novel by W.O. Mitchell." And he was in intellectual agreement with that but his heart was caught up with that Colleen Dewhurst and *Back to Beulah* stuff, and he spent so much time on the movie script and so much emotional time dreaming these Hollywood dreams. . . . He was constantly – I won't say taken in – but his hopes were constantly raised to an unrealistic level by cynical Hollywood people who operate that way and he would take it seriously. He would invest emotional time and real time in developing his treatments and that sort of thing and I would listen encouragingly but I would say, "Bill, I hope this isn't going to hold you back from finishing the novel." "Ah, [he would say] it will only take three months." Well, that three months became . . .[11]

— MITCHELL AT SEVENTY —

Mitchell turned seventy on March 13, 1984, and felt the pressure of how fast life was passing. Happy birthday wishes were not particularly welcome: "Would *you* be happy when you hit seventy!" he demanded fiercely. His birthday was also not the ideal time to ask about progress on the new novel. Although he generally suffered a crisis of faith with each new novel, on this one, and subsequent ones, he showed an increasing vulnerability. He wondered if this novel was trivial: "Am I saying something important?"; "Does it really matter that my guy gets the wrong skin back"; "Is the idea of the hunt weighty enough?"[12] For someone who had been relaxed about a weekly deadline throughout all the frenetic years of *Jake and the Kid*, he was unnerved by his May 31 promise to Gibson that he would have this book done. He had sent out a portion of the manuscript in early March, and by mid-March, recognizing that Bill was nervous that there had been no report from Gibson, Merna telephoned. Gibson assured them both that the story was "great" (or, as Merna recalled, "good").

Merna and W.O. joined us in April in Sitges, Spain, on the Mediterranean coast, where we presented papers at a Commonwealth Literature Conference on Autobiography and Biography. It was fascinating to watch how W.O. absorbed so much of what happened around him for later use in his novels. He carried home with him "after-images" (SD 82) that were quickly integrated into his manuscript — the scene of the nude sun-bathers, the architecture, the weather, the wife's disgust with the saltwater showers in the hotel, and his walks along the boardwalk.

It was about this time that we first realized that our interview sessions with W.O. throughout the 1980s were helping him bring to surface some recollections that became rough lumber for Since Daisy Creek *(and subsequently for* Ladybug, Ladybug . . . *,* For Art's Sake, *and* "Brotherhood, True or False"*). The papers we delivered at the conference (on biographical theory and on W.O.'s use of autobiography in his work) also became grist for his creative mill. On the way home, W.O. announced* *that he had decided to have his character, Colin Dobbs, return for a second visit to Spain to present a paper on biography at such a conference. As well, the discussions around biographical writing inspired him to think about a new novel in which his protagonist is a biographer.*

On the last evening of the conference W.O. read passages, from his novel-in-progress, including the sauna scene in which Dobbs encounters the woman with the mastectomy. The audience was very moved; there was laughter in the right places and sympathetic silence at the end. He was so wound up by the positive reception that he continued on past his allotted time, until, finally, Merna, stood up and signalled to him that it was time to stop.

The May 31 deadline fast approached and Mitchell found himself busy with events at the University of Windsor, including his appointment as honorary professor, only the second such appointment in the history of the university. He did not get as much finishing work done on the novel as he had hoped, so when Gibson received the final chapters he was disappointed: "It [was] terrible . . . it was just sort of reported as 'here's what happened in the court case,' and it was just sloppy and skimpy." Gibson was nervous about telling Mitchell that the last chapter would have to be redone. But when he telephoned and gently broke the news, Bill laughed and said, "I know. I just sent it off to you so I could say I got it in on time. But I'm reworking it, and I'm writing out the court scene."[13]

Mitchell had already attended some court sessions in Windsor earlier that year and, drawing on that research, he completed the court scenes, but, to make sure that he was not hitting any wrong notes, he asked his company lawyer in Calgary, Mac Jones, to read them over for him. Jones observed that Mitchell "had a pretty good grasp of a court procedure at the time."[14] Amazingly, it turned out that Jones had been the junior lawyer acting for Dr. Harry Jennings in the stolen bear hide case back in 1948, and he insisted on reading through the whole novel to make sure that Mitchell was not opening himself up to a libel suit.

Mitchell went on tour with the book in November. As usual he was irascible, and there was a hint of the Dobbs character invading his own when an interviewer recorded one of his more impatient moments with a telephone caller: "'When I was young,' said W.O. Mitchell as he slammed down the phone in his hotel room, 'I used to be impatient. As I get older, I get sweeter. But not with that son of a bitch.'"[15] His highs were getting higher; his lows lower. With unenthusiastic or inefficient interviewers he could be blunt or sarcastic, but for autographing sessions with the public he was ebullient. It was debatable whether he was getting any sweeter, as he claimed, but he was certainly still gathering positive reviews and interview spots across the country. The reviews for *Since Daisy Creek* were, four to one, very good, complimenting him on the storytelling aspect of his novel and on the daughter-father relationship, although the latter came in for some criticism as well. He was praised for his "priceless, irreverent humour, which briskly skewers pretension in lively dialogue," though some critics felt he overused dialogue in this novel.[16] Patricia Morley wrote that "*Since Daisy Creek* tops *How I Spent My Summer Holidays* and ties with *Who Has Seen the Wind* as Mitchell's best fiction."[17]

The novel received little attention from academic critics. In 1991, Dick Harrison, in a lengthy critical survey of Mitchell's career, took a relatively neutral position on this novel, praising "the storyteller's mastery of control and pacing."[18] On the other hand, in her comprehensive essay, "Quest in W.O. Mitchell's *Since Daisy Creek*," Catherine McLay concluded that it is "a rich, complex novel which shows Mitchell, at seventy, at the height of his artistic powers" (*ML* 191). This novel has more depth than initially meets the eye, although it is not as emotionally charged or as poetic as *Wind* or *Summer Holidays* or as symbolically and structurally complex as *The Vanishing Point.*

Mitchell sold U.S. rights for *Since Daisy Creek* to Beaufort Books, the first time he landed a U.S. publisher since *Who Has Seen the Wind* in 1945. He was offered $3,500 advance royalties, and it was published at the end of 1985. Unfortunately it was bad luck again, for the company went bankrupt before they could pay Mitchell the final $2,000 advance (which he took back in inventory). Only about 3,000 copies sold in the United States compared to more than 19,000 copies sold in Canada. The American market did not like the mixture of folksy humour and philosophic reflection, although, of course, the bankruptcy abruptly curtailed the marketing. However, there were a few nibbles from film companies in both the United States and Canada; indeed, the reader for Paramount Pictures found the book amusing, preferring the satire on academic life to the bear hunt story.

~ ITALY ~

In September 1984, Mitchell returned to Windsor for his sixth year. Part of *Since Daisy Creek*'s dedication reads, "WITH GRATITUDE TO THE UNIVERSITY OF WINDSOR." As he said in numerous interviews, Windsor had been a great boon to his career: "In five years I've done three books, two new stage plays and a feature film. . . . I never wrote that much in 10 years in my writing life before."[19] He geared up for his fall speaking engagements and for the beginning of a book tour that would keep him moving across the country for the month of November, but he was also thinking about a new film venture, "Burmese."

In the summer he had been approached by Pat Ferns of Primedia to write a ninety-minute television screenplay around Burmese, the Queen's horse, who had been born at the RCMP stables in Saskatchewan, trained for the Musical Ride and, in 1969, presented to the Queen, who rode her in numerous Trooping of the Colours Parades. As Mitchell described it, "This is a film about a young girl and a horse. Both were runts and it matters a great deal to Maggie and to the little mare, Burmese. . . . The narrative arc of the film twins the lives of Maggie and Burmese, both of whom, in the words of Maggie's grampa, will 'never settle for anything less'."[20] Although he raided material from some of his *Jake and the Kid* horse scripts and from *Wild Rose* for the character of Maggie, much of the story is freshly written. It has all the sentimental qualities of a popular film, as both Burmese and Maggie overcome their disadvantages and go on to prominence. Shooting on "Burmese" was to start by spring 1985. Mitchell finished a 168-page draft sometime in November or December 1984, but travel plans from February through April interfered with further work on it.

At the end of February 1985, the Mitchells went to Florida, and Bill gave a reading in Orlando. They were only back in Canada for two days before they flew off to Italy on March 3, 1985, where Mitchell had agreed to be writer-in-residence in Turin for a month. First, though, he landed in Rome and gave a lecture at the Canadian Cultural Centre, and then was a week at a conference on Canadian Studies in Fanzano. As with his trips to Germany and to the conference in Spain he was pleased to be gaining an international audience. He and Merna stayed in a small hotel, the Goya, near the university and had many amusing tales to tell about their language problems, particularly their difficulty in ordering anything other than pizza. Bill hilariously demonstrated how, on one occasion, he resorted to graphic body language to communicate to a pharmacist that he needed a laxative. In his letter of thanks to Guy Gervais at the Canada Council, Mitchell jokingly explained that Italians did not know what a writer-in-residence was, and he discovered that he was expected to teach all the North American and Canadian literature classes. He added, "The strange thing is that I didn't mind a bit." He humorously related how he broke the tradition of the formal lecture structure:

> The third day I stopped and asked them if it was true that Nietzsche had gone crazy in Turino and they all nodded. I said, "Are you sure he wasn't crazy <u>before</u> he got to Turino?" That thought had not occurred to them. Then Professor Gorlier said, "In Turino he kissed a horse." I said, "But everybody loves horses enough to kiss them, don't they. Oh! You mean he didn't kiss the horse's nose. He kissed the horse's ass!" From then on

for the rest of the seminars and lectures we had a nice back and
forth flow of discussion on Canadian and American literature
and I would not have missed it for the world.

He also explained how his various trips abroad had offered him
"lovely lumber" for his fiction: "New World artists can well use the
global vision afforded them in this way. I wish to hell that this sort
of thing had been afforded writers of my generation before we
became senior citizens."[21]

On his return in April, Mitchell was busy with reading engagements and did not get "Burmese" revised as had been expected. In
fact, another screenwriter was hired to finish the project, though
Mitchell did not seem to mind as he had with his other film scripts.
He, rather immodestly, liked to claim that he was a great screenplay
writer, yet each of his film scripts had been criticized in much the
same manner. While he had unique characters and situations and
fresh and realistic dialogue, he tended to overindulge in minor,
comic details, losing track of the overall focus.

In July Mitchell spent twelve days in Banff, finding it increasingly stressful, even though he enjoyed the enthusiasm of his
student-writers. Cora Taylor, who became an accomplished and
award-winning author of young adult fiction, had taken his class in
1972 at the University of Alberta and came to do a week with him at
Banff. She had heard it rumoured that he would not be returning to
Banff the following year. She could see that the course at Banff was
"nothing like the course . . . at U of A." Mitchell's great skill, she
said, was that he "allowed me to find my **own** voice"[22] and not be
imitative of other writers. But, this year she found some instructors
too directive and, in particular, she was "sorry" to discover that
Mitchell's free-fall method was not being encouraged: "Now it seems
more like a psychological group-grope session. The pieces that get
the rave reviews are the bleeding wounds, not the vivid writing or
insightful images."[23]

~ THE GREAT MARK TWAIN NOVEL ~

The working title of his new novel was "The Great Mark Twain Novel." The central character, Kenneth Lyon, like Colin Dobbs, is a failed writer, and for a number of years has been struggling with his biography of Sam Clemens/Mark Twain. Although the new novel was not a sequel to *Since Daisy Creek*, he reused the setting, because, as he said, "having found Livingstone University, I'd hate to waste it."[24] His two major characters emerged from *Since Daisy Creek*, where they had played minor roles: Lyon, a seventy-six-year-old professor emeritus; and Charles Slaughter, the sociopathic graduate student. Slaughter had taken such hold of Mitchell's imagination that even in *Since Daisy Creek* he had attempted to work him into the plot more prominently. In rough notes he thought about having Slaughter kidnap Annie and threaten Dobbs until Dobbs "baited a trap for this fellow and waited himself with the Weatherby." But he cut all that, realizing that this was "too damn much:" "Don't get carried away, Mitchell, for God's sake!"[25]

There were a number of elements that came together at this time that pushed him toward making Lyon a biographer of Mark Twain. He remembered a story he had heard from his friend and publisher John Gray more than thirty years before about Sam Clemens (Mark Twain) being the illegitimate son of William Lyon Mackenzie. This seemed like a fascinating theory that might even provide Lyon with a real biographical coup. The actual incident occurred much as Lyon describes it in *Ladybug* (254–261). An old army colonel came into Gray's office one day hoping that Macmillan would be interested in his theory and publish his book. The colonel may have "had only one oar in the water" (*LL* 59), as Mitchell wrote, but Gray was interested enough to tell Mitchell about it at some length. Mitchell spoke to the archivist at McMaster University where the Macmillan papers are located, but, unfortunately, they could not find any references to this man or his proposed book.

Even without that link, it seemed inevitable that Mitchell would one day put Mark Twain into a book. For a number of years now the media had called him the Mark Twain of Canada, and, of course, Mitchell had been brought up not only on his mother's stories about nursing either Mark Twain himself or his wife, Livy, in New York[26] but on *The Adventures of Tom Sawyer* and *The Adventures of Huckleberry Finn.* Having just attended a conference in Spain on biography, and with the constant immersion in the biographical process with his own biographers, it was an easy step to make his protagonist a biographer rather than a writer. He read Justin Kaplan's biography, *Mr. Clemens and Mark Twain* (1966), some of Bernard De Voto's books on Twain such as *The Portable Mark Twain* (1946), and hired a researcher to find out if there was any truth to the speculation about Twain's Canadian ancestry. In fact, this was the most external research he ever did for one of his novels.

In spite of all this free-falling, Mitchell was stalled: "I didn't have it, and I knew in my guts . . . I had to know what <u>was happening.</u>" For the past year he had filled pages with free-fall, with those "more ephemeral things [that] are the hardest to come by," but, as he self-critically noted, he had not found his plot: "I probably delay too long for that narrative, skeletal structure, and event structure." In the late summer an event occurred that suddenly provided him with the opening for his novel and the motivation for Lyon's action. Mitchell read that Hugh MacLennan, professor emeritus at McGill University, had been "kicked out of his office." This treatment of a friend and fellow writer truly upset and angered Mitchell, and it was that, along with memories of his own feelings when the University of Calgary casually let him go, which fed into his writing about Lyon's feelings of rejection: "I read that and, 'Hey, hey!' – that's what lights the fuse for everything that explodes along the line. . . . I think the novel is going to open with that goddamned memo, 'We will no longer need Dr. Lyon's office.'"[27]

After his Mabel Lake holiday, Mitchell was once again back at Windsor for the fall of 1985. It was busy as usual, so Merna attempted to erect the fortress and protect Bill from demands on his time. She declined invitations on his behalf, saying that he had to concentrate on his own writing. Unfortunately, her good intentions were frequently violated by Mitchell himself, who could not resist the temptation, both of money and excitement, on the speaking circuit.

About this time Bill and Merna became aware of a female student in the social work program at the University of Windsor who was being physically and verbally harassed by her partner to such an extent that the police were involved. When she moved to Calgary in the spring of 1986 and was once again attacked the Mitchells interceded on her behalf, contacting their own lawyer to draw up a restraining order. This situation continued to worry them for another year. Some of the details, and certainly this woman's fear, fed into Mitchell's new novel, *Ladybug, Ladybug . . .* , in which his young female character, Nadya, is harassed by Slaughter. Nadya, a young woman of Ukrainian descent with a six-year-old daughter, Rosemary, answers Lyon's ad for a housekeeper. She takes on the roles of housekeeper and daughter, becomes Lyon's pool-playing companion, and the researcher for his Twain biography. It is clear that Mitchell was interested in her largely for his revenge plot. She is the link to the Slaughter character from whom she is trying to escape after an earlier frightening encounter, and her daughter not only provides the young-old relationship that Mitchell enjoyed portraying but becomes Slaughter's victim.

From fall to spring 1986 he carved out writing time on the new novel. In March Bill was stunned to learn that Doug Gibson was leaving Macmillan, the company Mitchell had been with since the publication of *Who Has Seen the Wind* forty years earlier. He had been aware of the turmoil in the publishing business for the past few years, with Ron Besse taking over Macmillan in 1980 and Jack McClelland appointing Linda McKnight president at McClelland & Stewart in 1982 and then selling to Avie Bennett at the end of 1985. But he may not have been aware of the considerable downscaling of the fiction list at Macmillan and of the tension between Gibson and Besse. At M&S, Bennett needed an experienced publisher, and Gibson was ready to go: "I left Macmillan on a Tuesday and started work at M&S on Monday. The deal was that I would have my own editorial imprint, and W.O. was one of the very first authors who said, 'Wherever you go I want to go with you.' And so it was great."[28] A number of Gibson's authors, including Robertson Davies, Alice Munro, Mavis Gallant, and Jack Hodgins, followed him to M&S.

At the same time Mitchell was half-heartedly working on another film project for Eric Till and Meadowlark Films, a made-for-TV two-hour film that combined ideas from his stage play *Royalty is Royalty*, his musical *Wild Rose*, and his movie script *Alien Thunder*. Merna had bought him a dictaphone, which he thought would be ideal for this project because he was simply cobbling together past work. He dictated his plot outline and various scenes from his past work. He used it also to record some of his research on Mark Twain, but he never really liked it, needing the impetus of the words moving across the page. The story thread of *Royalty* was simply the one he had already exploited from his early *Jake and the Kid* radio plays – the story of a horse and, in this case, a young girl rather than the boy, the visit of the Prince of Wales in the late 1920s, and the controversy of who would hand up the royal flowers. It was tired material that even Mitchell did not seem excited about, except when he announced to the media that he was working on another film. Till was dismayed when he received the draft in June 1986 and called Mitchell's son, Orm, expressing a sadness that Mitchell's creative energy seemed to have flagged.

Much of the difficulty was that Mitchell, given his age, had too many shows on the road. His dabbling in film and his teaching took too much time and energy. Something needed to go. On July 3, *Centreletter*, the Banff School's newspaper, headlined his departure: "W.O. Mitchell's Curtain Call After 13 Years as the Head of Centre's Writing Programs."[29] Typically Mitchell exaggerated: "This is the fourteenth year, for God's sake, and Merna wanted me to drop out eight years ago" (*Centreletter*). Merna, indeed, had been urging him to retire for the last two or three years, and he should have listened to her, but that was not the prime reason why he left in 1986. Rather it was out of exasperation over what was happening at the school, and it was not a happy exit.

The tension that had been building for the past three years was due, ironically, to the success of the program. It had become too big for Mitchell to administer, and yet he insisted on being a part of all the decisions, especially the hiring of the writing instructors. When that did not happen, he felt betrayed by his staff and he exploded. He had little facility for moderation, and furiously stomped into the administration offices threatening resignation. They accepted. It was hardly a glorious ending to what had been, in fact, a remarkably successful and innovative program for thirteen years, grown from his personality and his concept of free-fall.

He returned for a final reading on July 8. Paul Fleck, president of the Banff Centre, paid tribute to him in his opening remarks: "There is a kind of enthusiasm and there is a kind of expenditure of energy which is like none other that we have experienced. He is one of those people who has made the Banff Centre what it is." Fleck recounted that someone, earlier that day, had said that "two days of W.O. is like a 100 days of almost anybody else anywhere."[30] Sometimes, as Mitchell would say, life follows art, and this was one of those times. Mitchell, like his character Kenneth Lyon in *Ladybug, Ladybug . . .* , suffered "exile wounds" (*LL* 15) for a few years.

Throughout the summer of 1986, Mitchell worked on his new novel, attempting to weave together the disparate strands of plot and character that had emerged for him. Around the character of Dr. Kenneth Lyon he developed his theme of "AGE," which, as he wrote in his free-fall notes for this novel, "is a sort of involuntary exile."[31] Mitchell asked himself why he had always in his writing "reached for the young end of the human-age stick and the old end?" The answer, he said, is very simple: "The young and the old are much more dramatic and colourful and vivid than the colourless in between. That's a simple answer, but . . . I think the man always retains in his magnitude the miniature boy" (the "opposite" he pointed out of Robertson Davies's statement in *Fifth Business* that the boy contains the man in miniature).[32]

It was worrying him that, once again, he had begun to develop an unsympathetic character. Perhaps with this in mind, Mitchell lightened Lyon, for he is not as bitter a man as Carlyle, King Motherwell, or Dobbs. At the time the novel opens Lyon is still grieving the death, five years earlier, of his wife, Sarah, and his biographical work on Sam Clemens constantly reminds him of other sadness in his life: the loss, about forty years earlier, of his three-year-old daughter, Susan (named after Twain's daughter who also died young); and the death of his brother Henry (who, like Clemens's brother Henry, caused him both guilt and sadness). His pain is still acute: "The memory ache for Sarah, for their little Susan, for his brother Henry, and the faster-growing number of friends who had reached the finish line ahead of him, would never leave him. Now it was going to be even lonelier here in the twilight" (*LL* 9). Age exacerbated the pain, and Lyon fears becoming cynical and miserable like Clemens.

Mitchell, himself, though not lonely or grieving, was frustrated by both the physical and emotional problems associated with aging. He ascribed to Lyon his own "feeling of being helpless," that his "links with an outer world were being destroyed." Mitchell wrote free-fall notes about his own diminishment of hearing, taste, smell, and sight and constructed some scenes that, although they did not end up in the novel, indicated his own frustration and sadness. "The most annoying loss," he wrote, was the loss of hearing and "in direct proportion to the loss there is a loss of patience – there is a turning up of the flame of annoyance." Mitchell was reluctant to admit to this loss of hearing, preferring to blame "some son of a bitch who was mumbling and smudging his consonants – who was lowering or turning away his head – especially at the ends of his sentences."[33]

The Slaughter character from his previous novel drew Mitchell into the realm of the psychological thriller. Mitchell made the risky decision to attempt to enter Slaughter's mind, and he sought help from his friend, Dr. Jack Fair, a child psychiatrist in Calgary, to make sure he was creating an accurate portrayal. He began exploring themes around "chaos and horror," the "manic depressive's high of laughter [which] precedes the depths of despair . . . [when] fun turns to danger."[34] One of the "insights" he was intrigued by was the way in which, even in so-called normal lives, "often horror is preceded by comedy and I think of [Orm] and Hughie and a manic little push shove game and [Orm] ending up with a long sliver up [his] spine and having to go into emergency." He commented that "Alice Munro is aware of it in one of her *Dance of the Happy Shades* stories – a pot of boiling water is pulled off the stove and scalds the infant to death."[35] It is this insight that is the basis for his creation not only of the character of Slaughter but of Duane, the six-year-old sadist who destroys everything at Rosemary's birthday, and even Rosemary herself who seeks vengeance on the squirrel that bites her. In this new novel he wanted to explore a range of violent behaviour, from that of the innocent child to the psychotic.

In the first half of the novel, Slaughter's encounters with his psychiatrist and his flashing at convocation are, on the surface, comic, but he is revealed to be a very twisted and destructive personality. Slaughter, in fact, was based in part on a graduate student at Windsor who wreaked havoc in a number of departments. Soon he becomes consumed with sociopathic revengefulness, and for much of the novel Mitchell achieves a graphic and convincing portrayal of this crazed personality. For the horrific scene following Rosemary's kidnapping, Mitchell drew on his experience of hazing at the University of Manitoba in 1931 when he was initiated into a fraternity and ordered to speak of himself only in third person singular, as "it."[36] Mitchell uses this sadistic and psychologically damaging ritual in the scene where Slaughter tries to intimidate and subdue Rosemary.

The Mark Twain thread running through the novel served three closely entwined purposes: it gave Lyon an occupation as a failed or frustrated writer; it allowed Lyon to slip over into autobiography and talk about his own life; and it allowed Mitchell to use the despair and cynicism that was evident in Twain's life as he grew older, especially in his book *The Mysterious Stranger*, as a parallel for Lyon's experience. Even though Mitchell assimilated the Clemens biographical material quite astutely and made only a few factual errors, Lyon often sounds more like a fiction writer and his role as a biographer is not always convincing. However, the biography angle is simply a conduit into Lyon's life-story, and it takes second place to Mitchell's real interest, which was an exploration of the degrees and facets of sadness, despair, and anguish exhibited by his three main characters: Clemens, who in old age turned cynical; Slaughter, who turned psychotic; and, finally, Lyon, who is saved from despair by Nadya and Rosemary. Clemens becomes a reminder to Lyon of what life would be without hope in humans.

At Mabel Lake that summer it was clear that W.O. was struggling to pull together all these ideas. We wrote him at the end of the summer, warning him "to be careful of pushing the new novel along too quickly." We had been concerned about the quick finish on Since Daisy Creek *and were hoping that W.O. would hold off on a deadline (March 1, 1987) with Gibson until he had all his disparate ideas truly working together.*[37] *In retrospect, however, it may have been that he was at a stage in his writing career and his life when the fine work of layering and weaving and honing incident and language was impossible. He was simply anxious to get a book out. We could see that he was less critical than he used to be, and he favoured the broad strokes of dialogue, which came easily to him, rather than the more difficult emotional inner monologues.*

Merna was not as involved with this book, which also may have affected his flow of ideas and his critical appraisal of the manuscript. As Mitchell told an interviewer, when he phoned Merna from the office and said, "Listen to this," Merna stopped him. "'Just a minute. You know what I would like? I'd like to read just one of your novels that I haven't been flayed with bit by bit over a three-year period. But don't mistake me. When you finish that goddamn thing I want to be the first to read it and have input before anyone else sees it.'"[38] *Merna had been nervous about his last novel, and she may have sensed more weaknesses in this new novel. Bill had less tolerance for her criticism now, and this was bothering her, although in public she explained it lightly: "We fight over bits and pieces again and again. If there's something I don't agree with, he resists. Frequently he comes around, but he's stubborn." Bill added, "It isn't stubbornness, it's just that I know better, dear."*[39]

Another explanation for her withdrawal may have been that she was sensitive about his presentation of the wife, Sarah Dobbs, in Since Daisy Creek, *who had an alcohol problem. Annie complains to her father, echoing conversations Willa had had with her father, "mother's the bad experience" because she drinks too much (SD 140). Though Merna would not have made the mistake of equating fiction and fact as a general principle, it might have been difficult for her to ignore aspects of this portrait and of Sarah Lyon in* Ladybug, *who, although much warmer and more loving than Sarah Dobbs (as was Merna), is slyly controlling. Bill's stubbornness and inability to negotiate without exploding into anger had forced Merna to find subversive ways to control him that, inevitably, fuelled a bigger explosion. Lyon's admission of how hard he was on his wife grew out of Mitchell's own self-reproach about his treatment of Merna: "God knows you spilled irrelevant annoyance over her for three decades. Often enough for her to have called you a wife-batterer once. Of the worst kind! Verbal! She asked you if you did it to your students, too, and that made you do some serious self-examination then, didn't it? Not very comforting to realize that you almost never had with your students. Saved it for the woman you loved most" (LL 111).*

~ FINAL YEAR AT WINDSOR ~

Mitchell liked to have at least one project waiting in the wings and, at the end of August 1986 he once again began thinking about his book, "The Devil is a Travelling Man." His idea was to complete a third short story to accompany "The Devil's Instrument" and "The Black Bonspiel," and he recalled his original idea about a fisherman meeting the devil. Thinking about these rogue figures initiated another project in the spring of 1987, a one-man stage play called "Scam and Be Damned" that satirizes medicine men, politicians, and TV evangelists who are, he said, all "the same rascals."[40] Prompted by Eric Till, he had also been thinking about a new series for television, based on the *Jake and the Kid* material. Mitchell felt that "the worst thing a writer can do is leave a gap; it's so hard to get the momentum . . . much better to slip into another mode." In fact, he thought that he almost "deliberately alternat[ed] novels and plays."[41] His creative versatility and abundant flow of ideas were both his triumph and his distraction.

In early fall Merna and Bill made the decision that this would be their final year at Windsor. It had been a warm and rewarding experience for both of them, and it was with mixed emotions that they made the decision. No doubt Bill's age and the travelling between Calgary and Windsor played a role in their decision. Merna, as in the past, may have been the initiator, thinking primarily about Bill's writing, but she admitted to homesickness, missing, in particular, her piano. Bill waited until the new year to write his formal letter of resignation to the vice-president: "With great sadness I must end my tenure at the University of Windsor as writer-in-residence. It is done also with great gratitude to the University for the eight years, during which I have written more than in any fifteen years of my writing life. I shall always be indebted to the University for the marvelous umbrella the English department has held over me during my years here."[42] He knew, as he wrote under cover of his character Kenneth Lyon in *Ladybug, Ladybug . . .* , that "he was going to miss coming down the hall from the elevator, rounding the corner to see the English Department office door always open and Bev framed there at her desk to look up and smile and wave to him as he went on to pick up his mail and then to his own office. He was going to miss the stir and nudge of university life all around him. . . . He was going to miss sandwich and tea for lunch at SUB with Alistair or Colin or Ed or Herbie or Charlotte" (*LL* 11). Most of those names were not even disguised. Bev Stahlbrand was his secretary, and he was so appreciative of her assistance that he nominated her for the President's Achievement Award.

Mitchell spent most of the month of March 1987 in the United States. He gave lectures and readings at universities and libraries in North Carolina, Georgia, and Florida. On March 19 he visited his daughter, who had moved to New York in 1985, and he gave a reading arranged by the Canadian consulate. He was always delighted to go south in the winter months, especially if he could couple it with some readings to new audiences. It was a rugged agenda, however, and he arrived back home with an infection that fatigued him miserably for months.

On May 24 Mitchell was honoured at a dinner for his eight years' contribution to the University of Windsor. Acknowledging their support, he indicated that the University of Windsor would be remembered on the dedication page of *Ladybug, Ladybug* . . . The Mitchells crated up the Victorian dining-room table and chairs, a corner cabinet, and other antiques they had collected during their time in Windsor. They had enjoyed searching through the antique shops and, although Merna located the prizes they found, Bill claimed he had made the spectacular deals. He enjoyed telling how he bargained and bargained but could get nowhere with the dealer on the Victorian walnut table until he pulled out his stash of bills, saved up from his Old Age Security pension cheques, and counted out twenty-five hundred dollars in twenty-dollar bills and said, "That's all I've got. Take it or leave it." The dealer took it.

15

FIVE BOOKS

~ 1987 to 1992 ~

MERNA LOVED her Calgary home – the space of it, the ever-fascinating park across the road, her neighbours. What a joy it was to play her grand piano once again in the room she had so daringly decorated in dramatic red and gold and to be touched again by her paintings, the lively Janet Mitchell, the Casson landscape, the Harold Town horse, the Emily Carr totem poles. The one concern, however, was Bill's health. He never totally recovered from the virus he had picked up in Florida in the spring.

Mitchell had one more talk on July 15, to the Workers' Compensation Board in Yellowknife, before he could get out to the lake and relax. This was a trip that had originally excited him because it included a couple of fishing trips. Merna was not interested in going, but the two other fishers of the family, Susan, his daughter-in-law, and Ben, his ex-son-in-law, were invited. As Susan noted, Mitchell opted to stay in his comfortable hotel room (watching the Iran-Contra hearings) rather than fly in to the remote fishing location. Whether this was due to his health, or to the frighteningly small plane they were to take, or to his infatuation with the Iran-Contra hearings was not clear, but he was not in good humour. However, he agreed to allow Max Ward, the legendary owner of

Wardair, to fly him in the larger Twin Otter up to Ward's fishing camp, where he fished for arctic grayling and lake trout – and where he cursed the horseflies, the DEET that he got in his eyes, the netted hats they had to wear, and the fact that there was no television.

It was obvious that he was not feeling well. Still blaming the virus, he finally went to his doctor, who diagnosed a sinus infection that would not clear up. It did not help his humour that the family constantly blamed his sinus problems on his snuff-taking and nagged him to quit. In September he was experiencing nausea along with his fatigue and sinus difficulties, and on September 24 he was admitted to the hospital for tests. After nine days of extensive examinations the doctors found an abdominal aneurysm, which did not seem to be the cause of his complaints nor too worrisome in itself. They also discovered a benign cyst in his nose, and he was advised to give up snuff, though he never admitted this to the family. He continued not only to use snuff, but to claim that it did him no harm. While it never led to cancer, it did contribute to his continual bouts of sinusitis and his unpleasant, well-recognized throat clearing.

In the end the doctors listed their number-one diagnosis as depression and exhaustion. Mitchell denied feeling depressed, except about feeling ill for so long, so in all likelihood he was exhausted from all his book tours and public performances. However, after six days in the hospital, with enforced rest, he begged to be released, as he had engagements to be met. On October 4 he was discharged, just in time to fly to Winnipeg on October 5 for rehearsals and then the opening, on October 8, of *Royalty is Royalty* at the Manitoba Theatre Centre. *Royalty* had not been performed since 1959 when it was staged for Saskatchewan's Golden Jubilee. Rick McNair, who had directed other Mitchell plays (*The Kite*, *Those in Peril on the Sea*, and *The Black Bonspiel*), rejuvenated it for the Manitoba Theatre Centre, and made it "shine like new."[1] It was on for one month and was warmly received by audiences, who especially liked the nostalgic 1950s set and the strong performance by Tom Jackson as Moses Lefthand.

Mitchell on book tour with the illustrated edition of *Who Has Seen the Wind* (Fall 1976).

Budge Crawley with his 1976 Oscar Award and Bill with his 1975 ACTRA Nellie Award (March 1976).

Mitchell leading a writing workshop at the Banff Centre.

Merna and Bill in Hawaii (December 1976). *Inset:* W.O. with his milk of magnesia sun block (Barbados, 1980).

W.O. performing a slip dive for grandchildren. Far left, Geoff; far right, Sara (1979).

Mitchell cottage at Mabel Lake, B.C.

Orm, W.O., Barb, and Merna at Mabel Lake.

W.O. and grandchildren Kaley, Jaime, and Tiree.

W.O. and grandchild Brenna.

W.O. canoeing at Mabel Lake (1985).

Merna and Bill sailing *The Kite* at Mabel Lake (1986).

Tying flies. Left to right: Hugh, W.O., and Orm.

W.O. fly fishing (1986).

Mitchell giving a performance at Trent University (around 1985).

UNIVERSITY OF WINDSOR

Bill and Merna at their University of Windsor farewell dinner (June 1987).

Merna rehearsing Bill for his role in the television series *Anne of Avonlea* (1989).

COLIN McKIM, *ORILLIA SUN*

At the Stephen Leacock Awards: Left to right: W.O., Pierre Berton, and Ben Wicks (June 2, 1990).

Bill and Alice Munro at the Blyth Festival for opening of *The Black Bonspiel* (1994).

Bill and Merna on their fiftieth wedding anniversary at Mabel Lake (August 15, 1992).

W.O. and Sir (around 1990).

W.O. and daughter, Willa (around 1990).

Bill and Merna and Chloe, their first great-grandchild (1992).

Mitchell performing at the Waterloo Seagram Museum (November 1990).

Around the end of August, Merna and Bill adopted a new family member – a purebred golden retriever puppy they named Professor, or Sir for short. Sir became the most loved and spoiled of all their dogs. Like a newborn baby, his every behaviour was commented upon, especially by Bill, who loved his comic grin, and who was greatly amused when Sir barked and then, tail between his legs, hid under the porch when the hot-air balloons, so common in Calgary skies, let out their loud, gaseous sighs. Sir became a major focus in their lives and, in fact, became a character in his next novel, *For Art's Sake*. But it was Merna who did the work, and October was a tough time for her, worrying about Bill's health, and juggling the puppy care with Bill's business calls and commitments, visits to the hospital, and household chores. Though she seldom complained, she was upset that her work was unnoticed and unappreciated by Bill.

Between January and May 1988, Mitchell cut down his speaking engagements to about four or five, and concentrated on finishing the novel. The two main events he allowed himself were the readings he did for the Margaret Laurence Tribute Gala Dinner at Trent University on March 11 and 12 (which were a big success) and the opening of *Back to Beulah* at Edmonton's Citadel on March 24 (which was a bomb). By March he seemed to have gathered together some of his old energy, and in spite of "Merna's Law" that he was not to talk about future projects, he did just that. He enthusiastically spoke of two plays he was eager to write. One was the "Scam and Be Damned" play he had already outlined; the other was "Royal Crown Derby," a play about his mother and her sister: "I can see the bloody set already. Especially the china. Nothing stands for the elite Victorian classes like Royal Crown Bloody Derby."[2] He was already enacting some of their arguments and imagining the tea party at which one of them breaks the precious china.

By mid-May most of the Mark Twain novel, now called "Three Are We," was in Gibson's hands. Mitchell still had work to do on the conclusion, but Gibson had only minor editing suggestions to make, and congratulated him on "a fascinating manuscript, with as many facets as an expensive diamond. It was very good at first reading and really stands up under the sort of tough scrutiny I've been giving it." He especially liked the relationship between the young child and the old man and commented that it was "a novel about a new kind of family."[3] A week later Gibson had edited the whole novel. He suggested that Mitchell "might want to amend" the ending "if you don't want to see yourself enthusiastically misquoted by Tories from Mulroney on down."[4] In Mitchell's original ending Lyon says to Sam Clemens, "your voice is the voice of *both* our American nations. You fellows down there below the forty-ninth never have been and never will be the *only* Americans on this continent" (*LL* 275–76). Given the current warming of Canadian-American relations through the rapport of Prime Minister Mulroney and President Reagan and the campaigning for the free trade agreement (which Mulroney would make the crux of his platform for the November 8 election), Gibson felt that Mitchell should tone down his ending. He did, adding "and we welcome you as one of us in our new world" (*LL* 276). Mitchell did not have as many reservations about free trade as did many of his writer friends and colleagues: "I wouldn't want to get tied in with Mulroney and those guys. But I studied classical economics. The free flow of commerce between nations – that's what made the British Empire. What the hell difference does it make if I wear Italian shoes and a Taiwan shirt and eat oranges from Florida? What does that have to do with my culture?"[5]

W.O. and Merna came to Toronto in June. Merna had more or less withdrawn from giving him feedback on his work, but she was worried about this novel and urged W.O. to have us read the manuscript, although it was too far along in the process for any major revisions to be done. We had reservations, particularly about the climactic scene near the end in which Slaughter guns his motorcycle over the escarpment and kills himself. It read like a Hollywood movie script. Although we did not question, as some critics did, the psychological validity of this character choosing suicide, we talked to W.O. about the way in which he was building to the climax. Slaughter's inner voices grow more frenetic as they should, but his invocation of God, like a malignant version of Saint Sammy in Who Has Seen the Wind, *was not convincing. The storm scene was predictably melodramatic, but just before that is a catalogue-like description of Slaughter's Triumph Bonneville: the 750 cc motorcycle with "low-rated sprocket for faster acceleration and free-flow exhaust for high decibel level" (LL 244). The tones jarred. The book lacked the layering of meaning, the sensuous detail, the freshness and rightness of character, and the restraint of his other books. He admitted that the death scene was melodramatic, but it was too late to change much and just a few touches were altered (such as the cliff becoming five hundred feet instead of one thousand).*

We were disappointed because he had such rich material in this book. His portrayal of a psychotic personality was for the most part brilliantly handled and fascinating, and his Mark Twain material had potential he had not fully tapped. Perhaps, though, he had lost some of the art of grace and restraint, those two qualities he so admired in writing, and, even with more time, it might have been impossible for him to have worked any longer at this manuscript.

Ladybug, Ladybug . . . was launched on September 19, 1988, at the annual McClelland & Stewart authors' reception at the Art Gallery of Ontario. Compared to his other books, this novel was less well liked by both readers and critics, although it sold well. By mid-November it had sold 25,000 copies and went into a second printing. The reviewers at the *Ottawa Citizen*, the *Globe and Mail*, and the *Toronto Star* gave it mixed reviews at best, noting that the Mark Twain and other more comic material did not blend well with the melodramatic kidnapping story. They found this latter material "out of control"[6] and even mawkishly sentimental.[7] When asked by critic Ken Adachi why he did not explore more deeply the Lyon/Twain relationship, Mitchell tellingly responded, "I'm not denying that my novel perhaps should have focussed more on the Twain/Lyon relationship. . . . but it wouldn't have worked. If a novel is to carry on for 276 pages, it needs energy and action."[8] That he had foregrounded action and backgrounded philosophy, lyricism, and symbolic structure was precisely the problem. On the other side, however, two reviewers quite familiar with Mitchell's work liked the "raw suspense"[9] and the "darker view of the human condition."[10]

Although considered a comic writer, Mitchell was always quick to retort that the "dark element has always been there." Indeed, since *Summer Holidays* his plots had taken a dark turn in tune with, as Mitchell noted, the prevailing world vision: "In the last couple of decades, we've grown more aware of the darkness under the thin skin of civilization. The threat is growing more and more vivid, getting louder. Until now, we've thought the cover of civilization is thicker than it really is." He was beginning to sound like Mark Twain with these prophetic words. But it was not the dark element that made this book less successful than his others; rather, it was the slip in style, depth of meaning, and coherence. However, he had set the bar very high for himself and seemed aware that this book might, even more than his others, draw comparison to the highly successful *Who Has Seen the Wind*: "In a way, it's unfortunate if the artist's first novel really does it. Then that title is leaning over his shoulder for the rest of his or her writing life. The landscape is littered with one-novel novelists, like J.D. Salinger. But all writers really only have a couple of really good novels in them." Although not every book can match that first success, he argued that "writing is an on-going flow. You keep doing it for its own sake. It ain't an Olympic event. Art is the only thing that humans do for its own sake. It doesn't matter who came first. It's not a contest."[11]

Mitchell began his book tour in Toronto on October 31 and travelled steadily through November. On November 25, he landed back in Calgary to attend the opening of *The Black Bonspiel of Wullie MacCrimmon*. This play was one of the most successful plays ever staged by Theatre Calgary and this production drew full houses for two weeks. November 28 was declared W.O. Mitchell Day by the city and at a benefit luncheon Mitchell said he was delighted to "shill" for Theatre Calgary. Pierre Berton sent a note of congratulation: "When the Lord fashioned Bill Mitchell he was careful to break the mould. Two of him would be too many. None of him

"going to lay it on the line" with Willa and Hugh that they must stay in touch. His concern extended to Merna, and he wished that she would do more interesting things than getting tied up with doing the company books. Maybe, he said, he had been partly to blame. He seemed poignantly aware of the shortness of life and the need to focus on meaningful things. Very soon after Dick's death he started writing about brotherhood. He had never before started so soon to write about something so close and so emotional. "I miss him like hell," he said.[17]

Mitchell buried himself in his work, and by May 24 the manuscript for *According to Jake and the Kid* was in Gibson's hands for editing: "It will be a great book," Gibson wrote encouragingly.[18] At this time, Mitchell told Gibson about the long-forgotten manuscript of "Roses Are Difficult Here," which he had just reread. Gibson was delighted at the prospect of a third Mitchell book on successive fall lists, and Mitchell immediately set to work revising it.

It was unusual for the Mitchells to head east rather than west to their cottage in July, but Bill had been offered a role as the curmudgeon Alexander Abraham in the *Road to Avonlea* television series based on the Lucy Maude Montgomery novels. Patricia Hamilton (who played Rachel Lynde) recalled that Mitchell seemed unfamiliar with the length of time it took to perfect and tape a scene and, on one occasion, took off in his taxi to head back to Toronto before the scene had been wrapped up. The crew had to send another taxi to bring him back.[19] He also caused "consternation" on the set with his snuff habit, for he continually covered his moustache and costume with brown stains. It was frustrating and uncomfortable waiting around for the calls in the hot, sticky Ontario summer weather, and the "all-woollen costume of long underwear, shirt and trousers had made him *genuinely* grouchy before the cameras."[20]

Merna and W.O. came to Peterborough for a few days before heading to Toronto for the filming. They sat outside on the picnic bench, practising W.O.'s lines for the Road to Avonlea *script, Merna smoking, W.O. doing snuff. Merna cued W.O., and he delivered his lines, muttering away at how Montgomery could not write dialogue, making it extremely difficult, he claimed, for him to act the lines with any naturalness and meaning. Merna, very patiently, demonstrated how the lines should be done. He repeated them – more bombastically. She would correct him: "Bill, tone it down. Don't overdo it." He would get cross, curse a bit, then "All right, all right, Merna." It paid off. The reviewers found the curmudgeonly Abraham "nicely underplayed by Mitchell."[21]*

In September 1989, Mitchell was offered an office at the University of Calgary with the Faculty of Social Work. He liked his new quarters and, as usual, made instant tea friends with a number of the staff and faculty. It was ironic, and appropriate, that he should be working on "Roses Are Difficult Here" among social scientists, since he had never had much time for sociology, which he considered a pseudo-science, and which comes in for a great deal of criticism in "Roses." He had also, twenty years earlier, not been very encouraging when Merna considered taking some sociology courses at the university. So here was Mitchell's opportunity to develop a more flexible view of the social sciences – and he did. In fact, he paid gratitude to them on the dedication page of his final novel.[22]

Mitchell was on book tour with *According to Jake and the Kid* from October 13 to November 24. *Ladybug* came out in mass paperback at the same time, so he had two books in the limelight. The reception of *According to Jake and the Kid* was warm. Some critics found the resolutions of the stories sentimental, but most Mitchell followers delighted in their nostalgia. Critics and readers alike saw Mitchell in terms of an aging icon now, and were gentler with him. Mitchell resisted that image and even grew impatient talking about his old radio days at the CBC: "God, I hate being this senescent old bastard reminiscing back 30 years."[23] The highlight of the tour was his reading at the International Authors' Festival at Harbourfront in Toronto on October 21, where he received a standing ovation for his reading of "Love's Wild Magic" from *According to Jake and the Kid.* It tickled Mitchell that he could make some sly remarks about the organizer of the festival, Greg Gatenby, through the character of his story, "old man Gatenby" who was so "stubborn . . . that once he gets an idea into his head, stumping powder won't blow her out of there" (*AJK* 212).

– "GLORIA CHORAL" –

Mitchell had two novels on the go. He had written about 150 pages on his brotherhood novel, at this stage called "For My Brother," but he felt overwhelmed and saddened by the theme so he put it away to concentrate on "Roses Are Difficult Here." "Roses" was more res-urrected than revised. Unlike the rewriting he did with *The Vanishing Point* where he virtually abandoned the original "Alien," *Roses Are Difficult Here* is primarily the same as its earlier manuscript. Of course, the "Roses" manuscript was in better shape, for, in 1959, it had been accepted for publication by Macmillan and was held back because Mitchell had wanted American publication as well.

Like *According to Jake*, the atmosphere of the book is distinctly 1950s, not in the sense of casting back to that period, but of it having been written in that time. However, in 1990, thirty-three years later, that became one of its virtues – that it portrays, emotionally and accurately, a bygone time of small towns and local newspapers with their earnestness, their dignity, their gossipy trivialities, and their prejudices. Mitchell had a serious theme about community life when he first wrote this in 1957. He saw small-town life composed of various voices, various storytellers (reporters, sociologists, gossips, sermonizers, tall-tale tellers, satirists, historians), not all of them, by any account, good and high-principled, but all of them contribut-ing to the community voice. To some editorial readers at that time the focus on the small town seemed hackneyed and sentimental, but, in the 1990s, perhaps helped by nostalgia, Mitchell's focus on story-telling, his look at the boundaries between fiction and fact and at the ways in which we construct ourselves through narrative, took on a fresh and significant appeal.

What Mitchell was concerned with in such storytelling was the ambiguous interplay between truth and lies and the implicit understanding that listeners have of storytelling conventions. For instance, tall-tale telling in Mitchell's opinion was not irresponsible, but had a role to play in building and preserving the heritage of the west. Looked at this way the stories in the novel resonate with purpose, and in the concluding pages Matt Stanley realizes that all the stories, the voices in the town, come together to create a unity, what he calls, a "GLORIA CHORAL" (*RD* 318).

In his 1990s revision he did more shifting of material than actual rewriting. The most significant changes were made at the beginning and the end. By slightly increasing the role of Uncle Ben, the first editor of the paper and long-dead uncle of the protagonist Matt Stanley, Mitchell was able to heighten the theme of responsible news/story telling. Uncle Ben in the older version of the novel had been not only a drunkard but a slacker, "content to make a living from job printing."[24] Now, in the new version, he becomes a model figure as he urges Matt to think about significant issues and become a meaningful voice for the community. The largest addition Mitchell made was the story of "Santa's Visit to Shelby." It was based, in fact, on a true story told to him by George McClellan, one of his creative-writing students in 1972.[25] This very amusing set piece came to be one of Mitchell's favourite reading selections.

Mitchell sent the manuscript to Gibson in February. He was pleased with his revisions, but Merna was concerned when they did not hear back.[26] The novel reopened old wounds for her as she sadly recalled that the community had let her down when she was working on the recreation board. There was also the deep, unspoken worry that Bill had not written a serious-enough novel. In 1959 Mitchell felt he had missed the trapeze with "Roses,"[27] although now he had convinced himself that his revisions had brought a new, sharper feel to the book.

Gibson returned the edited manuscript in mid-April and complimented Mitchell: "I came away struck by what a wonderful picture it is of the West at the end of an era, with the old Harry

Derrigan characters no longer around now to give us their picture of the West in the old days. That strength, and the portrait of the community (the real central character) and Matt and his family, the other characters in town and the comical set-pieces (Santa, and the invasion of the goats), make this a wonderful rich novel, that will be greeted with delight."[28]

Mitchell was in Toronto on April 20 and met with Gibson to do a final edit on *Roses*. He also discussed with Ron Besse, publisher for Macmillan, an extension of the 1982 Bantam Seal Paperback deal for five of his titles. Mitchell, in a "lapse of discretion," indicated that he was dissatisfied with "procedural delays" at McClelland & Stewart regarding the renewal of the paperback deal. Perhaps because of that, perhaps because his New York agent, Susan Schulman, was pushing him toward more assertive negotiations regarding his properties, he intimated to Besse that he might accept a bid on his next hardcover, which was to be based on the Calgary art scam. Although he was very happy working with Gibson, "the finest editor I have ever had,"[29] he was annoyed when he heard from his agent that other writers were cutting larger percentages. For the next six months he and his agent haggled with M&S over the *Roses* contract, and it was not until December 1991 that the paperback deal was concluded, and not favourably.

In the meantime, Mitchell heard the good news that *According to Jake and the Kid* had been chosen for the Stephen Leacock Award for Humour. He had won it in 1962 for his first collection, *Jake and the Kid*, so he confessed, "I wasn't ready for it. . . . I knew I was up for it, but I really didn't think I would get it."[30] The award ceremony was held in Orillia, Stephen Leacock's hometown, on June 2, with Pierre Berton hosting. In his thank-you speech Mitchell said, "I take humour to be a very serious matter. Its main quality has to be logical surprise, unpredictable as life itself. Its use must be responsible. If not, then satire becomes simply invective, directed against undeserving targets. Comedy turns into one-liner slapstick. No space given to irony." He went on to explain that he had been introduced to Leacock by his American teacher at St. Petersburg High School:

"Leacock hooked me instantly as he ever did any small mouth bass. I am still in his creel and I am delighted to receive this award. I hope that in my writing I have selected my targets of pomposity, misuse of power, adversarial selfishness, elite conceit, as carefully as he would. And as responsibly."[31]

We, and our daughter Sara, attended the award ceremony with W.O. and Merna. There were a number of W.O.'s Ontario cousins in attendance, two of them, women, seated at our table. As we listened to them and W.O. recalling family connections and stories, we were interrupted by a cousin from another table. He had obviously inherited the Mitchell ham genes, though they seemed somewhat diluted, and he began to hold forth on Mitchell genealogy. He exasperated W.O. with his interruptions and inaccurately recalled family stories. Merna giggled and whispered, "Bill's getting his own back." The other cousins, laughing, leaned over and explained to us that this cousin had CRAFT. "Oh?" we queried, not understanding. "Yes," they laughed, "he can't remember a fucking thing." W.O., his patience finally exhausted, turned in his chair and decisively said, "Shut up and fuck off!" Conversation at nearby tables stopped. Sara, who by this time was used to W.O.'s outbursts, was mortified and said, "You shouldn't be that mean to anyone." W.O. apologized, his cousin retreated, and, once more, all seemed sweetness and light in Mariposa-land.

Mitchell began his book tour on September 19 and was kept on the run until mid-December with more than forty-five events. When he spoke to the Women's Canadian Club in Edmonton in October he must have been amused when one of the organizers told him how much she had enjoyed reading his story "Opening My First Bank Account," confusing him with Stephen Leacock and his well-known story, "My Financial Career." *Roses* hit number two on the best-seller lists in its first week and remained on the list for at least fourteen weeks. This year was a coup: Mitchell had two books on the best-seller lists in the same year.

Mitchell cleverly avoided saying that the book had been written and nearly published in the 1950s. Rather, he explained, "this novel's been in my gut for 38 years."[32] Reviewers thought it was a nostalgic look back at the 1950s; in fact, it *was* the 1950s. The reviews were predominantly positive. This was a gentle book, "unfashionable" but "rich," commented one reviewer,[33] and another said Mitchell delves "into moments that really count in the lives of people."[34] It broke no new ground, but it did have an effect on the common reader. Two years after the book appeared Mitchell received a copy of a review of the book written by Martha Perkins, editor at the *Haliburton County Echo*, in which she concluded that, "*Roses Are Difficult Here* should make everyone sit down and write Mr. Mitchell a letter of thanks."[35] She did just that and reported to him that his book had a great impact on her, so much so that she had urged Trent University students, who had come to her town to do local research, to read the novel so as not to act like Dr. June Melquists. Mitchell's novel had inspired her: "Your words helped me form my thoughts. Not many people have that gift."[36]

The International Festival of Authors paid tribute to Mitchell on October 18, 1990, and it was a very proud moment for both Merna and Bill. Peter Gzowski introduced each of the eight speakers,[37] and then he summed up, saying there had been "many expressions of love . . . all of them genuine, all of them earned." After giving a reading, Mitchell responded, "I want to thank every one of you jokers. You didn't turn this into a roast. . . . I was quite, quite moved. There's been only one omission. You haven't heard from an important person in my life. She's my chief editor. She sees it first. For the past half-century she's been my down field blocker. It's my ass if I answer a telephone call first. She kept me from 'flake-ing.' She's a distant relative of mine from marriage. God, she's the only woman who could have stood living with me for 48 years. Come on up here, Merna."[38]

His last engagement on tour was a benefit reading for the Edmonton Symphony on December 15. Just before that event, in good spirits, he wrote, "Merna and I have just about reached the end of the hype and horror trail for ROSES. I say Merna and I because I think it's damn near as tough for her as it is for me. But I've made it – praise God – praise His Holy Name! I'll be reciting at the Edmonton symphony Christmas show the end of the week; they turned down my offer to play the pan flute while tap dancing to SHUFFLE OFF TO BUFFALO."[39]

The mock evangelical language in his letter was a reference to one of the characters in the new stage play, variously titled "Scam and Be Damned," "Bringing in the Sheaves," and "Bringing in the Shekels," that he had been working on between tour interruptions: "I am doing the con play that's been in my gut for five or more years. I have been hot and I have been cold."[40] This one-man play centred on a medicine man, an evangelist based on Amy Semple MacPherson, and a baseball player, about to engage in a celestial playoff (an obvious borrowing from *The Black Bonspiel*). Although he was amused by it as he wrote it, and finished it in January 1991, it was thin and repetitive material, which he willingly abandoned when a new novel took hold of him.

⁓ "ART FOR ALL" ⁓

Thinking about cons, he had begun a new novel earlier in the summer, called alternatively "Scamelot" and "Art for All," but had put it aside while working on the play and going on his book tour. Rather than a nostalgic look back to the 1930s medicine men and evangelists, the novel revolved around a series of art thefts that took place in Calgary from 1976 to late 1977. He had remembered the initial theft of twenty famous Albrecht Dürer prints from the University of Calgary Art Gallery in 1976 and had dug up all the newspaper reports of this case, which ended with the arrest and trial of the thieves in 1978. The judge at the trial had described the art thieves, a professor at the university and a junior high-school teacher, as having a "Robin Hood aura about them as they freely distributed their booty among friends and relatives."[41] Mitchell got going on this idea, echoing some of the phraseology from the *Calgary Herald*, including the "Robin Hood" description, although his thieves were much more altruistically motivated than the Calgary thieves. By January 1991, Mitchell had his theme – art for all – and his main characters. Professor, the Mitchells' slightly neurotic, overindulged golden retriever, was to be a significant character. As Mitchell said, Professor would probably never "achieve adulthood" although he was becoming "more and more articulate; indeed I think he has moved into doing sound poetry – much better than Stephen Scobie does."42

In mid-January Mitchell came east for the opening of *The Kite* at Hamilton's Theatre Aquarius, a very good production with Douglas Campbell playing Daddy. He also had good news about a proposed television movie based on the *Jake and the Kid* stories. In the fall of 1990, Fundamentally Film (Joe Green and Ron Singer) had approached Mitchell to be a script consultant on the movie with Ann McNaughton, a former creative-writing student of Mitchell, doing the adaptation. By March they had found a financier and this project looked as if it might fly.

In spite of work on an outline for the movie and a number of speaking engagements this spring, Mitchell kept working on the novel. He was amused by the plot and enjoyed the writing. Following on *Since Daisy Creek* and *Ladybug, Ladybug . . .* , he selected Livingstone University as his setting. Art Ireland, the main character, is a disgruntled sessional in the Faculty of Fine Arts who, within the first few pages of the novel, resigns – just before he is fired – providing ample ammunition for Mitchell to attack academe's old boys' network. His other target is the elitist, capitalistic art world, which favours collecting art in the hands of the rich rather than depositing it in public galleries. Ireland, a widower for five years, has established a rural art colony with three other men, Charlie, a sculptor, Darryl, a poet, and Win, an actor. They are all down-and-out, "victims of a materialistic, commercial, money-motivated society" (*Art* 72), but Ireland has a plan to get revenge on the dean who fired him and to redistribute art in public galleries. They will steal targeted paintings from private collections, stash them at his art colony, wait for the insurance payback option to expire, then drop them off in Europe to be rediscovered and put on the block at auction. Ireland assures his co-thieves that the moral point of these heists would then be achieved, for the art would assuredly be purchased by public art galleries throughout the world.

Although the scheme seems harebrained, and Mitchell does not quite convince readers that it is workable, the theory behind it, that art is done for art's sake and should be available for all to enjoy, is a serious one. In fact, it was his friend, the Montreal painter Louis Muhlstock, who talked to him about this philosophy. Mitchell first met Muhlstock at Banff during the 1980s, and his recall of conversations with Muhlstock over the years went directly into his fictional character Louis Simard, Ireland's mentor. In 1995 when Mitchell wrote to wish Muhlstock a happy birthday, he added a P.S.: "You were slightly upset when my novel, *For Art's Sake*, came out and you found yourself in it. Only a part of you was in Art. Like him you believe that art is for all, not just the wealthy few who can keep it to themselves for ego embellishment. You even turned me down once as a private owner of your work, later <u>gave</u> me The Pigeon of Sainte Famille and one of your innerscapes."[43]

We were living in England when W.O. sent us, in April 1991, thirty pages of the novel he was working on. He wrote, "This probably is the most autobiographical thing I've ever found for my fiction. With the very slight changes it is actually my summer of 1933, and as I have said possibly the beginning of what I have done with most of my time ever since."[44] The section he sent us (Art 45–65) concerned the misfortunes of young Art Ireland in England and France at the hands of a couple of con artists. The piece had intensity, good descriptive prose, crisp, well-differentiated dialogue, and it dealt, provocatively, with questions of innocence, corruption, the old world and the new. We felt that an exciting new novel was underway.

In April, Mitchell was nominated for the Stephen Leacock Award for Humour for the third time, but he did not win.[45] He was somewhat relieved: "Once was lovely, twice is plenty, but to make it a third time only affirms in idiots' minds that this guy is only a slapstick comic."[46]

By June he had finished 120 pages on the novel. The television movie deal was tantalizingly close, but Mitchell was being very cautious. He insisted that he and Eric Till were to retain artistic control, and that he would sell rights to only three stories for a movie, not rights to all the work for a television series. Ron Singer of Fundamentally Film even made a trip out to Mabel Lake to get Mitchell to look over another version of the agreement. Finally, in September, plans were set in motion to form a new company, Crocus Films, owned by Green, Singer, Mitchell, and Till, to produce the television feature film based on the three *Jake and the Kid* horse stories. Mitchell's diabetes and its related problems were taking their toll on him, and it upset him that one of the clauses in the film agreement stipulated that another writer could be brought in if he were unable to complete the work for health reasons. However, in August at the lake he persisted in keeping his annual rendezvous with the Chinook salmon.

For four mornings in a row — at 4:30 a.m. — W.O. and I went salmon fishing on the Shuswap River. He seemed to be in good shape for someone seventy-seven years old, given the physical demands made by salmon fishing. On the second morning as we were fishing the Cable Car hole, he stumbled on the rocks and fell in at the river's edge. I grabbed his arm and helped him to his feet. He had only scraped his shin, but I will never forget the look of panic and frustration on his face. He asked me not to tell Merna.

Merna tried to hide the deepening concern she had about Bill's health. Recently she had had a disturbing dream in which he was calling out for her help. She ran to the window, but he was outside, and she was inside. He was hanging on by his fingertips, shouting, and she could not find a way to help him.[47]

Her worry about Bill exacerbated her drinking problem. Always a happy social drinker like many of her era, she had begun drinking more over the years, and on occasion it brought out an angry side of her. In the mid-1980s her problem had caused concern and confrontations in the family. When she was asked to consider AA, she refused, and attempted to deal with the problem on her own. Bill did not know what to do. He had tried to talk to her, but she would not listen. Mostly he refused to confront her, which was both escapist and defensive on his part. He feared her reprisals, and would plaintively plead, "Why are you attacking me, Merna?" At times, though, he seemed oblivious to the situation. In the earlier years, their household disagreements had largely dissipated like smoke in the air, but now, at times, they lingered in a black cloud. One evening Merna lashed out at him, "You don't know me — you really don't know me." Though in so many ways theirs was a loving and complementary relationship, Mitchell seemed less and less able, in these latter years, with his own physical and emotional defences at a low point, to give to Merna the attention and support she needed.

Mitchell worked on his novel in September and October, keeping an eye on the progress of the film venture at the same time. In October he met with the co-writer, Ann McNaughton, and they discussed the outline. She was to structure the scenes while he filled in the text. Apparently he had already talked to Gibson about the possibility of this *Jake* film script being transposed into a novel that Gibson, rather optimistically, thought they could publish in November 1992. This excitement and scheming about other projects dissipated his creative energies, and they were not financially necessary, as they had been in earlier years. Now his annual company earnings, though not huge, were on average slightly better than $100,000 (before taxes, expenses, and support for Willa), from which he and Merna could draw salaries. But he simply could not resist spinning off new ideas.

November was a busy month with a shortened book tour for M&S's new edition of the full-length text of *Who Has Seen the Wind.* As with the 1976 coffee-table edition, the William Kurelek paintings were used, though in a slightly different format. Mitchell thought it was a handsome book and was thrilled, calling it "a literary Lazarus — a miracle,"[48] because the original Macmillan text that he had always preferred (seven thousand words longer than the Little, Brown version) was restored for the first time since its publication in 1947. By December it had sold out of the five thousand copies of the first run and was into a second printing of twenty-five hundred. It had also made it onto the best-seller list.

~ "THANK GOD FOR WHAT I DO" ~

The *Jake and the Kid* joint film venture was signed in March 1992, and Crocus Films was formally incorporated. There was strong hope for success on that front, though what materialized was a mixed blessing. Mitchell hoped to be finished his novel by April. He seemed dubious about it, and echoing the words of his character Art Ireland, he said that it might just turn out to be a "bucket of shit."[49] There was no doubt, though, that he was enjoying the writing – figuring out the mechanics of the art heists, writing the comic hot-air balloon scene, and concocting the sound-poetry lines for Professor.

Merna hid any worries she might have about the quality of the book because she felt it was essential for Bill to be working on a project. He had doctors' examinations and tests during February and early April. While he was completing the manuscript, his tests came back positive. He had prostate cancer, and, worse, it had spread to the bone. As with most serious matters in his life, Bill internalized it, withdrew, and could not talk about it. Merna was shattered by the news, and talked only to a few people for the first few weeks. She and Bill kept their minds preoccupied with the details of the medical procedures. He was put on hormones to battle the testosterone with the hope of slowing the progress of the cancer. The doctors felt that, given his age, the advancement through the body would be slow, and it would probably be some other health issue, such as his aneurysm, that would cause his death. Bill and Merna soon found, once again, the optimism and strength that had marked their lives and marriage from the beginning.

For nearly a month, Merna was too upset to inform us in England about W.O.'s condition. It was difficult simply to utter the word cancer *and was especially hard for her to tell Orm. On a Mother's Day telephone call she told me, but with instructions not to tell Orm. That was impossible. We dealt with the news, conferred with family members, and then called W.O. on May 17. When Orm spoke to his father, W.O. had found his equilibrium and discussed his cancer calmly, explaining that he was taking the hormone treatment and was feeling fine. "It's estrogen," he explained, "don't you notice that my voice is higher?" Orm continued in that vein: "No, I hadn't noticed," but since it was made from the piss of pregnant mares and was also used in birth control, had he started having regular periods? "We both enjoy a bit of black humour, don't we, son?" Then W.O. switched the conversation to the new book, explaining that he was redoing parts of the first chapter and also completely rewriting one of the characters. When Orm asked if he was pleased with it, he replied, "Not really, but Merna and Doug like it." Brightening up, he added, "Thank God for what I do. When I'm on the typewriter, I get into an inner world, and it doesn't matter what's going on in the outer world."*[50]

By telephone and then by letter, Gibson gently told Mitchell at the end of April that the manuscript needed considerable work. In fact, it was not up to Mitchell's standard at all. "When you get a novel of that level," Gibson later remarked, "there is no doubt you are weighing all sorts of other considerations, and the considerations include decency and humanity. If I were to say 'Absolutely not,' what would it do to the author?"[51] In his letter to Mitchell he pointed out many problems with the novel, its lack of "texture," some "shadowy" characters, only one "typical W.O. Mitchell comic set-piece," and "abrupt" and "stripped-down" narration, but he felt that it was "a good, interesting novel, not quite like anything you've done before."[52] And, of course, the Mitchell name was marketable.

Mitchell called *For Art's Sake* his art caper novel and, indeed, it had been somewhat of a caper for him to write, light-hearted and not deeply philosophical. Though there are some serious and dark issues touched upon – grief, suicide, murder – he only occasionally transcends the art heist plot to reach an emotional level. One of these occasions is a finely written reverie that Ireland has about his wife, Irene, as they are about to go swimming in the pond at the farm. This passage's sensuously detailed description of the natural world and its inherent emotional intensity show Mitchell at his best. He knew full well the power of this passage, for he used it to signify the dispelling of Ireland's five-year painter's block (*Art* 248–51).

Though Mitchell wondered whether this novel was good, as he had wondered about *Ladybug*, his concern was about the plot and the theme – which, in fact, may have been some cause for concern. But the problem was more that he had forfeited the depth and resonance of descriptive prose and rounded characterization for the lighter verbal sparring between characters. *For Art's Sake* went further down that stylistic road of dialogue and action than had *Since Daisy Creek* and *Ladybug*. Mitchell, however, was generally proud of this transition in his writing, indicative, perhaps, of how far he had fallen under the influence of stage and film script work.

~ CELEBRATIONS ~

Bill and Merna had booked flights to come to England on June 16 for three weeks. At the time they did not know that Mitchell would require an orchidectomy, which he had on June 1. This was considered a safety measure and, in fact, the biopsy showed no testicular cancer. When they arrived Mitchell was tired and unsteady on his feet, but able to join in on almost all activities including trips to Dunlop, Scotland, the birthplace of his great grandparents, Maggie Gibb and John Biggart. They also travelled up north to Hartlepool, the birthplace of Merna's mother, and on to Sunderland to visit with Merna's cousin where, much to Merna's annoyance, he was back in performance mode, and taking over conversations even with her side of the family.

Sixty years ago, when W.O. spent two days in London on his student trip to Europe, he picked up some of the verses of the English comic Stanley Holloway. Soon after we had arrived in our little village of Barmby Moor (in Yorkshire) in 1990, W.O. had written a letter that opened with a witty rendition of Holloway's verses: "EE bah goom, stay away from t'zoo there in Barfington Moor because that's where yoong Albert shooved his cane with horse's 'ead 'andle into ear of lion name Wally and Wally turned over with roll and swallowed yoong Albert oop 'ole."[53] *W.O. used to practise these skits with a friend during the 1930s. On our way home from Sunderland, in June 1992, we stopped at a pub, where we were amazed to hear W.O. and the landlord launch into various Holloway comic routines. Together they rhymed off the story of "Albert and the Lion," W.O. doing a credible Lancastrian accent. This was much more interesting to him than attending the York Cycle Plays or going to hear madrigals on the York Minster lawn.*

It was almost midnight when we arrived back at "Barfington Moor" from our trip north. We had just settled down to bed when the telephone rang: "This is the Prime Minister's Office calling. Is W.O. Mitchell there?" Thinking it was our son, I almost said, "Geoff! Stop kidding around." I called up to W.O., "Can you get up and take this call?" He yelled back, "Who the hell is it, Barbara?" Uncertainly, I said, "It could be – I think – the prime minister." W.O. took the phone, and, without missing a beat, casually asked the caller, "The Prime Minister of England or Canada?" He was soon chatting on a friendly first-name basis with Prime Minister Brian Mulroney, who asked if Bill would accept the honorary title of Member of the Privy Council and, if so, could he fly home to Canada in time for the presentation by the Queen on July 1. W.O. said he would be honoured to accept and quipped, "Couldn't the Queen just do it here?" He then said he was turning the phone over to Merna. Merna very definitively said no, they could not fly back for the July 1 presentation. When W.O. got back on the phone, Mulroney said, "I sensed the voice of authority in Merna." W.O. replied, "You are perceptive."

Later that fall he received the honour at a private ceremony at the Governor General's residence in Ottawa. Beside the letters O.C. (Order of Canada) he was now permitted to use P.C., and he made it perfectly clear to all and sundry that this did not signify Progressive Conservative. The title was a newly established honour for non-politicians: "It's the highest honour in terms of title you can have in Canada," stated Mark

Entwistle, the prime minister's spokesman.[54] *The family ribbed him for weeks, saying that he was certainly a wise choice for this position because, judging from his story about blowing up Melvin Arbuckle's grandpa in the backhouse, he knew a lot more about privies than most people.*

Merna and Bill were at the lake to celebrate their fiftieth wedding anniversary on August 15, 1992. This was the western celebration (there was to be another in the east in December), and all their friends from surrounding cottages congregated to celebrate this loving and adventure-filled marriage. Indeed they had many stories to tell of Bill's misadventures – and Merna's forbearance. Doug Gibson and friends at M&S arranged for fifty red roses to be delivered to the lake, no mean feat, and that could not have pleased Merna more. Merna and Bill would say it was good luck that brought them together and their mutual sense of humour that kept them together. Bill would add that no one else would have put up with him for so long – and he was probably right! Doug Gibson, teasingly, called it the "enduring power of mutual recrimination."[55] They were intensely loyal to one another, and that bond of affection had carried them through financial and emotional ups and downs for five decades. It seemed somehow fitting for them to be at Mabel Lake, for fifty years ago they had honeymooned at another green retreat, Sylvan Lake in Alberta, but Mabel, where the beds were not on wheels, was far more seductive.

The Mitchells returned to Calgary at the end of the salmon season, and Mitchell attacked the *Jake and the Kid* film project once more. It was not going well, and Eric Till could see that. On September 22, 1992, he wrote Bill, "When reading the latest draft I could see how tired and unwell you've been these past months and my heart went out to you. . . . The present draft won't sell with the louts at CBC and Telefilm." He suggested leaving the scripts entirely up to Ann McNaughton, for "you're much too important to all of us to get exhausted and stressed over the TV Jake."[56]

In October, Bill and Merna flew east for the launch of *For Art's Sake,* for a gala event marking the twenty-fifth anniversary of the

Order of Canada ceremonies, and to see their first great-grandchild. It was a cut-down book promotion tour, but Mitchell put on a good show at a reading at Harbourfront. The *Globe and Mail*, on October 31, led off the reviews of the novel: "Things are a little flat on the prairie." However, the reviewer commented, one flat book "need not be a diminution" of what Mitchell has accomplished with his other novels.[57] The book had a good run, and, in spite of a general slowdown in book sales, it sold about 11,500 and made the best-seller list for the next five months, rising as high as number five.

He was not quite sure where to turn his attention. The *Jake and the Kid* venture seemed to have "pissed away into the sand again."[58] He wanted to call the deal off and then settled down enough to allow Till to proceed, but he refused to do any more of the writing himself. Merna tried to get him interested in working on his Royal Crown Derby play, and there was his brotherhood novel. Then Merna had another idea. She urged him to take a look at the short-story version of *The Black Bonspiel of Wullie MacCrimmon* and see if it could be expanded to a novella. Mitchell had forgotten that he had written this as a short story sometime between 1945 and 1948 – before it ever came to radio (1950) and stage (1966) – and had lengthened it in 1961 to fifty-six pages for a trilogy entitled "The Devil's a Travellin' Man."[59] Every time it was produced on stage, small changes had been made to it, so it seemed like an enjoyable and easy project to blend the stage play additions with the trilogy version.

Before he could get to that, however, he was invited by Lawrence Cherney to put together some readings for a Christmas program in a series for young people called "Musical Magic" at the St. Lawrence Centre in Toronto. Mitchell chose a few Christmas-themed pieces from *Wind* and *Roses* and a couple of his *Jake* tales. He narrated them with all his former vigour and Billie Mae Richards took on the Kid's voice once again as she had in those golden days of *Jake and the Kid* radio. Louis Applebaum wrote the musical score, which served as a setting for the stories. The two afternoon performances, December 19 and 20, were a success, and he had the audience in tears with his reading of the *Jake* story "A Voice for Christmas."

Mitchell was looking and feeling better than he had for six months. He and Merna had requested a second anniversary celebration, so they could invite the family and their many Toronto friends who lived in the east. The event was held at Trent University in December. Merna was the star, telling the very amusing story of their honeymoon night on rolling hospital beds in the spartan and unromantic accommodation they had at Sylvan Lake fifty years earlier — fifty years together and they were still amused by what Mitchell appropriately called the "capsize quality of life."

16

"THE GREEN LUMINOUS BUBBLE"

~ 1993 to 1997 ~

MITCHELL MADE a concerted effort in the New Year to do some exercises that might help his balance and his hip difficulties. He despised doing fruitless exercises like riding a stationary bicycle. He had been an active man, but did not exercise for the sake of exercising. He sailed, hunted, and fished, and, as he constantly reminded Merna, walked miles in airport terminals. So, it was with great disdain that he sat upon the stationary bicycle in his family room, loading his nostrils with snuff, and watching the uninspiring *Murder, She Wrote* or *Columbo*. Like a little boy being punished, he cycled and pouted. January was a cold month and although Mitchell wanted to get back to work at his office, Merna said it was too cold so they "hibernate[d]."[1]

Imperial Oil Review had invited him to put together a piece on summer on the prairies and he did so, imaginatively transporting himself to the warm and "humming, living prairie of old." He wrote about going to his cottage at Carlyle Lake in the 1920s, and about Sheepskin, the Saulteau Indian, with whom he traded shoes for bows and arrows. Then he told about a canoeing incident with his brother Bob, when the canoe had tipped and they had found themselves mesmerized by the magic light of the "green luminous bubble" under the capsized canoe "with the water's slap, tap and gurgle amplified."[2] He had just written this section for his new novel about brotherhood, and it showed the nostalgic mood he was in. It is an evocative scene that returns to the style of writing that Mitchell used in *Wind* and in *Summer Holidays* and captures those aspects of boyhood that Mitchell was so good at conveying, and never lost in his own life – an innocent thrill of adventure, a delight in the sensuousness of experience, and a reflectiveness. He hoped he could weave that magic "luminous bubble" over the whole of his new novel.

In the meantime, he decided to go ahead with the idea of expanding "The Black Bonspiel" and, in early April, he sent Gibson the 1961 prose version. It would be a push to get this ready for fall publication, as Gibson wanted it to be at least twenty thousand words, which meant that Mitchell would have to write about twenty-five hundred more words. To lengthen it even more, he and Gibson were both scouting out an illustrator who could create black-and-white chapter headings. Mitchell added a beginning section, comically describing the history of the game of curling; he gave more context to the town, now called Shelby like the town in *The Kite* and *Roses Are Difficult Here*; and he expanded on Wullie (now spelled Willie) MacCrimmon's personal life. Mitchell noticed that, "as in *For Art's Sake*, I had neglected [at first] to give the lead character a wife. Now Willie has one and if he loses his soul to Cloutie he will never rejoin her in Heaven. Thanks to Merna, I now plagiarize Robbie Burns, who lost <u>his</u> Highland Mary."[3] For the ending, he decided on a newspaper report of the Canadian Brier under the byline of Bill Frayne, a nod to his sportswriter friend Trent Frayne. Gibson asked a knowledgable curler to check over the scoring, for Mitchell had not been accurate in his early versions. Gibson and Merna had really pushed Mitchell forward on this one, and he wrote him, "How I owe that woman and you!"[4] The ten full-page black-and-white illustrations, created by Wesley W. Bates, perfectly suited the old-fashioned, classical tone of the story and, as Gibson wrote, it was "a rich package."[5]

Bill and Merna were enthusiastic watchers of curling on television, even though Mitchell had failed miserably as a curler himself. Although he recalled curling, as a young boy, out on the frozen prairie sloughs or river with lard tins filled with ice, he had only played once or twice as an adult in Castor – and not impressively.[6] With some exaggeration, he told a reporter that he recalled "stepping backwards unto a curling rock, and riding it 'ten feet down the ice'" and, thus, getting his team disqualified.[7]

With the finishing of the book, negotiations over the contract not yet finalized, and constant worry over Mitchell's health, May and June were anxious months. Bill was to have another measurement of the aneurysm and hip X-rays, and they had to change doctors, all of which created a great deal of stress for Merna. On the night of June 27, without warning, as she was walking to bed, her leg gave out and she collapsed to the floor. Bill called for an ambulance, and she was admitted to hospital for a series of tests. She had suffered a minor stroke. Obviously the anxiety of the last few years had contributed to her hypertension, as, no doubt, had her smoking and drinking. But, like most crises in their lives, Merna dealt with it head-on. She stopped smoking, at once – and forever. She was soon impatient to be released from hospital, and, once stabilized on heart medication, she was discharged. As usual, she was more concerned about getting home to care for Bill than she was worried about her own health problems.

Then came another reminder of mortality. On July 6, Jack Mitchell, Bill's older brother, died. He was eight-six. Mitchell and his son Hugh went to Regina to attend the funeral. Bill was downcast, and sadly remarked, "I'm the last one."[8] It was a difficult journey, emotionally and physically. His hip was so painful now he could hardly walk a hundred yards.

It was not until October that Merna and Bill felt they could cope with some publicity for the launch of *The Black Bonspiel*. In fact, because Mitchell was not able to do much active promotion, Gibson asked him to sign one thousand bookplates that would be placed in both *The Black Bonspiel* and the illustrated edition of *Who Has Seen the Wind*, which was still selling well. The Mitchells arrived in Toronto on October 26 for four days of promotion, largely radio and television interviews, rather than public readings. His pared-down schedule was still rigorous, including eight interviews in two days and attendance at the opening night of *The Black Bonspiel* at Theatre Aquarius in Hamilton, where he autographed books; yet he felt stimulated by the activity.

The Black Bonspiel hit the best-seller list and sold 10,000 copies by January. A few reviewers, however, were critical and found it annoying that Mitchell was retreading an old story: "And now, as a novella . . . well, Willie MacCrimmon's rocks just don't seem to make the hog line."[9] Mitchell was not in the least embarrassed about reusing the story. He thought it was a great tale: "I think it is just one of those legends based on universal truth. The Faust legend reveals the vulnerability of humans wanting to score, to make the big gamble."[10] However, he never ranked it with his novels; it was "a cute little cookie."[11] Other reviewers saw it in that vein as well, commenting on the nostalgic tone: "It was a time when principles were still in touch with humanity. That's almost gone now. But you can still catch its echo in the sound of the pipes, and we have, in W.O. Mitchell's charming tale, a grand souvenir."[12]

In the fall of 1993 there had been an exciting change of direction with the *Jake and the Kid* television movie. The CBC had dropped the project, but the producers involved in Crocus Films, Green and Singer, had talked to Nelvana, the world's largest independent company specializing in animated films. Nelvana was branching out to live-action television, and the family quality of *Jake and the Kid* looked promising to them. To the Crocus producers the deal looked positive and lucrative. Mitchell was cynical, but after talking to Till about it and getting his lawyer to look over the details he agreed to an option with Nelvana that was signed on January 24, 1994. However, it was the old problem. Nelvana wanted much more than a television movie; they had plans for at least a one-year series of thirteen episodes, probably a two-year series, and there was talk of five years. For that reason, they wanted broad rights – to the *Jake* characters, themes, and stories – which Mitchell had been reluctant to give before. However, he was led to believe that Eric Till would have a great deal of control over the selection of the writers and the development of the scripts. Till would also be directing five or six of the episodes in the first series. This, and the payment of $10,000 per thirty-minute episode or $20,000 per hour episode, persuaded him.

In early March 1994, Mitchell went to Red Deer to read from *The Black Bonspiel* and to attend his first-ever brier, the Men's Canadian Curling Championships. Coincidentally, the MLA for Red Deer had just raised the issue of censorship by demanding that Steinbeck's *Of Mice and Men* be taken out of the schools. Mitchell had some testy words to say to the press about that issue. Merna had deliberately not told Bill that the ban was being requested by an MLA from Red Deer, in case Bill should run into him at one of the events and let loose with some of his usual expletives. Bill, however, though not less concerned about such issues, had less energy for outrage.

On March 13, 1994, W.O. turned eighty. He declared that his best present was the surprise party with all of the family gathered. Merna had invited a few neighbours and friends to a small reception, during which W.O. sat, regally, in his red velvet Victorian chair at the end of the living room and Merna conducted people individually to him so that he was not overwhelmed with too many voices at the same time. His vigour and showmanship were missing now, but he was still the centre of attention — and enjoyed it. Merna would come over and sit beside him and read the cards and the messages. She would look over at him adoringly as if to say, "What a life we have had," "What fun it has been." "I love you, Bill." "I love you too," he would answer. But W.O. at times now seemed to withdraw into his own world, although afterwards he would surprise us with evidence that he had noticed the goings-on. His spectator quality was still intact.

W.O. had begun to use the phrases "my brain's gone rotten" or "my mind has gone to mush" when he could not recall something. He said this, of course, with humor, but also with burning frustration. From

childhood, his absorption of incident, sensory experiences, faces, anec-
dotes, expressions had been phenomenal. But now he could not always
readily trigger these memories. For a person of eighty this was not
unusual, but he felt it strongly. Publicly he covered up, usually with
humour, or let others ask the questions while he answered, often with a
well-rehearsed track from the past. But privately, he battled these
declines in body and mind, railing and complaining like a child having
a tantrum. He did not like this mandatory retirement his mind and
body were imposing. Sometimes when hit with a memory lapse he would
fill in with fiction or with an exaggeration. At times, he seemed not quite
sure what he had written and what he had lived.

~ "BROTHERHOOD, TRUE OR FALSE" ~

Mitchell was giving very few talks now, only seven or eight during 1994. One was in Edmonton in May when he became the first winner of the Writers' Guild of Alberta Golden Pen Award for Lifetime Achievement. On August 6 he attended a production of *The Black Bonspiel of Wullie MacCrimmon* at Blyth Theatre in Ontario. He was the special guest at the fundraising country supper before the performance, and the next day he gave a reading of "The Day I Blew Up Grandpa" to start off their gala retrospective.

Just before he came east, Mitchell had finished about 180 pages on his new novel, now called "Brotherhood, True or False," and was pleased with the way it was developing. Merna, for the first time in a number of years, had been reading it and making suggestions. She was wisely encouraging him. There would be no trip to the lake this August because Mitchell's hip and unsteadiness would not allow him to manoeuvre into boats, and he could not bear to be there and not fish. Merna was relieved. It had been difficult the last few years, for she always worried when Bill went out fishing on his own. Furthermore, she had recently been stung by a bee and had gone into anaphylactic shock so she felt more secure at home in Calgary. By November, Mitchell had finished the manuscript and wanted feedback before sending it on to Gibson.

The novel concerns brotherly love and, for this, Mitchell drew on his relationship with his brother Dick, with whom he had been very close. It also concerns betrayal. That element is fictional, although the horror of the university hazing that culminates in the brothers' estrangement arises from Mitchell's experience at university in the 1930s.[13] Some of the writing in the first half of the novel has the tone and mood of *Summer Holidays*, for it too is about an older man revisiting his past, hearing, as all Mitchell's prairie people do, the sound of mortality, the "wind dirging through the great harp of telephone wires" (BTF 10). Faced with prostate cancer like Davie in the novel, Mitchell could not hold back his preoccupation with death, and there are six deaths in the novel, though it is not morbid in tone.

As well as betrayal, the novel explores other themes Mitchell had been attracted to throughout his career: bridging, guardianship, creativity, loss, and memory. Bridging is the other side of the coin to betrayal, saying "yes" to human solidarity, which is the central thematic destination in Mitchell's work. Bridging makes life worth living and death bearable. That is what he was working through in his last novel. Although he said it is about brother betrayal, death is more at its emotional centre. Just as his father's death was the genesis for *Wind*, so his brother's death was the genesis for this unfinished novel. Though the tone is not elegiac as in *Wind*, Allen ponders the same question Brian asks, "What was the good in being human?" (*WW* 342).

There is an ambivalence at the end of Mitchell's best novels. Hugh muses that just as a person thinks he has "caught it," it slips away, leaving "a feeling of loss and sadness" (*SH* 1). The elusive, indefinable "it" in *Summer Holidays*, Brian's "feeling" in *Wind*, the "vanishing point" in *The Vanishing Point* – these enigmas can only tentatively, only partially be "sorted out" (*SH* 224). "It" seems to be related to betrayal at times, a motif that dominates *The Vanishing Point, How I Spent My Summer Holidays, Since Daisy Creek, Ladybug, For Art's Sake*, and even the benign *Roses Are Difficult Here* – where one human, even a community, fails another.

The first part of the novel has great promise. It is a change from the rapid-fire dialogue of *Ladybug* or *For Art's Sake* and back to the lyrical, descriptive passages of *Wind, Summer Holidays,* and *The Vanishing Point.* But the second half lapses when Mitchell starts leaning on previous material. Nevertheless, at the age of eighty, he had got up on that trapeze one last time; he had made himself vulnerable again – though only to his first editor, Merna, and to family.

W.O. sent us the manuscript and we sent him a detailed critique in early January. We were disappointed with some aspects of it, especially the ending about which W.O. himself was uncertain. But it was clear that this novel had potential far beyond his previous novel, For Art's Sake. *We told him that, although he had staked out a lot of rich territory, he needed to free-fall more on it, get to know his characters better, and replace some used stories with fresh ones. Our criticism hit him hard, perhaps because he knew that he had not done it this time, perhaps because he knew this novel had potential and he could not do it. Whenever we asked how it was going, he would say he was going through a writer's block.*

  But, as Merna knew, it had not been wasted effort. Although he could not make it loop-the-loop, he was still trying to keep that kite up there. It was a personal victory in that he not only dealt psychologically with love and loss, he kept himself hopeful, contemplative, and mentally active. Like his character Allen at the end of the novel, W.O. was not sure what he had created but he does know that it has helped him: "There it was: 244 pages after three long years. What was it? A biography? Autobiography? It didn't stray very far from the actual. Just a touch here and there. . . . He had started first by remembering simply for catharsis sake; through recall of his and Davie's brotherhood it had softened his sorrow and loss." (BTF 240, 241).

Mitchell now turned back to his play "Scam and Be Damned," which he joked might be too blasphemous to be published although, he retorted, the "real blasphemers"[14] were the evangelical preachers like Heally Richards who con people into false hope. Cons and book banners were common targets for Mitchell, and the Klein government had recently shown itself to be on the side of the book banners.

Thus, Mitchell was more than happy to help out during the second year of the Calgary City Council's "Freedom to Read" week in February 1995. In fact, Mitchell's *Who Has Seen the Wind* was selected as the book for that year, and every noon hour various people would read from it. On a similar front he was willing to lend his voice to those asking the government to reconsider cuts to the funding of the Harbourfront Reading Series. Although doing very little public speaking he gave Harbourfront an endorsement on CTV national news in April.

⁓ BOSTON: JUNE 1995 ⁓

For many years Merna had wanted to visit the Boston area where she spent twelve years, from age four to sixteen. In June 1995, for ten days, it finally happened, and she travelled to Hudson, Massachusetts, where she visited her childhood home and her school, then to Newton where her father had trained in the seminary, and finally to Gloucester and Plum Island where she and her family used to holiday. This was an important trip for Merna, important to have Bill share in and validate her history, as she always had his.

We met up with Merna and W.O. in New Jersey. Bill could only walk for short distances, and he certainly let us know that he did not enjoy being pushed around Boston in a wheelchair and treated like an old invalid. His spirits were low, and he did not entertain us with his usual observations and stories.

However, as we toured around Merna's old haunts he began to make an effort to share her enthusiasm. He sat back and listened as she told her own stories and commented: "What a wonderful recovery for Merna of her adolescence!"[15] The trip boosted Merna's spirits immeasurably and even W.O. began to enjoy himself toward the end. At times he seemed to know that he was being difficult, thanking us for "putting up" with him.

He was better when we arrived back in Peterborough and even agreed to swim a few lengths each day in our pool. He would haltingly stumble across the lawn and patio, then, with childlike clumsiness, try front ways, then back ways to get down the pool ladder (he stubbornly refused help). In the water, though, he pushed forward in a slow graceful crawl with sure and rhythmic kick. He was like one of those amphibian animals – penguins, turtles, walruses – which look so vulnerable and move so awkwardly on land but that suddenly take on an amazing grace in water.

He watched television all day. When we suggested we could rent a typewriter for him to work on his "Brotherhood" novel, he became upset. "I'm blocked," he said. "It's happened before; I'll get through it. But now, whenever I go into my interior, there's nothing there. Whatever I come up with I've already used."[16] Like Daddy Sherry, Mitchell had raged against the slow decline of his body and mind and the tricks old age was playing on him. But now he seemed sadly resigned and became more and more withdrawn.

— THE POT OF GOLD – FINALLY —

In June, when the Mitchells were visiting in Peterborough, they heard upsetting news about the Nelvana *Jake and the Kid* television series. Eric Till, knowing that Mitchell was ill and not wanting to upset him, called Orm and said that Nelvana was going ahead next month with the production of thirteen hour-long episodes. In spite of the clause in the agreement specifying "meaningful consultation," Mitchell had seen no scripts. Worse, Till had been completely left out of the script-development phase of the project and had only recently been sent three scripts – and they were cause for concern. He said, quite bluntly, they were terrible and would not do. The five or six scriptwriters for the series had substantially altered Mitchell's original characters, invented new (and badly conceived) characters, and skewed the plots so that Mitchell's stories were unrecognizable. Till withdrew from the series after a stormy scene with the producers and the chief writer, Laura Phillips. This was a crisis. Mitchell had finally found his pot of gold at the end of the television/film-industry rainbow – more than $400,000 for each series – but it was now in jeopardy.

On June 26 at a meeting in Toronto with Patrick Loubert and Michael Hirsch, owners of Nelvana, Bill and Merna expressed their unhappiness about the situation. However, they were assured that consultation would take place and that scripts would be sent out immediately. When the scripts arrived two weeks later, Mitchell struggled through "Long Live the Queen" and was furious to find his original work so distorted. He refused to read the other two scripts. Mitchell had been caught both ways. For years he had struggled to retain artistic control over his property to the point of not getting financial backing and seeing his projects disappear down the drain. Now he had ceded control, and his nightmare came true. He not only lost Till as director, he had his name forever credited to a series that bore little resemblance to his original work.

The anxiety continued throughout the summer. It was agreed by Nelvana that Orm and Barbara would act as script consultants representing Crocus Film's interests. Orm flew out to Edmonton with Green and Singer to talk with the writers and to view the set being built outside Edmonton. It, too, was a disappointment. It was clear Nelvana and Global wanted slickness, not authenticity. Barbara and Orm continued to consult with the writers over the next three months, but to little avail. In desperation Merna telephoned Izzy Asper, chairman of CanWest Global, but he claimed that Global was only the financier and exhibitor, and that Nelvana, the producer, was in control of the scripts. All the letters, the calls, and the consultations proved futile, for both Global and Nelvana continued to believe that they had "golden" scripts, not to mention the "golden" name, W.O. Mitchell, on which to sell the series.

The writers made bland fare out of Mitchell's spicy, humorous, unique stories. They shied away from dealing with issues of racial discrimination, and they were so determined to be politically correct that Wong (a Chinese cook) and Moses Lefthand (a Blackfoot in one script, Cree in another) were not permitted to speak with accents. In their rewritten roles, Wong is a jazz aficionado, and Moses quotes Confucius. The writers and directors betrayed an eastern sensibility and ignorance of prairie landscape, its language, its small-town culture, and 1940s/50s prairie life. Nelvana's writers wanted a series that was innocuous and looked pretty. Principal photography began on July 31, 1995.

On September 30, Mitchell attended the University of Alberta Alumni Association Gala in Edmonton, where he was presented with the Distinguished Alumni Award. He made a short acceptance speech acknowledging the help of his first mentor, Dr. F.M. Salter. Shortly after this event, he was put on chemotherapy and by December he was feeling such weakness that he resorted to using a walker.

He was not happy as he watched the first *Jake and the Kid* show in the new year.[17] Ironically, a number of the reviewers believed that the episode was a "faithful adaptation" of Mitchell's story and praised the "wonderful" look of the film: "*Jake and the Kid* is satisfying television – pretty as the sun rising over wheat fields, and polite as church supper."[18] Mitchell did not consider that a compliment to his work – he had never been a "polite" or "pretty" writer. One of his early radio fans wrote to tell Mitchell that the television version took a bit of getting used to; indeed, he thought the suggested romance between Jake and Miss Henchbaw might even be heresy![19] Miss Henchbaw was no longer the strict, prickly spinster, but a very attractive feminist. It was hardly praise (in Mitchell's mind) when another reviewer commented, "relocate *The Waltons* to W.O. Mitchell's rural Saskatchewan. Add a dash of *Lassie* and *The Wonder Years*" and you have *Jake and the Kid*.[20] Nelvana, who was concerned that Mitchell might make damaging remarks to the media, subtly suggested that if he were not obnoxious the series might run to five years. Mitchell behaved himself, but not for that reason. He was too tired to do otherwise.

– SIT-DOWN COMEDIAN –

In January 1996, Mitchell accepted the invitation to give the Margaret Laurence Memorial Lecture for the Writers' Union to be held in Winnipeg on May 31, 1996. Though not well, he was looking forward to it. However, on February 29, when he was manoeuvring around the kitchen with his walker, he took a fall and had to be taken to the hospital. His recent chemotherapy treatments had severely weakened him.

The immediate physical consequences were a bruised elbow and back pain from the fall, but, more significantly, he seemed to recognize that he could expect no improvement to his health, and he withdrew into a depression, worsened by the medications he was on. In the hospital he was withdrawn and uncooperative. It was difficult to ascertain how much of his immobility was due to his state of mind. Merna was terribly worried and had many difficult decisions to make about the feasibility of looking after him at home, but on the surface she remained confident and optimistic.

Bill was still in the hospital when Willa came to visit for a few weeks on March 24, but was roused, temporarily, out of his depression. He talked, even animatedly, about the new book he was working on, a collection of his performance pieces, and moved from the bed to his chair. However, when he was finally discharged, on March 28, it was to go home to a hospital bed in his family room and to constant homecare.

Merna's idea was to spur him on with the goal of the Margaret Laurence Lecture, and, indeed, his spirits lifted somewhat. He wrote a few pages and made suggestions for Merna to gather together other material. She sent a draft to Orm: "See what you think. Is it good enough? It is good for Dad to feel he'll be delivering the lecture. . . . Dad is improving as he's at home. He's exercising every day and I'm hopeful he'll be back to some walking."[21] At home, Mitchell spent most of the day in the bed or in the wheelchair, but he tried to maintain his sense of humour. When Ken McGoogan from the *Calgary Herald* came to interview him, he described his fall, "I landed on my ass." He was trying hard to get his legs back under him, and Merna was optimistic, saying, "He's getting better every day." [22]

W.O. had never liked to do what he was told, and now he was sur-rounded by an army of people who were giving him orders – his wife, his family, the homecare nurses, the physiotherapists, the doctors. He was urged to try to walk a bit each day, to take care of himself, to sit up, converse, be more pleasant. Often he was a cantankerous and difficult patient. Judy, one of the homecare nurses, was very firm with him and that seemed to work. He would say, "Judy's like Merna; she makes me behave." Merna, in fact, asked Judy to accompany them to Winnipeg to help care for him. Previously, Merna and W.O. had been unable to afford extensive physiotherapy and round-the-clock care, but, now, with the payments from the Jake and the Kid *series, they could afford these services, which not only added to W.O.'s comfort but took some of the pressure off Merna. It was not a lost irony that the series, which bore little resemblance to anything he actually wrote, should pay him more money than anything else ever had.*

As much as W.O. was resigned, Merna was optimistic. She never let go of that. She orchestrated visits with people, tried to cook special things for him, sat with him all the time, attempted to keep him in the flow of life and conversation. When we arrived to help take W.O. to Winnipeg, we were shaken to see how much he had deteriorated in four months. By this time W.O. was not sure whether he could handle going to Winnipeg. It was a wonder that Merna did not relent when all around her doubted that he could go. It was a remarkable act on both their parts.

The Margaret Laurence Lecture was the final public address Mitchell gave. When he arrived at the Winnipeg Art Gallery and was wheeled away from the taxi, people broke into applause. Inside, people welcomed him with a standing ovation. He grinned and then gave a clenched-fist victory sign. After the introductions, he began with an ad lib: "My father was a performer. He died when I was seventeen." Merna shouted up from the audience, "Seven." Mitchell smiled and continued: "My father was a turn-of-the-century elocutionist, what today is called a stand-up comedian. I'm afraid that tonight I'll have to be a sit-down comedian."[23] Then he began in earnest: "We writers are travellers – all travelling through time from the time that we were born till the time we reach a common destination that all mortals have." To be speaking of death when he, himself, was so near the end of the journey, was especially poignant. He travelled back in time – to his childhood in Weyburn, to his adolescent years in St. Petersburg, Florida, to his university years in Winnipeg, and on to the beginning of his career, in Edmonton, with the writing of *Wind*. He ended with the exhortation that "we must have <u>artistic</u> life," and, quoting Shelley, said, we are even more in need today "of the shared gift of the writer, the 'poetry of life'" (*Eve* 252–261).

He performed well. Only a few times did he make a mistake, or lose his place. At one point he asked, "Did I already tell you that?" A woman yelled up, "That's okay. You just say it again. We don't mind." Once, he looked down at Merna and said, "Did I say that already. I'm sorry, Merna." He shared his confusion with the audience. In waves, he would suddenly be in complete control and get the audience laughing, then he would be serious and engage them with the various themes of his lecture. When he finished, there was a spontaneous and long standing ovation. There were tears. Pierre Berton gave the thank you, telling some of his old stories about Bill, then, very moved, he told the audience that Mitchell had got out of his hospital bed to come here to deliver this lecture, and that this speech would be talked about for a long, long time. He did not say what all knew, that this was W.O. Mitchell's last performance.

As W.O. was being wheeled to a room away from the crowd, an old woman followed him and fervently began telling him stories in a German accent, animating them with origami paper birds whose wings flapped when you pulled the tail. It was so unexpected, so overwhelming, that no one knew what to do. W.O., trapped in his wheelchair, looked bewildered. Finally, we began to wheel him away, but, still she followed, insisting that she had more to tell about "ze little soldier." Annoying as it was, the incident also seemed somehow natural, for W.O. had always attracted "characters" and unusual situations.

Mitchell's spirits were raised by the event. He was more engaged than he had been for four months, and was keen to discuss two new projects. Gibson was particularly interested in the collection of his reminiscential pieces, *An Evening with W.O. Mitchell,* the project that Mitchell, himself, had floated about thirty years earlier and never found time to do. The other project was a collection of his previously unpublished short fiction, including the novella "The Devil's Instrument" and two short stories from the 1940s, "What's Ahead for Billy?" and "Catharsis." Mitchell read critically the latter two pieces, noting that they needed work. Near the end of June test results showed that his cancer cell count was down.

Nelvana had begun shooting the second series of thirteen episodes, with exactly the same disregard for Mitchell's originals. There was no attempt at consultation now, though one of the writers approached Merna with the idea that it would be a fitting tribute to Mitchell if they used a few lines from his Margaret Laurence address in one of the episodes. They proposed that George Solway, a "sour puss undertaker,"[24] read Mitchell's lines, about humans being mortal travellers in time, in the eulogy he gives over the Kid's dead horse. Merna was outraged and asked Orm to draft a letter to Nelvana telling them they would be sued if they touched any of that speech or any other work of Mitchell not covered by the contract.

The collection of performance pieces was underway by July and, although Mitchell was very much a part of the decision-making, the administrative work and collection of manuscripts were left to Orm and Barbara. The first draft was prepared by the end of August, and Mitchell was very pleased. He had read over the pieces, commented on which he would like in and which removed. He was insistent that "Saint Sammy's Creation of the World" stay in, but less excited about "Jake Invents the Jumping Pound." Most importantly, he was mentally and creatively engaged.

At Christmas he got a present of a special order. An anonymous donor suggested establishing a W.O. Mitchell Prize in his honour. Already there had been a W.O. Mitchell City of Calgary Prize for $2,000 to be awarded annually, but this was to be a national and much more substantial prize. Bill and Merna were thrilled.

Another pleasure was being on the final Peter Gzowski *Morningside* radio show on May 30, 1997. Mitchell had been Gzowski's first guest of the first *Morningside* on September 6, 1982 (and had been on his *This Country in the Morning* many times before that), so Gzowski wanted Mitchell, once again, to be his first guest during the last hour of the final broadcast. Because of Mitchell's health, this was pretaped a few weeks earlier than the show. Bill congratulated Peter for his recent Peabody Award and added, "All Canadian writers are indebted to you, Peter. You brought them into the light." Mitchell sounded strong and sure with these words. Gzowski returned the compliment: "Well, I'll tell you something else, W.O. Mitchell . . . every Canadian is indebted to you. . . . you showed us ourselves. You inspired other people, you lifted our hearts, you described the landscape." Bill laughed as he told Gzowski that "The Day I Sold Lingerie in a Prairie Whorehouse" was one of the pieces in his new book, *An Evening With W.O. Mitchell.* Their mutual affection was evident. Gzowski said, "I'm very fond of you – you old coot," and Mitchell, laughing, responded, "Well, I'm very fond of you too."[25]

An Evening With W.O. Mitchell came out the end of May 1997. The black cover was striking with white lettering and six small dramatic photographs of Mitchell on the front, showing expressions from the devilishly comic, the innocently joyful, to the contemplative. This was Gibson's idea. He had recalled an earlier photography shoot for the cover of *Dramatic W.O. Mitchell.* At that time, knowing that a collection of plays was going to be a hard sell, Gibson decided to make "W.O. the product" with the emphasis on dramatic: "The joke there is that I went along to Peter Paterson's studio to get some shots of W.O. being dramatic, and I thought I might be needed to goad him into producing a suitable shot. But getting W.O. to be dramatic was like asking the Atlantic Ocean to be wet. It was a terrific session."[26] Mitchell wrote in the "Preface" that what he enjoyed most about performing was the interaction: "Here, on stage, is no *illusion* of bridging between story-teller and audience. And I know immediately when the darts hit the centre, when we are really flying together" (*Eve* x). The book featured Mitchell's favourite performance pieces – from the humorous "The Day I Sold Lingerie in a Prairie Whore House" to the serious ecclesiastical rhythms of the final pages of *Who Has Seen the Wind* to the reflective words of his Margaret Laurence Lecture.

— "I CANNOT BEAR THE THOUGHT" —

Merna had been suffering from stomach pains off and on for more than six weeks but had told no one in the family. She was so worried about Bill that she could not think of herself. She was sent for a sigmoidoscopy on July 24, and the next day was in dreadful distress with pain and nausea. Bill was so withdrawn that he could offer no help or comfort. The next morning the homecare nurse found her curled up on the couch by Bill's hospital bed in severe pain. She was taken by ambulance to the hospital and operated on that afternoon. The surgeon removed a malignant bowel tumour. It appeared that the operation successfully removed all the tumour, and Merna felt hopeful about her prognosis.

Nine days later, while she was still recovering in Foothills Hospital, Bill had to be taken by ambulance to the same hospital. He had been complaining about pain in his back and hip for a number of weeks, but the doctor suspected he was malingering and simply prescribed Tylenol. That morning he had screamed out at one of the health-care people who tried to turn him in his bed. Orm went with his father, and Merna, tough as always, came down from her hospital bed to provide admission information.

I sat with my father for four hours in one of the curtained-off cubicles in emergency. He was weak and in a lot of pain, but they wouldn't give him any medication until an admitting doctor had seen him. I tried to comfort him by recalling hunting and fishing stories. He got some pleasure from this, particularly the memory of fishing the canyon on the Highwood and the big rainbow that got away when I smashed my knee. He still had his sense of humour, and when I said, "I love you, you old fuck," he grinned and, thinking of his orchidectomy, said, "Well, you know I can't do that any more" — which broke both of us up. When the doctor arrived, I insisted on a CAT scan of his hip and back. A hairline hip fracture was discovered, and it was noted that his cancer had spread to more areas, accounting for his increased pain. It was also discovered that his family doctor had overdosed him on gliberide for his diabetes and weaned him too quickly off prednisone — both of which exacerbated his light-headedness and weakness.

He was in the hospital for nearly three weeks, not able to do much but sleep. His medications were adjusted, he was taken for radiation treatments and put on a low-morphine regimen to deal with the pain. Once stabilized, he was less concerned about pain, but was frustrated that at times he could not think and speak clearly. He described being in a fog, and was aware that the words uttered did not match his thoughts. "Things are all mixed up," he would complain.

By the end of August, by sheer willpower, Merna had resumed most of her daily chores. It was a very trying time. Bill required twenty-four-hour care, and she resented strongly the invasion of their private lives by the daily shifts of people she did not know. She desperately wanted time alone with Bill, though she knew full well she could not cope. Emotionally, this time was the worst for her, and though Bill could not be responsive and comforting as she wished, she devoted all her energy to him. She became obsessed with the thought that she might die before him. Somewhere she had come upon a few lines that expressed what she was feeling: "I cannot bear the thought you first may die/Or of your grief should I."[27] She could only think of him. "I'm losing him a little bit at a time," she said, already grieving.

W.O. withdrew more and more into his own internal world. All activity centred on the family room where Merna would sit near Bill's hospital bed, mostly silently, but occasionally trying to get him to talk. Frequently she simply said, "I love you, Bill." Sometimes, she urged him, hoping for that long familiar connection: "Say it, Bill, say I love you." Obviously the morphine was controlling his mind, and, more and more, he became childlike, speaking nonsense, watching movement or colour out the window, reaching his hands up to make random movements. Except for the paper-thin and purple blotched skin, he was like a baby trying to co-ordinate its movements. Occasionally he would be more alert and one afternoon we asked him to sign a copy of the new edition of Who Has Seen the Wind. *"I'll have to think about what to write,"* he replied quite coherently. *When we brought the book in he tried to write a little note, about three lines, but it overlapped and he trailed off, pen motionless on the page for half a minute.*

There were two new books published this fall to celebrate his career. The first was the commemorative fiftieth anniversary volume of *Who Has Seen the Wind* published, as originally, by Macmillan, using the same photo of the handsome dark-haired man standing beside the Highwood River. The second, *Magic Lies: The Art of W.O. Mitchell,* was a significant milestone. It was the first full-length book of academic criticism on Mitchell's work, although it also, appropriately, included more informal articles on Mitchell by people with whom he had worked in theatre, television, and radio, and by his fellow writers Timothy Findley, Frances Itani, and Peter Gzowski. The editors pointed out that Mitchell's post-1980 work had been virtually ignored by academic critics, and they hoped this collection would "redress the imbalanced attention to Mitchell's earlier work."[28]

By October, Merna's doctors had informed her that the cancer had metastasized in the liver, and she was offered an experimental drug treatment. Characteristically, she felt "lucky" to be put on this program. For a short time, it looked positive, and CAT scans showed shrinkage of two of the tumours.

On October 15, Mitchell was honoured by the PanCanadian WordFest in Calgary. He was too ill to attend, but this evening meant a great deal to Merna, who was there to represent him and to read from his work in his place. It was also the launch of the new W.O. Mitchell Literary Award, funded anonymously and administered by the Writers' Trust of Canada. It was a substantial prize of $15,000, making it, along with the Governor General's Awards, the second largest literary prize in terms of monetary value (the Giller Prize being the largest). Bill and Merna had been instrumental in formulating the guidelines for the award. Truly national in scope (including writers in French, which Mitchell insisted upon), it would be awarded to a fiction writer or a dramatist for having produced a substantial body of work, for having recently published a book or produced a play (in keeping with Mitchell's motto of "Don't quit"), and for mentoring other writers. The first award was to be made in the spring of 1998.[29]

Peter Gzowski, one of Mitchell's long-standing fans, who had famously announced at previous events that, along the way to growing up to be Paul Hiebert, he would like to be Bill Mitchell, hosted an evening of speakers who paid tribute to Mitchell: "There are probably more honored writers among us; there are certainly richer; there may be those who have sold more books, or may even be better known around the world; there is no writer in the country who is more or better loved than W.O. Mitchell."[30] Merna, with surety, grace, and a Mitchellesque sense of timing, concluded the evening with her reading of Bill's Christmas story "Take a Giant Step." For the moment she could retreat into a happier time: "I always wondered what that [performing] would be like. I should have taken that up long ago."[31]

Christmas 1997: a gathering for the last time with the masters of ceremonies, Merna and W.O. W.O. lay in his hospital bed, weak, white-bearded, but still the centring force, although only occasionally conversing. Merna sat, morning to night, on the sofa beside him, intermittently asking a question, making a small remark, reminding him of the flow of life. In all the photographs from this Christmas, Merna, like a maestro, had on white gloves because the experimental drug treatment had made her skin painfully sensitive. She directed the traditional orchestra of events — a tree, a dinner at the table with her presiding, presents (an orchid plant for W.O.). During the day, we would try to engage W.O. Once W.O. said to Barbara, with that lifted eyebrow and twinkle returning momentarily, "I've had a pretty interesting life, haven't I?"

Orm would sit with his father and, just as W.O. had with his brother Dick, he brought up times past: Grandmother McMurray's fried porridge, fishing the Highwood, hunting, sailing and salmon fishing at Mable Lake. On one occasion, when Orm read him a review of a play in which he had starred in 1936, he was at first amazed and then, "I'm not sure I like this, what you're doing." "What don't you like?" Orm asked. But he could tell by the look on W.O.'s face that it underlined what he had been sixty-five years ago, and where he was now.

17

"AND IT IS DONE"

~ 1998 ~

JANUARY AND FEBRUARY 1998 were hard. Merna turned seventy-eight on February 11 and, in the morning, Bill turned to her and said, "You look good. I love you." On February 25, at 2:30 in the afternoon, he died, with Merna by his side. "He's gone," she said to the family. "It was peaceful, a slipping away."

It was a motley group at his bedside. The family had been prepared for a month, but we had just returned to Ontario from a week with him; Willa had returned to New York; Hugh was teaching. No one knew he was so close to going. In that unexpected manner that so befit him, it was Merna, one of his homecare nurses, Bev (the large farmwoman of a nurse whom W.O. had first disliked and then grown used to), Anita (the Spanish cleaning woman), Ben (his ex-son-in-law), and Marcia (Ben's partner) who were near him at the time. When we arrived, Anita told Orm and me her story of W.O.'s death: "Mr. Mitchell was not well that morning. He couldn't speak; he couldn't eat. Please, God, I was saying to myself, let him go. I said to Bev, just leave him alone – don't turn him, don't feed him." Anita was upstairs cleaning the hallway when he died. "Just by the green bedroom, I felt someone walking by. I know it is Mr. Mitchell and that he is gone. He goes into the pink bedroom, his bedroom. He always liked the bedroom with the picture of the crocuses over his bed. Then he went through the window – I felt him, like air, like the wind."

When he died, Anita said to Bev, "Close his eyes and his mouth. Put a towel around his mouth." This was her Spanish custom. But Bev refused. Anita demonstrated all these things as she talked to us. "Merna was crying and saying that she would be joining him soon. I told her," *said Anita, "you must not say such things." Anita finished, "I saw it all – even when they came and put a white sheet over him. Then Eddie*[1] *– he is a nice man – came and took me home."*[2]

There was a tremendous amount of media attention that truly consoled Merna, who felt a justified pride in Bill's accomplishments. There were dignified and moving articles about the "master storyteller,"[3] the "prairie icon,"[4] and "the Canadian literary icon"[5] – but also personal, poignant memories such as "my pal Bill Mitchell,"[6] my "warm-hearted neighbour,"[7] "How I love this man . . . and I know that I always will."[8] Rex Murphy on *Cross Country Checkup* saluted him as "one of this country's most respected, most enduring, and most affectionate writers."[9] Because he had been made a member of the Privy Council, the Canadian flag was flown at half mast across the country, and there were tributes from the various political parties. Perhaps Mitchell would have been amused to hear Preston Manning, the son of Ernest Manning, premier of Alberta who had been the brunt of Mitchell's famous satiric, "Dear Mr. Manning" letter, say, no doubt quite innocently, that Mitchell "loved to gently poke fun at people consumed by their own sense of self-importance."[10] The public remembrances replaced a public funeral that Merna, given her health, felt she could not undergo.

Although it was a small private family funeral there were, as always, many arrangements to be looked after. And, befitting a funeral for a serious humorist, the four days of preparation were filled with moments that made us laugh and made us cry. On Friday, the day before the funeral, a few of us drove down to High River to choose the casket. On

the way we reminisced about W.O. "He should be buried with a snuff box
and a good supply of snuff," Hugh suggested. "He has enough snuff at
the house," said Orm, "to last an eternity! He could always use the snuff
to bribe St. Peter at the gate!" When we spoke about the casket it was
Merna who lightened the mood. "A very simple one," she said. "A pine
box?" we asked. "No," she said, laughing, "it should be damaged — a
coffin from Unclaimed and Damaged Freight Sales." This broke us up.
Larry Snodgrass, the appropriately solemn funeral director, led us to the
coffin room, a hushed room where it seemed impossible to speak in any-
thing but ghostly whispers as we examined the heavy wood caskets with
their white satin linings. The funeral director said he would leave us to
make our decision, and Merna asked, with a perfectly straight face, "Do
you have a damaged one?" Larry was stunned. "Oh no," he hastily
assured us, "we send those back!" "What a pity," said Merna, "Bill would
have liked a damaged one!" We had to explain the joke to Larry. Merna,
the wise matriarch, put death in its place that day, just as her husband
would have.

On Saturday, February 28, Mitchell was buried in the High River
Cemetery, attended only by the family. There was no service at the
funeral home. Merna asked the family to sign the Bible that Bill had
been given by his long-time High River friend Mrs. McCorquodale.
The family had a wreath of white and purple orchids made, which
rested on the casket and went into the grave with him. "Life is a
chord of high notes and low notes," Mitchell had said in an interview ten years earlier. "'Listen, if I could be at my own funeral, I've
got news for you. Something funny'll happen. Guaranteed.'"[11]

How did he know? As if he were orchestrating the scenes for comic relief,
there was an interlude from grief. Photographers from Calgary had
staked out the funeral home since early morning. At the wishes of the
family, Snodgrass had refused to give out information about the time of
the funeral. But the photographers and reporters were determined. At
1:30 they followed a funeral procession out to the cemetery and snapped
away. It was not until the end of the burial service, when the minister

said that Mr. so and so – not Mitchell – was committed to the earth,
that they realized they were at the wrong funeral. This was the first time
we saw the funeral director smile. We did not know until later, when the
photograph appeared in the paper, that the reporters had recovered from
their blunder and followed us out to the graveyard to get their shot.

Around the grave, Merna read I Corinthians 13: 1–13: "And now
abideth faith, hope, charity, these three; but the greatest of these is
charity." Orm read from Who Has Seen the Wind: *"A forever and*
forever sound it had, forever and for never. Forever and forever the
prairie had been, before there was a town, before he had been, or his
father, or his father, or his father before him. Forever for the prairie –
never for his father – never again" (WW 264). Most of us said a few
personal words of remembrance. Two-year-old William dashed around
between graves, "stepping over graves so [he] wouldn't tramp over top of
people" just as his great-grandfather had done when, in that "spring
ritual," he went with his mother to his father's grave in Weyburn.[12]

Merna had suppressed the news that her tumour had grown, and
that she was being taken off the experimental drug and switched to
radiation. While waiting in March for this program to start, she
decided to try Essiac, an herbal remedy for cancer. Throughout
she remained optimistic that she could be treated and talked of revisiting her birthplace, Mahone Bay, Nova Scotia. Gibson asked her
what she thought about a tribute for Bill in Toronto on April 30. She
suggested that a later date, possibly May, would be better. About
mid-April she began to deteriorate, and was unable to attend the two
tributes for Mitchell, one in Edmonton on April 22 and one in
Calgary on April 25.

We were in Calgary for the tribute and Merna was still optimistic that
her upcoming radiation treatments would make a difference. But, on
April 29, she was admitted to hospital. When it was clear there was no
hope, she wanted to go home. We again set up the hospital bed in the
family room where W.O. had been only two months ago, and we brought
her home on Tuesday, May 12. No one thought she had only a few more

hours. She died at 4:50 that afternoon. Though some said, romantically, after her death that she wanted to be with Bill, there was no doubt in our minds that she had the will to live – she was beaten by the disease. Merna's death was a shock and, in that way, harder to deal with than W.O.'s, over which we had time to reflect and prepare as we lost touch with him slowly over six years.

Merna's only expressed request for her funeral was that it have a lot of music. And so she had – at the United Church in High River where she had served as choir leader for a number of years in the 1950s and 1960s. Along with pieces by J.S. Bach, Samuel Barber, and Vaughan Williams was an anonymous little English folk song, "Sweet Nightingale," which Merna had loved to sing in harmony with Willa. Willa, accompanied by her daughter Brenna, sang it again in Merna's memory:

> *Pretty maid, come along,*
> *Don't you hear the sweet song*
> *The sweet notes of the nightingale flow?*
> *Don't you hear the fond tale*
> *Of the sweet nightingale,*
> *As she sings in the valley below,*
> *As she sings in the valley below.*[13]

Together Merna and Bill had made music for fifty-six years. She was buried beside him in the High River Cemetery, looking, forever, out to the prairie, "As clouds' slow shadows melt across the prairie's face more nights slip darkness over. Light, then dark, then light again. Day, then night, then day again. A meadowlark sings and it is spring. And summer comes. A year is done. Another comes and it is done" (*WW* 320).

ACKNOWLEDGEMENTS

This would have been a very different biography without the encouragement of W.O. and Merna, and without their willingness to be interviewed on tape over a fourteen-year period. Though they both died in 1998, before the first volume of the biography appeared, their voices can be heard strongly throughout both volumes. We were most fortunate to have other good storytellers in the family, and we thank Hugh and Sue Mitchell for their amusing anecdotes, especially of Mabel Lake, which they shared, more than any of us, with Merna and W.O. for thirty years. As well, we very much appreciated Willa's candidness and willingness to share personal experiences, particularly of the early years in Calgary when the other siblings had left home.

Overall we conducted taped interviews with eighty-five of Mitchell's friends and colleagues, and we thank them all for their time, their openness, and their genuine interest in the project. The following people contributed to our research on this volume: Sid Adilman, Betty and Gerry Anglin, Laurence Arnold, Ruth (Fraser) Bertelsen, Jan and Pierre Berton, Dr. James Black, John Clare, Georgie Collins, Dave and Rita Diebel, Larry Diebel, Dr. Tom Dilworth, Toots Dixon, Candas Dorsey, Janet Finlay, Peter and Ruth Francis, Frances Fraser, Fil Fraser, David and Dorothy Gardner, Don and Eady Garrett,

Douglas Gibson, Les Hannon, Arthur Irwin, Francis Itani, Mac Jones, Sandra Jones, Philip Keatley, Allan King, Webster Lefthand, Richard Lemm, Bonnie LeMay, Earl and Helen Lewis, Alistair MacLeod, Adam Marshall, Shirley (Northey) Missiaen, Barbara Moon, Gordon Morash, Farley Mowat, Leila (Danny) Pepper, Beth Proctor, Billie Mae Richards, Bert Shepherd, David Staines, Edna Staebler, Bev Stahlbrand, Donald Sutherland, Gordon and Margaret Swan, Claire (Drainie) Taylor, Eric Till, Patricia Watson, Robert Weaver, Ron Weyman, Rudy Wiebe, and Eddie Wong.

We are also grateful to those who provided reminiscences through letters, e-mails, or telephone conversations and/or sent us Mitchell material. Our thanks to Lawrence Arnold, Harry Boyle, A. Camozzi, James Forrester, Patricia Hamilton, Norma Hawkins, Francis Itani, John Jennings, Lois Laycraft, Sylvia Lennick, Pam McCorquodale, Rick McNair, Margaret Mitchell, Sharon Mitchell, Matie Molinaro, Gordon Morash, Marrie Mumford, Kay Parley, Linda Robbins, David Silcox, Rowena Sol, and Cora Taylor.

We thank Francis Itani and Allan King for granting us access to their papers held by the National Archives of Canada, and Farley Mowat for access to his papers at McMaster University. Ann Godard kindly assisted us at NAC with the Allan King papers.

Research on the *Jake and the Kid* radio series, on *Foothill Fables*, and other drama Mitchell wrote for radio and television was a special challenge because the material, particularly audio and audiovisual tapes, has not been systematically collected and catalogued in any one location. When we began this project we wanted to hear what the actual *Jake and the Kid* programs sounded like. Gail Donald, CBC radio archivist, was very helpful in setting us up (in the old Sumac Street CBC building) to listen to the original acetate sound-check disks of the radio shows. These are now at the National Archives of Canada and have been dubbed on audiocassettes. We appreciated the assistance of Sylvie Robitaille in helping us obtain audiocassettes of the programs. We would also like to acknowledge Mark Rheaume, CBC records manager, for locating additional *Jake and the Kid* paperscripts, and Roy Harris, CBC television archivist, for allowing us to view a number of Mitchell's television dramas. At the Centre for Broadcasting Studies at Concordia University, Montreal, we had the assistance of Howard Fink and John Jackson. Two theses written on the *Jake and the Kid* series provided valuable listings of the available radio scripts and their dates: Alan Yates's "W.O. Mitchell's Jake and the Kid: The Canadian Popular Radio Play as Art and Social Comment," Ph.D. Diss., McGill, 1979; and Timothy Zeman's "An Annotated Bibliography of the Radio Drama of W.O. Mitchell in the Special Collections of the University of Calgary Libraries," M.A. Diss., University of Alberta, 1993.

We are especially indebted to Appollonia Steele and Marlys Chevrefils of Special Collections, Information Resources, University of Calgary, who guided us through the largest and most significant collection of Mitchell material and who with cheerful patience and support dealt with our requests over many years. Dr. Carl Spadoni and Renu Barrett were most helpful with our research in the Macmillan Canada Archives at the William Ready Division of Archives and Research, Mills Memorial Library, McMaster University. Other archivists and librarians offered valuable assistance in specific areas: Lisa Atkinson, university archives manager, University of Calgary; Rebecca Cape, public services department, Lilly Library, Indiana University (for Bobbs-Merrill correspondence); Bernard R. Crystal, curator of manuscripts, and Jean Ashton at the Rare Book and Manuscript Library of Columbia University in New York, and with thanks to Grace Wherry at Curtis Brown Ltd. (for the Willis Wing correspondence); Edna Hajnal, the Thomas Fisher Rare Book Library, University of Toronto (for the Ernest Buckler letters); Jane Parkinson, archivist at the Paul D. Fleck Library and Archives, Banff Centre; The Calgary Health Region (for medical records); and Veterans Affairs Canada (for medical records concerning Spurgeon "Spud" Hirtle).

Permissions for correspondence were gratefully received from the following: Michael Benedict, editorial director of *Maclean's*; Jan Berton; estate of Harry Boyle; David Gardner; the estate of Bill

Glassco; John Gray; Arthur Hiller; Sean Kane; Allan King; the estate of William Kurelek; Richard Landon, Thomas Fisher Library; Pat Ljungh; Martha Perkins; Mrs. F.M. Salter; Page Stegner; Paul Surdin; Claire (Drainie) Taylor; Eric Till; and Edward Weeks, former editor of the Atlantic Monthly Press. We would also like to thank the following for their help in obtaining photographs for use in the biography: Lynda Barnett and Brenda Carroll (CBC Still Photo Collection); Alex Kaliszuk; Dorothy MacPherson; Colin McKim (*Orillia Sun*); Jane Parkinson and Liz Hay (Banff Centre Archives); Kay Parley; and Kelsey Robins (*Calgary Herald*).

We appreciated the work of Aurelie Treadwell in documenting all secondary material in book form written about W.O. Mitchell. We are indebted to the many excellent academic appraisals of Mitchell's work and, in particular, to the first book devoted entirely to Mitchell, *Magic Lies: The Art of W.O. Mitchell* (1997), edited by Sheila and David Latham.

We would like to acknowledge Trent University and the Department of English Literature, which provided assistance over a number of years through sabbatical leaves, unpaid leaves, and personally funded research grants.

We are most grateful to Douglas Gibson of Douglas Gibson Books, McClelland & Stewart, who edited this second volume of our biography. We very much appreciated his encouragement, his patience, and his wise guidance toward a book that is solidly researched yet, we hope, publicly accessible. Always maintaining a neutral position regarding his own involvement with our subject, he was able to offer first-hand knowledge. Our thanks to Heather Sangster, who copy-edited the manuscript with meticulous care, and to Kong Njo, who skilfully designed the book and its cover, which beautifully matches the first volume. Thank you also to Martin Boyne, Trent University, for preparing the index.

Writing this biography has been a long labour of love, interrupted by numerous work-related activities (as well as two major floods). We are grateful to our friends and relatives who supported and encouraged us throughout the project, especially through the final haul of writing and revising. Finally, we wish to thank our close family, Geoff, Bernadette, and Sara, our sisters, Linda, Willa, and Susan, and our brother, Hugh, not just for all their stories of Merna and W.O., but for keeping us sane and reminding us of the joys and value of family.

NOTES

Frequently Used Names:

DC   Dudley Cloud, managing editor, Atlantic Monthly Press (the coterie press of Little, Brown)

DG   Douglas Gibson, editor, Macmillan, then McClelland & Stewart

EB   Ernest Buckler

EW   Edward Weeks, editor, Atlantic Monthly Press

FMS   Frederick Millet Salter, University of Alberta

JMG   John Gray, publisher at Macmillan

MLM   Merna Lynne Mitchell

WOM   William Ormond Mitchell

Unpublished Material:

The W.O. Mitchell *fonds* at Special Collections, University of Calgary Library contains most of the unpublished material. The first accession, numbered MsC 19, includes material up to 1976 and is catalogued in *The W.O. Mitchell Papers* (1986). The second accession, numbered 980604, includes material up to 1998, and is inventoried. The *fonds* contains manuscripts for published and unpublished work, personal letters, business correspondence, scrapbooks (assembled by Mitchell's mother, Mrs. O.S. Mitchell), photographs, and other miscellaneous items.

W.O. Mitchell Ltd. (designated as Family) retains some material such as the W.O. Mitchell Ltd. business correspondence and papers, rough free-fall for the later novels, notes for speeches, a few unpublished manuscripts, and personal letters. It also holds video and audio cassette recordings of media interviews and live reading performances that Mitchell gave from 1975 to 1990. This material will be turned over to the University of Calgary for a third accession.

We hold approximately sixty hours of our taped interviews with W.O. and Merna Mitchell and approximately one hundred and twenty hours of interviews with relatives, friends, students, writer-friends, and business acquaintances. Alan Yates passed on to us (for eventual deposit with Special Collections at the University of Calgary) his interview tapes with members of the *Jake and the Kid* radio series, including the following: Harry Boyle, Fred Diehl, Claire Drainie, Peter Francis, Arthur Hiller, Esse Ljungh, W.O. Mitchell, Billie Mae Richards, Morris Surdin, and Robert Weaver. We also hold personal letters to and from the Mitchells and personal notebooks in which we recorded impressions or conversations.

Paperscripts of *Jake and the Kid* and other radio and television materials are held in the W.O. Mitchell *fonds*, in the Morris Surdin *fonds* (Special Collections, University of Calgary), at the Centre of Broadcasting Studies (Concordia University, Montreal), at the CBC (Toronto), and privately by the Family. Sound recordings are primarily held at the National Archives of Canada, with a few held in the W.O. Mitchell *fonds* and the Morris Surdin *fonds* at the University of Calgary. Audio-visual recordings of some Mitchell dramas can be found at the CBC and in the W.O. Mitchell *fonds*.

The William Ready Division of Archives and Research Collections, Mills Memorial Library, McMaster University in Hamilton, holds correspondence between W.O. Mitchell and the Macmillan Company of Canada. Correspondence between Mitchell and Douglas Gibson Books is located at McClelland & Stewart, Toronto, in the Douglas Gibson files. Atlantic Monthly Press in Boston, Massachusetts, holds W.O. Mitchell's and Edward Millet Salter's correspondence with Edward Weeks, Dudley Cloud, and Jeanette Cloud concerning *Who Has Seen the Wind*, some short stories, "The Alien," and "Roses Are Difficult Here." Columbia University, Rare Book and Manuscript Library, New York, holds Willis Wing's correspondence with W.O. Mitchell.

The following abbreviations are used in the Notes:

Atlantic Atlantic Monthly Press, Boston.

Columbia Willis Wing correspondence, Curtis Brown Ltd. Records, Columbia University, Rare Book and Manuscript Library, New York.

Family Manuscripts, letters, papers held by the Mitchell family and W.O. Mitchell Ltd.

Life Barbara and Ormond Mitchell, *W.O.: The Life of W.O. Mitchell: Beginnings to* Who Has Seen the Wind, *1914–1947* (Toronto: McClelland & Stewart, 1999).

McMaster Macmillan Papers, William Ready Division of Archives and Research Collections, Mills Memorial Library, McMaster University, Hamilton, Ontario.

ML Sheila Latham and David Latham, eds., *Magic Lies: The Art of W.O. Mitchell* (Toronto: University of Toronto Press, 1997).

NAC National Archives of Canada.

NFB *W.O. Mitchell: Novelist in Hiding.* Dir. Robert Duncan, National Film Board of Canada, 1980. Video recording, transcripts, and rushes are held at UCalgary. We quote from the unpublished transcripts of the film and the rushes.

PD The biographers' personal diaries and notes.

PI Personal untaped interviews.

PL Personal letters to or from the biographers.

PTI Personal taped interview conducted by the biographers. Unless otherwise noted the interview is with W.O. Mitchell.

UCalgary W.O. Mitchell *fonds*, Special Collections, University Library, University of Calgary, Calgary, Alberta.

UToronto Ernest Buckler *fonds*, Thomas Fisher Rare Book Library, University of Toronto.

W.O. Mitchell's Major Works (published and unpublished) are referred to within the text by the following abbreviations:

A Ms. (complete) in Family files. Unless otherwise indicated references are to this ms. Other sources: *The Alien* (condensed version of Part III): *Maclean's*, 15 Sept. 1953 to 15 Jan. 1954 (semi-monthly). Ms (incomplete) at UCalgary.

AJK *According to Jake and the Kid.* Toronto: McClelland & Stewart, 1989.

Art *For Art's Sake.* Toronto: McClelland & Stewart, 1992.

BTF "Brotherhood, True or False." Unpublished manuscript. UCalgary

BBW *The Black Bonspiel of Willie MacCrimmon.* Toronto: McClelland & Stewart, 1993.

DWO *Dramatic W.O. Mitchell.* Toronto: Macmillan, 1982.

Eve *An Evening With W.O. Mitchell.* Toronto: McClelland & Stewart, 1997.

FF *Foothill Fables.* CBC Radio series, Toronto. 25 Dec. 1961 to 19 Jan. 1964. Refers to scripts held at UCalgary unless otherwise stated.

JK *Jake and the Kid.* Toronto: Macmillan, 1961.

JKR *Jake and the Kid.* CBC Radio series, Toronto. 1950–56. Refers to scripts held at UCalgary unless otherwise stated.

JKT *Jake and the Kid.* CBC Television, Toronto. 1961. Refers to scripts held at UCalgary unless otherwise stated.

K *The Kite.* Toronto: Macmillan, 1962.

LL *Ladybug, Ladybug . . .* Toronto: McClelland & Stewart, 1988.

RD *Roses Are Difficult Here.* Toronto: McClelland & Stewart, 1990.

SD *Since Daisy Creek.* Toronto: Macmillan, 1984.

SH *How I Spent My Summer Holidays.* Toronto: Macmillan, 1981.

VP *The Vanishing Point.* Toronto: Macmillan, 1973.

WW *Who Has Seen the Wind.* Toronto: Macmillan, 1947. Unless otherwise indicated this is the edition to which we will refer. In 1947 the novel was also published by Little, Brown in an edition that was about seven thousand words shorter than the Canadian one. This version was used for subsequent editions, including paperback editions. In 1991 McClelland & Stewart published an edition illustrated by William Kurelek, which used the longer text version, and in 1997 Macmillan published a fiftieth-anniversary edition using the longer text.

Preface

1. Zs. Gartner, "In Conversation: W.O. Mitchell," *Booknews*, n.d. (ca. Nov. 1981).

Chapter 1 *(Pages 1–24)*

1. WOM to FMS, 21 Sept. 1948, UCalgary.
2. PTI, MLM, 2 Jun. 1982.

3. "W.O. Mitchell Takes Maclean's Editorship," *High River Times*, 1 Jul. 1948.

4. David Mackenzie, *Arthur Irwin: A Biography* (Toronto: University of Toronto Press, 1993) 5.

5. Mackenzie, 5.

6. PTI, John Clare, 24 Oct. 1987.

7. PTI, Pierre Berton, 19 Sept. 1987.

8. See *Life* 245–59.

9. PTI, Arthur Irwin, 18 Jun. 1984. See also David Mackenzie's *Arthur Irwin: A Biography* (Toronto: University of Toronto Press, 1993) 209–11.

10. PTI, 9 Jun. 1985.

11. See "See the Pattern Forming," *Eve*, 135–38 for Mitchell's full account.

12. PTI, John Clare, 24 Oct. 1987.

13. Mackenzie, 186: 1946 memo from Arthur Mayse to Irwin.

14. PTI, MLM, 16 Jun. 1982. The *Maclean's* fiction editors' correspondence files for the 1940s and early 1950s have disappeared.

15. PTI, Arthur Irwin, 18 Jun. 1984.

16. PTI, 11 Jun. 1984.

17. PTI, Pierre Berton, 19 Sept. 1987; see also Pierre Berton, *My Times* (Toronto: Doubleday Canada, 1995) 101: "More than anyone else on staff . . . Bill Mitchell . . . had a rapport with writers that endeared him to them and inspired them to excel."

18. PTI, 1 Jun. 1985.

19. PTI, Arthur Irwin,18 Jun. 1984.

20. Berton, *My Times* 8–9.

21. PTI, 8 Jun. 1985; 1 Jun. 1985.

22. PTI, Pierre Berton, 19 Sept. 1987.

23. PTI, 11 Jun. 1984. Barry Holloway was vice-president of Grolier Press in New York.

24. PTI, 8 Jun. 1985.

25. "The Long Years" (15 Sept. 1948); "The Mad Wizard of Mars" (15 Sept. 1949); "I'll Not Ask for Wine" (1 Jan. 1950); "The Rocket Man" (1 Mar. 1951).

26. "In the Editor's Confidence," *Maclean's*, Mar. 1951: noted that Bradbury's "stories have been appearing in the pulps and more recently in the slicks."

27. PTI, 1 Jun. 1985 and 8 Jun. 1985. The two stories used in *The Martian Chronicles* (Doubleday, May 1950) were "I'll Not Ask for Wine" and "The Long Years," which were retitled "February 1999: Ylla" and "April 2026: The Long Years."

28. *The Oxford Companion to Canadian Literature* (Toronto: Oxford University Press), 818.

29. PTI, 5 Jun. 1984 and 1 Jun. 1985.

30. It appeared in the 1 Nov. 1948 issue with the cutline, "Geoffrey dreamed of knightly deeds, of honour and wealth and Lady Gemma. Of these dreams, one had to die – it took a dream to slay a dream." Part of the story's suspense lies in whether Lady Gemma will be tortured and raped. Another of Hardy's stories appeared in *Maclean's* while Mitchell was fiction editor, "The Philistine," 15 Nov. 1950.

31. PTI, Barbara Moon, 19 Nov. 1987.

32. PTI, Pierre Berton, 19 Sept. 1987.

33. PTI, Pierre Berton.

34. PTI, 8 Jun. 1985.

35. FMS to DC, 28 Apr. 1945, Atlantic.

36. PTI, Les Hannon, 8 Oct. 1987.

37. PTI, 8 Jun. 1985; 9 Jun. 1985.

38. PTI, Edna Staebler, 22 Jul. 1999.

39. PTI, Edna Staebler, 22 Jul. 1999. Mitchell urged John Gray at Macmillan to publish Staebler's book on Cape Breton Harbour, but Gray told her that, although it was beautifully written and should be published, there was not yet a market for it in Canada. *Cape Breton Harbour* was finally published twenty-two years later by Jack McClelland following Staebler's success with *Food That Really Schmecks*.

40. PTI, 9 Jun. 1985.

41. PTI, Les Hannon, 8 Oct. 1987.

42. PTI, Arthur Irwin, 19 Jun. 1984.

43. Dudley Cloud was managing editor of *Atlantic Monthly* magazine and of Atlantic Monthly Press, the coterie press of Little, Brown.

44. FMS to WOM, 13 Sept. 1948, UCalgary.

45. Stanley Salmen, managing editor of Little, Brown.

46. WOM to FMS, 21 Sept. 1948, UCalgary.

47. WOM to DC, 21 Nov. 1948, Atlantic.

48. DC to WOM, 24 Nov. 1948, Atlantic.

49. PTI, Dec. 1981.

50. On a per capita/land basis Hutterites were, and have remained, the prairie provinces most productive farmers. See John Ryan, "Hutterites," *The 1999 Canadian Encyclopedia: World Edition.* CD-ROM. Toronto: McClelland & Stewart, 1998.

51. "The Devil's Instrument," ms., UCalgary, MsC19.19.23. f19, 24, 27, 39–40, 68, 41.

52. Hugh Garner, *One Damn Thing After Another* (Toronto: McGraw-Hill Ryerson, 1973) 49–50.

53. WOM to Hugh Garner, 10 May 1949, Queen's University archives; see also: WOM to DC, 11 Apr. 1949 and DC to WOM, 4 May 1949, Atlantic.

54. Garner, 104. It was published December 1950. Garner won the Governor General's Award for his first collection of stories, which included "One, Two, Three Little Indians" (*Hugh Garner's Best Stories*, Toronto: Ryerson Press, 1963).

55. WOM to EB, 19 Jul. 1948, UToronto.

56. EB to WOM, undated draft, UToronto.

57. EB to WOM, 28 Dec. 1948, UCalgary.

58. EB to WOM, 25 Jan. 1949, UCalgary.

59. WOM to EB, 18 Feb. 1949, UToronto.

60. EB to WOM, 19 Apr. 1949, UToronto.

61. PTI, MLM, 2 Jun. 1982.

62. Claire (Drainie) Taylor to Edna Staebler, 28 Mar. 2000. Family.

63. PTI, 13 Oct. 1986. The New Play Society, Toronto's first postwar professional theatre organization, was started by Dora Mavor Moore and her son, Mavor Moore, in 1946. *She Stoops to Conquer* played in the Museum Theatre 7–11 Oct. and 13–15 Oct. 1949. See Paula Sperdakos, *Dora Mavor Moore: Pioneer of the Canadian Theatre* (Toronto: ECW Press, 1995) 150, 186.

64. PTI, MLM, 2 Jun. 1982. She critiqued his novel *Peace River Country*, which was eventually published in 1958.

65. PTI, 8 Jun. 1985; Pierre Berton, *My Times* (Toronto: Doubleday Canada, 1995) 51–52.

66. PTI, Pierre Berton, 19 Sept. 1987.

67. PTI, Les Hannon, 8 Oct. 1987.

Chapter 2 (Pages 25-45)

1. Bronwyn Drainie, *Living the Part: John Drainie and the Dilemma of Canadian Stardom* (Toronto: Macmillan of Canada, 1988) 8–9.

2. "Radio Market for Canadian Dramas and Short Stories as Seen by Allan Sangster," in "Critically Speaking," *CBC Times*, 27 Mar.–2 Apr. 1948, 4.

3. Howard Fink and John Jackson, eds., *All the Bright Company: Radio Drama Produced by Andrew Allan* (Toronto: Quarry Press, CBC Enterprises, 1987) vi.

4. Mitchell later discovered that his next-door neighbour in High River, Jack Kelly, was Harry Boyle's uncle. Kelly was one of the main models for Jake Trumper in the *Jake and the Kid* stories.

5. PTI, Dec. 1981.

6. "The Comtesse," UCalgary 19.32.10.1–3.fi.

7. Quoted in Robert Weaver's "The Canadian Short Story," *CBC Times*, 31 Jul.–6 Aug. 1949, 10.

8. WOM to DC, 19 Mar. 1949, Atlantic.

9. K. Ellis to DC, Mar. 1949, Atlantic.

10. "On the Air," *The Standard*, Montreal, 9 Apr. 1949, 5.

11. "Chaperone for Maggie" was broadcast 1 May 1949. It was adapted from the story published in *Maclean's*, 15 May 1948.

12. Broadcast on 2 Jul. 1950.

13. WOM, taped interview with Alan Yates, Feb. 1977, Tape #2. Family. Yates taped various people for his Ph.D. thesis, "W.O. Mitchell's *Jake and the Kid*: The Canadian Popular Radio Play as Art and Social Comment" (Diss. McGill, 1979). Yates kindly gave us his taped interviews.

14. PTI, 8 Jun. 1985.

15. PTI, MLM, 2 Jun. 1982.

16. W.O. Mitchell, "He Lured Success," *Maclean's*, 1 Aug. 1949.

17. PTI, WOM and MLM, 1 Jun. 1985.

18. WOM to DC, 18 Mar. 1949, Atlantic.

19. WOM to DC, 20 May 1949, Atlantic.

20. JMG to DC, 27 Jun. 1949, Atlantic.

21. Winter did eleven sketches for various scenes on eight pages: see UCalgary, MsC 19.19.26.

22. DC to WOM, 22 Jul. 1949, Atlantic.

23. WOM to DC, 23 Jul. 1949, Atlantic.

24. During the 1920s Denison "was at the forefront of Canada's Little Theatre movement as designer, actor, and playwright for Toronto's Hart House Theatre." As a historian of Canadian commerce he wrote commissioned books on Massey-Harris, Molson, and the Bank of Montreal (L.W. Conolly, "Denison, Merrill," in *Oxford Companion to Canadian Literature*, Second Edition, 288–89). Denison later donated his Bon Echo property to the province and it became a provincial park.

25. Mary Savigny, *Bon Echo: The Denison Years* (Toronto: Natural Heritage Books, 1997) 57–62.

26. Merrill Denison to Mrs. O.S. Mitchell, 6 Aug. 1949, UCalgary.

27. Savigny, 4.

28. PTI, MLM, 2 Jun. 1982.

29. "The Alien," ms., UCalgary, MsC 19.14.3.f112, 114, 113, 21.

30. WOM to DC, 23 Jul. 1949, Atlantic

31. DC to WOM, 22 Jul. 1949, Atlantic.

32. "Trade Editorial Report," n.d, Atlantic.

33. DC to Little, Brown, 18 Aug. 1949, Atlantic.

34. Little, Brown report to DC, 8 Sept. 1949, Atlantic.

35. Dr. Marcus Bach was a professor in the School of Religion at the University of Iowa (where he also received his Ph.D. in creative writing and dramatic art). He published books and wrote stage and radio plays (he had a weekly radio show on WSUI) on various religious groups of America.

36. DC to WOM, 9 Sept. 1949, Atlantic.

37. WOM to Bobbs-Merrill, 15 Sept. 1949, Atlantic.

38. WOM to DC, 15 Sept. 1949, Atlantic.

39. Frank Steele was active in the Church of Jesus Christ of Latter-Day Saints and had written a book about early Mormon settlement so he would have been of interest to Bach.

40. PTI, Dec. 1981.

41. WOM to DC, 15 Sept. 1949, Atlantic.

42. DC to WOM, 22 Sept. 1949, Atlantic.

43. Our search of material in the Bobbs-Merrill archives indicates that Bach was working on the final draft of *The Dream Gate* for at least five weeks after the CBC aired *The Devil's Instrument* on 27 Mar. 1949.

44. PTI, 26 Dec. 1985.

45. WOM to DC, 17 Oct. 1951, Atlantic.

46. WOM to EB, 6 Oct. 1949, UToronto.

47. WOM to EB, 14 Nov. 1949, UToronto.

48. PTI, MLM, 16 Jun. 1982; and PTI, Mowat, 13 Mar. 2001, in which he says, regarding sending out "Eskimo Spring," "I had to sell something pretty soon or else get a job."

49. PTI, MLM, 16 Jun. 1982. In our interview with Mowat, he did not deny Mitchell's recollection of reading and giving him feedback on early ms portions of *People of the Deer* (PTI, Farley Mowat, 13 Mar. 2001).

50. Edward Weeks wrote to Orm that Atlantic was "enormously grateful to your father for having introduced us to Farley Mowat. . . ."

51. The series aired beginning 26 Mar. 1950.

52. Farley Mowat to WOM, 10 Apr. 1950, UCalgary.

53. Mowat wrote his father 19 Nov. 1949 that he was doing some writing for the CBC and *Maclean's* (Farley to Angus Mowat, Farley Mowat *fonds*, McMaster).

54. PTI, Dec. 1981.

55. PTI, WOM, 5 Jun. 1984.

56. PTI, Dec. 1981. "Eskimo Spring" was sold to the *Saturday Evening Post* 30 Dec. 1949 and published as "The Desperate People," 29 Jul. 1950, 31, 42, 44–46, 48.

57. WOM to EB, 27 Dec. 1949, UToronto.

58. EB to WOM, 13 Jun. 1950, UToronto.
59. WOM to EB, 19 Jun. 1950, UToronto.
60. EB to Curtis Brown, 25 Feb. 1950, UToronto.
61. DC to WOM, 29 Aug. 1950, Atlantic.
62. See EB to WOM, 30 Apr. 1951, UToronto.
63. PTI, MLM, 16 Jun. 1982.
64. Farley Mowat to WOM, 10 Apr. 1950, UCalgary.
65. Farley Mowat to WOM, 18 Oct. 1950, UCalgary.
66. WOM to DC, 28 Dec. 28, 1950, Atlantic.
67. DC to WOM, 20 Mar. 1952, Atlantic.

Chapter 3 (Pages 47-70)

1. WOM, "The Oldest Old-Timer," *JKR* (audiocassette), 27 Jun. 1950, NAC.
2. PL, Harry Boyle to biographers, 15 Dec. 1992.
3. PI, Harry Boyle, 13 Nov. 1992.
4. PTI, MLM, 2 Jun. 1982.
5. Bronwyn Drainie, *Living the Part* (Toronto: Macmillan, 1988) 179.
6. Lister Sinclair et al., *John Drainie: 1916–1966* (Association of Canadian Television and Radio Artists, 1966).
7. Andrew Allan et al., *John Drainie: 1916–1966* (Association of Canadian Television and Radio Artists, 1966).
8. See *Life*, 310–12.
9. William Munro, *The Critic*, Vol. 1, No. 3, May-June, 1950.
10. PTI, 27 Dec. 1985.
11. Mitchell later revised "The Liar Hunter" as a two-parter in the regular *Jake and the Kid* series under Peter Francis's direction, and it was improved: "Is that the Truth?" *JKR*, 17 Oct. 1950 and "Hair of the Dog," 24 Oct. 1950. See Yates, 226.
12. WOM to Harry Boyle, 17 Jan. 1952, UCalgary.
13. Claire acted under her maiden name, Claire Murray.
14. PTI, 27 Dec. 1985.
15. PTI, WOM and MLM, Dec. 1981.
16. PTI, Billie Mae Richards, 10 Sept. 2000. Billie Mae played the Kid throughout the first six years and returned to play the Kid opposite Fred Diehl's Jake in a twenty-episode revival in 1969–70.
17. J.G., "And now it can be told!" *CBC Times*, 12–18 Apr. 1953, 4.
18. Yates, 252, 250, 257.
19. WOM, taped interview with Yates, Feb. 1977.

20. PTI, Billie Mae Richards, 10 Sept. 2000.

21. Morris Surdin, taped interview with Alan Yates, Nov. 1977.

22. "Brokenshell Flood," *JKR*, 22.

23. "Gettin' Born," *JKR*, Family, 6.

24. "Auction Fever," *JKR*, CBC Archives,19.

25. "Lo, the Noble Redskin," *JKR*, 15, 14.

26. PL, Harry Boyle to biographers, 15 Dec. 1992.

27. J.G., "And now it can be told!" *CBC Times*, 12–18 Apr. 1953, 4.

28. WOM, taped interview with Yates, Feb. 1977.

29. "Old MacLachlin," *JKR*, Family.

30. PTI, Dec. 1981.

31. Yates, 236.

32. Peter Francis, taped interview with Alan Yates, Mar. 1977.

33. PTI, Dec. 1981.

34. Yates, 236.

35. Yates, 230.

36. Harry Boyle, taped interview with Alan Yates, 1978.

37. Peter Francis to Morris Surdin, 15 Nov. 1950. Morris Surdin *fonds*, UCalgary.

38. PTI, Claire (Murray) Taylor, 3 Nov. 2000; see also McKenzie Porter, "The Man Behind Jake and the Kid," *Maclean's*, 13 Sept. 1958, 46.

39. PTI, Ruth and Peter Francis, 15 Feb. 1986.

40. Cecil Crooks to WOM, 13 Jan. 1950, Family.

41. Rough notes for an article on Toronto, ca. 1978, Family.

42. PTI, Hugh Mitchell, 19 Jul. 1986.

43. This sequence of events is cobbled together from Merna and Bill's account (PTI, Dec. 1981), interviews with their friends (PTI, John Clare, 24 Oct. 1987; PTI, Gerry and Betty Anglin, 24 Oct. 1987; PTI, Adam Marshall, 24 Oct. 1987; Pierre and Jan Berton, 19 Sept. 1987), and published accounts by Berton (*My Times*, 35–36) and by McKenzie Porter ("The Man Behind Jake and the Kid," *Maclean's*, 13 Sept. 1958, 50).

44. PTI, Barbara Moon, 19 Nov. 1987; PTI, John Clare, 24 Oct. 1987.

45. Ralph Allen to Bruce Hutchison, 16 Oct. 1956, UCalgary.

46. PTI, 8 Jun. 1985.

47. PTI, 8 Jun. 1985.

48. PTI, 8 Jun. 1985.

49. Porter, 50.

50. WOM to EB, 22 Sep. 1950.

51. The following year he asked for a raise to $175, which he eventually received, and which was, according to Peter Francis, "higher than anyone else gets." Peter Francis to WOM, 30 Jan. 1952.

52. "The Tragic Trek of the Mennonites," *Maclean's*, 1 Mar. 1951, 7.
53. Gordon Sinclair, "Radio," *Toronto Daily Star*, 27 Feb. 1951, 7.
54. *The Black Bonspiel of Wullie MacCrimmon, CBC Stage*, radio script, broadcast, 3 Mar. 1968, Family, 4,7, 36, 37, 38. This is probably the same version as the 25 Feb. 1951 script.
55. *The Black Bonspiel* radio script, 5, 27, 30, 36.
56. *The Black Bonspiel*, quotations taken from 7–8, 12–14, 22–23.
57. See *Life* 269.
58. PTI, Dec. 1981.
59. PTI, Dec. 1981.
60. *CBC Times*, 4 Mar. 1951.
61. Jack Danylchuk, "Mitchell," *The Albertan*, 13 Feb. 1965, 16.
62. MLM, interview with Alan Yates, ca. Mar. 1978.
63. PTI, Billie Mae Richards, 9 Oct. 2000.
64. WOM, interview with Alan Yates, ca. Mar. 1978.
65. Peter Francis, interview with Alan Yates, Mar. 1977.
66. PTI, Pierre Berton, 19 Sep. 1987.
67. Pierre Berton to WOM, 24 Aug. 1951.
68. "Returns Home," *High River Times*, 19 Apr. 1951, 1.

Chapter 4 (Pages 71-101)

1. NFB, A-9.
2. WOM to EB, 9 Oct. 1951.
3. WOM to DC, 17 Oct. 1951.
4. PTI, 26 Dec. 1983.
5. PTI, Earl and Helen Lewis, 28 May 1984.
6. "Rotary Steak Fry is Held in Idyllic Atmosphere," *High River Times*, 21 Jun. 1951.
7. MLM to Elsie Park Gowan, 27 Feb. 1952.
8. "The Riddle of Louis Riel," *Maclean's*, 15 Feb. 1952, p. 45.
9. Historical Committee, *Leaves From the Medicine Tree* (High River, 1960) 35. See *The Kite* in *DWO*, 153.
10. PTI, 27 Dec. 1985; PTI, Dec. 1981.
11. PTI, 27 Dec. 1985; PD, 13 Jul. 1990; see *VP* 170.
12. PTI, Dec. 1981; see *Life* 344.
13. Peter Francis to WOM, 29 Jan. 1952, UCalgary.
14. "My Home Town: High River," *Toronto Star Weekly*, 22 Sept. 1962, 2.
15. PTI, 27, Dec. 1985; see *Imperial Oil Review*, October 1963 for the composite of Jake's character. See also *Life*, 256–57; 308–14 for a discussion of early "Jake and the Kid" short stories.

16. Jack Art, "Part of Mitchell's 'Jake' was from Red Deer," *The Advocate Farm News and Shopper*, Feb. 1975.

17. "Old MacLachlin Had a Farm," *JKR*, 1, Family.

18. Yates, 298.

19. PTI, Claire Taylor, 3 Nov. 2000.

20. PTI, MLM, 16 Jun. 1982.

21. PTI, Earl and Helen Lewis, 5 May 1984.

22. Surdin to WOM, n.d. probably 10–15 Oct. 1951, UCalgary, Surdin *fonds*.

23. WOM to Morris Surdin, 17 Oct. 1951, UCalgary, Surdin *fonds*.

24. PTI, 27 Dec. 1985.

25. NFB, Roll 2, 21.

26. In November 1951, Taylor became ill and joined his wife at Hobbema. In August 1952, he resigned his post at Eden Valley. Another teacher, Muriel Many Wounds, had been hired for Eden Valley (*High River Times*, 4 Sept. 1952). Records are unavailable, but it appears that Mitchell taught only in the 1951/52 school year and not 1952/53, although he was out at Eden Valley for February 1953.

27. PTI, Dec. 1981. See *VP* 88–91.

28. PTI, 26 Dec. 1985.

29. PTI, 26 Dec. 1985.

30. PTI, Dec. 1981.

31. PTI, 27 Dec. 1985. See *VP* 18–20.

32. PTI, Dec. 1981 and PTI, 27 Dec. 1985.

33. PTI, 27 Dec. 1985. PTI, Dec. 1981.

34. PTI, Dec. 1981. PTI, 27 Dec. 1985.

35. PTI, 27 Dec. 1985. PTI, Dec. 1981.

36. PTI, 27 Dec. 1985. John Laurie (1899–1959) was a teacher of the Stoneys, a secretary of the Indian Association of Alberta, and an honorary chief of various Alberta tribes.

37. PTI, Dec. 1981.

38. PTI, 27 Dec. 1985.

39. PD 21 Jul. 1986.

40. Harry Boyle to WOM, 23 Dec. 1951, UCalgary.

41. WOM to Harry Boyle, 17 Jan. 1952, UCalgary.

42. Peter Francis to WOM, 29 Jan. 1952, UCalgary.

43. Peter Francis to WOM, 30 Jan. 1952, UCalgary.

44. "Prairie Flower," 25 Nov. 1951, NAC.

45. PTI, MLM, 2 Jun. 1982.

46. WOM to JMG, 26 Jan. 1952 (misdated 1951), McMaster.

47. Toronto: University of Toronto Press, 1951.

48. Basil Dean, "All Things Considered," *Calgary Herald*, 13 Dec. 1951.

49. "Under the Microscope," *High River Times*, 20 Dec. 1951.

50. PTI, 26 Dec. 1983.
51. Peter Francis to MLM, 18 Feb. 1952, UCalgary.
52. "Crocus Under the Microscope," *JKR*, 19.7.f25.
53. Peter Francis to MLM, 18 Feb. 1952, UCalgary.
54. PTI, 26 Dec. 1983.
55. This correspondence is lost, but Francis details the contents in his 9 Mar. 1952 letter to WOM.
56. Oswald Hall to WOM, 28 Feb. 1952, UCalgary.
57. Oswald Hall to Peter Francis, 14 Mar. 1952, UCalgary.
58. Peter Francis to WOM, 9 Mar. 1952, UCalgary.
59. "Prairie Flower," *JKR*, 25 Nov. 1951, NAC.
60. Pierre Berton, "A Small Tribute to an Authentic Original," *Toronto Daily Star*, 2 Sept. 1960, 17.
61. "The Grim Gash of Death," *JKR* 14, 22.
62. Scott Young says there was always suspicion that "none of these things really happened, that he made them up as he went along." *Gordon Sinclair: A Life . . . and Then Some* (Toronto: Macmillan, 1987), 62, 76, 176.
63. Peter Francis to WOM, 29 Feb. 1952, UCalgary.
64. "Radio," *Toronto Star*, 23 and 30 Jan. 1951. Mitchell considered Sinclair's attack on the *At Home with the Lennicks* show to be personal and "unforgivable" (PTI, Dec. 1981).
65. Broadcast 4 Mar. 1951.
66. PTI, Dec. 1981.
67. McKenzie Porter, "The Man Behind Jake and the Kid," *Maclean's*, 13 Sept. 1958, 47.
68. PTI, Dec. 1981.
69. Mitchell wrote five episodes involving St. Clair Jordan: "Woman Trouble," 4 Mar. 1951; "The Grim Gash of Death," 17 Feb. 1952; "Hometown Laughter," 22 Mar. 1953; "Settin' Ducks," 3 Jan. 1954; "Sink or Swim," 9 Jan. 1955.
70. Gordon Sinclair, "Gordon Sinclair Says," *Liberty*, May 1959, 12.
71. PTI, Dec. 1981.
72. UCalgary, MsC 19.14.3. f77.
73. "The Alien," ms., UCalgary, MsC.19.12.5.f61.
74. P.S.B. Shelley, "Adonais," lines 464–5.
75. WOM to DC, 28 Dec. 1950, Atlantic.
76. Willis Wing to DC, 16 Jun. 1952, Atlantic.
77. WOM to DC, 17 Oct. 1951, Atlantic.
78. WOM to EB, 26 Jan. 1952, Buckler *fonds*, UToronto.
79. MLM to JMG, 11 Feb. 1952, McMaster.
80. WOM to DC, 22 Jul. 1952, Atlantic.

81. WOM to Gray, 6 Dec. 1952.
82. PTI, 26 Dec. 1983.
83. PL, Kay Parley to biographers, 16 Feb. 2000.
84. PL, Norma Hawkins to biographers, 25 Jan. 2000.
85. WOM, "Eulogy for Florence James," rough notes, ca. 18 Jan. 1988, Family.
86. WOM, taped interview with Yates, Feb. 1977.
87. WOM, taped interview with Yates, Feb. 1977.
88. 26 Aug. 1953.

Chapter 5 *(Pages 102-124)*

1. WOM to JMG, 23 Oct. 1952, McMaster.
2. Vicki Fremlin, *Farmer's Advocate and Canadian Countryman*, 26 Sept. 1953, 12.
3. WOM to EB, 9 Feb. 1953, UToronto.
4. WOM to JMG, 3 Mar. 1953, McMaster.
5. Pierre Berton, Reader's Report for Macmillan, Apr. 1953, McMaster.
6. JMG to WOM, 25 Mar. 1953, McMaster.
7. Readers' Reports Summary to DC, 17 Apr. 1953, Atlantic.
8. DC to WOM, 27 Apr. 1953, Atlantic.
9. WOM to JMG, 23 May 1953, McMaster.
10. "Mitchell Again Wins Award," *High River Times*, 18 Jun. 1953, 1. "The Princess and the Wild Ones," adapted from two *Jake* radio dramas, was published in *Maclean's*, 15 Mar. 1952. The President's Medal was presented 23 Jun. 1953 at a special dinner at the University of Toronto.
11. "How to be a Canadian Writer – and Survive," *Saturday Night*, 16 May 1953, 22–23.
12. WOM to JMG, 23 May 1953, McMaster.
13. WOM to JMG, 3 Aug. 1953, McMaster.
14. WOM to EB, 4 Aug. 1953, UToronto.
15. "A Back Door Philosophy Favored by Bill Mitchell," *High River Times*, 8 Apr. 1954, 6.
16. PTI, Larry Diebel, 29 Jul. 1999.
17. WOM to EB, 4 Aug. 1953, UToronto.
18. JMG to WOM, 5 Feb. 1954, McMaster.
19. WOM to JMG, 10 Sep. 1954, McMaster.
20. JMG to DC, 13 Oct. 1954, Atlantic.
21. WOM to Karen, 24 Jan. 1967, UCalgary.
22. PTI, 26 Dec. 1985.

23. Yates interviewed all the directors for his thesis. He cited "Goin' to London to See the Queen" (4 Oct. 1953) as an example in which the music was "obtrusive" and the mix was "jarring and confusing" (275) and comments that Ljungh "exploited the humour to the point of farce" (278).

24. PTI, 16 Jun. 1982.

25. "Duel at Dawn," a two-part story, 1 and 8 Feb. 1953; "Turn the Other Cheek," 27 Dec. 1953; "King of All the Country," 7 Nov. 1954; "Daddy and the Gander," 21 Nov. 1954; "Settin' Ducks," 3 Jan. 1954; "Not All Men Have a Price," 20 Mar. 1955.

26. "How to Shoot a Goose and/or a Movie," ms., ca. 1963, UCalgary, MsC 19.21.13,f3.

27. WOM, interview with Alan Yates, ca. 1978.

28. "King of All the Country," *JKR*, Family, 24, 25.

29. WOM, interviewed with Alan Yates, Feb. 1977.

30. WOM, interview with Alan Yates, Feb. 1977.

31. "The Goose Hunt," notes, ca. 1963, Family.

32. WOM to Willis Wing, 25 Feb. 1959, Columbia.

33. "Take Her Gentle – Take Her Easy," *JKR*, 21.

34. See Timothy Zeman, "An Annotated Bibliography of the Radio Drama of W.O. Mitchell in the Special Collections of the University of Calgary Libraries," Diss. University of Alberta, 1993, 6.

35. Yates, 320.

36. See Catherine McLay, "Crocus, Saskatchewan: A Country of the Mind," *Journal of Popular Culture*, No. 14 (1980): "Like Leacock's Mariposa, Crocus is not a real place but a country of the imagination" (347).

37. Nathan Cohen, "Critically Speaking," *CBC*, 3 Sept. 1950.

38. Peter Francis to WOM, 13 Jun. 1952, UCalgary.

39. PTI, MLM, 16 Jun. 1982.

40. WOM, interviewed with Alan Yates, ca. Feb. 1977. See also Robert Duncan, director of *W.O. Mitchell: Novelist in Hiding*, who asked Mitchell, "What would lead you to something which is on the surface as glib as *Jake and the Kid*?" (NFB, A-24).

41. WOM, interviewed with Alan Yates, ca. Feb. 1977.

42. PTI, MLM, 16 Jun. 1982.

Chapter 6 (Pages 125-153)

1. See *Life* 263–64.

2. WOM to Dr. Laing, 27 Apr. 1955, UCalgary.

3. PTI, 17 Apr. 1987.

4. PD.

5. "Famous Canadian Writer in Search of Early Alberta," *High River Times*, 23 Jun. 1955, 1. By this time Hutchison was known for *The Unknown Country* (1943) and *The Incredible Canadian* (1952).

6. JMG to WOM, 7 Sept. 1955, McMaster.

7. WOM to Robert Goldfarb, 29 Feb. 1956, UCalgary.

8. WOM and MLM, script for Mrs. McCorquodale Day, 24 Jun. 1956. Family.

9. WOM to Mac Jones, 9 Jan. 1957, UCalgary.

10. WOM to JMG, 30 Jan. 1957, UCalgary.

11. *Liberty*, Vol. 33, No. 12, Feb. 1957.

12. WOM to Mrs. O.S. Mitchell, scrapbook, n.d., UCalgary.

13. *CBC Times*, n.d., in scrapbook, UCalgary.

14. WOM to Goldfarb, 16 May 1957, UCalgary.

15. MLM to Dorothy Brown, 22 Mar. 1957, UCalgary.

16. "Roses" refers to the first draft (1957) and the revised draft (1959); *Roses* to the revised published book of 1991.

17. MLM to Frank Upjohn, 1 Apr. 1957, UCalgary.

18. Frances Fraser, with encouragement from Merna and Bill, published *The Bear Who Stole the Chinook* (Macmillan, 1959).

19. PTI, Frances Fraser, 9 Jul. 1984.

20. PTI, Frances Fraser, 9 Jul. 1984.

21. "Roses," 1957, Chapter VIII, 7.

22. "A Back Door Philosophy Favored by Bill Mitchell," *High River Times*, 8 Apr. 1954, 6.

23. WOM to Bernie Braden, 28 Nov. 1957, UCalgary.

24. "Honey and Hoppers," 19. 30. 1. f12, UCalgary.

25. "Memorandum of Agreement," between CBC and W.O. Mitchell Ltd., 25 Nov. 1957, 7. Family.

26. WOM to Nora McCullough, 20 Nov. 1957, UCalgary. Mitchell figured he would receive about three-quarters of a million dollars if all sales laid out in the contract materialized.

27. WOM to DC, 12 Dec. 1957, Atlantic.

28. MLM to Dorothy Brown, 22 Mar. 1957, UCalgary.

29. PTI, MLM, 16 Jun. 1982.

30. PTI, MLM, 16 Jun. 1982.

31. Peter Francis to WOM, 26 Sep. 1957, UCalgary.

32. Scott Young, "3-Alarm Chap: He Knew When He Was Right," *Globe and Mail*, 24 Sept. 1957, p. 15.

33. MLM to Scott Young, 30 Sept. 1957, UCalgary.

34. PTI, 16 Jun. 1982.

35. WOM to Pierre Berton, 29 Nov. 1957, UCalgary.

36. Quoted in Porter, 13 Sept. 1958, 14.

37. "Roses," 1959, 119.

38. PTI, Earl and Helen Lewis, 28 May 1984.

39. PTI, MLM, 16 Jun. 1982.

40. PTI, MLM, 16 Jun. 1982.

41. PTI, MLM, 16 Jun. 1982.

42. WOM to Willis Wing, 13 Mar. 1959, Columbia.

43. JMG to WOM, 17 Mar. 1958, McMaster.

44. "Roses," 1957, Chapter 16, 13.

45. The episodes were: "Crocus Under the Microscope," "Something's Gotta Go," "Scandal, Scandal, Scandal," "Nature Knows Best," "Murder Will Out," "King of All the Country," and "Documentary from the Banana Belt."

46. Reader's Report, 3 Apr. 1958, McMaster.

47. Atlantic Monthly Press Reader's Report, 15 Apr. 1958, Atlantic.

48. Willis Wing to WOM, 28 Apr. 1958, Columbia. Gray reported the opposite, that the book was "fine, and in spots wonderful fun." JMG to WOM, 21 Apr. 1958, McMaster.

49. JMG to WOM, 14 Apr. 1958.

50. JMG to WOM, 21 Apr. 1958, McMaster.

51. WOM to Bernie Braden, 17 Sept. 1958, UCalgary.

52. *Royalty is Royalty* is adapted from two *Jake and the Kid* episodes: "Royalty is Royalty" and "Prairie Flower."

53. WOM to Wing, 13 Mar. 1959, UCalgary.

54. "Royalty is Royalty," ms., UCalgary, MsC 19.34.4, 116.

55. WOM to Bernie Braden, 14 Sept. 1959, UCalgary.

56. *Star Phoenix*, 6 Jun. 1959, Margaret Lutecia Mitchell's scrapbook, UCalgary MsC19.1-2.

57. WOM to Bernie Braden, 14 Sept. 1959, misdated 1954, UCalgary.

58. WOM to Willis Wing, 8 Sept. 1959, Columbia.

59. Willis Wing to JMG, 23 Oct. 1959, McMaster.

60. JMG to Lovat Dickson, 29 Feb. 1960, Macmillan.

61. Frye to Gray, 6 Jun. 1956, McMaster.

62. WOM to JMG, 12 Nov. 1959, McMaster.

63. "The Shocking Truth about the Undefended Border," *Eve* 98.

64. Jack McIver, "Man of Flowers," *Saturday Night*, Mar. 1986, 52.

65. "Orchids," rough notes, possibly for *Close-Up* television show with Pierre Berton on 27 Jun. 1961, UCalgary, 19.32.13.f1.

Chapter 7 (Pages 154-178)

1. WOM to Gray, 1 Feb. 1960, McMaster.
2. PTI, MLM, 16 Jun. 1982.
3. JMG to WOM, 22 Aug. 1960, McMaster.
4. NFB, 56.
5. *The Kite*, rough notes, 19.32.3.f10, UCalgary.
6. Terry Poulton, "The Artful Codger," *Radio Guide*, Feb. 1983, 6.
7. PTI, 13 Oct. 1986. This scene between Margaret and her younger sister delighted Bill so much that, as he thought about it over the next few years, he developed the idea for a play about two sisters who get under each other's skin. He never wrote it, but had the perfect title: "Royal Crown Derby."
8. WOM to Mrs. McCorquodale, 18 Oct. 1961, Family. Mitchell enclosed a copy of "Lincoln, My Mother and Mendelian Law." It was later retitled "The Day I Spoke for Mister Lincoln" (*Imperial Oil Review*, Jun. 1962, 19–22), and also "Four Score Years and One Spittoon" (*W.O. Mitchell Reading Series*, CBC Radio, 8 Aug. 1962).
9. *W.O. Mitchell Reading Series*, 22 Aug. 1962.
10. *Maclean's*, Jun. 1961, 17.
11. "Take One Giant Step," *Imperial Oil Review*, Dec. 1960; *W.O. Mitchell Reading Series*, CBC Radio, 25 Jul. 1962; *Eve* 80–85.
12. See *Life* 85–86.
13. PTI, 16 Jun. 1981.
14. *Maclean's*, 5 Oct. 1963.
15. PTI, Larry Diebel, 29 Jul. 1999.
16. 14 Jul. 1957.
17. "Holiday Weekend in Calgary," *Maclean's*, 15 Oct. 1959.
18. JMG to WOM, 22 Dec. 1960, McMaster.
19. Kildare Dobbs to WOM, 16 Jan. 1961, McMaster.
20. PTI, Dec. 1981.
21. 4 Jul. to 19 Sept. 1961.
22. David Gardner to WOM, 30 Jun. 1961, UCalgary.
23. Gardner, *ML* 280.
24. PL, Gardner to biographers, 23 Apr. 2001.
25. Alex Barris, "The Barris Beat," *Toronto Telegram*, 6 Jul. 1961, 10.
26. Dick Newman, *London Free Press*, 7 Jul. 1961, 33.
27. *ML* 286.
28. Gardner to WOM, 17 Nov. 1961, UCalgary.
29. PTI, Dec. 1981.
30. "Missing Grizzly Puzzles Writer," *The Albertan*, 27 Aug. 1955.
31. PL, John Jennings to biographers, 12 Jan. 2005.

32. "Celebrated Hide Case Furnishes Movie Plot," *Calgary Herald*, 26 Aug. 1955.

33. "Missing Grizzly Puzzles Writer," *The Albertan*, 27 Aug. 1955.

34. Myron Galloway, "W.O. Mitchell," *Montreal Star*, 11 May 1974.

35. CBC, *FF*, 4 Feb. 1962.

36. *FF*, "Green Thumb – Red Finger," 15, 18, 19, 16.

37. "Jake's Genius: He Put Crocus on the Map," *Globe and Mail*, 25 Nov. 1961, 18.

38. "A Canadian Classic?," *Canadian Literature*, 11 (1962) 68–70.

39. Judith Carruthers, "More to Mitchell: The Elusive Art of W.O. Mitchell's *Jake and the Kid*," M.A. thesis, Carleton, 1986, Appendix A, 102.

40. WOM to JMG, 4 Oct. 1961, McMaster.

41. JMG to WOM, 10 Oct. 1961, McMaster.

42. WOM to JMG, 23 Jan. 1962, McMaster.

43. MLM to Orm, 21 Sept. 1961, Family.

44. "After Mary's Boy," Morris Surdin *fonds*, UCalgary, 4.

45. "After Mary's Boy," 17–18.

46. MLM to Mrs. McCorquodale, 19 Oct. 1961. The fear of nuclear war was very intense at this time and came to a head a year later during the thirteen days of the Cuban Missile Crisis in October 1962.

47. WOM to John Clare, 22 Jan. 1962, UCalgary.

48. 19 Jan. 1964.

49. "The Trophy," 3, 21, 22, UCalgary.

50. "Summer Cottages Are Wasted Status Symbols," *Maclean's*, 21 Apr. 1962, 27, 61–62.

51. PTI, Don Garrett, 29 Aug. 2001.

52. "In the Shuswap Country," *Maclean's*, Apr. 1970, 69–70.

53. "In the Shuswap," 70.

54. PTI, Hugh Mitchell, 26 Aug. 2003.

55. PTI, Hugh Mitchell, 26 Aug. 2003.

56. Roy Kervin, "Filled with the Joy of Living," *Montreal Gazette*, 6 Oct. 1962.

57. Hawley Black, "A centenarian quizzed for story of the West," *Ottawa Citizen*, 27 Oct. 1962.

58. Donald Stainsby, *Vancouver Sun*, 3 Oct. 1962.

59. Arnold Edinborough, *Toronto Daily Star*, 5 Oct. 1962.

60. George Baldwin, *Queen's Quarterly*, 70 (1963) 284; F.W. Watt, "Letters in Canada: Fiction," *University of Toronto Quarterly*, 32 (1962–63) 401.

61. Margaret Laurence, "Holy Terror," *Canadian Literature*, 15 (1963) 76.

62. Patricia Barclay, "Regionalism and the Writer: A Talk with W.O. Mitchell," *Canadian Literature*, 14 (1962) 55.

63. Michael Hornyansky, "Countries of the Mind," *Tamarack Review* (1963) 67.

64. Catherine McLay, "A Study in Immortality," *Journal of Canadian Fiction*, 2 (1973) 43.

65. "The Goose Hunt," *Man in the Landscape*, 8 May 1963.

66. "How to Shoot a Goose and/or a Movie," ms., n.d. 1963 UCalgary, MsC 19.21.13.f7. Mitchell attempted, unsuccessfully, to sell this article to *Weekend Magazine*.

67. "Roaming the Plains and Hills of Alberta," *CBC Times*, 4–10 May 1963, 7.

68. WOM to Orm, 5 Dec. 1962, Family.

69. WOM to John Clare, 22 Jan. 1962. Mitchell published: "The girls put on their spurs," *Star Weekly*, 13 Jul. 1963, photographs by Peter Varley, 10–11; "My Home Town: High River," *Toronto Star Weekly*, 22 Sept. 1962; "Summer Cottages Are Wasted Status Symbols," *Maclean's*, 21 Apr. 1962.

70. Broadcast 25 Jul., 1, 8, 15, 22, 29 Aug., 5 Sept. 1962.

71. Directed by Melwyn Breen, broadcast 7 Mar. 1962.

72. Broadcast 5 Nov. 1962.

73. PTI, Eric Till, 6 Aug. 2002.

74. "The White Christmas of Raymond Shotclose," 24 Dec. 1962.

75. WOM to Orm, 5 Dec. 1962.

Chapter 8 (Pages 179-209)

1. WOM to Orm, 22 Oct. 1962, Family.

2. Mitchell used this exchange in "Sons and Fathers," *FF*, 17 Nov. 1963, UCalgary, MsC19.25.5 f15.

3. WOM to Orm, 22 Oct. 1962, Family.

4. WOM to Hugh MacLennan, 21 Jan. 1966, UCalgary.

5. PTI, 17,18 Apr. 1987.

6. "Stopping Smoking," *Eve* 201; first printed as part of "Three Random Scenes," *Maclean's*, 2 May 1964.

7. Jack Danylchuk, "Mitchell," *The Albertan*, 13 Feb. 1965, 16.

8. PTI, MLM, 16 Jun. 1982.

9. Stewart Brown, "Hell, heartburn and hallelujah," *Hamilton Spectator*, 3 Nov. 1973.

10. PTI, 17 Apr. 1987.

11. PTI, MLM, 16 Jun. 1982.

12. PTI, 17 Apr. 1987.

13. PTI, MLM, 16 Jun. 1982.

14. PTI, 18 Jun. 1987.

15. PTI, Dec. 1981.

16. WOM to his brother Bob, 27 Jan. 1964, UCalgary.

17. WOM to Wing, Nov. 26, 1963, UCalgary.

18. Esse Ljungh to WOM, 27 Dec. 1963, UCalgary.

19. Hiller to WOM, n.d. ca. Nov. 1962.

20. WOM to Wing, 26 Nov. 1963, UCalgary.

21. Up to mid-May 1959 Wing had been Mitchell's literary agent for American rights only. When Mitchell asked him to take over negotiations with the CBC, Wing sent through a new contract, which Mitchell signed, not realizing that he was assigning the handling of *all* his rights to Wing.

22. "Who DOES own *Jake and the Kid*?" *Toronto Daily Star*, 6 Mar. 1964, 24.

23. WOM to Mac Jones (his Calgary lawyer), 11 Mar. 1964, UCalgary.

24. "The Soft Trap," *FF*, 8 Dec. 1963, Surdin *fonds*, UCalgary; "Hurrah for Civilization," *FF*, 24 Nov. 1963, Surdin *fonds*, UCalgary; "The Wrong Trail," *FF*, 22 Dec. 1963, Surdin *fonds*, UCalgary. Peter Powderface's and Moses Lefthand's (*Jake and the Kid* stories) desire to embrace the white way was based in part on Raymond Shotclose, who was one of the most successful of the Eden Valley community in accommodating white culture.

25. "The Wrong Trail," 13, 16,19.

26. PTI, Dave Diebel, 9 Jul. 1984.

27. Soberg to Mitchell, 28 Feb. and 27 May 1964.

28. PTI, Dec. 1981.

29. PTI, Dec. 1981.

30. "The People Who Don't Want Equality," *Maclean's*, 3 Jul. 1965, 9.

31. Rebroadcast, 15 Dec. 1963.

32. "100 Per Cent Vote Against District Hutterite Expansion," *High River Times*, 21 Dec. 1961, p. 5.

33. *Summer Fallow*, CBC, 13 Apr. 1964.

34. *The Strait Gate*, CBC Television, Dec. 1964. MsC 19.35.7, UCalgary. Title taken from Matthew 7:13, 14.

35. Peter Kappele to WOM, 28 Dec. 1964, UCalgary.

36. See *Eve* 221–23.

37. "The People Who Don't Want Equality," *Maclean's*, 3 Jul. 1965, 36, 37.

38. "For the Sake of Argument," 16 May 1964.

39. WOM to Peter Gzowski, 11 Mar. 1964, UCalgary.

40. WOM to JMG, 11 Mar. 1964, UCalgary.

41. *Maclean's*, 2 May 1964.

42. Paul Soles was the host. Some of the pieces were "The Day I Spoke for Mister Lincoln" (22 Jun. 1964), "Take a Giant Step" (21 Dec. 1964), "The Hired Man" (25 Jan. 1965), "Living with Grandmother" (1 Mar. 1965).

43. 26 Apr. 1965.

44. Bob Blackburn, "In Blackburn's View," *Toronto Daily Star*, 27 Apr. 1964.

45. 30 Jun. 1965.

46. "Ron Southern," ms., UCalgary.

47. "In the Shuswap Country," *Maclean's*, Apr. 1970, 69.

48. "East End Was Just the Beginning," *Telescope*, CBC, 17 Nov. 1966.

49. WOM to Wallace Stegner, 18 Nov. 1958, UCalgary.

50. Wallace Stegner to WOM, 11 Dec. 1958, UCalgary.

51. Ed. by Jack Livesley (Toronto: Macmillan Canada, 1966).

52. WOM to Hugh MacLennan, 21 Jan. 1966, UCalgary.

53. "Centennial Play," UCalgary, MsC19.19.12, Part III, 1.

54. PTI, 9 Jun. 1985.

55. "It Was a Crashing Bore," wrote *Ottawa Journal* reviewer Frank Daley (12 Jan. 1967, 5).

56. PL, WOM to biographers, 20 Feb. 1966, Family.

57. WOM to Surdin, 31 May 1966, Surdin *fonds*, UCalgary.

58. WOM to Bernie Braden, 30 Jun. 1966, UCalagary.

59. WOM to Mrs. Hewlett, 26 Oct. 1966, UCalgary.

60. "Century," 23.

61. PL, WOM to Karen, 24 Jan. 1967.

62. PTI, 24 Dec. 1985.

63. WOM to Bernie Braden, 23 Jan. 1967, UCalgary.

64. "Wild Rose 'Slick' Production, But Play Not without Flaws," *Calgary Herald*, 25 May 1967, 33.

65. PTI, Willa Mitchell, 29 Dec. 1985.

66. PTI, Georgie Collins, 26 Feb. 1984.

67. "Wild Rose 'Slick' Production, But Play Not without Flaws," *Calgary Herald*, 25 May 1967, 33.

68. "Wild Rose: A flower that died before ever blooming," *Toronto Star*, 25 May 1967.

69. John Searchfield, "Mitchell Reveals Humor at MAC Theatre," *The Albertan*, 22 Feb. 1965.

70. Jack Danylchuk, "Mitchell," *The Albertan*, 13 Feb. 1965.

71. "Debts of Innocence," *Saturday Night*, Mar. 1976, 36–37.

72. *The English Teacher*, 3 (1963) 5–15.

73. "Grace and Illusion," 6.

74. Broadcast on 18, 25 Apr. and 2 May 1968.

Chapter 9 (Pages 210-231)

1. PTI, 24 Dec. 1985.
2. Herb Armstrong to WOM, 30 Jan. 1968, Family. Mitchell's salary was $17,500.
3. WOM to Dr. A.W.R. Carrothers, 23 May 1970, UCalgary, University Archives.
4. PTI, MLM, 16 Jun. 1982.
5. PL, MLM to biographers, 10 Dec. 1967.
6. PTI, 24 Dec. 1985.
7. PTI, Hugh Mitchell, 19 Jul. 1986.
8. PTI, Dec. 1981.
9. WOM to JMG, 7 Jun. 1968, McMaster.
10. PL, WOM to biographers, 10 Dec. 1967. Orm Mitchell, "Prophecy in the Novels of John Steinbeck," Diss. U of Alberta, 1967.
11. PL, WOM and MLM to biographers, 12 Jun. 1968.
12. PL, WOM to biographers, 10 Dec. 1967.
13. WOM to JMG, 7 Jun. 1968, McMaster.
14. PTI, 24 Dec. 1985.
15. WOM to A.W.R. Carrothers, 23 May 1970.
16. PTI, 24 Dec. 1985.
17. There was a revival of *Jake and the Kid* the following year on *Theatre 10:30.*
18. PTI, 24 Dec. 1985.
19. Betty Belliveau in "Five Illusions from a writers' workshop," Family.
20. PTI, Bonny LeMay, 7 Aug. 1986.
21. "Machinery," ("She Looks so Easy") in *Magicians, Acrobats and Writers,* p 15. Rough notes for three-part television education series produced by Alberta Department of Education, directed by Larry Shorter, shown on the CBC. "Pebble in a Pond," 18 Apr. 1968; "Rabbit from a Hat," 25 Apr. 1968; "She Looks so Easy," 2 May 1968.
22. MLM to JMG, Christmas card, n.d., McMaster.
23. PTI, Willa Mitchell, 29 Dec. 1985.
24. PTI, Willa Mitchell, 29 Dec. 1985.
25. PTI, 26 Dec. 1983. Costa-Gavras's *Z* won the Academy Award for best foreign film in 1968. It is a film about a Greek political leader who is assassinated, and it explores the democratic struggle of the liberal and left elements in Greece.
26. See *Life* 92–93.
27. See also David O'Rourke's "An Interview with W.O. Mitchell," *Essays on Canadian Writing* 20 (1980–81), 153.

28. This was a similar breakthrough to his vivid recollection of standing with his mother at his father's grave, which was the genesis of *Who Has Seen the Wind*; see *Life*, 1–2.

29. PTI, Dec. 1981.

30. Hugh Cowan and Gabriel Kampf, "Acta Interviews W.O. Mitchell," *Acta Victoriana*, 98 (April 1974), 18.

31. See *Life* 105–8.

32. WOM to JMG, 20 Mar. 1970.

33. WOM to A.W.R. Carrothers, 23 May 1970, UCalgary.

34. PTI, 24 Dec. 1985.

35. PTI, MLM, 16 Jun. 1982.

36. WOM to A.W.R. Carrothers, 23 May 1970.

37. PTI, Jim Black, 9 Aug. 1986.

38. PTI, Gordon Swan, 10 Aug. 1986.

39. Carrothers to WOM, 8 Jun. 1970, Family. In the academic world a probationary appointment becomes a tenure appointment following a tenure hearing unless the university shows cause for not granting tenure. At the very least Mitchell should have had a tenure hearing in which the university would have to show cause for not granting tenure and, if they made a convincing case, given him two further years before terminating his appointment.

40. The panel consisted of Barry Callaghan, Morley Callaghan, George Grant, a historian, James Eayrs, a political scientist, Malcolm Muggeridge, a British social critic, and Mr. Justice Samuel Freedman from the Manitoba Court of Appeal.

41. "A Death in the Family," Family.

42. Barry Callaghan, "Acceptance speech for W.O. Mitchell Literary Prize," 10 Jun. 1998, Family. At the dinner following the prize, Callaghan recalled that there was not a dry eye in the CBC studio that day.

43. Jim Coutts, "Tribute," International Festival of Authors Tribute to WOM, 18 Oct. 1990, Family.

44. Robin Mathews, a professor of literature and strong nationalist, sent Mitchell a copy of a lecture he gave in 1972 arguing that Canadian literature should be an essential element in Canadian education. He pointed out that Canadian books are not only ignored or considered second rate compared to American or British literature, but are rejected by publishers "for not being enough like a U.S. novel." He tried to "awaken his listeners" to the fact that *Who Has Seen the Wind* is as good as *The Adventures of Huckleberry Finn* and should be "given its legitimacy" (11, "Canadian Literature: The Necessary Revolution," Laurier High School, London, Ontario, 18 Feb. 1972, 11).

45. WOM to JMG, 23 Jul. 1971, McMaster.
46. JMG to WOM, 4 Aug. 1971 McMaster.

Chapter 10 (Pages 232-250)

1. PTI, Ruth Fraser, 9 Jun. 2002.
2. PTI, Dorsey, 26 Nov. 1997.
3. PTI, Itani, 16 Feb. 1986.
4. In 2003 she published her first novel, *Deafening* (Toronto: Harper Collins), to international acclaim.
5. PTI, Rudy Wiebe, 10 Jun. 2002.
6. "University of Alberta Citation for W.O. Mitchell," 15 Nov. 1975, U of Alberta Archives.
7. *Stories From Western Canada*, Macmillan, 1972.
8. Alan Twigg, "W.O. Mitchell: I'm not dogmatically or ritualistically religious. . . . But I think I'm an honourable man," *Quill & Quire*, Oct. 1984, 6.
9. PTI, Rudy Wiebe, 10 Jun. 2002.
10. See *VP* 259.
11. Reg Vickers, "Storing up 'life's lumber,'" *Quill & Quire*, Oct. 1973.
12. Here is another example of Mitchell's researching to get his details right. When he was writing his description of Old Esau in the opening pages of *The Vanishing Point*, Mitchell phoned Dr. Bill Cochrane to find out what "an old man dying of T.B. would smell like." (Reg Vickers. This led to "the dough smell of infection, a faint pickle of age . . . A familiar and musty sweetness reminding Carlyle of rotten potatoes." (*VP* 7–8).
13. Mrs. Waggood, "Author's attitude rebuked," *Calgary Herald*, 16 Oct. 1973.
14. *Life* 120–21.
15. WOM to Gray, 21 Feb. 1972. McMaster.
16. *Alien Thunder* promotional pamphlet, 58, UCalgary.
17. Fournier went on to direct sixteen feature films, including *The Tin Flute* (1983) and *The Book of Eve* (2001), both adapted from Canadian novels.
18. "Sunday Supplement," CBC Radio, 13 Aug. 1972.
19. *Alien Thunder*, transcripts of taped conversations between Fournier, Raymond, and Mitchell, 27 Feb. to 26 Mar. 1972, MsC 19.15.5.7.f4, UCalgary.
20. *Alien Thunder* promotional pamphlet, 13–14, UCalgary.
21. W.O. Mitchell, "Alien Thunder," film script, MsC19.15.6.f93, UCalgary.

22. PTI, Donald Sutherland, 23 Mar. 2000.
23. Allan King to WOM, 28 Jan. 1972, UCalgary.
24. PTI, Willa Mitchell, 29 Dec. 1985.
25. UCalgary, MsC 19.8.21.16.
26. PTI, Willa Mitchell, 28 Apr. 2004.
27. David O'Rourke, "An Interview with W.O. Mitchell," *Essays on Canadian Writing* 20 (1980–81), 152.
28. George Malko, *Alien Thunder* script, MsC 19.16.3.f28, UCalgary.
29. This line was actually "I'm just doing what I gotta do." *Alien Thunder*, film soundtrack, retitled *Dan Candy's Law* (1973).
30. *Sunday Supplement*, CBC Radio, 13 Aug. 1972.
31. Sid Adilman, "Celebrated Novelist Dives into Movie Scripts," *Toronto Star*, 24 Jun. 1976.
32. See *Life* 113–48.
33. PTI, Dec. 1981.
34. From 8–10 Feb. 1973.
35. PTI, Dec. 1981.
36. PTI, Dec. 1981.
37. Emily Murray to WOM, 15 Feb. 1973.
38. 16 Feb. 1973.
39. See Peter Gzowski's interview with WOM, "One Hour in High River," *Peter Gzowski's Book About This Country in the Morning* (Hurtig, 1974), 18–25.
40. PTI, 24 Dec. 1985.
41. PTI, Rudy Wiebe, 10 Jun. 2002.
42. Hugh Kane memo, 11 Apr. 1973.
43. Old Esau is based in part on Jonas Rider from the Eden Valley reserve, who, in 1955, went to Calgary "to seek the aid of a faith healer there, but . . . died while the big meeting was in progress." ("Jonas Rider Dies in Calgary," *High River Times*, 11 Aug. 1955).
44. Dingle's term for the Stoney custom of trial marriages (*VP* 153).
45. NFB, A-19.
46. Interview with Reg Vickers, *Calgary Herald*, 12 Oct. 1973.

Chapter 11 *(Pages 251-272)*

1. NFB, 36–101, 34.
2. WOM to President J.R. Evans, 31 May 1974, Family.
3. WOM to Roberta Charlesworth, Board of Education, North York, 21 Mar. 1974, Family.
4. WOM to Robertson Davies, 7 Jun. 1974, Family.

5. William French, "Sometimes happiness is simply snails and orchids," *Globe and Mail*, 17 Jul. 1973.

6. Ed Ogle, "Choice of Defeats," *TIME* magazine, 12 Nov. 1973.

7. "W.O. Mitchell book on Indians' plight will stir anger," *Toronto Star*, 20 Oct. 1973.

8. *Saturday Night*, Jan. 1974.

9. *Montreal Star*, 26 Jan. 1974.

10. "W.O. Mitchell's new novel is about tolerance," *Toronto Native Times*, Jan. 1974.

11. WOM to Perrott, 22 Mar. 1974, UCalgary.

12. *Saturday Night*, Jan. 1974.

13. Buckler to WOM, 16 Jan. 1974. UCalgary.

14. From notes on book tours, probably for Gzowski's 4 Apr. 1974 show, UCalgary.

15. WOM to President J.R. Evans, 31 May 1974, Family.

16. Trent Frayne, "Being a writer-in-residence: 'ridiculous' – W.O. Mitchell," *Toronto Star*, 6 Jul. 1974, B5.

17. Robert Fulford, "Young Writers have advantage with W.O. Mitchell on campus," *Toronto Star*, 9 Feb. 1974.

18. William Kurelek to WOM, 16 Jun. 1974, UCalgary.

19. WOM to Jeremy Hull, Federation of Saskatchewan Indians, 21 Mar. 1974, Family.

20. Reg Silvester, "The 'aliens' wear red," *Leader-Post*, 23 Feb. 1974, 7.

21. Reg Silvester. It was later released in video under the title *Dan Candy's Law*.

22. Peter Gzowski, CBC Radio, 9 May 1975.

23. PTI, Donald Sutherland, 24 Mar. 2000.

24. See *Life* 96.

25. PTI, Molly Mitchell, 18 Jun. 1984.

26. PTI, Dick Mitchell, 25 Aug. 1984.

27. We first learned that Spud was schizophrenic in 1998 when researching Spud's army discharge records from 1942 and later followed up with research of the Shaughnessy Veterans' Hospital records.

28. Eric Till to WOM, 16 May 1974, Family.

29. *Back to Beulah*, television script, 52, 101, Family.

30. Jon Anderson, "Minding the Shop," *TIME*, 16 Feb. 1976, 8.

31. Donald Cameron, "Merna Mitchell Thinks This Man Is the Most Endearing, Hopeless, Fascinating Dolt She Has Ever Met," *Weekend*, 29 Mar. 1975, 7–9.

32. The radio play, directed by Ron Hartman, was broadcast on CBC Radio on 26 Oct. 1974.

33. PTI, Patricia Watson, 21 Feb. 2003.

34. WOM, "Debts of Innocence," *Saturday Night*, Mar. 1976.
35. "W.O. Mitchell's Address to Convocation," *Folio*, University of Alberta, 18 Dec. 1975.
36. "Introduction," W.O. Mitchell, *Free-Fall*, 1976.
37. "Mitchell's Messy Method," *Free-Fall*, Banff Centre, 1975.
38. "Introduction," *Free-Fall*, Banff Centre, 1979.
39. "Preface: Mitchell's Messy Method," *Free-Fall*, Banff Centre, 1975.
40. *Artist, Builders and Dreamers: 50 Years at the Banff School* (Toronto: McClelland & Stewart, 1982) 58.
41. PTI, Richard Lemm, 10 Aug. 1986.
42. Other published writers who went through the Banff program with Mitchell include Martin Avery, Victoria Freeman, Gail Greenwood, Bruce Hunter, Elona Malterre, Shirlee Matheson, Sheldon Oberon, Darlene Quaife, Ally McKay.
43. PTI, Gordon Morash, 8 Jun. 2002.
44. Agnes L. Florence, "The Writer in Residence," *Access*, Autumn 1975, 22.
45. "W.O. Mitchell: pied piper in our schools," *Winnipeg Tribune*, 9 Nov. 1974.
46. WOM, Rough notes, Family.
47. "W.O. Mitchell: pied piper in our schools," *Winnipeg Tribune*, 9 Nov. 1974.
48. Lynne MacFarlane, "Bill Mitchell's Pied Piper Caper," *Alumni Journal*, University of Manitoba, 35 (1975) 4–5.
49. PI, Shirley Missiaen, 21 Mar. 2002.
50. There is a copy of a letter in NAC's Allan King *fonds* from King to WOM and Merna saying that the third draft of the feature film is enclosed and asking Mitchell for his reaction (26 Mar. 1975, Vol. 17, folder 6). However, the letter is misaddressed and it is possible that the Mitchells never received it or the script. See also letter from Allan King to David Wright, 10 Nov. 1976, NAC, Allan King *fonds*, D243, Vol 17. Wright questioned whether Mitchell had approved of the script, and King's letter summarizes his falling out with Mitchell.
51. Hugh Kane to WOM, 23 Jun. 1975, Family.
52. Bill Musselwhite, "Radio and television," *Calgary Herald*, 3 Jan. 1978, A18.
53. PTI, 17 Apr. 1987.
54. Musselwhite, *Calgary Herald*, 3 Jan. 1978.
55. *Foothill Fables*, 28 Jan. 1962.
56. Musselwhite, *Calgary Herald*, 3 Jan. 1978.
57. Hugh Kane to DG, memo, 30 Dec. 1975. McMaster.

Chapter 12 (Pages 273-305)

1. Guy Sprung claimed Glassco "didn't really like the play" and "dismissed it as arch Canadiana" (*ML* 308).

2. PTI, 13 Oct. 1986.

3. Eugene Chadbourne, "W.O. discusses his 'three mad women,'" *Calgary Herald*, 26 Dec. 1975.

4. Helen Hughes played Harriet, Maureen Fitzgerald played Betty, Marrie Mumford played Agnes, Samantha Langevin played Dr. Anders.

5. "Back to Beulah," stage play, Act III, 52, Family.

6. *Arts Alberta*, CKUA, 10 Jan. 1988.

7. Carol Hogg, "Mitchell's new play finest entertainment," *Calgary Herald*, 10 Jan. 1976, 12.

8. Scott Beaven, "'Back to Beulah' – a repellent farce," *The Albertan*, 10 Jan. 1976, 8. Merna and Bill never realized that this reviewer, at the beginning of his career, was soon to depart to the *Globe and Mail* to write under the name of Jay Scott, whose reviews, particularly of movies, claimed considerable notice, though the Mitchells never warmed to his bravado style.

9. Bryan Johnson, "Back to Beulah: lots of laughs, but fuzzy core," *Globe and Mail*, 22 Feb. 1976, 15.

10. David McCaughna, "Back to Beulah a mix that doesn't blend," *Toronto Star*, 2 Feb. 1976, D6.

11. "Theatre: From Edwardian gentility to 1970s piety," *Saturday Night*, Apr. 1976, 77.

12. Fred Bodsworth received $75,000 in 1973 for *The Strange One* [Barbara Wade Rose, *Budge* (Toronto: ECW Press, 1998) 164] and Margaret Laurence received $30,000 for the screen rights to *A Jest of God* (*Rachel, Rachel*) in 1967 [James King, *The Life of Margaret Laurence* (Toronto: Knopf Canada) 236].

13. "Assignment between W.O. Mitchell Ltd. and Allan King Associates," 20 Mar. 1976. 3, Family.

14. Blair Kirby, "CBC dominates ACTRA Awards, but show itself slips," *Globe and Mail*, 22 Apr. 1976.

15. PTI, Allan King, 21 Feb. 2003.

16. PTI, Allan King, 21 Feb. 2003.

17. PTI, Laurence Arnold, 12 Feb. 2004.

18. Arnold to WOM, 28 May 1976.

19. George Miller (King's lawyer) to Arnold, 7 May 1976, Family.

20. PTI, Allan King, 21 Feb. 2003.

21. PD.

22. PTI, Allan King, 21 Feb. 2003.

23. Martin Knelman, "A night at the pictures in Arcola," *Saturday Night*, Sept. 1977, 30.

24. PTI, Allan King, 21 Feb. 2003.

25. WOM to Don Haldane, 31 Jan. 1957, UCalgary.

26. Sid Adilman, "Prairie novelist at 62 works harder than ever," *Toronto Star*, 25 Sept. 1976, H3.

27. PI, Willa Mitchell, 26 May, 2002.

28. PTI, Allan King, 21 Feb. 2003.

29. WOM to Allan King, 19 Aug. 1976, rough copy, Family. This was addressed to King at Arcola, Saskatchewan, where he was shooting. There is no copy in the NAC King *fonds*.

30. Tom Goldstein, "Disappointed yes, angry no," *Leader-Post*, 1 Nov. 1976.

31. PTI, Patricia Watson, 21 Feb. 2003.

32. PTI, Allan King, 21 Feb. 2003.

33. Sid Adilman, "Eye on Entertainment," *Toronto Star*, 9 Jul. 1976, E4.

34. "Story Threads," *Who Has Seen the Wind* screenplay, Family.

35. Martin Knelman, *This Is Where We Came In* (Toronto: M&S, 1977) 170.

36. Tom Goldstein, "Disappointed yes, angry no," *Leader-Post*, 1 Nov. 1976.

37. Les Wedman, "Who Has Seen the Wind undeniably the year's outstanding Canadian film," *Vancouver Sun*, 5 Nov. 1977.

38. Robert Martin, "Who Has Seen the Wind," *Globe and Mail*, 5 Nov. 1977.

39. Clyde Gilmour, "Who Has Seen the Wind a likeable movie," *Toronto Star*, 7 Nov. 1977.

40. *New York Times*, 29 Apr. 1982.

41. The film, however, still has not recouped its costs. The 1995 unaudited financial statement for Souris River Films shows that investors were still owed $601,000, half of the film's total budget.

42. PTI, DG, 27 Jul. 2003.

43. Pat Barclay, "Another Milestone for Mitchell Classic," *Victoria Times*, 15 Jan. 1977.

44. Sid Adilman, "Prairie novelist at 62 works harder than ever," *Toronto Star*, 25 Sep. 1976.

45. NFB, 54.

46. Dave Wesley, "W.O. Mitchell and Wullie MacCrimmon host a black bonspiel in Peterborough," *Peterborough Examiner*, 4 Jun. 1977.

47. DG to WOM and MLM, 24 Mar. 1977.

48. Wayne Grady, "Life Ain't Art," *Books in Canada*, Nov. 1981, 5.

49. Free-fall for *SH*, UCalgary, Acc. 980604, Box 35, File 4.

50. See *Life* 94–95, 99–100.

51. Joseph Erdely, "Film expanded into play," *Ottawa Citizen*, 22 Oct. 1977.

52. *SH*, Acc. 980604, Box 36, File 12. UCalgary.

53. See John Keats's famous "negative capability" letter to Richard Woodhouse (27 Oct. 1818).

54. PTI, 17 Apr. 1987; see *Life* 70.

55. PTI, 17 Apr. 1987.

56. Bill Glassco to WOM, 2 Jul. 1977, UCalgary.

57. Ray Conlogue, "Mitchell again triumphs with cargo of lost souls," *Globe and Mail*, 24 Feb. 1982.

58. "Radio and Television," *Calgary Herald*, 3 Jan. 1978, A18.

59. *Turn Up the Contrast* (Vancouver: UBC Press, 1987), 338.

60. Arlette Francière, the translator of *Who Has Seen the Wind* (1974), did the translation, *Aux Hirondelles*.

61. NFB, roll 36–101, 36.

62. Myron Galloway, *Montreal Star*, 17 Mar. 1978, B1.

63. PL, from A. Camozzi, ca. 1976.

64. *SD* freefall, Acc. 980604, 44.6, 5, UCalgary.

65. 11 Jul. 1978.

66. "Pentecostals seek ban of books from schools," *The Albertan*, 30 Aug. 1978.

67. The program was taped 17 Nov. 1978.

68. PD.

69. Mitchell attacked Campbell's book banning on various occasions over a number of years: in his talk at the National Book Festival in Saint John in April 1979; in May during his address at Sir Wilfred Laurier University; at Trent University. On January 8, 1985, on the CBC's *Sunday Morning*, he said his new year's wish was that the Rev. Ken Campbell, Mrs. Trotter (active book banner in Laurence's Lakefield area), and Gerry Falwell will stop trying to get books banned, especially Margaret Laurence's.

70. n.d., Family.

71. NFB, A-34.

72. PTI, Fil Fraser, 5 Jun. 2002.

73. PTI, Eric Till, 6 Sept. 2002.

74. "Back to Beulah" film script rough notes, ca 1976, 52 (203), Family.

75. Alan Kellogg, "W.O. Touched many lives," *Edmonton Journal*, 26 Feb. 1998.

76. MLM to A. Camozzi, 30 Aug. 1980, Family.

77. NFB, film opening, videocassette, Family.

78. Gordon Morash, "W.O.: There's more to Mitchell than *Jake and the Kid*," *Calgary Magazine*, (Oct. 1979) 24.

79. NFB, 36–101, pp 58–59.

80. NFB, 21, 13, 53.

81. NFB, 53.

82. NFB, A-31.

83. NFB, 8.

84. Kildare Dobbs, "Jake and kid – with difference," *Ottawa Citizen*, 14 Jan. 1989, C3.

85. NFB, A-10.

86. Terry Poulton, "The Artful Codger," *Radio Guide* (Feb. 1983) 8.

87. Morley Walker, "New biography questions Mitchell's dedication to art," *Winnipeg Tribune*, 29 Apr. 1980, 63.

88. Poulton, 8.

89. NFB, 56.

Chapter 13 *(Pages 306-331)*

1. Sid Adilman, "Tireless W.O. Mitchell has writing jobs galore," *Toronto Star*, 25 May 1981.

2. PTI, Alistair MacLeod, 20 Nov. 2002.

3. Brad Liptrot, "The Mitchells," *Windsor, This Month*, Oct. 1987, 15.

4. PTI, Dilworth, 26 May 1987.

5. NFB, roll 68.

6. PTI, 1 Feb. 1986.

7. PTI, 1 Feb. 1986. See also free-fall for *SH*: "Miss Rossdance's is the halfway to heart of darkness place where people are breaking the rules – but openly – for the Victorian pretence of abiding by the rules – the elite can break them." UCalgary, Acc. 980604, Box 36 File 12.

8. *SH* free-fall, Family.

9. David O'Rourke, "An Interview with W.O. Mitchell," *Essays on Canadian Writing* 20 (1980–81) 153–4.

10. See *Life* 52: "I was a good boy."

11. PTI, Fil Fraser, 5 Jun. 2002.

12. PTI, Fil Fraser, 5 Jun. 2002.

13. August 30, 1980.

14. WOM, "Acceptance speech for the Banff School of Fine Arts National Award," 11 Jul. 1980, Family.

15. Canada's famous medallist whose portrait of the Queen appears on Canadian coins and who has created many award medals.

16. *SH* free-fall, Family.

17. *SH* free-fall, Family.

18. PTI, 17 Apr. 1987.

19. "Report on Writing Symposium November 8 & 9," 1 Dec. 1980, 4, Banff Centre archives.

20. PTI, Frances Itani, 16 Feb. 1986

21. Ruth Griffiths, "Says books are the foundation of civilization," *Prince Albert Herald*, 31 Mar. 1981.

22. MLM to Frances Itani, 6 Apr. 1981, Frances Itani *fonds*. NAC.

23. Martin Knelman, "Old Hams," *Saturday Night* (Oct. 1981) 73–74.

24. Maria Pavlik, "Roses Are Difficult Here," *Prairie Bookworld* (Winter) 1990, 28.

25. PTI, DG, 27 Jul. 2003.

26. PD

27. *SH* galleys, UCalgary, Acc. 980604, File 38, 230.

28. PTI, DG, 27 Jul. 2003.

29. DG to WOM, 2 Jul. 1981.

30. PTI, DG, 27 Jul. 2003.

31. In these half-hour episodes, Watson interviewed historical figures such as Queen Elizabeth I (played by Frances Hyland), Galileo (Chris Wiggins), Billy Bishop (Cedric Smith), Confucius (John Neville), and Nefertiti (Marilyn Lightstone).

32. Ken McGoogan, "Writer casts spell over audience," *Calgary Herald*, 12 Sept. 1981.

33. PTI, Farley Mowat, 13 Mar. 2001.

34. See John Orange, *Farley Mowat: Writing the Squib* (ECW Press, 1993) 61. Mowat also told the story for the CBC *Life and Times* documentary (1997), but, because the writer, Silver Don Cameron, knew Mitchell's side of the story, it was edited out. James King included it in his *Farley: The Life of Farley Mowat* (Toronto: Harper Collins Canada, 2002), which appeared two years after our interview with Mowat.

35. PTI, Farley Mowat, 13 Mar. 2001.

36. "Honesty is best, author claims," *Edmonton Journal*, 24 Oct. 1979.

37. WOM to Cloud, 28 Dec. 1950, Atlantic.

38. Matthew Clark, *Quill & Quire* (Nov. 1981).

39. DG to WOM, 16 Dec. 1981, McMaster.

40. Mrs. Young to WOM, 11 Sept. 1982, Family.

41. George Woodcock, "Jake and the id," *Books in Canada* (Nov. 1981), 7.

42. "W.O. Mitchell rich in oral tone," *Winnipeg Free Press*, 4 Nov. 1981, 19.

43. Robert Fulford, "A Pastoral myth, but inside out," *Toronto Star*, 24 Oct. 1981, F10.

44. William French, "Mitchell returns in raunchy style," *Globe and Mail*, 22 Oct. 1981, E1.

45. Jamie Portman, "Mitchell returns to Prairies," *Calgary Herald*, 24 Oct. 1981, F20.

46. Barbara Amiel, "Fiction's brightest season," *Maclean's*, 5 Oct. 1981, 40–43.

47. Sid Adilman, "Mitchell tired of complainers," *Toronto Star*, 11 Nov. 1982.

48. Barbara Amiel, "Fiction's brightest season," *Maclean's*, 5 Oct. 1981, 43.

49. James Adams, "Age hasn't slowed down W.O. Mitchell," *Edmonton Journal,* 27 Nov. 1981.

50. PTI, DG, 26/27 Jul. 2003.

51. PTI, Frances Itani, 16 Feb. 1986.

52. Frances Itani, International Festival of Authors' Tribute for W.O. Mitchell, 19 Oct. 1990, cassette, Family.

53. Barbara Gunn, "Author's past is the stuff of fiction," *Globe and Mail,* 5 Dec. 1984, M12. He used it anyway for his sociopathic character, Charles Slaughter, in *LL* . . . 142.

54. "Convocation Address," *Windsor University Magazine,* 24 Jun. 1982.

55. PTI, Jan Finlay, 7 Sept. 1986.

56. DG to WOM, 13 Oct. 1982, McMaster.

57. DG to WOM, 18 Mar. 1983, McMaster.

58. Urjo Kareda, "Dramatic," *Globe and Mail,* 15 Jan. 1983.

Chapter 14 (Pages 332-356)

1. Stratford Celebrity Lecture Series, 3 Jul. 1983, Family.

2. Ally McKay to WOM, 12 Aug. 1983. McKay published her first novel, *Human Bones,* five years later (Ottawa: Oberon, 1988; also Toronto: HarperCollins, 1990).

3. Mitchell's last three novels (excepting *Roses Are Difficult Here*) are set at Livingstone University, which, physically and in terms of incident, is a blend of the Universities of Calgary, Toronto, and Windsor, and Trent University.

4. Audrey M. Ashley, "Author Mitchell likes to combine actuality and illusion," *Ottawa Citizen,* 3 Nov. 1984.

5. Myron Galloway, "W.O. Mitchell," *Montreal Star,* 11 May 1974.

6. Alan Twigg, "W.O. Mitchell: 'I'm not dogmatically or ritualistically religious. . . . But I think I'm an honorable man,'" *Quill & Quire,* Oct. 1984, 4.

7. PD.

8. PTI, Willa Mitchell, 29 Dec. 1985.

9. Gulkin had produced *Lies My Father Told Me* (script by Ted Allan) in 1975.

10. Mitchell noted to his lawyer, "Over two years nothing is locked in – we are not moving forward . . . there has been cash outlay by Meadowlark and there is no more money" (W.O. notes to Arnold, dated 11/6/83, Family).

11. PTI, DG, 26/27 Jul. 2003.

12. PD.

13. PTI, DG, 26/27 Jul. 2003.
14. PTI, Mac Jones, 22 Jan. 1999.
15. Audrey Ashley, *Ottawa Citizen*, 3 Nov. 1984.
16. Alan Twigg, "W.O. Mitchell: I'm not dogmatically or ritualistically religious. . . . ," *Quill & Quire*, Oct. 1984, 4.
17. Patricia Morley, "Mitchell Matches his best," *Ottawa Citizen*, 3 Nov. 1984.
18. *Canadian Writers and Their Works*, Eds. Robert Lecker, Jack David, Ellen Quigley, (Toronto: ECW Press, 1991) 189.
19. Wendy Roy, *"W.O. Mitchell," Western people*, 10 Jan. 1985. The three books were *How I Spent Summer Holidays, Dramatic W.O. Mitchell*, and *Since Daisy Creek*; the two plays were "For Those in Peril" and the premiere stage production of "The Kite" on 30 Apr. 1981 at Theatre Calgary; and the feature film was "Burmese."
20. "Burmese" treatment, Family.
21. WOM to Guy Gervais, draft, n.d., Family
22. PL, Taylor to biographers, 6 Jul. 2004.
23. Cora Taylor to WOM, 3 Aug. 1985.
24. Kenneth McGoogan, "W.O. Mitchell," *Calgary Herald*, 17 Nov. 1984.
25. Free-fall, UCalgary, MsC 19.44.5.
26. See *Life* 33.
27. PTI, 26 Dec. 1985.
28. PTI, DG, 26/27 Jul. 2003.
29. Rick Caulfield, 3 Jul. 1986.
30. Paul Fleck, opening remarks for W.O. Mitchell Reading, 8 Jul. 1986, CD, Paul Fleck Library and Archives, Banff Centre.
31. *LL* free-fall, Family.
32. PTI, 18 Apr. 1987.
33. *LL* free-fall, Family.
34. *LL* free-fall, Family.
35. PTI, 13 Oct. 1986.
36. See *Life* 150–52.
37. PL, Orm to WOM, Aug. 1986, Family.
38. Brad Liptrot, "The Mitchells," *Windsor This Month*, Oct. 1987.
39. Wilder Penfield III, "Pooling Talent," *Sunday Sun*, 4 Dec. 1988.
40. "After 8 years, W.O. Mitchell is heading west," *Globe and Mail*, 21 May 1987.
41. Liz Nicholls, "Art garners no reverence from Mitchell," *Edmonton Journal*, 24 Mar. 1988.
42. WOM to Dr. Gordon Wood, 12 Jan. 1987, Family.

Chapter 15 (Pages 357-383)

1. Jamie Portman, "W.O. Mitchell's Royalty is Royalty shines like new," *Windsor Star*, 16 Oct. 1987.
2. Liz Nicholls, "Art garners no reverence from Mitchell," *Edmonton Journal*, 24 Mar. 1988.
3. DG to WOM, 31 May 1988, Family.
4. DG to WOM, 6 Jun. 1988, Family.
5. Paula Simons, *Western Report*, 7 Nov. 1988.
6. Kildare Dobbs, "Jake and kid – with a difference," *Ottawa Citizen*, 14 Jan. 1989.
7. William French, "The puppet-master steps out," *Globe and Mail*, 29 Oct. 1988.
8. Ken Adachi, " 'Writing novels ain't an Olympic event'," *Toronto Star*, 12 Nov. 1988.
9. Patricia Morley, "Sweetness and light with black edges," *Books in Canada*, Jan./Feb. 1989.
10. Dick Harrison, "A tale of mortality and isolation," *Western Report*, 7 Nov. 1988.
11. Paula Simons, "The trials of an icon," *Alberta Report*, Nov. 1988, 30.
12. Pierre Berton to Theatre Calgary, 18 Nov. 1988, Family.
13. McLay has written a number of articles on Mitchell's work, including "Novels Are Difficult Here: W.O. Mitchell's Unpublished Fiction," in which she says "Roses" is "not a great novel, but it is a good one and deserving of publication." *Essays on Canadian Writing* (Spring 1989) 97.
14. PD.
15. Lynne Van Luven, "Mitchell rewrote CBC radio scripts for new book," *Sun Times*, Owen Sound, 25 Nov. 1989.
16. Family.
17. PD.
18. DG to WOM, 24 May 1989, Family.
19. PI, Patricia Hamilton, Sep. 2004.
20. "Itching to play the part," *Maclean's*, 1 Jan. 1990.
21. Christopher Hume, "On the road again," *StarWeek*, 6–13 Jan. 1990. It was shown on the CBC on 21 Jan. 1990.
22. In Jun. 2000, the Faculty of Social Work held a ceremony in honour of Mitchell. They permanently named his office the W.O. Mitchell room and fixed a glass panel of a prairie scene above the door.
23. H.J. Kirchhoff, "Mitchell's Messy Method," *Globe and Mail*, 21 Oct. 1989.
24. "Roses," 1959 ms version, 6, UCalgary.
25. McClellan was a young RCMP officer in a small Alberta town when this incident occurred.

26. PD, 13 Mar. 1990.
27. Hugh Cowan, Gabriel Kampf, "*Acta* Interviews W.O. Mitchell," *Acta Victoriana* (Apr. 1974).
28. DG to WOM, 16 Apr. 1990, Family.
29. WOM draft letter to Besse, 24 Aug. 1990, Family.
30. H.J. Kirchhoff, "W.O. Mitchell wins Leacock humor award," *Globe and Mail*, 19 Apr. 1990.
31. Leacock acceptance speech, Family.
32. Verne Clemence, "W.O. Mitchell's rural upbringing resurfaces," *Saskatoon Star Phoenix*, 24 Nov. 1990.
33. Candas Jane Dorsey, "Who has seen the chinook," *Globe and Mail*, 13 Oct. 1990.
34. Marty Gervais, "Where a brighter side of the human spirit lives," *Windsor Star*, 27 Oct. 1990.
35. Martha Perkins, "A small town's pettiness and dignity revealed," *Country Life*, 14 May 1991, 9.
36. Martha Perkins to WOM, 20 Aug. 1992.
37. The speakers were Willa Mitchell; the Right Honourable Joe Clark, external affairs minister at the time; Frances Itani; Jim Coutts, former secretary to Pierre Trudeau and friend of the Mitchells; Douglas Gibson; June Callwood; David Staines, professor of English at University of Ottawa; and Alistair MacLeod.
38. Gzowski and WOM, IFOA, 19 Oct. 1990, audio cassette, Family.
39. PL, WOM to biographers, 17 Dec. 1990, Family.
40. PL, WOM to biographers, 17 Dec. 1990, Family.
41. Bob Poole, "Artistic 'Robin Hoods' get six years," *Calgary Herald*, 14 Sept. 1978.
42. PL, WOM to biographers, 17 Dec. 1990.
43. WOM to Muhlstock, 20 Apr. 1995, Family.
44. See *Life* 163–172.
45. Howard White won for *Writing in the Rain* (Madeira Park, BC: Harbour Publishing, 1990).
46. Marke Andrews, "Working up a head of steam," *Vancouver Sun*, 30 Nov. 1991.
47. PL, Frances Itani to biographers, 15 Mar. 2004.
48. Barb Gustafson, "Book to become a family heirloom," *Rural Roots*, 5 Dec. 1991.
49. *Art* 150; PI, WOM to biographers, 15 Mar. 1992.
50. PD, 17 May 1992.
51. PTI, DG, 26/27 Jul. 2003.
52. DG to WOM, 27 Apr. 1992, Family.
53. PL, WOM to biographers, 17 Dec. 1990, Family.

54. "Hockey star, scientist among 22 appointees to Privy Council," *Globe and Mail*, 2 Jul. 1992.

55. DG to WOM and MLM, 15 Aug. 1992, Family.

56. Till to WOM, 22 Sep. 1992, Family. Till hoped that Mitchell had some fresh project that would renew his spirit, and, indeed, Mitchell was slowly working on his brotherhood novel.

57. Terry Goldie, "Things are a little flat on the prairie," *Globe and Mail*, 31 Oct. 1992.

58. PD.

59. An abridged version of this was published in *The Curler* (Dec. 1964), and in 1976 it was published as book number ten in a thirteen-book series of Alberta literature and history (Frontier Unlimited, Calgary).

Chapter 16 (Pages 384-405)

1. PL, MLM to biographers, 11 Jan. 1993, Family.

2. "Prairie Summer," *Imperial Oil Review* (Summer 1993) 17, 8.

3. WOM to DG, 17 May 1993, Family.

4. WOM to DG, n.d. ca. 17 May 1993. McClelland & Stewart files.

5. DG to WOM, 28 Jun. 1993, Family.

6. See *Life* 269.

7. Lana Michelin, "Mitchell muses on curling, book bans," *Red Deer Advocate*, 7 Mar. 1994.

8. PD.

9. Tim Wynne-Jones, "There's hell to pay when Willie plays," *Globe and Mail*, 30 Oct. 1993.

10. Alan Kellogg, "Bill and Merna show offers some very entertaining theatre," *London Free Press*, 9 Dec. 1993.

11. Ken McGoogan, "Mitchell battles back to health," *Calgary Herald*, 11 Dec. 1993.

12. Anthony Hyde, "W.O. Mitchell's satiric spiel as Canadian as curling itself," *Ottawa Citizen*, 30 Oct. 1993.

13. See *Life* 150–52.

14. PI, 13 Nov. 1994.

15. PD.

16. PD.

17. It premiered in the east on 16 Dec. 1995 and in the west on 25 Jan. 1996.

18. Joe Chidley, "A Classic reborn," *Maclean's*, 18 Dec. 1995.

19. Don Ewing to WOM, 4 Mar. 1996, Family.

20. "New series Jake for the '90s," *Globe and Mail*, 14 Nov. 1995.

21. PL, MLM to biographers, ca. Apr. 1996, Family.

22. Ken McGoogan, "W.O. Mitchell's fighting back," *Calgary Herald,* 6 May 1996.
23. *Eve* 253. See also Philip Marchand, "Mitchell moves writers to tears," *Toronto Star,* 3 Jun. 1996.
24. "Jake Bible," *Jake and the Kid,* 2 Jul. 1996, 17, Family.
25. *Morningside,* 30 May 1997.
26. PTI, DG, 27 Jul. 2003.
27. PL, A. Camozzi to Barbara Mitchell, 14 Feb. 2003. Family. We were unable to discover the author of the poem.
28. Edited by Sheila Latham and David Latham (Toronto: University of Toronto Press,1997). Mitchell's work has received quite a bit of attention from the academic world, including about forty-five masters and doctoral theses, thirty articles, and full chapters in a dozen books.
29. The award was given six times and, unfortunately, lapsed in 2004.
30. Gzowski, "A tribute to W.O. Mitchell," PanCanadian wordfest, Calgary. 15 Oct. 1997. Writers included Sandra Birdsell, David Carpenter, Rick McNair, Holley Rubinsky, Rachel Wyatt, and the Calgary musician James Keelaghan.
31. Gordon Morash, "W.O. Mitchell remembered," *Legacy,* May-Jul. 1998, 9.

Chapter 17 (Pages 406-410)

1. Eddie Wong, the China boy from *Who Has Seen the Wind.*
2. PD.
3. Douglas M. Gibson, "Requiem for a master storyteller," *Globe and Mail,* 28 Feb. 1998.
4. Philip Marchand, "Author, humourist W.O. Mitchell dead at 83," *Toronto Star,* 26 Feb. 1998.
5. Ken McGoogan, "W.O. Mitchell," *Calgary Herald,* 26 Feb. 1998.
6. Sid Adilman, "Fishing those fond memories of my pal Bill Mitchell," *Toronto Star,* 27 Feb. 1998.
7. Don Braid, "Financial footnote for a great writer," *Calgary Sun,* 6 Apr. 1998.
8. Frances Itani, "W.O. Mitchell and me," *Ottawa Citizen,* 1 Mar. 1998.
9. Rex Murphy, "Eulogy for W.O. Mitchell," *Cross Country Checkup,* 1 Mar. 1988.
10. Hansard.
11. "Art garners no reverence from Mitchell," *Edmonton Journal,* 24 Mar. 1988.
12. See *Life* 1.
13. English folk song, unknown writer.

INDEX

456

OTHER TITLES FROM
DOUGLAS GIBSON BOOKS

PUBLISHED BY MCCLELLAND & STEWART LTD.

JAKE AND THE KID *by* W.O. Mitchell
W.O.'s most popular characters spring from the pages of this classic, which won
the Stephen Leacock Award for Humour.
Fiction, 5½ × 8½, 211 pages, trade paperback

HOW I SPENT MY SUMMER HOLIDAYS *by* W.O.Mitchell
A novel that rivals *Who Has Seen the Wind*. "Astonishing . . . Mitchell turns
the pastoral myth of prairie boyhood inside out." *Toronto Star*
Fiction, 5½ × 8½, 276 pages, trade paperback

ALICE MUNRO: Writing Her Lives. A Biography *by* Robert Thacker
The literary biography about one of the world's great authors, which shows
how her life and her stories intertwine.
Non-fiction, 6½ × 9⅜, 604 pages plus photographs, hardcover

RUNAWAY *by* Alice Munro
The 2004 Giller Prize-winning collection of short stories by "the best fiction
writer now working in North America. . . . Runaway is a marvel." *The New York
Times Book Review*
Fiction, 6 × 9, 352 pages, hardcover

THE QUOTABLE ROBERTSON DAVIES: The Wit and Wisdom of the Master
selected by James Channing Shaw
More than eight hundred quotable aphorisms, opinions, and general advice for
living selected from all of Davies' works. A hypnotic little book.
Non-fiction, 5¼ × 7, 176 pages, hardcover

CRAZY ABOUT LILI: A Novel *by* William Weintraub
The author of *City Unique* takes us back to wicked old Montreal in 1948 in this
fine, funny novel, where an innocent young McGill student falls for a stripper.
Fiction, 5½ × 8½, 272 pages, hardcover

TO EVERY THING THERE IS A SEASON: A Cape Breton Christmas Story *by*
Alistair MacLeod, with illustrations *by* Peter Rankin
A "winsome tale of Yuletide past" (*Toronto Star*), almost every page of this beautiful little book is enriched by a perfect illustration, making this touching story
of a farm family waiting for Christmas into a classic for every home.

STEPHEN HARPER AND THE FUTURE OF CANADA: *by* William Johnson
He could be our next prime minister, and this is "a thorough, compelling, and
balanced look at the life and career of one of Canada's most enigmatic politicians." *Calgary Sun*
Non-fiction, 6 × 9, 418 pages, hardcover